D1784566

New Innovations in Teaching and Learning in Higher Education

New Innovations in Teaching and Learning in Higher Education

Anne Hørsted, Paul Bartholomew
John Branch and Claus Nygaard

THE LEARNING IN HIGHER EDUCATION SERIES

LIBRI
PUBLISHING

First published in 2017 by Libri Publishing

Copyright © Libri Publishing

Authors retain copyright of individual chapters.

The right of Anne Hørsted, Paul Bartholomew, John Branch and Claus Nygaard to be identified as the editors of this work has been asserted in accordance with the Copyright, Designs and Patents Act, 1988.

ISBN 978-1-911450-14-6
All rights reserved. No part of this publication may be reproduced, stored in any retrieval system or transmitted in any form or by any means, electronic, mechanical, photocopying, recording or otherwise, without the prior written permission of the copyright holder for which application should be addressed in the first instance to the publishers. No liability shall be attached to the author, the copyright holder or the publishers for loss or damage of any nature suffered as a result of reliance on the reproduction of any of the contents of this publication or any errors or omissions in its contents.
A CIP catalogue record for this book is available from The British Library

Cover design by Helen Taylor

Design by Carnegie Publishing

Printed by Edwards Brothers Malloy

Libri Publishing
Brunel House
Volunteer Way
Faringdon
Oxfordshire
SN7 7YR

Tel: +44 (0)845 873 3837

www.libripublishing.co.uk

Contents

Foreword

Higher education across the globe has been a great success story of the post second war period. Huge growth in student numbers and research income, and expansion of facilities, faculty and even geographical reach, have created for most institutions a glow of success.

Yet at the same time, there has been a drift from classic, often not formalised, academic values both as a result of marketisation and, of course, on the volatile dependence on student fees and governmental and business funding. Some nations have been able to retain their historic university cultures, many have not.

One area which has yet to come under close scrutiny is, in countries such as the UK, the ongoing subsidy of research by teaching. But the introduction in the UK of the much challenged (indeed derided) Teaching Excellence Framework, has highlighted that not all research universities are delivering the same high quality of teaching as they are of research.

At the same time as there are externally driven pressures on higher education, there are in parallel some other radical changes taking place. One of the most clear cut relates to incoming student skills. The curriculum and expectations of secondary education have shifted markedly, but one implication is that there is more passive learning and less critical thinking emerging from school leavers, a particular problem when it comes to assessing the value or otherwise of plausible online materials.

One of the implications of the huge investment in research is that the half-life of knowledge is very much shorter than when universities started up a thousand years ago. In some areas, not least arts and humanities, the idea of transmitting a fixed body of knowledge was never central to higher education. But certainly in the optimistically titled social sciences, the dream of discovering clear-cut facts has been displaced by much more ambiguous positions. Even the physical sciences are not able to ignore moral and ethical dilemmas.

The modern European university was created in Bologna, and some argue that teaching and learning methods have not changed radically since then. A closer analysis of teaching history shows this is simply not true. The small scale classes and lectures of Bologna were challenged by medical education in particular. The need for medical students to be as close as possible to the corpse being dissected led to innovation in learning space design. The model that served best was the Renaissance theatre (like the Globe in London) which used circular or oval galleries to achieve physical proximity. This was copied by anatomy schools, hence the invention of the term "lecture theatre" still in use today.

By the mid 19th century, the magic lantern, a slide projector, was used not least in presentations on science, and the invention of photography enabled very large images to be displayed and shared. By the 20th century, the model of the lecture room had shifted from physical proximity, towards the audience being able to see a large projected image. This was the era, which we are still in, of the lecture room as cinema (darkened room, all facing a screen).

Though educational technology evolved steadily from the magic lantern onwards, the most significant innovation of large high quality distance learning did not depend on computer technology, but more on applying manufacturing principles to the production and use of learning materials, not least quality management. The UK Open University and other mega-universities have of course steadily exploited computer technology, but it was their willingness to rethink the educational process which was their real innovation.

I remain a strong believer in integrated learning management systems such as Moodle, Blackboard, Sakai and Canvas. But these systems, some approaching 20 years old, have not fulfilled their potential. They were conceived as a radical challenge to transmissive education, but most studies of the actual use of such systems suggest 90% of the functions used are those most closely linked to transmissive education. This is not the fault of the software providers. It reflects the remarkable ability of universities to conserve their traditional teaching and learning methods.

The overall success of universities in the later 20th century has created a situation where they appear to be reluctant to invest in innovation, and this is not simply down to top managements creating an educationally conservative culture around teaching and learning, and retaining the imbalance between research and education resourcing. It is also down to many if not most academics preferring to use the methods through which they were themselves taught. In most professions, the professional body demands that initial entrants have basic training and qualifications in all their key functions. An accountant is expected to know about both financial accounting and management accounting.

Many university systems do not apply this to academics, and reward systems globally tend to be based only or primarily on research competence, with teaching and learning competence placed second (if at all). Most academics are competent to teach in the traditional manner, but if they lack expertise in the basics of learning, and indeed in how our understanding of learning is constantly being enhanced, then they are much less likely to be willing or able to innovate outside the transmissive tradition.

Fortunately, there are many enlightened university teachers who can and do innovate even in the absence of any formal training in education. But looking at other professions where innovation is important, such as science, engineering and architecture, it is clear that continually upgraded personal skills and knowledge are a fundamental aspect of the personal capability needed for innovation.

Higher education teaching as a whole needs as a matter of urgency evidence-based exemplars and role models of innovation, both successes and failures, so that we are collectively much better placed to meet stakeholders' expectations and indeed in some cases, if institutions are to survive.

Not only does this book meet this urgent need through its individual chapters, the process through which it has been produced is itself a model for accelerating innovation in higher education. Firstly, the book is global in scope with contributions from five continents, all the more notable given that participants had to meet physically. Secondly, it is cross disciplinary if not actually indisciplinary. Methods which are not innovative in any given discipline are potentially innovative if applied in a different discipline for the first time. Thirdly, the whole process used to produce the book, of appreciative inquiry and feedback, intensive and face to face peer review, and new content emerging out of the event itself, all are role models of what can and should be done within much more of higher education itself. Finally, though there is coverage of high profile topics that gain the oxygen of publicity, MOOCs being a good example, the contributors in this book approach such topics through a more reflexive approach than comes from those who are simply high-profile cheerleaders.

It is also striking how many of the contributions identify themselves as being learner-centred. It is clear from the chapters that this is not simply the rhetoric deployed widely deployed in higher education marketing materials. It arises out of genuine beliefs by the authors that university students should not simply be recipients of standardised facts and methods, but also able to challenge and change what is standardised.

This book is an important and welcome contribution to the debate on innovation in university education and both its chapters and overall approach demonstrate how much bottom-up innovation is possible even in traditional academic cultures.

Clive Holtham is Professor of Information Management at the Cass Business School, City, University of London. He is the Director of the Cass Learning Laboratory, and a UK National Teaching Fellow.

A Possible Conceptualisation of Innovative Teaching and Learning in Higher Education

Anne Hørsted, Paul Bartholomew, John Branch
and Claus Nygaard

To Be Innovative Requires a Valuable Invention

Higher education has several individual and yet integrated purposes. To improve the knowledge, skills, and competencies of its students is one. To prepare its students for the job market is another. To benefit society by raising the educational level of its citizens is still another. Visit the website of any university, and you will doubtless find a section which states its purpose(s).

But whereas the purpose of higher education is one thing, another thing altogether is how the university aims to fulfil its purpose(s). And for far too long, we argue, the dominant paradigm for this fulfilment has characterised the university as a responsible provider of expert knowledge. The competition between universities to be among the best in class, however, has led to national and international ranking games based on the size of the student population, the quantity of external research funding, academic qualifications of instructors, and sometimes even the popularity of instructors. The result is an input-driven model of higher education, in which the measure of success is driven by the quality (and quantity) of a university's resources.

Under this paradigm, teaching and learning in higher education focuses on the university as provider of academic knowledge, taught by experts who 'curate' this knowledge, within the subject domains embraced by the university. This focus on the university as provider of academic knowledge was valid in the era of industrialisation, and was labelled by Best (1991) as *the old competition*. It involved pre-programmed large-scale transactional activities and appropriate support services. Simply stated, universities set the curriculum, then packaged and delivered it to students like over-the-counter products.

OLD COMPETITION:

SUCCESS OF EDUCATION = QUALITY OF ITS RESOURCES

And for years, this paradigm worked. Indeed, it has been argued that the key to the success of universities, their long-term survival even, has been an institutionalised distrust of radical innovation of their own structures and processes (Nygaard *et al.*, 2011). Universities have seemingly have avoided rocking the boat. For example, in 1980 Blackburn *et al.* found that up to 83% of instructors chose lectures as their primary method of teaching and learning. Twenty years later, Lammers and Murphy (2002) reported that the lecture continued to be the most dominant instructional tool at universities.

Like other sectors of the economy and society, higher education has entered a post-industrial era, triggering that which Best (1991) labelled *the new competition*, and a transformation of society from the production of physical goods to the production of information. The Internet, for example, has enabled rapid communication and the exchange and transaction of knowledge. Markets have become more open, global, and inter-connected. In general, technology has given instant access to information from every corner of the world and universities, as a consequence, lost their monopoly as providers of expert knowledge.

It follows, therefore, that universities must play a different role, summarised by Tinkler *et al.* (1996) as 'learning for the future'. Instead of acting as experts transferring expert knowledge to students with no prior information, universities must teach students how to learn. They must prepare students for an unknown future, developing within them the capacity to adapt, to be resilient, and the ability to manage change. As a consequence, the success of a university will not be measured solely by the quality of its resources, but instead on the quality of its innovative methods of delivery too.

NEW COMPETITION:

SUCCESS OF EDUCATION = QUALITY OF ITS INNOVATIVE METHODS OF DELIVERY

The obvious question is thus: What exactly is innovation? We (the editors) define innovation with the following equation:

INNOVATION = INVENTION (within a context) + VALUE

As such, an innovation is never guaranteed simply because it is new. On the contrary, an innovation must be more valuable than an existing solution. In the marketplace, value is judged by the customer (who, to a university, might be a prospective student or the company to employ its graduates). In other words, the market is the arbiter of innovation. Consequently, the university does not innovate, it invents. It puts a new educational product or offering on the market and hopes that it 'catches on' among customers. And if it does, the new product diffuses in the market, displacing previous instantiations—a process which Schumpeter (1975) called 'creative destruction'.

So, what exactly is value? Value can be defined as the outcome of the valuation of an exchange, with valuation as a process by which a customer estimates the consequences of an exchange. If a customer were to go to the corner store to buy ice cream, for example, he/she would expend both time and energy to walk to the corner store, would spend money to acquire the ice cream, would grin with gustatory pleasure at the first lick, would regain some energy from the ice cream's sugar content, and would maybe add a little fat 'around the middle'. These are all consequences of the exchange. Value, therefore, can be written as:

VALUE = ΣCONSEQUENCES (OF THE EXCHANGE)

You might notice from the ice cream example, however, that some of the consequences are negative and some of them are positive. In marketing, consequences which are positive are often referred to as consumer benefits, while those consequences which are negative are referred to as consumer detriments (or costs). It is not unlike weightlifting, in which there is both 'pain and gain'. Innovation, therefore, is about inventing something new (within a context) which, hopefully, will increase benefits and/or decrease detriments to the customer.

Extending this discussion to the higher education context, this definition of innovation suggests that any new teaching or learning practice is not an innovation but is instead an invention. And a practice becomes an innovation not because it is new, but because it adds value by increasing benefits or decreasing detriments. More precisely, it becomes an innovation because it improves the activity of teaching or, more importantly, because it adds value by enhancing student learning.

In this book, we build upon these three central equations as summarised in Figure 1.

Three equations central for this book:	What the equation means for this book:
NEW COMPETITION: SUCCESS OF EDUCATION = QUALITY OF ITS INNOVATIVE METHODS OF DELIVERY	We have invited authors from all over the world to give examples of teaching and learning practices which they (and their peers and students) consider to be a success. We have asked them to describe in detail their innovations.
INNOVATION = INVENTION (within a context) + VALUE	We have asked authors to explain their innovations in terms of the practice (the invention) and the value which it adds.
VALUE = ΣCONSEQUENCES	We have asked authors to demonstrate the value in terms of the consequences for student learning and student attributes (such as knowledge, skills, competencies, abilities, capabilities, personalities, etc.).

Figure 1: The three equations central to this book.

The Writing of This Book

This book is a collaborative product of the 2017 Copenhagen Symposium on Innovative Teaching and Learning Practices in Higher Education. The symposium was organised by the Institute for Learning in Higher Education (LiHE)—an international academic, not-for-profit association founded in 2007 for the advancement of learning-centred higher education. LiHE works explicitly as a network organisation, bringing together international researchers and practitioners within higher education to advance research on the design and implement of learning-centred higher education for the benefit of students' learning outcomes, self-development, and employability. It operates in close collaboration with universities from around the world, including Stellenbosch University,

University of Michigan, University of Technology Sydney, University of Akureyri, Birmingham City University, University of Adelaide, Stockholm School of Economics in Riga, Copenhagen Business School, and Cass Business School London.

The main activity of LiHE is the symposium. The unique LiHE symposium model was invented in 2007 by professor Claus Nygaard, then at Copenhagen Business School. He noted that academics often attend conferences at which they present their scientific research in a 15–20-minute session, get a few comments, and apart from that receive no academic input or collegial support at the conference. Therefore, Claus proposed an alternative conference format, the Ancient Greek symposium, at which academic collaboration and co-creation are the key aspects. An LiHE symposium is output-driven, which brings together scholars and practitioners to co-create a book-manuscript on a specific aspect of learning-centred higher education. Each book is published worldwide by the publishing house Libri Publishing Ltd., Oxfordshire, UK. LiHE was founded to challenge the conventional academic conference with its hundreds (if not thousands) of delegates, and parallel streams of short presentations…and even shorter discussions. LiHE is devoted to bringing together small groups of experts in ways which encourage joint research, collaborative publications, professional networks, and lasting friendships across geographic and disciplinary boundaries.

The symposium in Copenhagen, Denmark, from 8–10 May 2017, was the 17th LiHE international symposium. The symposium itself was the culmination of a long writing and review process which began about 14 months prior to the symposium, when the call for chapter proposals was announced. Following the call, authors submitted for double-blind review a template which showcased their innovative teaching and learning practices. If accepted, they then submitted their full chapter for a second double-blind review. If accepted after the second review, authors were invited to participate in the symposium. Before meeting in Copenhagen, invited authors were divided into collegial work groups, sent a collegial review plan, and asked to give supportive collegial reviews of the other chapters in their work group – all in the service of helping other authors finalise their chapters for publication. During the symposium, authors met and worked not only on their own chapters, but also wrote, on the fly, an introductory chapter for their sections of the book. In other words, the collegial work group whose chapters clustered around e-learning, wrote the introductory chapter for e-learning. Consequently, each author left Copenhagen with two book chapters in this book. In addition to the academic symposium activities, authors also explored some of Copenhagen's main attractions, sailed on the city's canals, sampled Denmark's gastronomical delights, and acted like children again at the world's oldest amusement park.

A Framework for the Book

For this book, we sought primary examples of innovative teaching and learning practices in higher education. During the double-blind reviews and subsequent symposium activities, six themes emerged, resulting in the following six book sections:

1. Engaging Students through Practice;

2. Student-Centred E-Learning;

3. Technology for Learning;

4. Simulation;

5. Effective Transformation; and

6. Curriculum Innovations.

Section 1: Engaging Students through Practice

The book opens with a section on student engagement. This section has five chapters. Chapter 2, *Engaging Students Through Practice*, by Brook *et al.*, is an introductory chapter to the section itself. Here, authors argue for the value of engaging students through various innovative practices. It is a preamble to the book, a philosophical statement, and a wider call for student engagement.

Chapter 3, *Teaching Business Communication through Collaborative Project-Based Learning*, written by Pather, takes us to Johannesburg in South Africa. This chapter addresses innovations in teaching and learning by revealing the efficacy of the oral presentation in addressing most of the difficulties which black African students encounter as a result of their lack of fluency in English, such as mastering written and academic English and speaking in front of large audiences. The innovation offers a practical strategy to assist students who have learnt English as a second or third language. It is user-friendly and can be used by virtually all higher education institutions. The most important lesson of the chapter is that students enjoy the collaborative problem-based approach to teaching and learning and that the outcomes are measurable. The strategy is particularly useful for those instructors who teach large groups of students.

Chapter 4, *Employer Engagement: Accounting Standards in Action*, by Johal, brings us to Birmingham in England. This chapter addresses innovations in teaching and learning by introducing an employer-led intervention in order to encourage accounting students to engage better with the module content through practical application. The employer is an integral part of this innovative practice and creates a strong link between the module content and how it is relevant to the workings of a live organisation. The innovation is designed to enable students to further develop their knowledge and skills, be creative and discursive, apply and challenge, and to practice deep rather than just surface learning. The chapter inspires readers because it addresses the relevance of accounting knowledge that is sometimes considered by students as knowledge that they do not perceive as useful after their university experience. In doing so, it describes a practice that connects the classroom to the workplace through employer engagement. The most important lesson in the chapter is the recognition that even the most tedious (for some) aspects of accounting can be brought to life by linking them to how they perform in the workplace. This in turn enhances student engagement and develops a curious interest that translates into a better student experience.

Chapter 5, *Practice Framework Enhancement for Supervising Research Students*, by Brook and Eley, also brings us to Birmingham in England. The innovation here is incremental in that it is based on selected existing frameworks and develops them into a new, integrated approach. It aims to better reflect a collegial yet structured approach to research supervision. This chapter provides a bridge between existing frameworks that provide some familiarity and the innovation of an integrated development of them. The basis of it is well established and grounded, whereas the integrated approach offers something new aimed at better understanding and progress between candidate and supervisor. The most important lesson from this chapter is to stress the need to be flexible at the same time as following a structured framework or approach. In doing so, it moves established approaches forward into a more collegiate and yet still guided approach.

Chapter 6, *The Art of Seduction: Designing Innovative Curriculum that Engages and Retains Reluctant Bachelor of Arts Students,* by James and Midford, takes us to Melbourne, Australia. This chapter addresses innovations in teaching and learning through the development of a first-year core programme that improves student success and engagement in the first year of their Bachelor of Arts. The innovations work together to convince students of the value of an arts degree. The student experience is improved through the scaffolded development of academic skills embedded in engaging subject content in an innovative module format. The small classroom environment facilitates cohort-building and fosters a connection between students and their lecturers. Through collaborative learning and mentorship, pass rates are improved and students are encouraged to progress to the second year of that particular degree through better engagement. The chapter inspires readers because it shows that even students who are disengaged, unprepared, or reluctant about their course can be motivated to continue through innovative approaches to teaching and curriculum design. The coordinated approach to student success and engagement convinces students that it is worthwhile getting an arts degree and that there are jobs for arts graduates at the end of their degrees. The innovation could be employed in any subject discipline in any degree. By preparing students adequately, they can more deeply engage in subject content and focus on achieving better results. This leads to greater student confidence, which then leads to better student success and retention. The most important lesson from this chapter is that building student confidence, creating a cohort experience, and providing engaging and active learning exercises in the first year of an arts degree is just as important as delivering subject content. In an era when there is increasing emphasis on employability, arts degrees have a stigma attached to them, and students need to be convinced of the value of their degree early if we are to retain them. The more curriculum focuses on maximising student engagement, the more confident students feel and the better they perform. This gain in student achievement and performance leads to better student retention.

Section 2: Student-Centred E-learning

Chapter 7, *Student-Centred E-Learning*, written by McGuire *et al.*, is the introductory chapter to section 2. Each of the chapters in this section addresses student-centred learning with digital solutions, using e-learning tools, to ensure the purposeful use of technology, as opposed to innovation for innovation's sake. The projects discussed in these chapters emanate from contexts that are geographically, culturally, and educationally diverse: Australia, Hong Kong, and Scotland. They also deal with students at both undergraduate and postgraduate levels. The approaches introduced can be utilised across the academic spectrum.

Chapter 8, *Revitalising the Past: Crafting a Digital Engagement Model to Innovate Humanities Curriculum*, written by Midford and Evans, brings us again to Melbourne, Australia. This chapter addresses innovations in teaching and learning by finding an innovative way to make use of resources which are familiar and accessible to students. Students are frequently interested in historical narratives in popular culture, and they find the Internet an easy first port of call for research; they also respond better to the flexibility of material that can be accessed digitally (podcasts, vodcasts, etc.). The innovation described in the chapter makes use of this existing interest and helps students to question these resources, thus learning good historical practice. It also shows them how to create their own resources and to engage with societal perceptions of their subject by using popular culture and social media as resources. It does so by outlining a theoretical teaching model, based in scholarship of teaching and learning, that facilitates the development of digital literacies and better understanding of the past. It shows them a (potentially simple) method of engaging students in complex historical scenarios. It is easily replicable for completely different historical periods and other disciplines too, and it involves watching films in which Russell Crowe gets to fight to the death. The chapter outlines tested methods that allow students to customise their curriculum and learn academic material from a position of familiarity and interest. This results in a more comprehensive understanding of the subject matter and how popular entertainment is crafted using historical sources. The most important lesson from the chapter is that digital sources and resources that might seem attractive, but not always appropriate, for students, can actually be exploited to give students a better sense of how they approach the past as 21st century researchers. Student-led learning results in enthusiastic student participation and better success rates and the digital engagement model can be broadly applied across disciplines and subject areas to achieve similar results.

Chapter 9, *MOOC→SPOC via F2F: It's a Flipped Hybrid, SPOC!*, by McGuire, takes us to Glasgow, Scotland. This chapter looks at a number of different innovations in one package: How is a MOOC converted to a SPOC? What are the differences? What is Flipping? What is hybrid learning? And how does all of this fit together? The chapter inspires readers for a number of reasons. It takes as its subject two of the most recent and innovative methodological designs. It shows others how to take the most useful lessons that we have learnt from MOOCs and how to convert them for use in a SPOC. It combines a number of current innovations in the final design, including hybridised learning and flipping, in addition to the innovations already mentioned. The most important lesson to learn from the chapter is that supporting the student is key to curriculum design. The needs of the student must come first as opposed to simply advancing a new innovation for its own sake.

Chapter 10, *Whiteboard Animation: An Innovative Teaching and Learning Tool for Flipped Classrooms*, by Li *et al.* takes us to Hong Kong. In their chapter, they address innovations in teaching and learning by using tailor-made storytelling whiteboard animations for the flipped classrooms. Instead of recorded lecture videos for flipped classrooms, whiteboard animations are engaging short video clips to introduce prerequisite knowledge and to clarify concepts in a fun and enjoyable way. The authors believe that their chapter inspires readers because it introduces the use of engaging whiteboard animations for teaching and learning in higher education. It describes the details of how to design and produce tailor-made whiteboard animations according to the needs of the course. Readers can easily follow the chapter to produce the whiteboard animations and use them to facilitate discussion in tutorial classes. In general, whiteboard animation can be applied to nearly any subject in a more engaging fashion. The most important lesson in the chapter is to produce teaching materials to facilitate teaching and also help students in learning to use attractive methods.

Section 3: Technology for Learning

Chapter 11, *Technology for Learning: Something Old, Something Borrowed, and Something New*, by Klopper *et al.*, introduces the third section of the book. In their chapter, they position technology for learning in the extant literature; and they borrow from the task-technology fit theory as an organiser for four new applications of technology: 1) a learning management system for professional education; 2) digital learning activities for student engagement; 3) the Web 2.0 platform for English as a second language; and 4) virtual reality integration into the classroom in higher education. This sample of applications makes a useful contribution to the advancement of technology for learning in higher education by illustrating the need for 'fit-for-purposeness' and showing some of the key roles that technology can play to support learning and teaching.

Chapter 12, *A New Tool for Improving Learning in Professional Education Programmes*, by Gillett and Hamori-Ota, takes us to Ann Arbor, USA. Their chapter addresses innovations in teaching and learning by introducing a new online tool that focuses on the learner's journey through a professional education programme, starting before the face-to-face training, continuing through it, and extending beyond it. They wrote this chapter because they wanted to share how they were able to improve the delivery of professional education programmes. The authors realised that learners would benefit from having one central location (an online home) for all course materials (e.g., presentations, readings, bios) that would also be a place for them to share thoughts and resources with each other. At the same time, instructors would benefit from being able to see this information and communicate with participants. They argue that creating such a learning community improves student and instructor engagement, making it more likely that students will reflect, share learnings, and apply what they learn back on the job.

Chapter 13, *Socrative: A 'Smart Clicker' for Teaching and Assessing Engineering Students*, by Salama, brings us once again to Birmingham, England. She wrote this chapter to show how she has successfully added a technological component to her course. Previously, she had taught in a traditional manner through lecturing, and had noticed that students were disengaged. She brought in an element of technology, which is what Millennials are practically born with, and at the same time made it interactive to keep them on their toes. After her trial with Socrative, she noticed how students would come to class showing more enthusiasm and also saw how their grades improved. The chapter might inspire others because the technology described is free; it can be used with any type of device whether it is a smart phone, iPad, or laptop; and lastly, it is very easy to set up and use without spending too much time beforehand on learning how to use it.

Chapter 14, *The Influence of Web 2.0 on Language Learning Motivation to Foster Learner Autonomy: A Vietnamese Case Study*, written by van Rensburg and Van Han, takes us to Ho Chi Minh City in Vietnam. The authors report on the evaluation and assessment of the influences of a Web 2.0 learning management system in an EFL (English as a foreign language) course. Through this innovative technology, the EFL students have acquired numerous opportunities for the expression of ideas, advancing their involvement in the learning activities, as well as affirming their confidence in virtual interaction. Such advantages connect to the elements of a learning environment that motivates the learners to learn English, leading to the advancement of learner autonomy. As such, this chapter reports on the evaluation and assessment of the influences of this Web 2.0 learning management system. Referencing both intrinsic and extrinsic motivation, the qualitative data collected from interviews comprising eight undergraduate learners in a tertiary college was assessed to determine the possible impacts of the LMS on the learners.

Chapter 15, *Virtual Reality in the Classroom and the Mandate to Bring Edutainment to Adult Learners*, by Klopper and Burt, brings us to Queensland, Australia. This chapter addresses innovations in teaching and learning through the explicit narration of the use of digital technologies into a programme of study in higher education. The authors wrote this chapter in response to a teaching challenge of delivering a traditionally face-to-face teaching course as an online delivery. They designed a virtual reality learning experience to provide initial teacher education students the opportunity to participate in the observation of water management in a local environment through a custom-made 'hands-on' virtual reality field excursion. They believe their chapter will inspire readers because it narrates first-hand experience, provides guidance to produce an educational virtual reality learning experience, and shares their insight into the application of a virtual reality learning experience in initial teacher education. The most important lesson in their chapter is that students who are active agents in the construction and acquisition of their knowledge will achieve greater learning outcomes and realise the relevance and impact to their own lives.

Section 4: Simulation

Chapter 16, *Stimulating Critical Thinking through Simulation*, written by Louw *et al.*, is an introductory piece to the fourth section of the book, showcasing innovative teaching and learning through the use of simulations. In their chapter, they discuss the benefits of using simulations to enhance student learning. As well as passing on factual knowledge, higher education needs to prepare students to fulfil all sorts of active professional roles. In addition to a thoroughly developed repertoire of specific skills, such real-life roles frequently demand further abilities—to engage effectively alongside others in existing practices whilst thinking critically about them, to make quick decisions under pressure, and to build collective learning from shared experiences. The authors argue that such higher-order cognitive abilities cannot be effectively developed in lectures and tutorials, but require hands-on experience.

Chapter 17, *Court-Proofing Professional Records – An Innovative Simulation Teaching Resource*, by Andrews and St. Aubyn, brings us again to Birmingham, England. This chapter addresses innovations in teaching and learning by providing a safe learning environment to explore as realistically as possible the experience of being questioned in a legal arena. The principles learned are applied directly in an engaging and innovative way. The authors are on a campaign to improve record-keeping skills in the field of nursing. Record-keeping can, they explain, be difficult to teach and engage students in, and can be viewed as a dry topic. They have developed a simulation approach as an appropriate way of engaging students and developing a lasting understanding of the underpinning principles. The authors believe their chapter inspires readers because it discusses a low-fidelity simulation teaching resource that is easily transferable to different disciplines within higher education. The method engages students and facilitators by being memorable but 'scary' in a safe way. The most important lesson in their chapter is that record-keeping is an essential element of nursing practice and many people are removed from the professional register because their records are of a poor standard. Teaching record-keeping in an engaging and memorable way ensures that students remember this important lesson before they find themselves in the witness box defending their livelihood.

Chapter 18, *High-Fidelity Simulation-Based Training in Radiography*, by Louw, brings us again to Johannesburg, South Africa. In her chapter, the author addresses innovations in teaching and learning by giving a description of how the author applied the principles of layering and scaffolding of learning material to enable easy retrieval of basic knowledge from students' long-term memory to facilitate problem solving in stress-laden scenarios. A problem was designed to activate students' higher cognitive critical thinking, multi-level communication, and teamwork skills. The case scenario was built on well-known basic skills and was complicated by the introduction of various elements to increase the cognitive load of students and force them to function on a new, not-yet-comfortable professional level. She wrote the chapter because she believes that the innovative strategy she shares here with colleagues will make for new and exciting approaches to teaching and learning in a variety of educational domains. The author believes her chapter inspires readers because, even though it involves ample planning and preparation, the simulation-based training strategy described was received very well by the students and achieved not only the targeted learning outcomes but also some unexpected positive outcomes. The most important lesson in the chapter is that educators ought not to hold back on the basic information which they give their students, and that when they do so in a structured manner, students are surprisingly effective in coming to insights and understandings that will shape their future performance, skills, and attitudes in a positive and advanced manner.

Chapter 19, *A Political Solution to Stimulate Creative Group Work in a Large Class*, by Dawson, takes us to Lugano, Switzerland. In his chapter, the author illustrates a mechanism for providing a structure within which university students are stimulated to produce creative work together whilst reinforcing their language skills. The underlying motivation for writing the chapter is his belief that university teaching in general needs to become increasingly learner-centred. It is clearly in the process of doing that, the author argues, but it is often difficult to make it happen quickly enough for universities to be able to continue to offer much better learning opportunities than students can find easily enough without a university course. The author believes his chapter inspires readers because they will be able to get an impression of the range of learning experiences students can create together for themselves when given the chance to do so and of the kind of structure that can potentially allow them that opportunity.

Section 5: Effective Transformation

Chapter 20, *Changing Frames of Reference though Effective Transformation*, by Cermak-Sassenrath *et al.*, introduces the fifth section of the book. In their introductory piece, they argue for the use of innovative teaching and learning practices that lead to transformational learning for students—a process of change that transforms their frame of reference. Students who have the ability to change their assumptions about the world benefit from more reliable and critical beliefs, they argue. They see the globalisation of education and the adoption of a holistic approach to teaching and learning as a recent driver for the introduction of a transformative model. It is their argument that to remain responsive to future challenges, students must be able to synthesise the proliferation of information available through new technologies and objectively evaluate the credibility and reliability of the information. The interaction of focus, synthesis, and creativity can lead to new innovations and knowledge. As they show in this section of the book, there are various ways to achieve effective transformation of student learning and subsequent assumptions, beliefs, attitudes, and values.

Chapter 21, *Creative Reflection: Thoughts from Two Vocational Programmes*, by Jack and Lewis, takes us to Manchester in England and Cardiff in Wales. The authors present two cases of innovative teaching and learning in higher education. In their chapter, they address innovation by discussing a creative way to support students to reflect on their practice experiences. Rather than writing traditional reflective pieces, students have the freedom to create pieces of art or creative writing. The motivation for writing this chapter was that the authors both found that students did not engage fully in the experiential learning process when tied to a traditional essay format of reflection. They wanted to investigate alternative forms of expression to support deeper and more meaningful levels of learning. The chapter inspires readers by providing real-world examples of students' creative work and offers practical guidance on the implementation of the approach and other alternatives for consideration. The most important lesson is that if students are given freedom to reflect in creative ways, they will come back with more meaningful and insightful work than if they are restricted to the traditional format. The work created through these methods serves as a gentle reminder of the real-world anxieties faced by students on a daily basis, which this is important for educators to remember.

Chapter 22, *Course-Based Undergraduate Research for Student Success and Equity*, by Hensel, brings us to Laguna Woods, California, USA. From there, Hensel—the president of The New American Colleges and Universities—has written a chapter reflecting on the expansion of undergraduate research to American students by including research in first- and second-year courses. Undergraduate research, she argues, is a powerful pedagogy that supports student success and career preparation by developing critical thinking and problem-solving skills, comfort with ambiguity, persistence, and self-confidence. Typically, undergraduate research experiences have been limited to a few students in their junior or senior year. Low-income and first-generation students are not always able to access research experiences that are not embedded into the curriculum, since they may not have the time or financial resources for summer or out-of-class research experiences. The chapter addresses innovations in teaching and learning by embedding undergraduate research into the curriculum for first- and second-year students. Course-based research introduces students to the research methodology of the discipline. Course-based research stimulates curiosity and questioning that can lead to deeper engagement in learning. The author believes that her chapter inspires readers because it addresses the issue of pedagogical equity by providing all students opportunities to engage in research. First-generation and low-income students may not initially understand the value of engaging in research or see themselves as researchers or scholars. Course-based research introduces students to the excitement of research and discovery. The most important lesson in the chapter is the concept of adapting pedagogy, in this case the pedagogy of undergraduate research, to the needs of low-income and first-generation students and thereby making the education experience more inclusive and equitable.

Chapter 23, *From Material Construction to Cognitive Construction—On* the Roles of the Artefact in the Learning Process, by Cermak-Sassenrath, takes us to Copenhagen, Denmark. The author investigates the connection between material construction and cognitive construction from a dialectical constructivist position. He starts the chapter with the hypothesis that physical making and conceptual thinking can happen together, inspire each other, and build on each other. In the chapter, the author defines material construction as the creation of all kinds of artefacts, from software applications such as games to websites, films, electronic gadgets, and woodworking. The innovation presented in the chapter is the *BreakIT* workshop series at the IT University of Copenhagen. *BreakIT* is a hands-on, practical workshop series about electronics, mechanics, interfaces, and dangerous things. Workshops are offered monthly during the (taught) semester, for a total of six to eight workshops per year. A different practical project is built in each workshop. The projects differ considerably in their difficulty, scope, and materials; participants may explore, search, assemble, model, experiment, take apart, shape, manufacture, test, discuss, perform, and play. But each project has to involve an *artefact* that can be built or made or fixed, and which people *want to have*. The workshop series is extracurricular and not (in the author's estimate) conceived of by the facilitators or perceived by the participants as an educational event. In the chapter, the author makes specific observations of students' material and cognitive constructions, and documents those with photos taken during six seasons of *BreakIT*, from March 2014 to December 2016. The method of data collection is participatory observation by the author in the roles of workshop host, facilitator, and participant.

Section 6: Curriculum Innovations

Chapter 24, *Collaboration as a Vehicle to Curriculum Innovation*, by Bendriss *et al.*, introduces the final section of the book. In their introduction, they provide a brief discussion of curriculum alignment between secondary education and university study. They also describe the results of a collaborative partnership between faculty and librarians in integrating information literacy into a writing course. Furthermore, the concept of creating an active learning community through a "horizontal communication approach" is presented and, finally, the authors introduce a framework that enables collaborative and collegial evaluation of curriculum for quality as well as research into its impact and effectiveness for student learning.

Chapter 25, *Curriculum Alignment: Opportunities for Cross-Sector Collaborations*, by Nzekwe-Excel and Ladwa, takes us to Birmingham, England. This chapter addresses innovations in teaching and learning by extending the idea of curriculum alignment across modules and programmes to include sector alignment as the big picture and an individual's education in its entirety. They wrote this chapter because they wanted to investigate how students and academics felt about students transitioning into higher education studies. The authors believe their chapter inspires readers because it is student-focused and gives academics the opportunity to collaborate with colleagues across sectors in an exciting way in order to reduce transition anxiety within the transitioning student population and the issues that this can raise. The most important lesson in this chapter, they argue, is quite simple. At its core, it is about raising awareness and communicating issues to achieve 'joined-up thinking' for a student's education in its entirety.

Chapter 26, *The Flipped Classroom: Strategies for Building Students' Information Fluency in the ESL Curriculum*, by Bendriss and Saliba, takes us to Doha, Qatar. This chapter addresses innovations in teaching and learning by introducing the flipped classroom model as a pedagogical tool to facilitate students' self-directed learning. This chapter also addresses the results of a successful collaborative relationship between faculty and librarians to co-design an outcome-based writing curriculum and integrate information fluency strategies. The authors wrote this chapter because they noticed that students lacked basic research skills when they joined their medical college. Therefore, they decided to embed information literacy strategies in the ESL curriculum throughout the entire academic year to develop students' information fluency competencies. They believe their chapter inspires readers because it provides them with tangible tools to replicate in their classroom. It suggests an effective model of practice for a productive collaboration applicable across multiple disciplines. The most important lesson in the chapter is the positive outcomes of embedding information fluency strategies in a defined course context to equip students with the research skills necessary for academic and career readiness.

Chapter 27, *Student Engagement, Metacognition, and Self-Regulated Learning in Higher Education: Implementing Interactive Learning Logs as a Formative Assessment Technique*, by Lloyd, takes us to Tennessee, USA. This chapter addresses innovations in teaching and learning by engaging higher education students in an interactive practice during class. The activities provide an opportunity for faculty and students to engage in rich dialogue as students reflect on course content, professional competencies, and occasional misunderstandings. The author wrote this chapter because it highlights an innovative practice, interactive learning logs (ILLs), which can be implemented across disciplines as a formative assessment technique. ILLs are a collection of written, in-class activities housed in a notebook and are designed to actively engage students. As a professor of undergraduate methods courses in teacher education, the author noticed the need for impromptu activities to complement larger course assignments, as well as to scaffold the learning process in the higher education setting. The author believes her chapter inspires readers because of the importance of student engagement within the context of higher education. ILLs emphasise self-regulated learning, as students reflect on personal and professional experiences related to course content. ILLs may also be used to alleviate students' misunderstandings or misconceptions. The most important lesson in the chapter is the simplicity of ILLs, their broad application across disciplines, and their ability to enhance students' cognitive processes. In addition, ILLs promote students' use of metacognitive strategies and self-regulated learning as they build on prior knowledge and apply new learnings.

Chapter 28, *Embedding Evaluation and Scholarship into Curriculum and Teaching: The Curriculum Evaluation Research Framework*, by Kelder and Carr, brings us to Hobar, Tasmania. This chapter addresses innovations in teaching and learning by presenting a solution to a pressing problem for academics in higher education: how to meet a range of expectations for quality improvement, quality assurance, and scholarship of teaching and learning while also delivering educational curriculum to students that meets their expectations. The authors have developed a curriculum evaluation research (CER) framework that guides a way of thinking and provides a method for developing a teaching-team practice that is underpinned by commitment to routine evaluation for quality improvement and quality assurance, as well as scholarship for innovation and contribution to higher education knowledge. The authors wrote this chapter because they believe that teachers are key to the quality of students' learning experiences and the ability to ensure learning outcomes. In particular, they think that quality outcomes and experiences are directly related to how teachers approach designing and strengthening their curriculum and their ability to build and use an evidence-base for their decision-making. They also believe that the most efficient and effective context for building such capability is the teaching team. The most important lesson in their chapter is that teaching teams can use the CER framework to collaboratively plan the evaluation of their curriculum as well as publish the innovations they implement. The authors believe their chapter inspires readers because a key feature of the CER framework is that it solves a pressing problem through a collegial approach of sharing academic workload by using a distributed leadership model and providing a method for activity directed towards the quality of their work.

About the Authors

Anne Hørsted is Adjunct Professor at the University of Southern Denmark, Senior Consultant at cph:learning in Denmark, and Adjunct Professor at the Institute for Learning in Higher Education. She can be contacted at this e-mail: anne@lihe.info

Paul Bartholomew, Professor, is Pro-Vice-Chancellor (Education) at Ulster University, Northern Ireland. He can be contacted at this e-mail: paul.bartholomew@ulster.ac.uk

John Branch is Academic Director of the part-time MBA programmes and Assistant Clinical Professor of Business Administration at the Stephen M. Ross School of Business, and Faculty Associate at the Center for Russian, East European, and Eurasian Studies, both of the University of Michigan in Ann Arbor, USA. He can be contacted at this e-mail: jdbranch@umich.edu

Claus Nygaard, Professor, PhD, is Executive Director at the Institute for Learning in Higher Education and Executive Director at cph:learning in Denmark. He can be contacted at this e-mail: info@lihe.info

Bibliography

Best, M. H. (1991). *The New Competition. Institutions of Industrial Restructuring.* Garden City, N. Y.: Doubleday.

Blackburn, R. T.; G. R. Pellino; A. Boberg & C. O'Connell (1980). Are Instructional Programs Off-Target? *Current Issues in Higher Education.* Vol. 1, pp. 32–48.

Lammers, W. J. & J. J. Murphy (2002). A Profile of Teaching Techniques Used in the University Classroom: A Descriptive Profile of a US Public University. *Active Learning in Higher Education.* Vol. 3, pp. 54–67.

Nygaard, C.; N. Courtney & C. Holtham (2011). Effectiveness in Higher Education Demands Innovations in Teaching that Progress Beyond Transmission. In C. Nygaard; N. Courtney & C. Holtham, *Beyond Transmission – Innovations in University Teaching.* Oxfordshire: Libri Publishing Ltd., pp. 1–9.

Schumpeter, J. (1975). *Capitalism, Socialism and Democracy.* New York, USA: Harper.

Tinkler, D.; B. Lepani & J. Mitchell (1996). *Education and Technology Convergence. A Survey of Technological Infrastructure in Education and the Professional Development and Support of Educators and Trainers in Information and Communication Technologies.* Commissioned Report No. 43, National Board of Employment Education and Training. Canberra: Employment and Skills Council, Australian Government Publishing Service.

Section 1: Engaging Students through Practice

Chapter 2
Engaging Students Through Practice

Martin Eley, Sara James, Parminder Johal, Sarah Midford and
Magas R. Pather

Introduction

The university sector has undergone significant transformation since
the turn of the 21st century, which has resulted in changes to student
access and the expansion of the sector internationally (Altbach, 2015).
As more students enter the higher education sector, it has been necessary to augment curricula to cater for students with greater academic
skills needs and lower motivation levels, and to better direct our students
within their discipline. In order to help address ever-increasing student
drop-out rates, student expectations, employability, and career development, universities have prioritised curriculum development that enhances
student engagement (Altbach, 2013).

This section includes four case studies that employ innovative practices to engage a diverse student body. The case studies from Australia,
Britain, and South Africa, are at both undergraduate and postgraduate
level, and demonstrate that despite many differences, there are common
challenges across continents, disciplines, and levels, but there are also
shared solutions. Each chapter in this section presents a curriculum innovation that enhances interaction; encourages in-depth learning; connects
students and their skills to the wider market; and/or develops confidence,
aspiration, and articulation. By identifying and addressing gaps in our
students' knowledge and skills, the authors have engaged students and
improved their outcomes.

Defining Our Approach

Student engagement is a broad concept, and for the purpose of this
section it refers to the degree of interest that students demonstrate in

the learning process. Engaged students display passion for what they are learning, which motivates curiosity and facilitates success. Jang (2010) describes three engagement-fostering aspects of tutors' instructional styles: autonomy, support, and structure. He discusses how engagement is at its peak when high levels of autonomy are provided in a supported environment. Student engagement ultimately impacts retention, perseverance, and completion (Zepke, 2005). Halm (2015) suggests that at the core of student engagement is a bond between teacher and students. A relationship of mutual respect and trust heightens student engagement, as does a variety of active learning experiences. This is probably best summed-up as *"the condition that occurs when learning becomes the unavoidable by-product of a desired activity or process"* (Dueck, 2014:n.p.). Common to each chapter in this section is the implementation of curriculum structure to support students to act independently within an active learning framework.

Each chapter outlines ways that learning environments can be redesigned and how teaching practices can be augmented to enhance student engagement (McCormick *et al.*, 2013; Kuh, 2003). The authors of each chapter outline their practice as a vehicle for active learning that has been implemented within their specific institution. Whilst these practices are different, there is a commonality in their purpose which is twofold. The first relates to the use of active learning practices that foster opportunities for students to actively engage in subject content rather than to just sit and listen. This is demonstrated through collaborative learning, active participation, introduction of dialogue, interdisciplinary awareness, oral presentation, and embedded employer-led activity.

The second commonality relates to these practices not just engaging students with subject content but also inculcating skills and competencies that will benefit students beyond the curriculum, and perhaps more importantly, better enable them to articulate their disciplines. It is widely accepted that in order to further enhance the process of engaging students, it is necessary to create the opportunity for students to be able to link the relevance of their learning to their lives beyond the curriculum (Bundick *et al.*, 2014; Frymier & Shulman, 1995). Consequently, each practice enables students to apply their learning to an aspect of their life outside the university.

The practices that are introduced in this section all fall under the umbrella of active learning. Prince (2004:1) defines this as an *"instructional method that engages students in the learning process"*. Students are engaged through the completion of structured or layered meaningful tasks. Each practice in this chapter encourages students to participate actively in their learning, which provides time for reflection and eliminates the passive reception of information prominent in more traditional student-teacher relationships.

Another key component of the practices outlined in this section is collaborative learning, which is a common strategy for developing student autonomy in a supportive environment. Peer-to-peer interaction engages students through participation in discussion and socially with their fellow students (Crouch, 2007). Collaborative learning at undergraduate and postgraduate level is evident in each chapter, which outline practices that benefit students through working together or with their supervisor.

The key theme across the four chapters in this section is the development of practice within the curriculum that will better engage students in their learning. The practices take different forms, ranging from collaborative assessment and activities, embedded employer-led practice, and individual involvement in systematic investigation and research. The diversity in practice reflects the different skills deficits and learner traits across the different universities where these practices were applied, as well as the differences in the institutions' priorities and challenges.

Introduction to the Chapters in This Section

This section consists of four chapters that we have divided into undergraduate and postgraduate practice. Chapter 3 and Chapter 6 in this section focus on the entry point of students into university at the undergraduate level, whereas Chapter 4 and 5 describe initiatives introduced in postgraduate courses at the exit point of university.

Undergraduate Practice

As mentioned, Chapter 3 and 6 in this section discuss innovations employed in undergraduate courses: one in the Bachelor of Arts at La Trobe University in Australia (see Midford & James in this volume) and the other in a number of business diplomas at the University of

Johannesburg in South Africa (see Pather in this volume). The common challenge in both of these contexts is engaging and building the skills of increasingly diverse cohorts of students that are attending university as a consequence of a widening participation agenda (Warren, 2016). As part of the democratisation of access to university, many of the students enrolled in these courses are the first in their family to attend university and may not be as prepared for study as those students who have the benefit of family experience; they are *"travelling in uncharted waters"* (O'Shea *et al.*, 2017:3). The innovations in both chapters aim to create a cohort experience for students through collaborative learning, which assists them with the transition to higher education.

Students in these courses come from urban, rural, and remote areas, and there is considerable diversity in ethnic background. In Chapter 3, Pather focuses on the challenges faced by non-native English speakers in business communication and describes how an innovative approach to oral assessment builds the confidence of these students while engaging them in an assessment methodology that is new to the African context. The innovation described by Midford and James in Chapter 6 also addresses student confidence and unpreparedness by introducing two core interdisciplinary subjects in the first year that embed academic skills into engaging subject content in an innovative module format.

A crucial difference between these two contexts is the issue of motivation. At the University of Johannesburg, students completing business diplomas are generally highly motivated to succeed in their course due to financial compulsion and family pressure; many of the students attending come from neighbouring countries and feel great pressure from their families to succeed. They enrol in a vocational course that has an obvious pathway to employment. By contrast, in the Australian context, while some students at La Trobe University come from low socio-economic backgrounds, it is rare for them to experience significant financial distress. A bachelor of arts is not a vocational degree, and students often experience a lack of motivation and disengagement due to uncertainty about future career pathways.

Postgraduate Practice

Chapters 4 and 5 in this section describe innovations that have been implemented at the postgraduate level at universities in the United Kingdom (UK) and demonstrate how practice is utilised to engage students and to further enhance skills and competencies that are transferable during and beyond the student's university experience. The practice in Chapter 4 relates to a module on the MSc Accounting and Finance programme at the University of Derby in the UK (see Johal in this volume). The programme attracts a diverse student body from the domestic and international student market, of whom most, if not all, aspire to enter the workplace following their postgraduate experience. So, whilst they may be keen to complete the programme, sometimes they question the relevance of parts of the programme. It is important, therefore, to ensure that the learning experience employed encourages the student body to continue to engage with all parts of the programme. In Chapter 4, Johal elaborates on how an employer-led intervention is extended beyond just a guest address, in that the employer activity is embedded within the module to create a teaching, learning, and assessment practice that is designed and delivered in consultation with the employer. This not only confirms the relevance of the module content for the students but also encourages engagement and therefore a move towards a deeper learning approach. Furthermore, the embedded employer approach broadens the student's understanding, application, and appreciation of competencies and soft skills that are deemed necessary and desirable in the workplace (de Villiers, 2010).

In Chapter 5, Brook and Eley share an innovative practice of collaborative working, not only between the student and his/her peers but also between the lecturer and student. The chapter focuses on the relationship between a supervisor and their postgraduate research student. It brings together two robust frameworks: Tannenbaum and Schmidt's *leadership continuum* and Lee's *supervision framework*. The marriage of the two, which come from the higher education and the business sector, enables a new framework to be developed: the Brook-Eley *business applied research supervision model*. This was developed to further the discussion on supervision methods, in particular to help address the expectations gap between supervisors and students, and thus better engage the students in the supervision process. By having a flexible but clear framework, the student is encouraged to take responsibility for their research project and to motivate themselves, with encouragement and advice from their supervisor. The CBI (2011:n.p.) developed a list of competencies required by employers and stated that *"under-pinning all these attributes, the key foundation must be a positive attitude: a 'can-do' approach, a readiness to take part and contribute, openness to new ideas and a drive to make these happen"*. Therefore, the experience gained by the student during their research project is transferable into their future career, and knowing this will ensure that the student is motivated to do well.

Conclusion

In section 1 of this anthology, the key focus of all the chapters is to demonstrate how creativity within teaching, learning, and assessment can result in practices that move away from a more traditional learning approach so that a broader, more engaged learning can begin to take shape. Each of the chapters employ active and collaborative learning approaches, embedded in practice, to engage students. While the innovations described in this chapter come from very different contexts across three continents, they respond to a need to improve student motivation, teach transferable skills and prepare students to confidently articulate their discipline after university.

At the heart of these four innovations that are designed to engage is the development of the crucial competency of communication, be it between students and other students, students and supervisors, students and lecturers, or students and employers. This notion is supported by Trowler (2010:2): *"With higher education institutions facing increasingly straitened economic conditions, attracting and retaining students, satisfying and developing them and ensuring they graduate to become successful, productive citizens matters more than ever …. If student engagement can deliver on its promises, it could hold the magic wand making all of this possible."* Innovative practices within higher education are therefore a crucial phenomenon if we are to better engage our students, and if academics can engage students better through the adoption of such practices, then this would be truly magical.

About the Authors

Martin Eley is associate professor in management practice, Birmingham City University. He can be contacted at this e-mail: martin.eley@bcu.ac.uk

Sara James is a cultural sociologist and a lecturer in interdisciplinary studies in the School of Humanities and Social Sciences at La Trobe University. She can be contacted at this e-mail: s.james@latrobe.edu.au

Parminder Johal is a senior lecturer in accounting and finance and post-graduate programme leader at the Derby Business School, University of Derby, UK. She can be contacted at this e-mail: p.johal@derby.ac.uk

Sarah Midford is a lecturer in interdisciplinary studies in the School of Humanities and Social Sciences at La Trobe University. She has received a university and an Australian national teaching award for outstanding contributions to student learning. She can be contacted at this e-mail: s.midford@latrobe.edu.au

Magas R. Pather is head of the Department of Applied Communicative Skills at the University of Johannesburg. He can be contacted at this e-mail: magasp@uj.ac.za

Bibliography

Altbach, P. (2013). *The International Imperative in Higher Education*. Rotterdam, The Netherlands: Sense Publishers, pp. 21–24.

Altbach, P. (2015). Globalization and Forces for Change in Higher Education. *International Higher Education*, Vol. 50, pp. 2–3.

Bundick, M.; R. Quaglia; M. Corso & D. Haywood (2014). Promoting student engagement in the classroom. *Teachers College Record*, Vol. 116, No. 4, pp. 1–34.

CBI (Confederation of British Industries) (2011). *Building for Growth: business priorities for education and skills*. CBI Publication. ISBN: 978-0-85201-740-1

Crouch, C.; J. Watkins; A. Fagen & E. Mazur (2007). Peer instruction: Engaging students one-on-one, all at once. *Research-based reform of university physics*, Vol. 1, No. 1, pp. 40–95.

De Villiers, R. (2010). The incorporation of soft skills into accounting curricula: preparing accounting graduates for their unpredictable futures. *Meditari Accountancy Research*, Vol. 18, No. 2, pp. 1–22.

Dueck, M. (2014). *Response: The best ways to engage students in learning.* Education Week Teacher. Online Resource: http://blogs.edweek.org/teachers/classroom_qa_with_larry_ferlazzo/2014/12/response_the_best_ways_to_engage_students_in_learning.html [Accessed on 9 May 2017].

Frymier, A. & G. Shulman (1995). "What's in it for me?": Increasing content relevance to enhance students' motivation. *Communication Education*, Vol. 44, No. 1, pp. 40–50.

Halm, S. (2015). The Impact of Engagement on Student Learning. *International Journal of Education and Social Science*, Vol. 2, No. 2, February 2015.

Jang, H.; J. Reeve & E. Deci (2010). Engaging students in learning activities: It is not autonomy support or structure but autonomy support and structure. *Journal of educational psychology*, Vol. 102, No. 3, p. 588.

Kuh, G. (2003). What we're learning about student engagement from NSSE. *Change: The Magazine of Higher Learning*, Vol. 35, No. 2, pp. 24–32.

McCormick, A.; J. Kinzie & R. Gonyea (2013). Student engagement: Bridging research and practice to improve the quality of undergraduate education. In M. B. Paulsen (Ed.), *Higher education: Handbook of theory and research*, Vol. 28, pp. 47–92. Netherlands: Springer.

O'Shea, S.; J. May; C. Stone & J. Delahunty (2017). *First-in-family students, university experience and family life. Motivations, Transitions and Participation.* Palgrave MacMillan UK.

Prince, M. (2004). Does Active Learning Work? A Review of the Research. *Journal of Engineering Education*, Vol. 93, No. 3, pp. 223–231.

Trowler, V. (2010). *Student engagement literature review.* Higher Education Academy (HEA), UK. pp. 2–52.

Warren, D. (2016). Curriculum design in a context of widening participation in higher education. *Arts and Humanities in Higher Education*, Vol. 1, No. 1, pp. 85–99.

Zepke, N. & L. Leach (2005). Integration and adaptation: Approaches to the student retention. *Learning in Higher Education the Journal of the Institute for Learning and Teaching*, Vol. 6, No. 1, pp. 46–59.

Chapter 3

Teaching Business Communication through Collaborative Project-Based Learning

Magas R. Pather

Introduction

This chapter contributes to the book *New Innovations in Teaching and Learning in Higher Education* by showing how collaborative project-based learning is used as an innovative educational methodology to improve the courage and audacity of non-native English-speaking African under-graduate students to face an audience and "have their say" – in English. The undergraduate students follow a business communication course at the University of Johannesburg (UJ), Gauteng, South Africa. The course is taught in English. Most of our undergraduate students come from rural South African schools, where the language of teaching and learning is isiXhosa or another Nguni language (there are nine official traditional languages in South Africa). Some come from other African countries speaking Mashi/Swahili, for instance. Overall, our undergrad-uate students have minimal skills in writing and speaking English. This is a challenge to both teachers and learners of business communication.

There is a rareness of literature on teaching and learning business communication in the African academic context. Therefore, I see my chapter as a significant milestone in the advancement of business commu-nication in African universities, because for the first time it brings an African perspective to that discourse. It highlights the non-native English speakers' hesitations for oral communication in English. And oral communication is, of course, a major part of teaching and learning business communication. Oral communication is often considered one of the most difficult aspects of learning a second language (Brown & Yule, 1983). In particular, non-native English-speaking students find it difficult to express themselves in English in front of an audience. Speaking seems to be the most important of the four skills in business communication (listening, speaking, reading, and writing) (Ur, 1996). The major goal of all English language teaching should be to give learners the ability to use English effectively and accurately in communication scenarios (Davies & Pearse, 2000). This is why I focus on how to teach oral communication skills to students through collaborative project-based learning in our Business Communication course. Reading the chapter, you will gain at least three important insights:

1. an insight into the way in which we use collaborative project-based learning as our innovative teaching method;

2. an insight into how oral presentation becomes on of multiple innovative learning methods for our non-native English-speaking students;

3. an insight into how Business Communication students acquire the necessary oral communication skills.

My chapter is structured in four main sections. In the first section, I present the background for using collaborative project-based learning at UJ. In this section, I also address two contextual challenges of teaching business communication in a South African university. In the second section, I describe my practice in more detail. In the third section, I describe the outcome in terms of student learning. In the fourth and final section, I look forward as I end the chapter by discussing what is yet to be done to further improve business communication learning.

Section 1: The Background

At UJ we revised the Business Communication undergraduate curriculum in 2015 to better prepare our non-native English-speaking black African students for the challenges they will meet in the workplace. As head of the Department of Applied Communicative Skills in the Faculty of Humanities, I have taken this seriously, and I have been rather instrumental in integrating business needs into our curriculum, because I find this to be of particular importance for the future of our students. We are a service department, and business communication is offered as a required course in national diplomas, and in the bachelor of commerce and engineering degrees.

The format and content of our Business Communication course has changed over time. It used to be a traditionally taught course with an emphasis on intercultural business communication, focusing on cultural challenges. Today, the intercultural dimension has been integrated in a way that sees interculturality as a natural consequence of globalisation, and therefore not as something that needs to be addressed uniquely but rather as a fact of life in the world inhabited by a diverse population of students and faculty. New topic areas are still being introduced to the course content when the development in the business environment calls for adjustments to the curriculum. Most recently, in 2015, we introduced the role of social media and the vital role of oral communication in the workplace.

At UJ, we currently experience two major contextual challenges in relation to teaching and learning business communication: 1) a change process of the educational model; and 2) possible deficiencies of African university education.

A Change Process of the Educational Model

Currently, African universities are involved in a wide-reaching change process of their educational model, stemming from different student protest actions demanding the decolonisation of knowledge. The problem is not the absence of "African voices" or indigenous knowledge but its epistemological subordination within the mainstream economy of knowledge. African students wish to make knowledge a broader good for society. The perceived problem is that a large bank of knowledge produced in colonised and postcolonial societies has never been incorporated into the mainstream economy, or is included only in marginal ways (Sydney, 2016). This economy has been profoundly shaped by what the Peruvian sociologist Quijano (2000) has called the "coloniality of power". A careful look at the history reveals that the hegemonic forms of knowledge in the global economy are far from being simply an expression of "Western" knowledge. Thus, there is a call for making knowledge a common good, for sharing knowledge in broader parts of society, and for using non-Westernised knowledge. Whatever educational model is adopted, one thing should remain unaltered in the university: *"the incessant search for truth in which the teacher teaches what he discovers day to day, subjecting his own knowledge to permanent criticism, with a marked vocation for service to the society in which he is immersed"* (Cazorla et al., 1996:5). This "outspoken confrontational" attitude defines students in many South African universities. Tulgan (2008:n.p.) says: *"This is a generation of multitaskers, and they can juggle email on their tablets, while talking on cell phones as well as trolling online"*. They believe in their own self-worth, which challenges conventional ways of presenting ideas to potential clients in the workplace.

UJ is currently reviewing everything we do through the lens of decolonisation of knowledge. Our drive towards decolonisation was given impetus by our Institute for Pan-African Thought and Conversation (IPATC), and the library, who are collaborating to tell African stories about key figures from our past – people whose contributions to the continent will also guide its future. For example, one discussion was centred around Ali Mazrui (1933–2014), the Kenyan political thinker best known in the West for writing and presenting a groundbreaking television series *The Africans: A Triple Heritage* (1986). On the panel to discuss a new publication in tribute to Mazrui *A Giant Tree Has Fallen* were Ms Rose Francis (African Perspectives Publishing), Mr Abdul Bemath (Ali Mazrui's bibliographer), Prof Mathatha Tsedu (School of Literature, Language, and Media, Wits), Prof Gilbert Khadiagala (Department of International Relations, Wits), and Prof Adekeye Adebajo (Director: IPATC), (UJ-Vice Chancellor's message, 2017).

This focus on decolonisation of knowledge means that our Business Communication course is taught across disciplines, levels, and programmes where new students are courted into contributing to the conversations on decolonisation of knowledge.

Possible Deficiencies of African University Education

Currently in South Africa, workplaces have pointed out the following to be the main deficiencies of university education:

1. insufficient preparation for research and creation;

2. excessive theoretical instruction with a reduced practical component;

3. knowledge that is too general with poor specialisation and outdated knowledge;

4. insufficient preparation in directing human teams.

This was close to what came to the fore in European universities over a decade ago (Commission of the European Communities, 2003). One of the great challenges of the African university system is to demonstrate capacity for adaptation to the changes in the 21st century and its new demands for professional competencies. In our redesign of the Business Communication course, we have done our best to take into consideration these deficiencies of African university education, which is why we pay much more attention to working with the method of collaborative project-based learning.

Following this short background section, where I briefly touched upon the Business Communications course and two of the contextual challenges related to delivering this course in a South African context, I will turn to section 2 and describe the collaborative project-based learning in more detail.

Section 2: The Practice

In this section, I elaborate on the details of our Business Communication course and discuss the practical aspects of collaborative project-based learning as we practice it. Whereas project-based learning is commonplace in first-world countries like the USA. and UK, it is considered an innovation in the African educational context, chiefly because it exposes and provides a space for particularly black African students to experience what mirrors work in a real workplace situation. This is why in the African academic environment, collaborative project-based learning is an important and yet innovative educational methodology. In collaborative project-based learning, students collaborate with one another; use social media; and engage with employees, employers, and their lecturers. This is not something they have been taught or have been trained to do during their formal schooling before university. To our students this is a completely new way of teaching and learning.

The goal of our Business Communication course is to enable students to be able to communicate socially and formally in the workplace. Oral communication skills are fundamental to their development of literacy and essential for their thinking and learning. It is the glue that puts all the components of a language together. Through talk, students not only communicate information but also explore and come to understand ideas and concepts; identify and solve problems; organise their experience and knowledge; and express and clarify their thoughts, feelings, and opinions. Listening and speaking skills are essential for interaction at home and in the workplace. *"Tell me and I forget, teach me and I may remember, involve me and I learn"* – this quote by Benjamin Franklin rings true in the project-based learning approach. The Business Communication students at UJ particularly enhance their English oral communication skills on a whole new level by becoming involved in a collaborative group project that has as its output an oral presentation to the class. Whereas in a Western university, where students may have English as their mother tongue, the concept of oral presentations in English to the class is not a new innovation, I may again point to the demographics of our student population, who come from rural South African schools where the language of teaching and learning is isiXhosa or another Nguni language. In our educational context, it requires an innovative practice to develop the courage and audacity of non-native English-speaking African under-graduate students to face an audience and "have their say" – in English.

We teach large undergraduate classes at the UJ – in some cases 250 students in a class. In the Department of Finance, Economic and Finan-cial Science, we service a cohort of on average 1,500 students. These are mainly black African students from South Africa and Africa who have done English as a second or third language at school. Their deficit in oral communication skills places them at a disadvantage in the workplace, and that is why our innovative teaching approach involves collaborative project-based learning where students become active participants rather than passive recipients of knowledge.

2a. Our Methods

In our Business Communication course, we use collaborative project-based learning in ways that support different learning strategies, merging different methods: intuitive, comparative, inductive, case study, problem-solving (Cazorla *et al.*, 1996). We use different activities inside and outside the classroom: lectures, group activities, collaborative learning, online and face-to-face tutoring, project exhibits, and oral presentations among project teams. Our Business Communication course is a melting pot of teaching methods and student activities. We use these to mirror what we believe our students will meet in the workplace.

Most functions in the workplace require oral communication skills interspersed with written communication. Students, as the biggest users of sites like YouTube and Flickr, engage well with images and video. They turn business screensavers into interactive billboards and bring internal communication messages to life by communicating visually and in written format, albeit in what has become known as "mobile language".

In keeping with these abilities of our students and the demands of the business community, the Department of Applied Communicative Skills at UJ focuses in both semesters on an oral communication project, which encompasses as many digital platforms as possible in its attempt to teach oral communication skills through collaborative project-based learning. In example box 1, a lecturer from the Department of Applied Communicative Skills explains the project-based teaching method used in the Business Communication course given to Engineering students on the Doornfontein Campus, UJ.

I have graded over 500 students' oral presentations and was convinced that oral presentations as an assessment form needed to be improved on. When given more information and guidelines on the presentation, it was encouraging to see that students generally improved most aspects of their presentation skills. For example, presentation style including eye contact, body language and overcoming stage fright were factors that improved. However, the audience's understanding of the topic was lacking in many cases. The average student seemed to adopt a surface approach to preparing for presentations and usually by-hearted a 5-minute speech and delivered it to a bored class. The problem that then becomes apparent is that the class loses out on valuable teaching/learning time as oral presentations are held in class time. In a class of around 100 students where a group of 5 is presenting, 95 bored students waste their time by not participating and engaging in the learning process. Audience participation is therefore vital for the presenter and audience and innovation in this area of business communication was vital. Improving audience participation is important in enhancing the value of time spent on presentations. Otherwise, a majority of the class is left out of the whole learning process.

To overcome these problems, I introduced video oral presentations in my Business Communication classes in 2015. I gave students detailed guidelines about the format, as they were new to video production. The subject outline delineated the requirements: You are required, in small teams of 4–5 people, to create a video on a topic related to your specialised field of study and business communication. The video should not be a 12–15 minutes' presentation of "lecture material". Instead, ensure you include activities to keep the class interested, while demonstrating your understanding of relevant business communication concepts. Be creative, use multimedia music, audio accompaniments, and visual effects. Students were told to make it interesting and to consider including debates, role-plays, demonstrations, team games and competitions. They also needed to ensure that the video was a well-prepared team effort, not a collection of separate video sections by each group member. Each member of the group had to contribute equally to the preparation and presentation of the video. Group members were awarded marks as a group based on their contribution to the preparation and performance during the video. The oral presentation presents an opportunity for students to develop capacity for self-directedness and improve communication skills. Working in groups enables students to develop collaborative abilities such as appreciating alternative viewpoints, decision-making skills and empathy towards other group members.

Example box 1: Video production as a project-based learning method.

As the example shows, we use video production as the vehicle for engaging students in collaborative project-based learning where the output is both self-directedness and improved communication skills. During theory classes, students are introduced to a range of innovative applications in the field of speech language pathology. Integrated learning takes place when students apply the skills they have acquired from this collaborative learning experience in their core discipline, such as human resource management or entrepreneurship and business management. Two vital skills that are developed are *creative problem-solving* and *critical thinking*. As facilitators, we are convinced that these skills are enhanced, because during the practicum, students experience the process of creating an innovative concept themselves by going through a structured work process. In example box 2, I explain how we work with student groups:

Students are divided into groups and choose a realistic context for the practicum (followed by the proposal and formulation of an innovative concept which addresses the findings from the fieldwork). Groups are supervised with regular meetings, discussions and evaluation sessions. Finally, the groups summarise their findings and prepare their final presentations. The process of approximation to reality is complemented with group activities in class and participatory workshops using active methods (Johnson, 1999) to achieve direct participation of the students in the development of the projects in a way similar to real professional work. In these sessions, the lecturer acts as a guide in the tasks students undertake and provides incentive for learning. During these sessions, an active learning process is obtained instead of a passive absorption of knowledge. The active method of learning by doing is of special relevance in the area of projects with enormous potential for originality, creativity and common sense that can fit perfectly with the scientific and technical knowledge students have previously received during their coursework (Bartkus, 2001).

Example box 2: Students working in groups.

The lack of motivation among the non-native English-speaking students because of their aversion to address an audience was one of our great challenges. A large part of the problem of learning to think – and thought – is a problem of motivation. Thinking can be hard work and undoubtedly the main reason that people do not think is simply because they are unwilling to make the effort (Nickerson *et al.*, 1985). The main ingredients of the solution to overcome this obstacle and motivate these students was the eminently practical approach, contact with real agents, ensuring that groups were well-balanced with students that express themselves well in English and the revelation that they were performing useful work that solves real problems. A group made this discovery during their research about the efficacy and usefulness of the oral presentation in the business world:

> *"Pharmaceutical giant, GlaxoSmithKline used a mixture of satellite broadcasting and webcasting for its research and development presentation to analysts and at its round-up of the firm's activities. The latter reached 37,000 employees worldwide, says Business internal comms V-P Elaine Macfarlane. GSK plans to show future presentations on every employee's computer."*

This way of putting our teaching and learning of business communication into practice and reflecting what goes on in the business world is a way to enhance student motivation.

2b. Presenting

Proper guidelines are provided and students are given adequate time to select a topic related to the themes being studied in Business Communication, such as "Topic Six: Managing Generations at work":

> *"We are all familiar with the challenges of different generations working together, but it is not only the different expectations and attitudes, even the means of communication may be different between Generation Y and the older generations. Discuss this important issue in an oral presentation."*

They meet regularly to strategise, research the topic, and audio visual material are created by the group. They acquire best practice skills in communication, which form an integral part of an employee's work life. Public speaking skills are highly prized in the employment market and are well worth taking the time to develop. Oral presentations can have a greater impact than written presentations and require a wide range of skills, not only the skills required to stand up and deliver a talk, but also skills in research:

1. the ability to organise ideas and construct logical arguments;

2. the ability to develop handouts and aids;

3. the ability to field impromptu questions from the audience.

Students are also required to write an accompanying paper. The key areas that groups have to focus on to deliver an oral presentation include:

+ preparing the presentation;

+ delivering the presentation.

Preparatory oral presentations in the Business Communication course take place in various forms. These include:

1. giving a public talk in the form of a lecture or seminar presentation;

2. delivering a presentation on the outcomes of a class exercise or on an assigned reading;

3. actively participating in a tutorial, discussion group.

This is also accompanied by a written component. Good communication skills help to reduce the barriers erected because of language and cultural differences. The following outcomes inform the assessment criteria:

1. The group will practice writing as a process of motivated inquiry, engaging other writers' ideas as they explore and develop their own.

2. Students will develop an appreciation of how the formal elements of language and genre shape meaning; they will express their own ideas as informed opinions.

3. Students will be able to identify topics and formulate questions for productive inquiry; they will identify appropriate methods and sources for research and critically evaluate the sources they find; and they will use their chosen sources effectively in their own writing, citing all sources appropriately.

4. Students will be able to prepare, organise, and deliver an engaging oral presentation. They will appreciate the expressive use of language as an activity, mimicking an actual oral presentation in the workplace.

2c. Props

Video, interviews, research, and mock workplace props are regularly designed and created by groups to mimic what is found in the workplace. YouTube and live interviews are used to make the presentation authentic. Depending on the topic that is selected, the group will employ prop(s) that enhance their presentation and convey the message clearly.

Section 3: The Outcome

While at first it is a dread, once completed the students feel armed to "take on" other oral communication challenges. We need linguistic competence, an adequate vocabulary, and mastery of syntax to speak in another language (Nunan, 1999). However, linguistic competence is not sufficient for someone who wants to communicate competently in another language. The practitioner must also display confidence in conversation and during interviews.

After having conducted class observation, informal interviews, and received feedback from lecturers in the Department of Applied Communicative Skills, we consider our innovation a success. Our students do too. Why do our students consider our innovative teaching and learning practice a success? The oral presentation, among other merits, was expected to:

1) increase quantity and quality of speaking;

2) improve class participation;

3) permit individual assessment in a large class;

4) encourage in-depth learning; and

5) offer immediate feedback to students.

The merits of the oral presentation are many. It encourages higher-order learning and, as Biggs (2000:43) comments, *"the most likely kind of learning, assessed by oral presentations is concentrating on relevance and application"*. Koshy (2008:n.p.) evaluates oral presentation sessions as an alternative to term assessments and argues for the choice of oral presentation sessions. It *"allow[s] lecturers the opportunity to avoid reading/grading students"*; secondly, it permits *"students to work collaboratively in groups"*; and thirdly, the various merits suggested in an article by Watkins *et al.* (2006). Dunn *et al.* (2004) list many advantages in the use of this type of assessment, including student motivation, generated by an innovative assignment and peer learning. Oral presentations are less threatening than written tests, since, with the latter, sections to be tested and questions are unknown, whereas with the former there is interaction between lecturers, tutors, and students during the sessions, resulting in better evaluations.

Another major merit is that students cannot memorise material and work in tandem for a written test, which requires the application of attained knowledge. However, they easily recall the content of the oral presentation because it is their creation. The entire group of students must be au fait with the content of the whole presentation in order to respond to questions posed by an audience of their peers and not rely on the cue cards so that it becomes a reading exercise of the whole research.

A series of interviews of 40% of students enrolled in Business Communication 1 (N=520) was done to evaluate their responses to the innovative assessment. The interview consisted of 19 ordinal questions on a 5-point Likert scale and 1 ranking question about the preferred type of assessment. The core areas covered were: working on the oral presentation; viewing other presentations; delivering the oral presentation; and a comparison with other assessments.

To questions about working on the oral presentation:
- 80% of the students agreed that they enjoyed working on the oral presentation;
- an overwhelming 97% of students said they like to work on new types of assessments;
- 78% said they would like to work on oral presentations again.

On their views about viewing other oral presentations:
- 96% said they enjoyed listening to other oral presentations;
- 83% said they learned from other oral presentations;
- 83% agreed that the topics covered in the oral presentations were interesting; while
- 94% agreed that the topics were useful;
- 42% said the number of oral presentations presented in a session should be around 3, while
- 36% said they would like to see 3–5 oral presentations per session;
- the rest said they would like to view 5–7 oral presentations per session.

Table 1: Student evaluation of oral presentations.

In short, an analysis of the interviews shows that students enjoyed working on the assessment and benefitted greatly from it. When Kirkpatrick's four-level evaluation framework (Kirkpatrick, 1975) is considered: lecturers note that the outcomes have been achieved; learning has taken place as evidenced by students being more confident in their oral presentations during the second semester; feedback from other staff members and students attest to the fact that students are more positively inclined to the oral presentation as a form of assessment; through informal conversations with ex-students that are employed, it has been noted that the oral presentation gave them the required skills to do similar presentations in the workplace. Thus, we contend that performance at all four levels of evaluation has been enhanced.

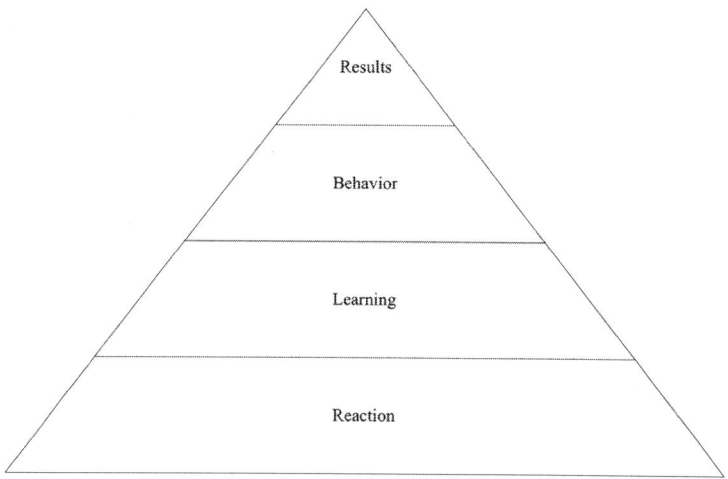

Figure 1: Kirkpatrick's (1975) four-level evaluation framework.

Walker (2005:43) also reports similar findings: "*students maintained that an Oral Presentation provided stimulating satisfaction and feel that the assessment method enhances their learning of the subject*". To the questions about presenting the topic, 36% agreed that they were afraid to speak in public, and 91% said the one-to-one speaking in the oral presentation gave them confidence to speak in public. About the discussion session with presenters, 89% agreed that presenters handled questions well and gave detailed responses, while 64% said they were asked stimulating questions by their peers. In the interviews, 75% said it was easy to score marks in the oral presentation. An overwhelming 86% said that oral presentations helped them to understand difficult topics; 84% said oral presentations were preferable to written assessments. For the ranking question, which asked students to rank in order of preference the assessment they liked best, 54% chose the oral presentation as their preferred assessment. Farber and Penhale (1995:12) suggest that oral presentation sessions "*not only provides educational benefits, but also elicits enthusiastic participation and positive response from students*". Akister *et al.* (2000:231) observe that students "*seem to enjoy exploring a different mode of presentation. Overall the experience of using this method of assessment has been extremely positive. It seems an efficient way of teaching through assessment and of developing verbal and presentation skills*". Informal interviews with 89 students studying the National Diploma in Entrepreneurship (ATK 11A1/11B1) were also conducted to analyse their motives, beliefs, attitudes, and feelings in relation to the assessment. The interviews were recorded, transcribed, and analysed. This yielded very encouraging feedback. One major observation was that it was a fun assessment to do. Some students also said it was easier than other assessments. Some students felt it was too much work to be done by a small group of students, while others responded that working on an oral presentation in a group would be difficult as there would be "too many conflicting ideas". A group of students that produced one of the best oral presentations entitled *Computer Mediated Communication* in the workplace said that they felt like they were at an exhibition: "*We've been a part of many Business exhibitions and it feels great when you present your topic and you get your views from your lecturer, it tells how you should improvise on your presentation skills*". The need to make the information "come alive" was highlighted during the interviews. Colleagues and I have received feedback from ex-students employed in various capacities in businesses in Johannesburg, Gauteng, South Africa, complimenting us on the usefulness of particularly oral communication skills taught in Business Communication and its efficacy in the workplace:

Ms F. Darsot, who offers Business Communication for sophomore Bachelor of Commerce students, received the following e-mail, evidencing that our outcomes in teaching verbal communication skills had to a large degree been achieved:

> *"Morning Fatima, you know when I chose to do Business Communications this semester, I was just avoiding to do Computer Systems. It got real this weekend even I was at the Herbalife Extravaganza and I saw some speaker doing all the wrong things, her hands moving all the time and I couldn't focus on what she was saying. I then remembered how you made us practice and you would correct us. I then knew that I made the right choice when I chose to do Business Communications. A big thank you goes to you, for being patient with us at all times and preparing us for the business world. Your student Tracy."*

An African student's (Lebo's) written response gives an insight into why our students consider this practice innovative:

> *"Dr. Pather's approach to teaching is rather interesting and unconventional. He uses humour to pass on knowledge and makes learning fun. Through his humour, we are more relaxed during lectures and more eager to learn than if we were tense and agitated. Dr Pather has a skill to simplify the content using the most outrageous practical examples of which you are guaranteed to remember when you have to do your presentation. With regards to oral presentations, he always makes sure he tells us well in advance, giving us enough time to prepare."*

Section 4: Moving Forward

The execution of the project has been an interesting chance for both students as well as the project facilitators to reflect and innovate. The project helped the students to integrate more quickly into their core studies. The oral presentation experience is a lifelong learning experience. The oral presentation model becomes a benchmark that students build on and use to improve their oral interactions at work and socially. This project remains indelible on the student's mind because it was a lived experience. This helps our lecturers control the relationship between theory and practical experiences. Long after the project, students from the oral presentation groups still maintain contact with each other as well as spend time together on and off campus. Lecturers work intensively for protracted periods throughout the academic year with these freshman, which fosters a sense of camaraderie and trust between student and lecturer.

This new learning environment at UJ is stimulating and motivating, and student class attendance and performance is bolstered. This can be used as an advantage in the promotion of our diploma and degree programmes. The dean of Humanities has been informed of the benefits of this collaborative group project. Law students now have a compulsory oral presentation component in mock scenarios in their curriculum. The number of degree programmes including the oral presentation in their work plan has increased. Thus, this type of student-integration-through-involvement model can be imported to other universities.

Businesses were approached to partner in this project. Topics related to business practice were given in advance and my students prepared and presented to a sample of that business's management and staff. As Paloma and Banta (1999:46) write:

> "Assessment must be seen as an activity done with and for students, rather than to them. Students need to be active partners in assessment. If educators are thoughtful about how they include students in the assessment process, they can help overcome motivation problems that hinder assessment."

Biggs' (2000:13) observation, "being active while learning is better than being inactive: activity is a good in itself", supports the involvement of students in the assignment. Though the oral presentation was successful in overcoming some of the drawbacks of oral communication experienced by non-native English speakers, there are areas that need revision to improve this assessment. In the future, it would be feasible to follow what Mulnix and Penhale (1997) did during the poster session they organised. A section based on the best oral presentation content can be used in the final examination in the Business Communication written examination. This would ensure the active participation of students in the oral presentation. A major drawback is that students feel that oral presentations call for hours in the library, critical thinking, and interpretation. In the interviews, many students raised this concern. It is interesting to note that the students who participated in the sessions identified four reasons for the effectiveness of oral presentations:

1. the design and format of the oral presentation;

2. the visuals supporting the oral presentation;

3. the content of the oral presentation;

4. the overall audience participation.

We can deduce that many students relate successful oral presentations to creative research and critical thinking skills.

Conclusion

The 10-year experience with collaborative project-based learning described here is an innovative educational methodology for the development of competences, linking teaching and practice with the professional sphere. This learning technique is based on collaboration, active participation, and interaction, offering multiple possibilities for developing technical, contextual, and behavioural competences. Arising out of this experience is a learning/student-centred process that requires that both lecturers and students assume a more active role, greater shared commitment, and, in the case of the students, greater responsibility for their own learning. Throughout the different phases, the scientific basis of project-based learning is maintained to generate learning strategies in which students are not submissive recipients of knowledge but are absorbed in a pre-professional experience – thanks to the link between the Department of Applied Communicative Skills and the business world defining projects with workplace content that require students to integrate the knowledge they have already gained from other courses with new knowledge attained in developing the project. Personal competences are also developed. Students learn to work in teams, potentiating their personality and taking them closer to reality. The methodology arouses a spirit of investigation and innovation, creativity for the generation of new knowledge, productive thought, and motivation to learn and solve problems.

About the Author

Magas R. Pather is head of the Department of Applied Communicative Skills at the University of Johannesburg. He can be contacted at this e-mail: magasp@uj.ac.za

Bibliography

Akister, J.; A. Bannon; H. Mullender-Lock (2000). Poster Presentations in Social Work Education Assessment: a Case Study. *Innovations in Education and Training International*, Vol. 37, No. 3, pp. 229–233.

Bartkus, K. R. (2001). Skills and cooperative education: a conceptual framework. *Journal of Cooperative Education*, Vol. 36, No. 1, pp. 17–24.

Biggs, J. (2000). *Teaching for quality learning at university: What the student does.* Open University Press.

Brown, G. & G. Yule (1983). *Teaching the Spoken Language.* Cambridge: Cambridge University Press.

Cazorla, A.; J. L. Marco & I. De Los Ríos (1996). *El ciclo de los proyectos y la docencia: aplicación a una comarca rural.* Paper presented at the VI Nacional Conference on Project Engineering, June 26–29, in Almagro, Ciudad Real, Spain.

Commission of the European Communities (2003). *The role of the universities in the Europe of knowledge.* Commission of the European Communities.

Davies, P. & E. Pearse (2000). *Success in English Teaching.* Oxford: Oxford University Press.

Dunn, L.; C. Morgan; S. Parry & M. O'Reilly (2004). *The Student Assessment Handbook.* New York: Routledge.

Farber, E. & S. Penhale (1995). Using Poster sessions in Introductory Science Courses: An Example at Earlham. *Research Strategies*, Winter.

Kirkpatrick, D. L. (Ed.) (1975). *Evaluating Training programs.* Alexandria, VA.

Koshy, S. (2008). *Group work for freshmen students: A positive learning.* Presented at the Research Across the Disciplines conference sponsored by the International Journal for Arts and Sciences, 1–4 Dec, 2008.

Mulnix, A. & S. J. Penhale (1997). Modeling the Activities of Scientists: A Literature Review and Poster Presentation Assignment. *The American Biology Teacher*, Vol. 14, No. 8, pp. 482–487.

Nickerson, R. S.; D. N. Perkins & E. E. Smith (1985). *The Teaching of the Thinking.* New Jersey: Lawrence Eribaum Associates.

Nunan, D. (1999). *Second Language Teaching & Learning.* Boston, Massachusetts: Heinle & Heinle Publishers.

Paloma, C. A. & T. W. Banta (1999). *Assessment Essentials: Planning, Planning, Implementing, and Improving Assessment in Higher Education.* 1st edition. New York: Wiley.

Tulgan, B (2008). https://www.youtube.com/watch?v=s-Jicy_xm5A. Uploaded by APBSpeakersInc. [Accessed on 4 April 2017].

Ur, P. (1996). *A course in Language Teaching. Practice and Theory.* Cambridge: Cambridge University Press.

Walker, S. (2005). Poster, poster on the wall: whose is the fairest assessment of all? *Journal of Family Therapy*, No. 27, pp. 285–288.

Chapter 4
Employer Engagement: Accounting Standards in Action

Parminder Johal

Introduction

This chapter contributes to the book *New Innovations in Teaching and Learning in Higher Education* by demonstrating how pedagogy practice in the accounting subject discipline can positively contribute to the student learning experience. Both the changing landscape of higher education institutions (HEIs) and the changing role of the professional accountant, with businesses calling for greater emphasis not only technical but also ethical and interpersonal skills and competencies (ACCA, 2016), has placed a spotlight on the provision of quality teaching, learning, and assessment (TLA) practice at the subject discipline level within higher education (HE). Both HEIs and employers are moving in parallel to adapt to the fast pace of change in HE and the global market. Constructivist and student-centred learning approaches (Gagnon & Collay, 2001) have been mooted as approaches that can better deliver to this parallel transition through a greater focus on learning over teaching.

In light of this transitional journey and the UK Government's manifesto to deliver on the implementation of a teaching excellence framework (TEF), the University of Derby (UoD) has recently drafted a revised TLA strategy with a clear focus on transforming student lives with a broader focus on the student experience. The transformational experience is embraced under three pillars: employability, teaching quality, and research in the curriculum. As part of this strategy, the UoD is actively encouraging and supporting staff to continue to develop innovative teaching, learning, and assessment methods. It is a combination of the revised UoD strategy, the changing HE landscape, and the increasing demands on the role of the professional accountant that has encouraged the introduction of an embedded employer-led intervention at module level. This chapter will enable you to adapt your current teaching practice so that the following may be addressed:

1. a move towards a deeper learning approach in the accounting subject discipline;

2. effective employer engagement;

3. enhanced student experience and employability skills.

This chapter is divided into five sections. The first section will set the context for the innovative practice. Sections 2 and 3 will focus on the practice itself and the related outcomes, whilst section 4 outlines the way forward, and section 5 presents the conclusion.

Section 1: The Background

The accounting subject discipline remains a popular choice for students at the UoD as they start to plan for their journey in HE and beyond. The MSc Accounting and Finance programme at the UoD attracts a diverse student body from the domestic and international student market. For many, it is a choice that provides a structured career trajectory and creates the opportunity for graduate employment and/or further study at postgraduate level or study towards professional accountancy qualifications. Being a vocational programme, and one that is heavily guided by the various professional accountancy bodies, has restricted the creativity of the accounting curriculum design and its delivery within HE.

As a consequence, quite often the teaching of accounting modules (the units of study that make up a degree), such as, corporate reporting, can be restrictive in that the students are required to learn the accounting standards as a set of guidance rules that govern how organisations construct their financial statements. The application and impact of these standards is limited to question-based scenarios with little or no opportunity to experience how this process would work in reality for any given organisation. The transfer of this factual knowledge lends itself to a teaching practice that is predominately following a traditional class-based approach (with the lecturer at the front of the classroom delivering to a silent student cohort), and thus learning theories very clearly position the accounting discipline amidst the positivist or traditionalist perspective in its approach to student learning. Not surprisingly, this is reflected in a curriculum design that depicts a pyramid approach to the subject content, moving from a generalist to a specialist level of content, and this may force the learner towards a certain learning approach (Emes & Cleveland-Innes, 2003). The pedagogy practices associated with the accounting subject discipline tend to conclude that accounting students adopt a surface learning approach (Chan et al., 1989; Eley, 1992; Gow et al., 1994; Booth et al., 1999) and this in turn may significantly impact the quality of student learning and therefore student experience (Biggs, 1987a, 1987b; English et al., 2004). A surface learning approach is characterised by a process of rote learning and a regurgitation of facts as opposed to a deep learning approach, which lends itself to the more curious, engaged student who will probe, explore, integrate, and question the relevance and application of the subject content.

In response to the increasing emphasis on student experience and its link with pedagogy practices, it was decided to introduce employer engagement within an accounting module as an innovative practice to direct students towards a more engaged and deeper learning approach that will contribute towards a better student experience. The innovative practice will also serve as a suitable vehicle to develop competencies and skills that are necessary beyond the curriculum and desirable in the workplace (de Villiers, 2010).

Section 2: The Practice

The practice described in this chapter incorporates a change in the learning approach as an attempt to better engage the students and enhance their HE learning experiences through an employer-led intervention. The emphasis of the practice was to enable the student to connect the module content and learning to its practice and impact for a live organisation and thus engage with a deep learning approach. The practice orchestrated a move away from the traditional class-based teaching method towards an extension to the purpose of a guest speaker from industry, such that the employer is engaged with the module even before the students commence the module and continues to be engaged after the guest address. Students are set activities that will enable them to develop further their knowledge and skills, be creative, discuss, research, apply and adapt to a live situation, and practice deep and not just surface learning. In addition, this shift in approach is a step towards the university's emphasis on prioritising the student experience.

2a. A General Introduction to the Innovative Practice

The innovative TLA practice was relevant for postgraduate accounting students and in particular relevant to the Corporate Reporting module with a focus on accounting standards and the impact of these standards for organisations. It was felt that a fuller understanding, through employer engagement, of how developments in accounting standards impact organisations, their financial information, and therefore internal and external stakeholders, would add more value and insight for a student from a learning perspective. It would also better prepare them for the realities of the impact of emerging developments in the workplace. The practice was therefore providing the students with experience from the "coalface" (the lecturers who are face to face with the students) and the opportunity to engage with an employer on a work-based development. Whilst it may be possible to mirror this practice for accounting students at undergraduate level, the challenge would lie in how much "assessment space" (in the curriculum) would be available for this practice, since at undergraduate level most accounting programmes have a significant proportion of the assessment strategy dedicated to exams so that professional exemptions are applicable.

The module delivery pattern was amended to expose the students to a live organisation that needed to address an emerging corporate reporting issue, one that would mean potential changes to the way in which it constructed and reported the financial statements. The students were introduced to the financial resources director (FRD) of a local organisation, who introduced the organisation and the current challenge it faced due to changes imposed through the emergence of new accounting standards. The students were then required to work in groups to analyse and advise the organisation on the application and implications of these changes.

2b. The Curriculum

The practice was applied in the postgraduate Corporate Reporting module in the MSc Accounting and Finance programme. It is a core module and runs alongside two other modules and a series of research sessions, delivered as part of the Independent Study module, that are delivered throughout the year. The research sessions complement the assessment practice in that the students are equipped with the necessary research skills. It also meant that the learning from this module could be utilised to refine future outputs as students' progress through the programme, in particular the end product for the Independent Study module.

The Corporate Reporting module also sits in the fourth year of the four-year Integrated Masters in Accounting and Finance programme – again, it is a core module that runs alongside one other module and an independent study module that covers research methods. Sharing this module across these two programmes will enable the two cohorts to benefit from peer feedback.

The key learning outcome addressed by the innovative practice:

1. Critically discuss the impact of contemporary and emerging corporate reporting issues on strategic business decisions (the assessment carries a 40% weighting).

In addition, the employer engagement was introduced and embedded in order to:

+ enhance overall student engagement and therefore student experience;

+ develop teamwork and communication skills;

+ enhance student employability;

+ reinforce the relevance of the module content;

+ encourage deeper learning.

2c. Organisation of the Practice

Prior to addressing the students, the financial resources director (FRD) of a local organisation and I, as module leader for the Corporate Reporting module, discussed a potential assessment idea that was challenging, topical, and relevant to the module learning outcome. It was decided that the topic would be "Accounting Standards and the challenge for SMEs" (small and medium-sized enterprises). The challenge was essentially the requirement for SMEs to now fall in line with international accounting standards (IAS) and therefore prepare their accounts in accordance with the new standards FRS 101, 102, 103, as appropriate.

The assessment was crafted by the lecturer, and the FRD was consulted for feedback. Following this process, the lecturer delivered a lecture to introduce the topic, and following this the assessment was launched to the students (see assessment requirements below). The FRD was then invited (three weeks after the lecturer input) to deliver an overview of the organisation he worked for and a more in-depth lecture and discussion that related to the topic. The topic had been covered by the lecturer prior to the employer-led session, and the latter added a real-life, work relevant, company-specific dimension to the content. The FRD ended the session by making himself available for the students should they need to discuss any of the assessment requirements in the context of his organisation.

Example of Assessment Requirements on the Corporate Reporting module:

Assessment Requirements

During the semester, as a group, you will produce a presentation and write a paper that addresses the following current issue in financial reporting, using the organisation as a case study:

There has been a lot of activity to harmonise accounting standards so that a common set of standards can be used internationally. The aim of this is to enhance consistency, comparability and ultimately result in a set of financial statements that are an efficient decision making tool for a potentially wide ranging group of stakeholders.

In 2005 all listed companies were required to adopt International Financial Reporting Standards (IFRS's). This has meant that some companies still have the option to follow national accounting standards rather than the international standards. Recently there has been the launch of a number of new standards which will impact such companies.

As a group you will research the current issue outlined above. And then prepare a group presentation and a paper in which you will critically discuss the progress and impact of the current issue, on strategic business decisions for the case study organisation.

(At this stage of your studies you will predominately be researching secondary data and therefore carrying out an extensive literature review of the current issue topic. You will also attend a session on this current issue delivered by the Financial Resources Director for the cases study organisation. You may use this session to ask questions that may help you with your assessment. To get the maximum benefit of this session you should ensure that you have researched the assessment topic and the case study organisation prior to attending the session).

Your assignment submission will comprise of the following:

- an abstract and full paper (2500 including abstract) as outlined above;
- a 20-minute presentation of your full paper (this includes 5 minutes for questions) as though you were addressing an audience of Finance Managers from SMEs. (The FRD will be invited attend the presentation).

Your abstract will:

- Be no more than 250 words, it will be a short but concise summary of your full paper.
- The abstract will generally have the following features:
  1. An informative but short title;
  2. Clear statement of the research question or issue being addressed;
  3. The key points and/or arguments of the proposed paper, with generalised supporting information;
  4. Logical outline of the connections between material included; and
  5. Concluding point(s).

Lecturer's Role

In addition to liaising with the employer/FRD to formulate a topical and relevant assessment, the lecturer delivers a lecture on accounting standards and harmonisation. This will ensure that students are knowledgeable of the move towards universal accounting standards, who this applies to, and how this has progressed to include the SMEs.

Following this session, the lecturer launches the assessment and advises the students to form groups comprising of up to three to four students and to begin to research the assessment topic. Students are advised that the FRD of the case study organisation will deliver a session to the students specific to the assessment topic and that they will have the opportunity to ask questions. They are reminded that this opportunity will prove most beneficial if they have researched the impact of the new accounting standards on SMEs and researched the case study organisation. They are advised to read widely around the topic so that they can discuss and question the FRD on key issues, the practice followed to date, and the impact for stakeholders by relating to what they have identified through their research. The students and lecturer will also discuss student progress weekly by stealing 15–20 minutes of the regular timetabled class, where students can benefit from formative and peer group feedback.

Student's Role

Following the initial lecture on accounting standards and harmonisation by the lecturer, it is expected that the students undertake further reading to develop a fuller narrative and deeper comprehension of the integral role that accounting standards play in corporate/financial reporting and how this has evolved over time and affected organisations and stakeholders. This research will form the basis of their lines of enquiry for when they meet the FRD in three weeks' time. It is essential that the students engage with wider reading and study outside of the taught sessions. They must also decide how they will share the research activity amongst the group and the various sources they will each review and, finally, on how they will pull this together to formulate a series of questions for the FRD, a final paper, and a presentation. This teamwork, preparation, and allocation of tasks and planning will mirror behaviour that they would experience in a workplace environment and will further develop lifelong skills that will enhance their career potential and the student experience.

2d. Preparation

The table below provides some guidance around what preparation is useful with the practice of employer engagement in order to obtain the maximum benefit from this practice.

Preparations for this module started as early as the induction phase of the programme, during which time the students take part in a library induction event "Murder in the Library". The induction introduces the students to the digital resources, journals, and how to access articles, papers, and similar. Students worked in groups to solve the mystery of the "murder in the library" by utilising the range of resources available to them. The students can also book the meeting rooms in the library for study, presentation practice, and group meetings.

The employer-led session is a key part of the exercise, and the opportunity to approach the employer with further questions is also available to the student. The employer is therefore a key resource. The module content and assessment requirements (as outlined earlier) are also key materials that the students need. In addition, students are directed to abstracts/papers written by academic staff as examples of good practice that will help them structure their approach. These are populated on the Accounting Research Team (ART) noticeboard, prominently displayed within the business school.

Timely negotiation with the employer and release of the assessment will allow the students to maximise their research time and learn from peer feedback, reflection on teamwork, and formative feedback. It will also enable the students to plan their group meetings and independent study time. In addition, staff engagement with continuous professional development (CPD) and/or research in the relevant subject area is vital to the preparation stage, as this helps identify the current developments, challenges, and/or opportunities that organisations are faced with from an accounting and finance perspective. Current knowledge will enable the lecturer to contextualise the module content so that students can benefit from engaging with application and practice of their knowledge to reflect how it would happen in the workplace.

Semester timeline	Activity	Preparation
Period before the semester in which the module is delivered.	*Liaise with the employer to discuss identified recent developments in accounting standards in the context of a student assessment.	The lecturer's engagement with CPD activity is essential to identify current issues / developments. The lecturer will propose potential assessment ideas for discussion with the employer.
Week 2	Lecturer to introduce accounting standards and harmonisation and then launch the assessment.	Lecture preparation. Moderated assessment brief. Examples of staff/student research papers. Essential that the students have undergone a library induction so that they are aware of and comfortable accessing available resources. This usually takes place in the induction period.
Weeks 3–5	Independent research and task allocation by the student groups. Formative lecturer feedback.	Sometimes it is possible (depending on timing) to direct students to attend related (free) workshops by professional accounting bodies. Lecturer to provide flip chart paper/ markers and Post-its so that students can present an overview of how they plan to proceed as a group.
Week 6	Employer-led session by the FRD, followed by Q&A session.	Students to undertake independent/ group research. Each group to have at least two questions.
Weeks 7–8	Allocating tasks for the write up of the paper and presentation. Use of part of the seminar to reflect on progress and peer feedback.	Planning by students, setting their own deadlines and meetings. Sharing progress; peer feedback; formative feedback; reflection. Lecturer to provide flip chart paper/ markers and Post-its so that students can share their progress.
Week 12	Submission of paper and then a presentation to a panel of two staff members (FRD was also invited and agreed to attend, subject to availability).	Staff to make facilities available to students so that they can practice their presentation (e.g., booking a room with recording facility so that students can reflect and learn from their performance).

Table 1: Preparation.

*It is noteworthy that this practice relies on established links with employers. This may be an activity that is engaged with at university, school, and/or programme level. The key is for the programme team to be engaged with and to be aware of the employer engagement practice within their institution. I established my initial link with the employer through an employer networking event that was organised at Derby Business School level.

Section 3: The Outcome

The employer-engaged approach differs from the traditional teaching and learning approach in that an external and relevant perspective is introduced to the module from an industry expert, which adds credibility to the module content and brings real-life business decisions/scenarios into the classroom.

As a lecturer, this approach enhances relevance and means that the lecturer does not have to convince the students as to why they are learning about the development of accounting standards. Contextualising the module content to real life is made a lot easier, and the lecturer can enjoy discussion that is informed by student research, and therefore a greater level of interaction, challenge, and discussion is experienced. In addition, this approach of setting an assessment in collaboration with an external employer augmented the theoretical aspects of the module and provided scope for and encouraged deeper learning.

3a. Student Outcome

The deviation from traditional teaching and learning practice through collaboration with an embedded external employer added variety for the students and encouraged students to adopt a more professional approach, as it meant that they were accountable not only to themselves but now also to an external party. A break from the lecturer and the opportunity to access the expertise of an external employer provided an internal insight of an external environment. Having to address a live issue required the students to delve further into the information-gathering process and explore multiple implications relating to their decisions. This process was also an opportunity for students to recognise how the knowledge and learning from prior studies has a place in future modules.

Time management, communication, networking, research, and teamwork competencies were an integral part of this exercise; peer learning and reflection following the practice presentations and in class discussions also added to the learning experience. Discussions around the transfer of these competencies to other parts of the programme and beyond the programme itself left the students feeling confident and better equipped for future challenges. A deeper approach to learning through analysing the impact for the organisation was key to progressing students to better articulate their discipline.

The approach has been valuable to the students and the practice has contributed to an enhanced student experience in a number of ways, such as:

+ developing a range of skills needed in the workplace;

+ application to a live business situation;

+ stronger relationship with peers;

+ greater confidence to approach/network with employers;

+ being better equipped to complete their final dissertation project;

+ greater uptake of finance internships alongside university study;

+ greater exposure to industry expertise and feedback;

+ having to move out of their comfort zone.

3b. Teacher Perspective

By working collaboratively and engaging an employer with this module, I provide students with a greater opportunity to enhance their learning experience. The employer engagement provides the student not only with an insight into how their module content is relevant to the workplace but also of the key competencies/skills that are needed in the workplace. This approach therefore addresses, to some extent, the criticism that the accounting profession is lacking in "soft skills". The level of discussion, teamwork, and research skills required for this module can be developed and transferred to complete the independent study dissertation project that students are required to undertake. The approach therefore feeds forward, as it equips the students with skills for other modules. I feel the success of this practice is therefore not limited to this module but in fact provides an essential springboard from which the student can develop further and build his/her skill set for practice beyond university study.

The student engagement and interest is heightened by an insider's view of what is happening in the sector, which is confirmed in the feedback from module evaluation questionnaires. Students are connected with an employer and have the opportunity to network in order to apply for potential future projects, this is a success for both the student and the employer. As a consequence of this innovation, some students have successfully undertaken voluntary and/or paid internships with the organisation. The employer is now connected with the University Careers Employment Service and regularly advertises short-term finance internships to our students.

My final point relates to the emphasis on deep rather than surface learning, as the student is required to delve into the literature on the development of these long-standing standards and then to articulate the application of their discipline to a live situation.

Section 4: Moving Forward

The university has invested a considerable amount of time and resources to become an integral part of the city. The benefits of this transformation can be realised through the many networking events that take place at the university, sometimes at university level and sometimes at college/school level. Such an infrastructure has enabled innovative practices such as the one described in this chapter. To continue to meet the module learning outcomes and to enhance the student experience in an innovative way, a future consideration for the teaching and learning strategy of this module is to create a simulation exercise that will enable groups of students to work as a team to address, challenge, debate, and recommend a financial strategy for an organisation.

The aim will be to continue to encourage:

+ deeper learning within the accounting subject discipline;

+ further development of "soft skills";

+ confident articulation of one's subject discipline;

+ employer consultation in the simulation design;

+ employers providing constructive feedback as panel members at the presentation stage.

In addition, the aim is to continue working collaboratively with employers and to extend this collaboration to working in partnership with the student to deliver research projects as required by the employer. The outputs may also be designed for submission to the College of Business in-house journal.

Conclusion

The chapter findings conclude that, through an employer-based case study approach, the adoption of a shift in TLA towards a constructivist learning approach has displayed improved student performance and engagement. The innovative practice of embedded employer engagement created an opportunity to influence the students' approach to learning so that rote learning of accounting standards was discouraged. Instead, the learning context required students to adopt a deep learning approach, to apply knowledge and demonstrate its application in the workplace. This practice supports the conclusion by Laurillard (1984), Biggs (1985), and Ramsden (1992), who claim that learning activities and assessments can be used to move learners towards a deeper learning. Furthermore, the positioning of this practice within the programme (i.e., at postgraduate level) reinforces the findings of Hall *et al.*, (2004:502), who state: "*in accounting, students first must learn terminology, basic concepts and procedures before being able to apply knowledge to novel problems and reflect/evaluate on the appropriateness of various treatments and methods*". Therefore, it would seem that there is a place for surface learning in the accounting subject discipline, and some would argue that this is necessary at the early stages of the programme so that, at later stages, opportunities for deep learning can be phased in. It is the creation of an appropriate learning context that will enable this transition and therefore provide the benefits to the student, as has been described in this chapter.

About the Author

Parminder Johal is a senior lecturer in accounting and finance and postgraduate programme leader at the Derby Business School, University of Derby, UK. She can be contacted at this e-mail: p.johal@derby.ac.uk

Bibliography

Association of Chartered Certified Accountants (ACCA) (2016). *Professional accountants – the future: Drivers of change and future skills.* London: ACCA.

Biggs, J. (1985). The role of metalearning in study processes. *British Journal of Educational Psychology,* Vol. 12, No. 1, pp.73–85.

Biggs, J. (1987a). *Student Approaches to Learning and Studying.* Hawthorn VIC: Australian Council for Educational Research.

Biggs, J. (1987b). *Study Process Questionnaire Manual.* Hawthorn, VIC: Australian Council for Educational Research.

Booth, P.; P. Luckett & R. Mladenovic (1999). The quality of learning in accounting education: the impact of approaches to learning on academic performance. *Accounting Education: an international journal,* Vol. 8, No. 4, pp. 277–300.

Chan, D.; R. Leung.; L. Gow & S. Hu (1989). *Approaches to learning of accountancy students: some additional evidence.* Proceedings of the ASAIHL Seminar on University Education in the 1990s, Kuala Lumpur.

De Villiers, R. (2010). The incorporation of soft skills into accounting curricula: preparing accounting graduates for their unpredictable futures. *Meditari Accountancy Research,* Vol. 18, No. 2, pp. 1–22.

Eley, M. (1992). Differential adoption of study approaches within individual students. *Higher Education,* Vol. 23, No. 3, pp. 231–254.

English, L.; P. Luckett & R. Mladenovic (2004). Encouraging a deep approach to learning through curriculum design. *Accounting Education,* Vol. 13, No. 4, pp. 461–488.

Emes, C. & M. Cleveland-Innes (2003). A Journey Toward Learner-Centered Curriculum. *The Canadian Journal of Higher Education,* Vol XXXIII, No. 3.

Gagnon, G. W. & M. Collay (2001). *Designing for learning; six elements in constructivist classrooms.* Thousand Oaks, CA: Corwin Press.

Gow, L.; D. Kember & B. Cooper (1994). The teaching context and approaches to study of accountancy students. *Issues in Accounting Education,* Vol. 9, pp. 118–130.

Hall, M.; A. Ramsay & J. Raven (2004). Changing the learning environment to promote deep learning approaches in first year accounting students. *Accounting Education: an international journal,* Vol. 13, No. 4, pp. 487–505.

Laurillard, D. M. (1984). Learning from problem solving. In F. Marton (Ed.), *The Experience of Learning,* pp. 124–143. Edinburgh: Scottish Academic Press.

Ramsden, P. (1992). *Learning to Teach in Higher Education.* London: Routledge.

Chapter 5

Supervising Research Students Using the "Business Applied Research Supervision" Framework

Ann Brook and Martin Eley

Introduction

This chapter contributes to the book *New Innovations in Teaching and Learning in Higher Education* as we present an innovative approach to supervising research students that we have developed at Birmingham City University. Our innovative approach is intended for use primarily for master's- and doctoral-level research supervision. We name it the *Brook-Eley BARS framework*, where BARS is an acronym for business applied research supervision and Brook-Eley refers to our own surnames. The Brook-Eley BARS framework has been piloted specifically in the MSc Internal Audit Management and Consultancy programme and with particular doctoral supervisions at Birmingham City University. The Brook-Eley BARS framework integrates the Tannenbaum-Schmidt's (1973) leadership model with Lee's (2011) supervision framework to create a differentiated approach (integration of a leadership and a supervision model) to supervision for candidates from a business environment. Supervision is a key factor in a student's success in completing their research degree (van Dinther, 2011; O'Keeffe, 2013; Nygaard, 2014).

There is an increasing growth in the number of students completing master's and doctoral degrees in the UK and many other countries, and growth from the international market in particular is strong (Universities UK, 2012). Brown (2007) supports this specifically in relation to international students, who also have barriers of culture and language to contend with as part of the supervision process. To help address this, the real innovation here is the integration of leadership and supervision models to provide a rounded approach.

Personal experience of the authors has supported these challenges (including culture, ownership, and many more), as well as anecdotal feedback from colleagues. This can often lead to frustration when an able student fails due to a lack of understanding of the nature of the supervision and engagement in this (Clarke, 2007). Conversely, a student can also feel unsupported by a supervisor who fails to engage in a robust framework of supervision, often leading to a lack of direction and engagement. The model developed here provides a framework of progression that can be seen and used by both the candidate and supervisor, thus helping to bridge any potential gap between them (Humphrey, 2012). When reading this chapter, you will gain the following:

1. insight into different approaches to research student supervision and reflections on their use;

2. a detailed presentation of the Brook-Eley BARS framework and reflections on its use;

3. inspiration on how to supervise research student using the Brook-Eley BARS framework.

Our chapter is divided into four sections. In the first section, we briefly explain the idea with our construction of an integrated leadership and supervision framework. In section 2, we describe our supervision practice in more detail. We show two different approaches to research student supervision that have led to the construction of our own Book-Eley BARS framework, and we present our framework in detail. Section 3 is devoted to a brief discussion of the possible outcomes of using our framework, whereas section 4 is looking forward and signposting what is yet to be done to further improve our work.

Section I: The Background

In this section, we will explain what inspired the idea of the integration of a leadership and supervision framework. Within Birmingham City University (BCU), we have a strong internal audit and governance practitioner presence in an official centre on this subject. Teams have been managed for many years collaboratively across this centre, where the supervision issues considered here have been commonly seen. Training on mentoring, coaching, and leadership, including a course accredited by the Institute of Leadership Management have been applied as a solution, at least in part – much of which has been very usefully adopted into day-to-day activities.

It was found that several tutors, when moving up to master's degree level, had limited practical experience of this level of supervision yet were allocated supervisions in the same way as greatly experienced staff. BCU supports new academics on a postgraduate certificate programme in learning and teaching in higher education. During this developmental programme the nature of learning, and in particular independent learning, and the expectations of students is often put into postgraduate relevance as well as, and in contrast to, undergraduate relevance. After completing the postgraduate certificate, tutors can enrol on a SEDA (Staff and Educational Development Association) accredited course Supervising Master's Level Research. This is often identified as an area for further development but also of interest and relevance. As part of this programme, an assignment is required that focuses on an area of interest, the authors selected issues around the nature of the relationship between the supervisor and the student/candidate, and the differing expectations.

As part of this, a focus group was conducted on the expectations of students/candidates, which prompted reflection on personal experiences of supervision, which at that time was not extensive but was nevertheless sufficient to demonstrate the challenges identified earlier. After investigation, the Tannenbaum-Schmidt leadership continuum (Tannenbaum & Schmidt, 1973) was identified as a connection between supervising in a working environment as a manager and supervising a student. The commonality of the two scenarios made it highly appropriate for practice or work-based learning and programmes.

Section 2: The Practice

There are a number of quality frameworks (Bartholomew, 2015) that can guide the work of dissertation supervisors, such as the SEDA Professional Development Framework (Janes 2016; Nicholls, 2014) and the HEA's UK Professional Standards Framework (UKPSF) (Law, 2011; Higher Education Academy, 2011). Both of these have common elements and themes, such as personal development of the education professional and the provision of high-quality teaching and learning support for students. It is these types of frameworks that drive the professionalism of the sector and ensure that high-quality standards are clearly defined, understood, and facilitate the sharing of best practice amongst practitioners.

The Brook-Eley BARS framework that we have developed integrates the Tannenbaum-Schmidt's leadership model (Tannenbaum & Schmidt, 1973) with Lee's supervision framework (Lee, 2011) to create a differentiated approach (integration of a leadership and a supervision model) to supervision for candidates from a business environment. We chose Lee's model because it has a high degree of correlation with the QAA model, and the Tannenbaum-Schmidt model because it is a well-grounded and accepted approach. Below is an overview of the structure of the Brook-Eley BARS framework. Later in the chapter, we discuss it in more detail along with an explanation of how this framework has been developed and how it can be applied.

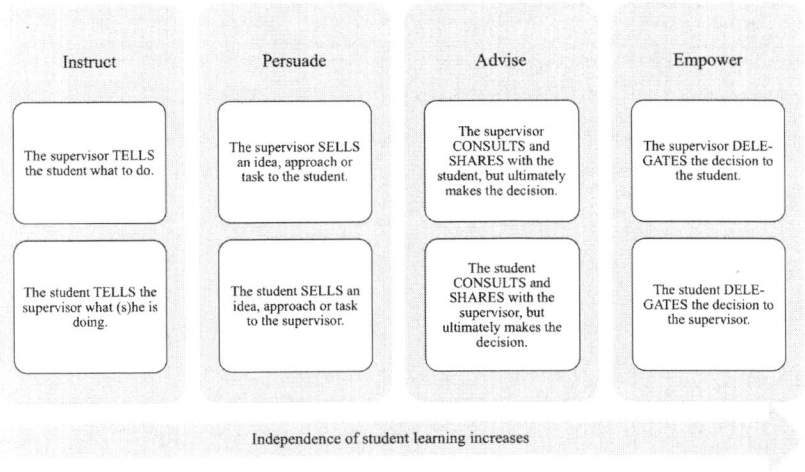

Figure 1: Structural overview of the Brook-Eley BARS framework.

What may emerge is the opportunity for the supervisor's development to be related to the student's development through a shared approach and understanding. However, such a shared or collegial approach does require some overall responsibility to be taken as, for instance, in the "empower" section they are each delegating the decision to each other, and so any effective impasse will need to be addressed.

Tannenbaum and Schmidt (1973) developed the continuum of leadership from 1973 onward. This looked at the decision-making power within organisations and how this is balanced between leaders and their subordinates. This leadership model can be specifically related to supervision if you consider the roles of supervisor and student/candidate as having many similar attributes to the roles of leaders and their subordinates. It categorised the shift of power in the decision-making between the two levels into five different types, namely: tell, sell, consult, share, and delegate. In particular, this approach provides significant links into key components of coaching and mentoring frameworks and techniques.

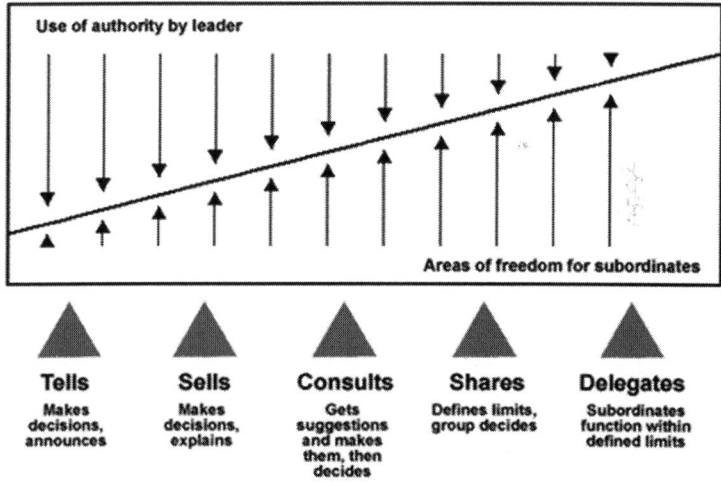

Figure 2: Tannenbaum and Schmidt's (1973) leadership model.

Lee (2011) proposes a number of different approaches that supervisors can use. Figure 3 seeks to demonstrate these:

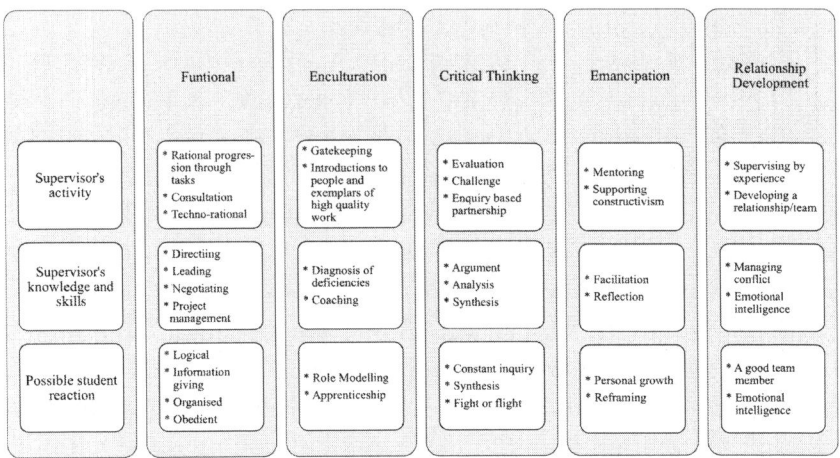

	Funtional	Enculturation	Critical Thinking	Emancipation	Relationship Development
Supervisor's activity	* Rational progression through tasks * Consultation * Techno-rational	* Gatekeeping * Introductions to people and exemplars of high quality work	* Evaluation * Challenge * Enquiry based partnership	* Mentoring * Supporting constructivism	* Supervising by experience * Developing a relationship/team
Supervisor's knowledge and skills	* Directiing * Leading * Negotiating * Project management	* Diagnosis of deficiencies * Coaching	* Argument * Analysis * Synthesis	* Facilitation * Reflection	* Managing conflict * Emotional intelligence
Possible student reaction	* Logical * Information giving * Organised * Obedient	* Role Modelling * Apprenticeship	* Constant inquiry * Synthesis * Fight or flight	* Personal growth * Reframing	* A good team member * Emotional intelligence

Figure 3: Successful research supervision: advising students doing research (Lee, 2011).

Lee (2011) proposes that the supervisor needs to assess themselves and the needs and expectations of the student in determining which approach to adopt for the supervision. In introducing the framework, she also explains that the frameworks are not as discrete as they appear from the table and that supervisors should identify which approach to use for which student and in which circumstance. It is not a case of picking one framework and sticking to it throughout. So, you could start with one approach and then move to another, forward or backward, as the supervision progresses, since it is not intended to be simple linear progression. Whether some elements are especially essential to the supervision is dependent on the experience and style of the student/candidate. An established executive undertaking a part-time doctorate will be significantly different in needs to a 22-year-old starting a master's-level programme immediately after their undergraduate degree.

An integration was made of the Tannenbaum and Schmidt (1973) learning continuum to the different appropriate roles in Lee's (2011) approach, from early concepts through to submission. Resulting in guidance to help both the supervisor and student on what to expect and therefore potentially closing the experienced expectation gap.

The two models are titled using different terms and there is therefore a need to first consider whether these two terms are related or not. With no relation, the overlay into an integrated approach would remain fundamentally questionable. Tannenbaum and Massarik (1957:5) provide a definition of leadership as *"interpersonal influence, exercised in situation and directed, through the communication process, toward the attainment of specified goal or goals"*. They comment that this is a strong definition due to its generality, as it is based on the notion of people interacting, rather than any hierarchical relationship within an organisation.

In contrast, Lee (2008, 2011) does not attempt to provide a definitive definition or purpose of supervision. Instead, she explains that a high proportion of past research in this area has been functional in nature – the activities and tasks that a supervisor should perform – however, she was focusing on the influences of the supervisor and student relationship on the success of the research.

Therefore, both Lee (2008, 2011), Tannenbaum and Massarik (1957), and Tannenbaum and Schmidt (1973) are using relationships as the foundations of their frameworks. They are not concentrating on the practical, but more the interpersonal. Therefore, this allows us to make the fundamental connection between the two frameworks that leads on to considering the elements in detail.

Lee's (2011) framework has five elements that are not independent of each other:

1. functional: where the issue is one of project management;

2. enculturation: where the student is encouraged to become a member of the disciplinary community;

3. critical thinking: where the student is encouraged to question and analyse their work;

4. emancipation: where the student is encouraged to question and develop themselves;

5. developing a quality relationship: where the student is enthused, inspired, and cared for.

This high-level description provided by Lee (2011) has a number of key terms that are describing the nature of the interaction between the supervisor and the student. The term "encourage" is used on several occasions and alternatives provided by a thesaurus include inspire, reassure, embolden, which can all result in increased confidence. If we consider the Tannenbaum-Schmidt (1973) model, it uses different elements to describe where the power lies in the specific interaction, and all, except tell, would encourage the student in their endeavour.

In the final element, Lee (2911) also talks of inspiration, enthusiasm, and a feeling of being supported. Again, the connection to Tannenbaum-Schmidt's (1973) continuum is evident in that advice and consultation can certainly create enthusiasm from the student and knowledge that the supervisor is supporting them. The delegate element can also lead to a feeling of being trusted by the supervisor, and this can also inspire and enthuse.

Lee (2011) does include a functional element to her framework; however, Tannenbaum and Schmidt (1973) made a conscious decision to not limit their framework to functional tasks and activities. So, while this does remain an important part of any supervision, whether business or research, the specifics can vary greatly depending on the reason why the supervision is in place.

In Lee's graphical representation of her framework, she includes some examples of how this would transpire. She uses words such as *consultation, negotiating, obedient, coaching, challenge, inquiry, mentoring, facilitation*.

Tannenbaum and Schmidt (1973) use terms such as *tell, sell, advise, consult, delegate, buy-in, involve*. The following diagram seeks to map the relationship between these two sets of terms in order to demonstrate that there is a connection between them:

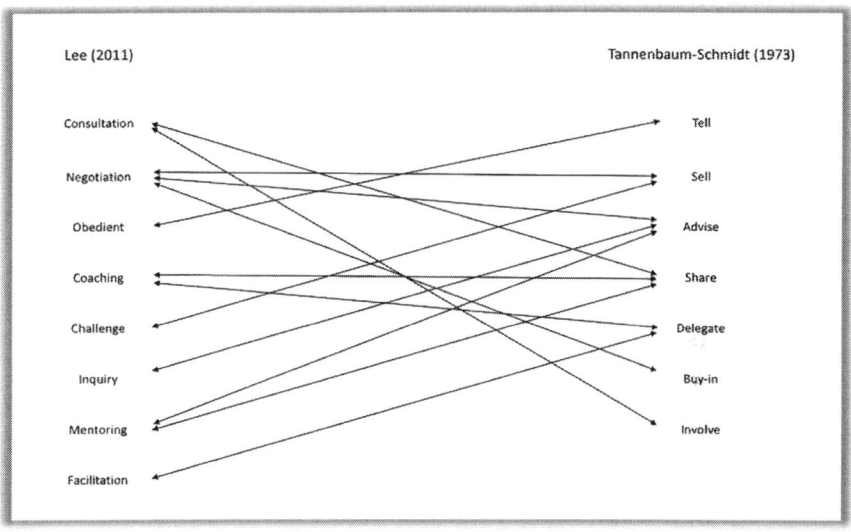

Figure 4: Relationship map of terms.

This analysis of the terms used by both to describe their framework, coupled with consideration of the terms used and the resulting mapping, highlights that there is a connection between the two frameworks when considering supervision as a form of interaction between the two individuals. This integration approach was based on practice results from a research supervision community of practice within BCU. This allowed for the collation of feedback across multiple supervisions. It was then progressively trial tested on subsequent supervisions to ensure that it suited practice or work-based students/candidates. A simple overview of the emergent integrated approach, but using the original contextual descriptors, is provided below.

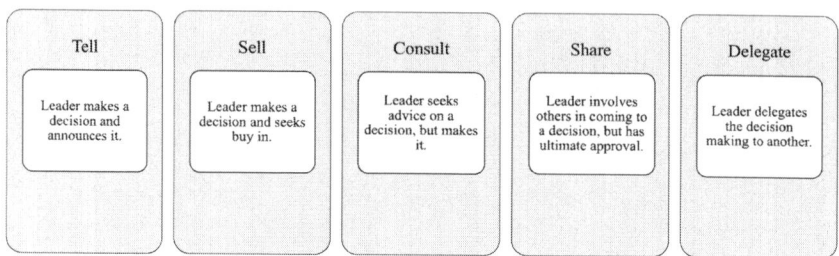

Figure 5: The integration of the different approaches.

This integrated approach is then transformed into appropriate supervision terminology (which has established academic meaning and intent) for postgraduate research candidates and becomes: The Brook-Eley Business Applied Research Supervision (BARS) Framework.

	Instruct	Persuade	Advise	Empower
Proposal	The supervisor TELLS the student WHEN the proposal needs to be submitted and WHAT should be included (i.e., the format).	When discussing the initial idea for the research, the supervisor will try to SELL a different research objective and aims if they do not feel it will meet the learning outcomes. However, the decision remains with the student.	When discussing the research proposal, the supervisor will CONSULT with the student on how they feel they are meeting the learning outcomes. However, when this is assessed, the supervisor makes the decision as to whether or not they do.	The student ultimately makes the decision as to what research they are going to do.

	Instruct	Persuade	Advise	Empower
Planning	The supervisor TELLS the student WHEN the research needs to be completed by and when it needs to be submitted for assessment.	The supervisor will ENCOURAGE the student to write a project plan with clear milestones. However, the student can decide whether or not to do this.	Where a project plan is written, the supervisor can provide ADVICE on the plan and make recommendations to the student on how to change this. However, the plan remains the student's, and it is their choice whether to update it or not.	Ultimately, it remains the student's DECISION whether to write a project plan or not, and if they do whether to make the changes recommended by the supervisor.

	Instruct	Persuade	Advise	Empower
Research Method	The supervisor INSTRUCTS the student on the format of the write-up for this and when a draft is to be submitted for review.	Through discussions with the student, the supervisor will ENCOURAGE them to consider different research methods where they feel it would be an improvement. Typical suggestions are usually focused on addressing difficulties with access to data or ethical consideration. The student still makes the decision.	When assessing the methodology use, the supervisor will DECIDE whether or not the methodology demonstrates the achievement of the learning outcomes and to what extent. There may have been discussions earlier with the student on this where ADVICE was given, but the supervisor ultimately decides whether it meets the requirements.	The student decides on the methodology that they follow. They may do this without any input from their supervisor, particularly experienced students who have completed research before.

	Instruct	Persuade	Advise	Empower
Literature Review	Again, the supervisor will TELL the student when they expect to see a draft and provide a format and word count target.	When discussing the literature review, prior to write up, the supervisor may SUGGEST particular sources for the student to consider for their literature review. The student may then look at them but can choose whether to include or discount them.	When assessing the literature review, the supervisor will DECIDE whether or not it meets the learning outcomes and to what extent. The supervisor decides what mark is merited.	The student will retain POWER over the content of their literature review and which sources are used. Again, experienced students may need very little advice and persuasion when they have both experience and a sense of empowerment.

	Instruct	Persuade	Advise	Empower
Primary Research	The supervisor will TELL the student what consent is required from the university before any primary data research is carried out. Again, they will also set deadlines for the students to follow.	When the student creates an interview or questionnaire, then the supervisor may ADVISE the student on changes to make; however, the ultimate decision to do this remains with the student.	Here, the supervisor may decide to retain all decisions relating to the issue and final versions of questionnaires and interviews. This may be required, as the student has little experience or there are concerns around ethical practice. Therefore, the supervisor may CONSULT with the student but retain the right to approve the primary research before it is implemented.	Again, students with vast experience and who are performing research with few to no ethical requirements can be empowered to design and implement their own.

	Instruct	Persuade	Advise	Empower
Conclusions	When drawing up conclusions, the only INSTRUCTION from the supervisor will be to have points that are logically drawn from the research conducted (i.e., to meet a key learning outcome).	As the research progresses, it is likely that conclusions and recommendations will be discussed at every stage. The supervisor may try to PERSUADE the student to a certain view, but ultimately the decision remains the student's.	This is the only time when a supervisor SHOULD NOT retain any decision-making power. This would be a conflict of interest, as they would then be marking their own outcome to the research rather than the student's.	Students should be fully empowered to decide what conclusions and decisions come out of their research.

Figure 6: The integrated Brook-Eley BARS framework.

The Brook-Eley BARS framework is intended for master's- and doctoral-level research supervision. It has been piloted specifically in the MSc Internal Audit Management and Consultancy and with particular doctoral supervisions. It should also be noted that these supervisions have been delivered across both face-to-face and remote methods with equivalent feedback and findings. The use of any framework will of course be tempered with the level of experience of the supervisor. At this stage, it is not necessarily anticipated that any amendment or modification is needed to use the Brook-Eley BARS framework when being used across business-related master's- and doctoral-level research. This will however need to be reassessed over time to see if it is appropriate or requires further development before it becomes a fully justified position.

The framework can be used at every stage and at every interaction between the student and the supervisor. One of the key challenges that prompted the development of the Brook-Eley BARS framework was that of differing expectations of students and supervisors (Manathunga, 2007; Malfroy, 2005). Therefore, to help educate the students on what they can expect, the framework should be shared with them and explained before it is used. This greater understanding of what they can expect from the supervisor and what they expect of the student should have the potential to increase the success of the supervision and ultimately the student, and this is supported by initial anecdotal feedback from the trials. However, if it is to be used, it is important that, during the supervision, the BARS framework is discussed with the student at an early stage as part of a developmental process, rather than presented as a fait accompli. This will mean that the supervisor is already adopting the *advise* approach from the BARS framework.

When preparing for a supervision meeting, the supervisor can refer to the framework and identify at which point in the research project the student has reached. The supervisor can analyse the progress both in terms of time and quality of work to that point and determine which role they need to adopt for that meeting. For example, if a student has not submitted an interim draft by a pre-agreed deadline, then the supervisor may wish to move toward *instruct*; however, if they are aware of mitigating circumstances for the student, then they may wish to *persuade* the student into a particular course of action.

Finally, at the end of the research project, the supervisor and student should take an opportunity to reflect on their use of the framework. This will be beneficial to both parties, as supervisors will be able to implement different ways of using the framework with future students and students will be able to take their experience into their future role as an employee/practitioner.

Before using BARS, the supervisor may wish to review it in light of their own experiences of supervision to identify which of the four techniques they tend to use, why, and when. Analysing their own preferences against the BARS framework may prompt consideration and investigation of some other techniques or frameworks that they may wish to try with their students and that will expand the range of approaches they have at their disposal. Another area of preparation, as highlighted above, is that the approach used should be shared with students/candidates.

Finally, where there are a number of supervisors for one degree, it will be beneficial for all supervisors to consider adopting the framework at the same time. This will lead to a consistent approach for all student supervision, while still allowing for flexibility due to personality, circumstances, and experience.

Section 3: The Outcome

Initial indications in the following list have already been observed, although largely through the experiences of the authors, early feedback from students/candidates, and other supervisors who have helped to trial elements of the framework.

Initially, it appears that there are a number of outcomes that the use of this framework may well achieve:

+ improve supervisor satisfaction regarding the relationship with their students/candidates;

+ improve student/candidate satisfaction regarding the relationship with their supervisors;

+ improve productivity of both parties to the supervision process;

+ improve success rates and achievement levels of students/candidates.

Outcomes for students/candidates:

+ A key outcome for students/candidates will be certainty of how their research will be supervised. Many postgraduate students/candidates have little or no experience of research, as they are often mature students or from other countries where the educational experience is different to that in the UK. Therefore, being clear at the outset on how the supervision will take place will take away the fear of the unknown (Vilkinas, 2002).

+ Robust supervision will also create a strong relationship between the student/candidate and the supervisor (Mainhard, 2009). This can only drive greater support from the supervisor, and therefore the student will be able to capitalise on the supervisor's willingness to guide them due to this positive environment – ultimately, improving the mark of the student for their work and therefore their success.

+ Students/Candidates will also see consistency of supervision for the degree they are studying, ensuring that students do not feel undervalued or poorly supported compared to their peers. This will increase their satisfaction and reduce the number of supervisor changes which can impact negatively on the research project and the student's success (Fernando, 2005).

In many ways, the outcomes for supervisors mirror those of the students/candidates. Outcomes for supervisors:

+ Having a framework to follow will support the professionalism of the supervisor, who will have confidence in the way in which they work and provide a benchmark against which they can assess their own performance. This self-assessment can also identify the need for further training and support promotion.

+ The professionalism of all supervisors using the same framework will also make the university attractive to others to work and study there, as the integrity of the degree is consolidated.

+ A stronger relationship with the student will result in stronger discussion and debate, which will lead to higher-quality research. This could also lead to supervisor-student collaboration during and after the research, and the publication of research in academic journals, improving productivity in a wider sense (Marsh, 2002; Pearson, 2002).

Overall, the fundamental outcome is the integration of leadership and supervision models into a new framework for supervision.

Section 4: Moving Forward

Wider application of the framework is currently planned with colleagues across the university and at other higher education institutions in the UK and internationally. This will be instigated by presentation of the Brook-Eley BARS framework at conferences and articles in appropriate journals/publications. From this, greater feedback will be gathered, allowing for further enhancement and refinement of the framework. It is also anticipated that there could be potential for an additional overlay of project management theory onto this framework. This would be to recognise that successful research projects frequently involve what is effectively robust project management. This will add disciplined timeline and resource management approaches to the supervision framework in order to deliver a more complete programme approach. To this end, interested parties are encouraged to contact the authors to provide feedback on the proposed framework development and also to participate in research studies by applying it to their supervisory practice.

Conclusion

The Brook-Eley BARS framework for supervision has been developed with the relationship between the supervisor and student firmly at its core in the context of encouraging independent learning as much as possible. In doing so, it will extend more traditional learning approaches and encourage a more holistic and integrated approach to supervised learning. Van Hout-Wolters (2000) takes an in-depth look at self-directed learning and independent work and its relationship to active learning, saying that in addition to relationships it is really about how much activity is asked from the learner. Together, this engenders quality and, coincidentally, supports the next-level integration of supervision and project management into the framework. Independent learning is generally encouraged through use of the integrated framework, which can inherently assist in pushing-up the quality of the resulting work. This results in improvement in satisfaction, quality, and, as discussed in the outcome section, productivity.

This combination of improvement is a laudable goal, which is achieved through application of the integrated (leadership and supervision models) framework. It is this integrated framework that is really innovative, and at the heart of this is a crucial competency of communication. The motivation for this integration occurred because the authors fully appreciate that the success of the student/candidate has a direct correlation with the success of the supervision, which effectively become shared goals. Finally, this new framework is probably applicable to other areas, making it part of a longitudinal development and range of application.

About the Authors

Ann Brook is programme director, Centre for Internal Audit, Governance and Risk Management, Birmingham City University, UK. She can be contacted at this e-mail: ann.brook@bcu.ac.uk

Martin Eley is associate professor in management practice, Birmingham City University, UK. He can be contacted at this e-mail: martin.eley@bcu.ac.uk

Bibliography

Brown, K. & F. Medway (2007). School climate and teacher beliefs in a school effectively serving poor South Carolina (USA) African-American students: A case study. *Teaching and Teacher Education*, Vol. 23, No. 4, pp. 529–540.

Clarke, A. & S. Collins (2007). Complexity science and student teacher supervision. *Teaching and Teacher Education*, Vol. 23, No. 2, pp. 160–172.

Fernando, D. & D. Hulse-Killacky (2005). The relationship of supervisory styles to satisfaction with supervision and the perceived self-efficacy of master's-level counseling students. *Counsellor Education and Supervision*, Vol. 44, No. 4, p. 293.

Guerin, C.; P. Bartholomew & C. Nygaard (Eds.) (2015). *Learning to Research – Researching to Learn*. Oxfordshire: Libri Publishing Ltd.

Higher Education Academy. (2011). *The UK Professional Standards Framework for teaching and supporting learning in higher education*. Higher Education Academy.

Humphrey, R. & B. Simpson (2012). Negotiating a 'Scary Gap': Doctoral candidates, 'writing up' qualitative data and the contemporary supervisory relationship. *Journal of Education and Training Studies*, Vol. 1, No. 1, pp. 1–10.

Janes, G.; D. Nutt & P. Taylor (2016). *Student Behaviour and Positive Learning Cultures*. SEDA Special 38.

Law, S. (2011). *Recognising excellence in teaching and learning: Report from consultation on the UK Professional Standards Framework (UKPSF) for teaching and supporting learning in higher education*. Higher Education Academy.

Lee, A. (2008). How are doctoral students supervised? Concepts of doctoral research supervision. *Studies in Higher Education*, Vol. 33, No. 3, pp. 267–281.

Lee, A. (2011). *Successful research supervision: Advising students doing research*. London: Routledge.

Mainhard, T.; R. van der Rijst; J. van Tartwijk & T. Wubbels (2009). A model for the supervisor–doctoral student relationship. *Higher Education*, Vol. 58, No. 3, pp. 359–373.

Malfroy, J. (2005). Doctoral supervision, workplace research and changing pedagogic practices. *Higher Education Research & Development*, Vol. 24, No. 2, pp. 165–178.

Manathunga, C. & J. Goozée (2007). Challenging the dual assumption of the 'always/already' autonomous student and effective supervisor. *Teaching in Higher Education*, Vol. 12, No. 3, pp. 309–322.

Marsh, H. & J. Hattie (2002). The relation between research productivity and teaching effectiveness: Complementary, antagonistic, or independent constructs? *The Journal of Higher Education*, Vol. 73, No. 5, pp. 603–641.

Nicholls, G. (2014). *Professional development in higher education: New dimensions and directions*. London: Routledge.

Nygaard, C.; N. Courtney & L. Frick (Eds.) (2014). *Postgraduate Education – Form and Function*. Oxfordshire: Libri Publishing Ltd.

O'Keeffe, P. (2013). A sense of belonging: Improving student retention. *College Student Journal*, Vol. 47, No. 4, pp. 605–613.

Pearson, M. & Brew, A. (2002). Research training and supervision development. *Studies in Higher education*, Vol. 27, No. 2, pp. 135–150.

Tannenbaum, R. & F. Massarik (1957). Leadership: A frame of reference. *Management Science*, Vol. 4, No. 1, pp. 1–19.

Tannenbaum, R. & W. Schmidt (1973). How to choose a leadership pattern. *Harvard Business Review*, Vol. 51, No. 3, pp. 162–180.

Universities UK (2012). *Patterns and trends in UK higher education*. Universities UK.

van Dinther, M.; F. Dochy & M. Segers (2011). Factors affecting students' self-efficacy in higher education. *Educational Research Review*, Vol. 6, No. 2, pp. 95–108.

van Hout-Wolters, B., Simons, R. & Volet, S. (2000). Active learning: Self-directed learning and independent work. In R. J. Simons; J van der Linden & T. Duffy (Eds.), *New learning*. Netherlands: Springer, pp. 21–36.

Vilkinas, T. (2002). The PhD process: the supervisor as manager. *Education+ Training*, Vol. 44, No. 3, pp. 129–137.

Chapter 6

The Art of Seduction: Designing Innovative Curriculum That Engages and Retains Reluctant Bachelor of Arts Students

Sarah Midford and Sara James

Introduction

This chapter contributes to the book *New Innovations in Teaching and Learning in Higher Education* by demonstrating that a student-centred approach to embedding academic skills, combined with personal support in first-year subjects and engaging interdisciplinary curriculum, can lead to improvements in student success and retention. Creating a high-quality learning environment through these measures improves the first-year experience and results in greater student success both with regard to pass rates and student satisfaction (Kuh *et al.*, 2005:9), while engaging curriculum encourages students to progress to the second year.

Across Australian universities, it is common for students to enrol in a bachelor of arts as a pathway into another degree or as a stopgap measure until they have clarified their future career path. In order to retain these students in the course, bachelor of arts curriculum needs to seduce students into completing their arts degree. Innovative curriculum leads to increased student engagement, which in turn leads to retention and student success. At La Trobe University, in Victoria, Australia, the introduction of two core interdisciplinary subjects to the first year of the Bachelor of Arts, that have been explicitly designed to enthuse students about their degree and demonstrate its vocational application, has effectively seduced more students into completing their arts degree, which is broadly applicable to a number of vocational pathways in an ever-changing job market. This aligns with the provost and deputy vice chancellor at

Sydney University Stephen Garton's statement that *"the message we are getting from employers more and more is that they want graduates with good generalist degrees"* (Graduate Careers Australia, 2016). Our job is convincing students that the value of their generalist arts degree comes from its flexibility.

In this chapter, we define new innovations in teaching and learning in higher education as the development of new curriculum that employs progressive methods that lead to better pass rates and greater student satisfaction and course retention. More specifically, our innovation is the development of a first-year core programme in the Bachelor of Arts that employs embedded skills acquisition, cohort building, and enquiry-based and collaborative learning principles to convince students to remain in the course, despite an initial, general disinterest in the degree.

Our innovation has been achieved through the development of two core interdisciplinary first-year subjects ("Rethinking Our Humanity" and "Ideas that Shook the World") that are compulsory for all Bachelor of Arts students at our multi-campus university. These subjects teach interdisciplinary content to approximately 1,000 students per semester across the five La Trobe University campuses in regional and metropolitan Victoria. Each semester, a teaching team of around 14 staff work together to deliver the subject. Teaching a subject on four regional campuses and one urban campus poses a particular challenge because the student cohorts and teaching facilities vary considerably between campuses, as do the motivation and preparedness levels of the students.

Each subjects' content is organised in an innovative module structure, departing from chronological and theory-based models of teaching. Instead, the dialogue between individual modules introduces students to true interdisciplinary thinking by asking them to recognise manifestations of concepts or themes across different disciplines. The curriculum embeds foundational academic skills (e.g., essay writing, research, teamwork) and employs incremental assessment within the module structure so that, when they complete their first year, students feel confident, capable, and engaged, and want to continue their studies in the degree.

The innovative approach taken in these subjects has resulted in greater student success and retention. Pass rates in both of the subjects have increased each year. This is particularly significant when the concurrent 20-percentile-point drop in admission rankings for the course between

2013–2016 is taken into account. In this context, a decline in pass rates would be expected, but the success of our innovative curriculum has, instead, led to an increase. These results demonstrate that the subjects are supporting student success in spite of factors, including the decline in admission rankings, lack of preparedness, and the course being used as a pathway degree, that would normally lead to its decline.

Before elucidating how our two interdisciplinary core subjects were developed to address sector-wide changes, this chapter outlines the background of these changes to the Australian higher education sector. It goes on to demonstrate the success of our first-year programme, and, finally, discusses the future direction of interdisciplinary core subjects at our institution. When reading this chapter, the reader will gain the following insights:

1. interdisciplinary core subjects can increase student engagement;

2. embedded skills lead to higher student confidence;

3. increased student engagement and confidence leads to greater student success and higher retention rates, and;

4. an interdisciplinary approach to subject matter facilitates the construction of foundational knowledge in the arts that students can build on throughout their degree, regardless of their chosen disciplinary major.

Section I: The Background

In recent years, the Australian tertiary education sector has experienced radical change (Baird, 2010; Coates & Mahat, 2014; TEQSA, 2013), for instance:

+ increased access to campus-based and online learning;

+ the rise of credentialism;

+ a shift in funding models;

+ introduction of transparent government performance standards.

In 2008, the Australian government set targets that by 2020 40% of 25–34-year-old Australians would have a university degree, an 8% increase over a decade (Bradley *et al.*, 2008). From 2012, regulations were changed so that universities could increase their intake of students to anyone who was qualified for the degree. This "uncapping" of university places was an opportunity for growth for those universities perceived by students as more prestigious, but for those institutions with lower student preferences, this change resulted in fewer student enrolments. In an attempt to retain their market share, many of these universities lowered the entrance requirement for their courses. Five years on, there are now more students in university overall and student cohorts are increasingly diverse.

La Trobe is a young university with a diverse cohort of students, including those from low socio-economic backgrounds and regional areas. More than half of the students enrolled in the Bachelor of Arts at La Trobe are the first in their families to attend university, which means that they do not have access to the same support networks outside of university as those students who have family members who have attended university (Arvanitakis, 2014). Approximately three quarters of students enrolled in this degree are school-leavers (age 18–21 years) with the remaining quarter being mature students. Around two-thirds identify as female and one third male. The cohort is almost entirely studying full-time (95%) and there are very few international students (approximately 1%) (James & Midford, 2017). At La Trobe, we retain about 60% of students who start a Bachelor of Arts, while 10% transfer into another course at the university after their first year (Harvey & Luckman, 2014:22). Almost one-third of our Bachelor of Arts students leave the university at the end of their first year. On the metropolitan university campus (Melbourne), 14.5% of Bachelor of Arts students have commenced, but not completed, another degree (at La Trobe or elsewhere) before enrolling.

La Trobe University is one of the institutions that has lowered its entry requirements for many courses. For the Bachelor of Arts, the entry requirement dropped by 20 percentile points between 2013 and 2016. This was an attempt to keep student numbers at the same level, but also led to students devaluing the degree because of ease of entry. Consequently, student preferences for the course at La Trobe declined.

Furthermore, student retention in the Bachelor of Arts after they enter the degree is a challenge, both at La Trobe and across the sector (Mestan,

2016). In the La Trobe Bachelor of Arts, the course retention rate is consistently more than 10% lower than other courses in the university (Harvey & Luckman, 2014). Students who enrol in the Bachelor of Arts often use it as either a stopgap measure or a pathway into another degree (Long *et al.*, 2006). Many students who commence their bachelor of arts at La Trobe intend to transfer to another course, with Law and Education being the most popular alternatives (James & Midford, 2017:3). This is consistent with sector-wide research into Australian bachelor of arts students; students in the field of society and culture are the second most likely, of any field of study, to change courses (McMillan, 2005).

While some students see entry into the course as a pathway, others view the Bachelor of Arts as something that will fill their time until they work out what they want to do. One student said of their choice to enrol in a bachelor of arts: *"I suppose the choice of my degree was based on the lame excuse of 'I've got nothing better to do', as opposed to a clearly defined goal of 'this is what I want to do with my life'"* (James & Midford, 2017:5). These students have low attachment to the course. Moreover, some students enrolled in a bachelor of arts feel that it carries a stigma among their families and within society; as one student describes it: *"There is a certain stigma in society with regard to studying arts. It's labelled a waste of time, a directionless self-absorbed act of navel gazing, and a one-way ticket to the service industry"* (James & Midford, 2017:6–7).

The challenge we face is convincing students who have commenced a bachelor of arts at La Trobe that it will benefit them to continue the course. We need to engage students in their degree, excite them about what they are learning, and demonstrate that the skills they acquire in their degree will help them gain employment and lead to career success. Therefore, our curriculum innovation involves grabbing students' attention from their very first class, building a sense of belonging, establishing social networks, and showcasing the vocational value of the humanities and social sciences.

Execution of the Idea

To achieve this innovation, in 2014, our two compulsory first-year interdisciplinary subjects for the Bachelor of Arts were introduced as part of fundamental degree and curriculum reform. The subjects were specifically designed to combat attrition rates by providing a year-long orientation to disciplines within, methodologies used, and skills required in the humanities and social sciences. The programme is designed to ease student transition into university, build student confidence in their abilities, and convince students of the benefits of completing their bachelor of arts degree. Through innovative curriculum, the subjects addressed academic and pastoral challenges by introducing the increasingly diverse student body to complex academic concepts and theories, while embedding both academic and transferable skills acquisition into the curriculum (Gibbs *et al.*, 1994).

Each year, we have modified the assessment structure to include more incremental assessment tasks that build towards a larger assignment. Many assessments involve an in-class component to encourage attendance, collaboration, and active participation. For instance, the group project in Rethinking Our Humanity takes place over several weeks and culminates in a class presentation. Students begin with a research skills worksheet that they complete in groups during class (see Figure 1). They are then provided with a group workbook, which has sections that they complete in class each week over a three-week period. In addition, students organise two meetings outside the classroom physically or virtually using an online meeting tool such as Zoom. Students also provide feedback on each other's presentations by completing a marking rubric and delivering verbal comments. These activities help students to build confidence in their speaking skills and encourage them to participate actively in future conversations in both our classroom and their other subject classes. The teamwork component of this assessment replicates a professional teamwork experience, as each group member takes on a role with a position description that it is their responsibility to fulfil over the course of the project, helping students to begin developing their employability assets (Hillage & Pollard, 1998).

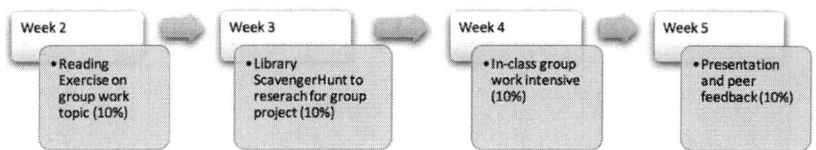

Figure 1: Staged group assessment for Rethinking Our Humanity.

A major part of the second semester subject Ideas that Shook the World is also a group assignment: Campaigning for Change. This task requires students to research and present to their classmates a campaign that addresses a real and current challenge to freedom in Australia. Students choose the type of campaign they wish to create, for example, organising a rally, creating an online petition, or producing a viral awareness video. Whether students choose to make their campaign "live" or just treat the exercise as an assessment, they are evaluated on the feasibility of their campaign to address the challenge to freedom based on quality research and the appropriateness of the campaign's direction (i.e., to politicians, newspapers, the general public). Students are encouraged to include this assessment in a portfolio of their work, which they can show to prospective employers to demonstrate their employability assets (Hillage & Pollard, 1998), including teamwork, problem-solving, communication, and research. Portfolios of students' work make a clear link between assessment tasks and the tangible and transferable skills (Gibbs *et al.*, 1994) acquired in their arts degrees.

Over the three years that these subjects have been taught, coordinators have drawn on feedback from students and the teaching team and have continually revised the curriculum and assessment structure of the subjects to ensure our students have the best experience possible. This facilitates successful transition into the later years of their degree, and, eventually, employment. Some examples of these improvements include:

- removal of the essay from the first semester subject and replacing it with a critical analysis assessment, which develops component essay writing skills through an iterative process rather than providing summative feedback at the end of semester;

+ removal of online quizzes because they were not contributing to effective student learning, as students were Googling the answers rather than reading the set subject materials;

+ introduction of student-led assessment topics to further engage interest in subject matter;

+ a clear articulation of each assessment task to a skill set required throughout their degree, and transparency of learning outcomes so that students can identify what they are learning and how it will be useful in their future employment;

+ introduction of cumulative assessment, so each assessment task employs skills and content from an earlier assessment task;

+ introduction of online lectures to ensure there is more in-class time for active and enquiry-based learning.

Section 2: The Practice

The Innovation

At a time when personal contact between teachers and students is declining due to the rise of blended and online subjects, combined with funding cuts (Gooch, 2011; Winefield *et al.*, 2008), our subjects are bucking the trend by being taught as two-hour seminars to small groups of students (ideally 25–30 students per class). Seminars are proven to be an effective method of promoting student engagement and collaborative learning (Kuh *et al.*, 2005:69–70), and our seminars are designed to facilitate students making a meaningful connection to a member of staff in their first year of university. They also encourage students to socialise with their peers and make a friend. First-year students often experience difficulties establishing social support networks and a student identity. This problem is particularly acute in large generalist degrees like the Bachelor of Arts. Students may struggle to develop peer cohorts when they are "just a face in a crowd" (Wilcox *et al.*, 2005; Scanlon *et al.*, 2007). Academic advising and cohort building encourage student engagement and subsequently increase retention (Pascarella & Terenzini, 2005; Thomas & Hixenbaugh, 2006; Reason *et al.*, 2007).

The two interdisciplinary core subjects address two essential questions for students: "What is the Bachelor of Arts?" and "What can the Bachelor of Arts do for you?" The subjects do this by providing first-year students with a year-long curriculum that offers them an overview of key ideas and debates in the humanities and social sciences. This would be difficult to achieve at the disciplinary level because disciplines have to be concerned with covering concepts and theories relevant to their field of scholarship. Interdisciplinary subjects, however, can take a bigger picture approach, explaining the degree as a whole, and can teach broader critical thinking and analytical skills embedded within subject content. The subjects have been designed as the mortar that binds the disciplinary subject bricks together; concurrent disciplinary and interdisciplinary learning can strengthen students' capacities and build their confidence to complete the Bachelor of Arts.

To engage students, we teach complex concepts using current issues that are familiar to students and relevant to their lives (Arvanitakis, 2014:742). Doing so stimulates vibrant discussions that enable students to understand the concepts as well as different disciplinary perspectives. In the classroom, students practice real-world applications of the theoretical concepts taught. For example, after introducing students to the concepts of imperialism and orientalism, students then apply these concepts in a critical analysis of the phenomenon of voluntourism or volunteer tourism (Simpson, 2004) that many of them have themselves participated in. This increases confidence and teaches students, experientially, to apply their critical thinking and analytical skills, which in turn leads to a better understanding of the real-world applications of an arts degree by fostering a belief in each student's ability to apply their newly acquired skills in a vocational context.

As well as critical thinking and analytical skills, the subjects also incorporate systematically embedded academic skills acquisition. Academic skills are embedded because research shows this to be more successful than stand-alone generic academic skills programmes (Chanock, et al., 2012). As students learn new skills, such as research or critical thinking, we make explicit what they are learning and how skills can be transferred into a vocational setting. By openly discussing skills acquisition and showing students the relevance of their skills in the real world, we seek to answer the question "what can a bachelor of arts do for you?", and encourage students to see the value of their degree, and thus remain enrolled in it.

The combination of small classes, time given to think through, discuss, and ask questions about an idea within a multi-disciplinary framework, addresses the students' question "what is a bachelor of arts?". Students are informed throughout the subjects that the degree offers them the skills to better understand their world and see it critically. This transparency contributes to their success.

The Curriculum

In their first semester, students study the subject Rethinking Our Humanity. The subject examines the human experience, the complexity of human identity, and the shape of our human future. It encourages students to see themselves and the communities in which they live from a critical and academic perspective. We begin with current issues that are in the media, including artificial intelligence, gender identity, and non-human-person rights. Disciplines studied in this subject include Australian aboriginal studies, anthropology, archaeology, English, gender, sexuality and diversity studies, history, legal studies, philosophy, politics, and sociology.

In their second semester, the students study Ideas that Shook the World. This subject explores some of the most influential ideas in the history of the West, including: freedom, imperialism, secularisation, and the individual. Students trace the origins of these ideas and their manifestation in the world today. The subject teaches students to critically evaluate central ideas underpinning public discussion on a range of political and cultural issues, and provides them with a solid foundation of cultural knowledge, which is invaluable as they continue their studies. The disciplines included in this subject are: Australian aboriginal studies, anthropology, archaeology, classics and ancient history, English, history, media and communications, philosophy, politics, sociology, and sustainability and development.

The curriculum is designed to include students with different knowledge bases and different skill sets, without "teaching to the top" or "teaching to the bottom". Through collaborative learning, students learn from their peers as well as their teachers, which stimulates further participation through socialisation and enjoyment.

Over a 12-week period, both subjects teach four topics. Each topic is referred to as a "module" and is taught over a two-week period so that the subject matter can be covered in depth and detail, and from multiple disciplinary perspectives. In Rethinking Our Humanity, the four modules are: the human animal, values, identity, and the human machine. These modules work together so that students can think critically about how humans establish the boundaries of their species between animals (nature) and machines (technology), and how these boundaries are fortified by complex social structures (see Figure 2 below). The second semester subject follows a similar format; in Ideas that Shook the World, the four modules are: the individual, freedom, imperialism, and secularisation. These modules work together to introduce students to the Classical, Renaissance, and Enlightenment periods and consider how ideas from the past have shaped contemporary Australian society. Although the topics are different to Rethinking Our Humanity, the modules function in the same way demonstrated in Figure 1. At the core of each module is the interrelationship of Enlightenment understanding on the development of contemporary Australia. Focusing on this from multiple disciplinary perspectives and tracing ideas from their origins to their manifestation over a two-week period ensures that students exit the subject knowing which ideas shook (and continue to impact) Australian society.

All the modules taught in both subjects are interconnected and allow students to relate what they are learning to their discipline major, regardless of what it is. This makes the subjects more relevant to the students, who can apply the knowledge acquired within their degrees but also to their lives outside the university. In each subject, the topic of each module has been crafted to fit into a broader subject "arc" that students are introduced to in their first week and follow throughout the semester. Different module topics could be employed in either subject, but the subject "arc" would then need to be revised. Outlining a clear trajectory to students and a central subject question allows them to better stay on track with subject learning outcomes throughout the semester and sharply focuses the complex and interdisciplinary subject matter.

Semester 1: Rethinking our Humanity

Key question: What does it mean to be human?

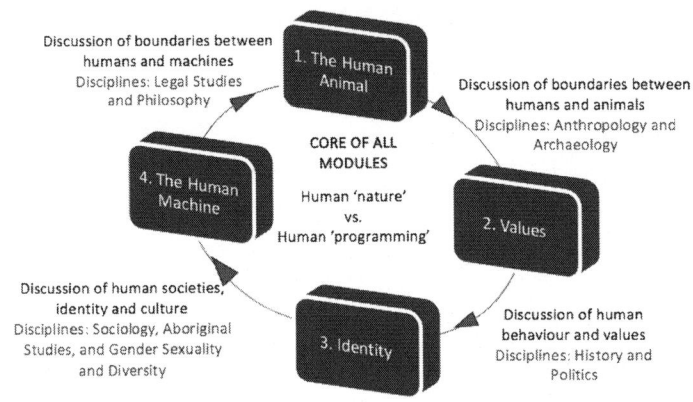

Figure 2: Module Structure of Rethinking Our Humanity.

The module structure allows each topic to be covered in depth and detail, and gives the students time to develop their understanding of a single idea or issue. The dialogue between individual modules introduces students to true interdisciplinary thinking by asking them to recognise incarnations of concepts or topics across different disciplines. This encouragement of cross-disciplinary approaches better equips students to think dynamically as they progress in their degrees and ensures their graduate capabilities are more broadly applicable beyond the academy.

Organisation

Qualified academic staff, experienced in interdisciplinary teaching, coordinate and teach the interdisciplinary core subjects. Additionally, a large team of casually employed teachers is recruited each semester to cover those classes that ongoing staff members cannot teach. These teachers are selected based on their teaching experience, and the coordinators try to ensure that a range of disciplinary fields is represented among the team so the teachers can learn from each other before passing it on to their students. The interdisciplinary nature of the subjects means that different staff contribute expertise that assists their colleagues. Because the curriculum changes each semester to accommodate current events in the media – ensuring the subject remains dynamic and relevant to students – building and maintaining a core team of teaching staff engaged in the pedagogy of the subjects is essential to the success of the interdisciplinary studies programme.

In addition to online lectures, coordinators spend their time writing detailed lesson plans that instruct the large teaching team what to cover in the classroom. These lesson plans are broken into 10-minute blocks and more material is provided to the teachers than is required so they have an opportunity to craft their lessons according to their specialties while still ensuring all students receive consistent learning outcomes. Further readings are made available to staff wishing to supplement their disciplinary knowledge and bolster their confidence before teaching.

Fortnightly meetings contribute to strengthening the mutual support amongst the teaching team across campuses, and sharing classroom experiences positively impacts on the preparedness and confidence of teaching staff. The group also debriefs on their classes and discuss upcoming assessment and the outcomes of assessment that has already taken place. The subject coordinator collects this informal feedback, and each semester it is used to further improve the curriculum. For example, when the teaching staff have indicated that an essential subject reading has not helped students to understand a module topic sufficiently, the subject coordinators have removed and replaced that reading in the next iteration of the subject. Assessment is also revised in consultation with teaching staff to ensure student learning outcomes are maximised. Social events are arranged to strengthen bonds between team members and so the coordinators can express gratitude for a job well done. The teaching team has indicated that a supportive and collegial work environment contributes to their job satisfaction, which has a positive influence on their teaching.

The lesson plans, supplementary reading, and team meetings are resources that casually employed staff would not receive when teaching most other subjects within our school, college, or university. Our casual staff frequently remark on the benefits of this for their own pedagogical development and greatly appreciate the supplementary materials provided.

Before attending their weekly seminar, staff and students are expected to work their way through an online lecture produced in the Microsoft programme Sway and delivered through the learning management system (LMS) and read one or two essential scholarly readings prior to attending their two-hour seminar. Further readings and resources are also made available for students wishing to extend themselves and gain a more in-depth understanding of the subject content. The preparatory materials are aimed at capturing student interest in the subject matter and are modified each semester by the teaching team based on what did and did not interest students as well as current events in the media.

In the seminar, concepts that the students were introduced to in the pre-class materials are elucidated in more detail through well-supported collaborative and active learning tasks. It is important for success that students clearly understand the relationship between what they are learning and how they are being assessed (Jessop *et al.*, 2014). Often, students are asked to bring an assessment to class, which forms the basis of an active and collaborative learning task (Dochy *et al.*, 1999). This incentivises classroom attendance, which is not compulsory at La Trobe, and ensures that students receive immediate feedback on their work from both their peers and their teacher.

Preparation

In order to effectively teach our subjects, collaborative learning spaces with moveable chairs and large tables for group work are required. Students are delivered content through a weekly PowerPoint presentation that is made available to them after their class has concluded, so a digital projector and computer are required. Whiteboards are also used in the classroom by both the teacher and the students to document discussion outcomes.

Students are regularly asked to complete peer feedback, worksheets, and workbooks in the classroom. This requires a lot of printing, which might be replaced with digital forms if the coordinator could rely on their students having a device in the classroom (at La Trobe, for equity reasons, it is not possible to assume all students have a tablet and/or laptop to use in the classroom). All of these materials are prepared by the subject coordinator in advance of the semester and are available on the subject LMS for the teaching team.

The assessments are designed to engage students, but also to ensure that they acquire skills that will assist them as they continue in their studies and transition into employment. The first assessment for both subjects is an activity that teaches effective reading skills. The students are informed that they should employ the technique used in the assessment when reading for the subject in subsequent weeks. These exercises are submitted very early in the semester (week two and three) so that they can be used as a diagnostic tool. Those students who have demonstrated a lower-level skill set than will be required throughout the semester will be referred to a subject support tutor for assistance.

Group-based treasure hunts are also employed in both subjects. In the first semester, students undertake an "Amazing Race"-style task that teaches them to reference using the subject-preferred style. In the second semester, students are given a campus map with clues that will lead them to a historical figure that features later in the subject. These assessment tasks both occur early in the semester (week three and week one) so that students have an opportunity to share a positive experience with someone in their class, encouraging them to attend classes in future weeks.

In Rethinking our Humanity, the traditional end of semester essay has been replaced with a critical analysis assessment that teaches students how to independently analyse a primary and secondary source before synthesising this analysis into a well-referenced essay paragraph. Students are informed about how the process teaches them the "building blocks" of essay writing so that they get the most value possible from the assessment.

In Ideas that Shook the World, students are encouraged to engage in real-world problems and seek solutions through activism. This is achieved in a group work assessment that requires students to create a "Campaign for Change" relevant to their community. The process is designed to show students that the skills they are learning in their degree have real-world application and that they have the agency to effect change in their worlds through the skills and knowledge gained in their bachelor of arts.

Section 3: Outcomes

Student Outcomes

The subjects aim to prepare students for university while engaging them in the Bachelor of Arts through stimulating content. Qualitative student feedback indicates that we are achieving this aim. One student commented of Rethinking Our Humanity:

> "This is a devilishly clever subject! I cannot express just how surprising this subject is. I have enjoyed it from the very first class … I DO feel this subject has achieved its aim and turned me into a better, more skilled student. I DO feel having completed this subject I will now take these skills with me and use them for the rest of my academic life and work life as well. The structure is spot on. The variety of Assessments develop a range of critical skills, analysing, essay writing, habit forming, public speaking, debating. The content is perfect in order to engage students while instilling skills. Receiving feedback on assessments during the course has been very important for knowing how we are going in the new academic life and what needs improving … I want to repeat, this subject has made me a better student."

These sentiments are also evident in student feedback for Ideas that Shook the World, with students commenting that they *"feel more capable"*, *"feel more developed as a global citizen"*, that they have been taught *"good habits"*, and that the topics are *"engaging"*, *"interesting"*, *"stimulating"*, and *"provide a good background for an arts degree"*. Students also expressed gratitude for being taught academic skills. One student commented: *"I find in other first year subjects we're already expected to be scholars, whereas this subject helps us become better writers by taking us through the research/essay process"*.

Moreover, students claim that the subject and its classroom and assessment structure has given them confidence and has prepared them for the future. One student commented of Rethinking Our Humanity: *"The highest praise I can give this subject is that it's brought my confidence back that I AM capable of passing and even possibly, doing well at University"*. And of Ideas that Shook the World, one student expressed: *"All subjects should be layed [sic] out like this one. It puts the responsibility of understanding content in your own hands and prepares an academic to actually do the readings".*

Students consistently report that they have learned proportionally more from these subjects and that they have enjoyed doing so. A student in Ideas that Shook the World stated that, *"I have learned more from this subject as a result of its structure than any other subject I have taken this year, or any year for that matter".* Many other students commented on the transferrable nature of the analytical and academic skills acquired in the subjects, both to other university subjects, but also to current and future employment.

Overwhelmingly, student comments focus on their love of the in-class discussions, where they practice their analytical and critical thinking skills in a supportive and respectful environment. The students' enjoyment of the subject content and their classroom experience, coupled with their recognition that they are acquiring knowledge and skills relevant to their degrees and their lives beyond the university, is testament to their consideration that these innovative subjects are successful. This success is further evidenced by the quantitative feedback received on the subject, which is consistently above the university and school averages in all categories.

As we have modified the curriculum and assessment structure of the subjects each year, pass rates have also increased. In Rethinking Our Humanity, pass rates increased from 77.9% in 2014 to 81% in 2016. As noted previously, this is a significant result when we consider the concurrent 20-percentile point drop in admission rankings for the course between 2013–2016. Similarly, in Ideas that Shook the World, pass rates have increased from 70% in 2014 to 73% in 2016.

Teacher Outcomes

Teachers in these subjects have frequently commented on the high level of student engagement and attendance in the core interdisciplinary subjects. Some members of the teaching team have remarked that this positive experience of teaching has increased their confidence in the classroom. Teachers have also remarked on the benefits of attending the fortnightly team meetings as an opportunity to learn about the pedagogical approaches of their colleagues and to troubleshoot any difficulties. The subject coordinators have found that this has led to improvements in their own teaching, which is being passed on to their peers through scholarship of learning and teaching symposia, curriculum development communities of practice, and the dissemination of pedagogical research. They have also taken on a leadership role within the school in innovative curriculum development.

Staff members who teach other first-year subjects in the School of Humanities and Social Sciences have commented that they have noticed a difference in students' greater competency in academic skills since these two new core subjects were introduced. This flow-on effect to other staff has been a significant achievement of the subjects.

Section 4: Moving Forward

Following the success of these subjects, the School of Humanities and Social Sciences at La Trobe will introduce core subjects for the Bachelor of Arts on the second and third year from 2018 onward. In addition, this model is being considered and implemented in other schools based on consultation with curriculum designers.

To ensure that Rethinking Our Humanity and Ideas that Shook the World continue to support students using the most innovative and cutting-edge curriculum, we are now focusing on further developing structured online content, open access resources that can be taken beyond the subjects, and integrating gamified assessment into the classroom.

The authors are also currently writing an e-textbook *Key Concepts in the Humanities and Social Sciences* to accompany the subjects. This open access resource will guide students through the myriad of complex terms they are exposed to over their first year and offer clear definitions to help them in the classroom and when they are writing their assessments. The textbook will be thoroughly referenced and include an extensive bibliography, which will assist students in the research process and in the navigation of interdisciplinary subject content. The authors are writing the book with the intention that students will take the resource with them into their second and third years of study, and perhaps even beyond.

Perhaps the most innovative improvement to the subject on the horizon is the creation of a gamified assessment task using an augmented reality app. This app will encourage students to learn more about the key thinkers around whom the subject Ideas that Shook the World has been developed. Students will walk through the university in pairs/ small groups looking for key thinkers in locations across the campus. As students find each personality in a relevant location on campus, they will be asked a series of questions about them in order to score points. The more key figures they find, and the more questions they get right, the more points a student will receive. These points will then be converted into an assessment score. As students play the game, they will learn about their university campus, the key thinkers in the subject, and also get to know their classmates.

These three new innovations all align with the pedagogical theories already embedded in each subject, but seek to extend our successful work engaging students in their degrees and exciting them about the subject content, ensuring success and commitment to completing their bachelor of arts.

Conclusion

The implementation of two interdisciplinary core subjects into the first year of the Bachelor of Arts at La Trobe University has increased student retention, engagement, and success. Student pass rates have increased each year, and improvement in academic skills has been noted by other academic staff in the school. Students have remarked on the way in which the subjects build their confidence and make them feel like capable scholars. They also frequently comment on the engaging subject matter and collaborative learning approaches that encourage them to attend class and participate actively. Stimulating and lively classes have similarly built the confidence of teaching staff, and weekly discussions amongst the teaching team have prompted many of the staff to modify their pedagogical approach based on discussion with their peers. In sum, introducing subjects that orient students to the arts, increase their academic competency, and convince them of the value of their skills is an exciting new innovation in teaching and learning in higher education. While the development of these subjects incorporated a number of innovative components, any one of them could be introduced in isolation, depending on what kinds of challenges are being addressed in a particular course. Following the success of these subjects, it is likely in the near future that other courses with retention challenges will implement similar subjects in an attempt to maximise the number of students who complete their course. The success of our innovation in the Bachelor of Arts at La Trobe has shown that the introduction of interdisciplinary core first-year subjects with an innovative module-based curriculum delivered in a seminar format can engage and seduce reluctant students to embrace their course choice and complete their degree.

About the Authors

Sarah Midford is a lecturer in interdisciplinary studies in the School of Humanities and Social Sciences at La Trobe University. She has received two university and an Australian national teaching award for outstanding contributions to student learning. She can be contacted at this e-mail: s.midford@latrobe.edu.au

Sara James is a cultural sociologist and a lecturer in interdisciplinary studies in the School of Humanities and Social Sciences at La Trobe University. She can be contacted at this e-mail: s.james@latrobe.edu.au

Bibliography

Arvanitakis, J. (2014). Massification and the large lecture theatre: From panic to excitement. *Higher Education*, Vol. 67, No. 6, pp. 735–745.

Baird, J. (2010). Accountability in Australia: More power to government and the market. In B. Stensaker & L. Harvey (Eds.), *Accountability in higher education: Global perspectives on trust and power*. New York: Routledge, pp. 25–41.

Bradley, D.; P. Noonan; H. Nugent & B. Scales (2008). *Review of Australian higher education*. Canberra: Department of Education, Employment and Workplace Relations.

Chanock, K.; C. Horton; M. Reedman & B. Stephenson (2012). Collaborating to embed academic literacies and personal support in first year discipline subjects. *Journal of University Teaching & Learning Practice*, Vol. 9, No. 3, pp. 1–13.

Coates, H. & M. Mahat (2014). Threshold quality parameters in hybrid higher education. *Higher Education*, Vol. 68, No. 4, pp. 577–590.

Dochy, F.; M. Segers & D. Sluijsmans (1999). The use of self-, peer and co-assessment in higher education: A review. *Studies in Higher Education*, Vol. 24, No. 3, pp. 331–350.

Gibbs, G.; C. Rust; A. Jenkins & D. Jaques (1994). *Developing students' transferable skills*. Oxford: Oxford Centre for Staff Development

Gooch, L. (2011). Staff cuts in Australia worry academics and students. *New York Times*. Online Resource: http://www.nytimes.com/2011/12/05/world/asia/05iht-educSide05.html [Accessed on 21 April 2017].

Graduate Careers Australia (2016). http://www.graduatecareers.com.au/careerplanningandresources/exploringyourcareeroptions/careerprofiles/generalistdegreegraduates/ [Accessed on 10 May 2017].

Harvey, A. & M. Luckman (2014). Beyond demographics: Predicting student success within the Bachelor of Arts Degree. *The International Journal of the First Year in Higher Education*, Vol. 5, No. 1, pp. 19–29.

Hillage, J. & E. Pollard (1998). Employability: developing a frame work for policy analysis. *Research Brief No. 85*. London: Department for Education and Employment.

James, S. & S. Midford (2017). *Report on the BA cohort: Report for marketing, La Trobe University*. Melbourne: La Trobe University.

Jessop, T.; Y. El Hakim & Gibbs, G. (2014). The whole is greater than the sum of its parts: a large-scale study of students' learning in response to different programme assessment patterns. *Assessment and Evaluation in Higher Education*, Vol. 39, pp. 73–88.

Kuh, G. D.; J. Kinzie; J. H. Schuh & E. J. Whitt (2005). *Student success in college: Creating conditions that matter*. San Francisco: Jossey-Bass.

Long, M.; F. Ferrier & M. Heagney (2006). *Stay, play or give it away? Students continuing, changing or leaving university study in first year*. Melbourne: Centre for the Economics of Education & Training, Monash University.

McMillan, J. (2005). Course change and attrition from higher education LSAY Research Reports. *Longitudinal surveys of Australian youth research report*. Melbourne: Australian Council for Educational Research.

Mestan, K. (2016). Why students drop Out of the Bachelor of Arts. *Higher Education Research & Development*, Vol. 35, No. 5, pp. 983–996.

Pascarella, E. & P. T. Terenzini (2005). *How college affects students*. San Francisco: Jossey-Bass.

Reason, R. D.; P. T. Terenzini & R. J. Domingo (2007). Developing social and personal competence in the first year of college. *The Review of Higher Education*, Vol. 30, No. 3, pp. 271–299.

Scanlon, L.; L. Rowling & Z. Weber (2007). 'You don't have like an identity… you are just lost in a crowd': Forming a student identity in the first-year transition to university. *Journal of Youth Studies*, Vol. 10, No. 2, pp. 223–241.

Simpson, K. (2004). 'Doing development': the gap year, volunteer-tourists and a popular practice of development. *Journal of International Development*, Vol. 16, No. 5, pp. 681–692.

Tertiary Education Quality and Standards Agency (TEQSA) (2013). *Draft standards for course design and learning outcomes*. Online Resource: http://www.HEstandards.gov.au [Accessed on 1 April 2013].

Thomas, L. & P. Hixenbaugh (2006). *Personal tutoring in higher education*. Stoke on Trent: Trentham Books.

Wilcox, P.; S. Winn & M. Fyvie-Gaul (2005). 'It was nothing to do with the university it was just the people': The role of social support in the first-year experience of higher education. *Studies in Higher Education*, Vol. 30, No. 6, pp. 707–722.

Winefield, A.; C. Boyd; J. Saebel & S. Pignata (2008). *Job stress in university staff: An Australian research study*. Bowen Hills: Australian Academic Press.

Section 2: Student-Centred E-Learning

Willie McGuire, Rhiannon Evans, Ming Li and Sarah Midford

Chapter 7
Student-Centred E-Learning

Introduction

Each of the chapters in this section address student-centred learning with digital solutions, using e-learning tools, to ensure the purposeful use of technology, as opposed to innovation for innovation's sake. The projects discussed in these chapters emanate from contexts that are geographically, culturally, and educationally diverse: Australia, Hong Kong, and Scotland. They also deal with students at both undergraduate and postgraduate levels. The approaches we introduce here can be utilised across the academic spectrum.

Commonalities

One of the key issues underpinning each of the chapters is the attempt to address knowledge gaps in student bodies in a constructive manner and to employ technology purposefully in order to address student needs. These methods also function as support mechanisms for teachers who face increasing workloads and expanding student cohorts (with less predictable preparedness and different needs). Another salient issue is the prominent position of flexibility in each of our chapters, which is represented by curriculum design features such as choice, customisation, and accessibility.

Each of our curriculum models is responsive to the needs of students, and each simplifies abstruse concepts in order to make subject content more accessible to students. The three innovations can be characterised by their evolution over time, often using the tried and tested process of trial and error. Each chapter in this section demonstrates adaptations to curricula that accommodate the changing backgrounds of the student body and provide easy-learning tools to increase motivation, engagement, and confidence. In each case, the change in methodology has resulted in a more actively engaged cohort.

We firmly believe that innovation alone does not necessarily lead to successful teaching and learning, as the innovation must be secondary to the needs of the students.

Overview of Chapters

Midford and Evans' Chapter 8 demonstrates how popular culture and accessible digital resources facilitate student engagement and provide an entrée into complex historical ideas. These sources then become the object of study for students, rather than simply entertainment, and provide the foundation for historical enquiry so that students can make their way through scaffolded assessment. Midford and Evans' innovation has revitalised historical studies at their university through student-led learning in an online environment (Bean, 2011; Tsay & Brady, 2010; Prince, 2004).

Classics and ancient history is a new discipline of study at La Trobe University, moving from elective subjects to a minor, and now building a major. Because of this, teachers cannot assume prior knowledge in our students, who come from a wide range of educational backgrounds and may never have encountered the ancient world in a scholarly setting. Their unfamiliarity with the subject matter means they are particularly prone to accepting the first search item in an Internet search and do not have the tools to question web sources.

La Trobe University's move towards blended and online learning has provided the catalyst towards forming the digital engagement model, which incorporates the creation of high-quality online resources, builds digital literacies, and champions student-led learning. Midford and Evans started to develop this model by uploading traditional learning resources to the Internet, but they quickly discovered that simply uploading lecture recordings and PowerPoint presentations engaged students poorly. To more effectively engage students, Midford and Evans commenced building tailor-made online resources. As they created digital resources, they also crafted a digital literacies framework that came to inform the digital engagement model.

Midford and Evans have applied their model to newly-developed subjects within their discipline and extended it to subjects outside their discipline. Each iteration of the model has resulted in continuous improvement, particularly because digital resources are built specifically for their newly developed subjects, rather than reshaping traditional curricula and uploading it to a digital space. Midford and Evans are now being encouraged to share their curriculum developments with peers developing subjects offered online, and to extend their subject offerings to non-traditional learners outside their institutional student catchment areas.

Chapter 9 has been named "MOOC→ SPOC via F2F: It's a Flipped Hybrid, SPOC!" to encapsulate McGuire's fascination with futurity and, in particular, the extant technology evident in all 79 original Star Trek episodes. Warping forward from Star Trek, when McGuire started writing his first MOOC, it was an attempt to create an online PGDE course for English teaching students to address a gap in the market caused by the comparatively remote geographical location of the area.

Some years following this, McGuire wrote a second MOOC, this time on online CVs, to support non-"digital natives" come to terms with translating their traditional CVs into the online medium, which was, essentially, the reverse of the movement described by Combefis et al. (2011), who describe the process of translating SPOCs to MOOCs.

Shortly after their introduction, it became apparent that MOOCs, while still popular, were perhaps not fulfilling their expected potential, particularly in terms of student retention (Jordan, 2014; Atchley et al., 2013). Additionally, the paper by Fox (2013) "From MOOCs to SPOCs" presented the idea of downsizing large MOOCs to smaller, more compact SPOCs, which are specific online private courses aimed at a particular audience. It was as a result of these ideas, that McGuire began to think about how the advantages presented by MOOCs could be adapted for other online forms and, in this case, the SPOC. This "repositioning" was referred to by Dillenbourg et al. (2014). Once this conversion process from an existing MOOC to a new SPOC began, it became apparent that the prevailing methodologies of lecture, seminar, follow-up activity also needed to be adapted to fulfil the potential of the project. As a result of this, McGuire decided to flip this normal structure to something quite different. The result was the removal of the lecture component, which was replaced by a pre-seminar student activity, which usually involved them working in groups to review an artefact and then to create a new variation of that artefact in order to more fully understand its workings.

The second flip lay in an alteration of the conventional seminar format; now students led the teaching and the learning by presenting their own artefacts to the rest of the class, who would then critique those presentations. Within this revised framework, the role of the teacher then became one of organising the dialogue matrices that emerged from the new format and also in ensuring that the discussions were nuanced and as effective as they could be. The final stage of the process lay in the addition of the new artefact to the new SPOC. This would then become an integral part of the learning materials for the next session's cohort, with the idea being that the SPOC becomes student-driven and student-generated in future iterations.

Chapter 10 by Li *et al.* presents the use of whiteboard animation as an innovative teaching and learning tool for flipped classrooms in the general education foundation course "In Dialogue with Nature", taught at The Chinese University of Hong Kong. This subject requires all university year one and two students from different major disciplines to read science-related classic/core texts before having discussions in a series of interactive tutorial classes (General Education Foundation Programme, 2017). As a matter of fact, many students find it challenging to understand the classic/core texts mainly due to the lack of pre-existing knowledge to grasp abstruse ideas in the texts.

In order to fully utilise the time in class for discussion, the classroom was flipped so that the pre-requisite knowledge was accessible to students online to review at their own pace before tutorial classes. It is desirable that the online materials should be tailor-made and presented in a relaxing and entertaining form so as to better engage the students and ease their anxiety regarding scientific concepts. Consequently, instead of video recordings of short lectures, Li *et al.* used whiteboard animations to explain the complicated concepts in a simple and straightforward way. Whiteboard animations are video clips that mimic teaching on a whiteboard in a cartoon style. They consist of step-by-step illustrations with voice-over narrations, which help to make complicated concepts understandable and allow students to learn better (Sparkol VideoScribe, 2015).

Chapter 10 demonstrates the practice of using short whiteboard animations to aid teaching and learning, which are tailor-made to address students' learning needs. The chapter also describes in detail the workflow of the production and implementation: from storyboard development, whole-picture design, voice-over recording, animation production, to post-production. Feedback from students has shown that whiteboard animations are helpful for improving student learning. Most of the students agreed that whiteboard animations are more interesting than lecture recordings (Li *et al.*, 2016). The precise and concise explanations in the whiteboard animations helped students to frame reflective questions for discussion in class. There is no doubt that whiteboard animations are efficient and effective teaching and learning tools for flipped classrooms.

Thematic Interrelationships

This section focuses on curriculum practices that place student needs before the engine of delivery of those needs (Brown & Adler, 2008). A key feature of each project is the purposeful use of e-learning. In Chapter 9, for example, a variety of e-learning and innovative strategies are combined (MOOCs, SPOCs, flipping, hybridisation), not for their own sake but rather to improve the student learning experience. This can be seen in the re-purposing of existing MOOC materials for a smaller f2f audience. In Chapter 8, this same idea is evident; there are a variety of e-learning tools (podcasts, e-books, vodcasts), but these are deployed with a clear and focused purpose: to use modern technologies in order to ease students' immersion into the past. Equally, in Chapter 10, while whiteboard animation is clearly a new innovation, its deployment here is designed to solve a specific challenge faced by students: how to improve their understanding of new concepts in an engaging manner.

Another commonality between each of the projects described in this section is the concept of the evolution of ideas over time. Perhaps the clearest case of this is evident in Chapter 9, in which an e-learning form, the MOOC, was gradually transformed from a purely online artefact to a hybridised information delivery platform involving both f2f and online elements. This idea of evolving methodologies can also be found in Chapter 8 in the strategies used to encourage student customisation of the learning by making their own selections of popular entertainment texts to critique, thus putting students at the centre of their learning. The project described in Chapter 10, too, could not have come into existence in one movement; it had to be constructed over a series of iterations, for example, with the inclusion of additional narrations in English and Chinese to meet the needs of a diverse student body.

Each chapter in this section positions active learning at the heart of effective learning. In Chapter 10, a clear example of the application of active learning strategies is evident in the flipping of curriculum so that students understand concepts that they otherwise would not be able to grasp in their own time before class. In Chapter 9, the conventional methodological structure is reversed and students are positioned in such a way that they must engage in a meaningful way with the learning materials in order to translate them into alternative forms. This is also evident in Chapter 8 through the authors' use of the digital engagement model, which has three core components: the creation of digital materials, the development of digital literacies, and the flexibility for students afforded by the use of a customisable curriculum.

Another comment element of each project in this section is the responsiveness to students' needs, ranging from curriculum design to course material development, as well as imparting specific concepts. For example, the digital engagement model described in Chapter 8 engages students in historical subjects through student-led customisation of the curriculum in which a modern text can be selected by the students according to their interests. The SPOC via f2f described in Chapter 9 encourages students to collaborate and co-create teaching materials for the next session of the course via the centrality of teamwork and collaboration. Students bring their own experience to bear on pedagogic problems so that the materials are made to cater to their needs in real teaching practice. In Chapter 10, the theme of each whiteboard animation is tailor-made to the students' need in order that they have the necessary scientific knowledge for class discussions.

In addition to benefiting students, the development of e-learning tools helps to ease teachers' workload. For example, the online resources (podcasts, e-books, vodcasts) described in Chapter 8 and the tailor-made whiteboard animations described in Chapter 10 can be reused so that the preparation of future iterations of the online subjects can be reduced. Although the development stage may require a significant time commitment, the long-term pay-off is a good investment.

One of the advantages of e-learning is the capability to simplify difficult concepts using modern technologies. In Chapter 10, for instance, the whiteboard animations provide step-by-step illustrations with voice-over narrations to explain concepts in a simple and straightforward fashion. The animation tool is especially helpful when grappling with difficult concepts, for example, the coding mechanism of DNA and the interaction between gene regulation and environmental influences. Another digital innovation described in Chapter 8 engages students studying historical subjects with sophisticated digital tools (e.g., the downloadable short podcasts), also makes learning interesting and easier. Making complicated concepts simple can also be done via self-studying online materials followed by f2f discussion described in Chapter 8.

The student-centred approach to e-learning provides students with flexibility. In Chapter 10, whiteboard animations are constructed around student knowledge gaps that have been observed in the classroom. Chapter 9 positions the students' interests at the centre of their learning experience, allowing students to tailor their studies by bringing resources to class.

A component of flexibility is accessibility. All authors have developed accessible learning tools for their students that can be accessed more readily than traditional learning resources. Midford and Evans have made a conscientious effort to produce open access resources for their students so that they can be accessed after they leave university. This allows students to benchmark quality online resources beyond their studies and to continue to develop their digital literacy skills. Li et al.'s whiteboard animations allow students to learn at their own pace and review complex information at their leisure before class. Furthermore, the resources have been designed to make knowledge that students have traditionally found difficult to access, more accessible. Similarly, McGuire has brought a swathe of disparate information together for his students and made it accessible in a single location so that students can better understand what is expected of them and more quickly achieve their learning outcomes.

Each innovation was developed using a process of trial and error. Each innovation in this section has been developed over time and refined through an iterative process. McGuire has collected online resources over time and brought them together to provide students with an integrated learning space. Midford and Evans have spent five years developing their curriculum resources and refining the digital engagement model within their digital literacies framework. Li et al. have learned from previous iterations of their subject where student knowledge gaps exist and then devised a staged roll out of whiteboard animations that address those gaps.

Differing student experience is key for the authors of all three chapters; indeed, this is a growing issue for tertiary education globally. As the pre-university experiences of our students are increasingly diverse, we have sought to fill the inevitable knowledge gaps with our innovative digital curricula. Li *et al.* were motivated by their students' misconceptions about key scientific issues and, in response, created whiteboard animations that explicated these issues attractively and succinctly. A lack of previous student engagement with reliably sourced history led Evans and Midford to exploit historical fictions so that students were encouraged to use digital resources to seek out texts that might verify or invalidate history. In so doing, their students were engaging digital tools in order to research rather than imbibe historical narrative (Sipress & Voelker, 2008). And the postgraduate students discussed in McGuire's chapter faced national educational changes that required them to become experts in a curriculum that they themselves had not experienced as secondary school students. In all three cases, there was a need to "flatten out" inequalities so that effective learning could take place in the classroom. These studies show how digital technology can be recruited in order to enable subsequent active learning, yet also that it is essential to accomplish this by means of more than simply uploading lecture recordings.

All of the chapters in this section give practical advice on the creation of inventive and attractive resources. Teachers should note that the time investment needed for this makes it imperative that these resources should be easily repurposed for other student cohorts, potentially at the same or at other undergraduate and postgraduate levels. This of course relates to the theme of easing teaching workload. Designing curriculum and resources is less onerous if both can be minimally altered to fit other courses and levels. Thus, the whiteboard animations designed by Li *et al.* could easily supply interesting background information for other subject areas, such as philosophy or cultural studies, where understanding scientific concepts is helpful but not the central area of study. They might also be repurposed for students at secondary level whose focus is science, but who have not yet met these issues. With slight alterations of emphasis,

McGuire's SPOC formulation could feed the needs of almost any post-graduate coursework, as its key aim is to encourage students to research, share, and explain complex subject matter to peers. And with more guidance and less challenging subject matter, undergraduates could navigate their way through a similar process, with the instructor modifying the skeleton of the SPOC interface to enable more scaffolding.

Following its successful use in "The Roman World", Midford and Evans have already retooled and reused their digital engagement model in additional first-year, and now second-year, university subjects. This model has several components that can be modified or (de)emphasised; for example, the more incremental aspects of source collection and peer review might not be necessary with higher-level students. Student engagement is always at the core of this and the other chapters, and it is crucial to recognise that seeing the curriculum from the students' point of view wherever possible will make clear whether the repurposing and reuse of engagement tools is feasible and desirable.

Moving Forward

To progress the repositioning of e-learning as a facilitator of student-learning, as opposed to being an end in itself, the authors of this section would recommend the following: there needs to be institutional support to place student learning at the centre of teaching practice. This might be enabled in a number of ways, one of which is the advancement of scholarship into achievable and scalable methodologies that support students through the purposeful deployment of e-learning with the aim of supporting effective learning. Additionally, support for academics at the institutional level to encourage them to dip their toes into e-learning and apply one or two of the strategies found in these chapters in order to lessen the demands on their own teaching would be helpful. Indeed, this process might be enhanced through the sharing of good practice in relation to e-learning, for example, by making access to such projects easy and straightforward. One way in which this might be done would be through the adoption of online teaching tips, which would, of course, require effective cross-college communication. Another potential area for exploration lies in the domain of staff-student co-operation to examine ways forward in relation to the developing needs of students to capture their ideas on how their own uses of e-learning might be developed. In doing this, though, it is also clear that balancing the needs of students against the increasing demands on teachers is necessary in order to create the best equilibrium between the two. Institutional recognition of the time commitment involved in creating *and sharing* student-centred e-learning would be an enormous step forward in encouraging teachers to further develop these resources. In taking forward these ideas, the development of fora for the incubation of staff-friendly methods to support their use of e-learning strategies is vital in order to explore the full potential for e-learning to transform student learning.

About the Authors

Willie McGuire is a senior lecturer in the School of Education at the University of Glasgow, Scotland, and a senior fellow of the Higher Education Academy. He can be contacted on this e-mail: william.mcguire@glasgow.ac.uk

Rhiannon Evans is senior lecturer in Classics and Ancient History at La Trobe University, Melbourne, Australia. She was recently awarded an Australian Federal Government Citation for Outstanding Contributions to Student Learning for her work in digital engagement. She can be contacted at this e-mail: r.evans@latrobe.edu.au

Ming Li is a lecturer in the General Education Foundation Programme at The Chinese University of Hong Kong. He can be contacted at this e-mail: liming@cuhk.edu.hk

Sarah Midford is a lecturer in interdisciplinary studies in the School of Humanities and Social Sciences at La Trobe University. She has received two university and an Australian national teaching award for outstanding contributions to student learning. She can be contacted at this e-mail: s.midford@latrobe.edu.au

Bibliography

Atchley, W.; G. Wingenbach & C. Akers (2013). Comparison of Course Completion and Student Performance through Online and Traditional Courses. *The International Review of Research in Open Learning and Distributed Learning*, Vol. 14, No. 4.

Bean, J. C. (2011). *Engaging Ideas: The Professor's Guide to Integrating Writing, Critical Thinking, and Active Learning in the Classroom*, 2nd ed. San Francisco: John Wiley & Sons.

Brown, J. S. & R. P. Adler (2008). Minds on fire: Open Education, the Long Tail, and Learning 2.0. *EDUCAUSE Review*, Vol. 43, No. 1, pp. 16–32.

Combefis, S.; A. Bibal & P. Van Roy (2011). *Recasting a Traditional Course into a MOOC by Means of a SPOC*. Conference presentation.

Dillenbourg, P.; A. Fox; C. Kirchner; J. Mitchell & M. Wirsing (2014). *Massive Open Online Courses: Current State and Perspectives*. Dagstuhl Perspectives Workshop 14112.

Fox, A. (2013). From MOOCs to SPOCs. *Communications of the ACM*, Vol. 56, No. 12, pp. 38–40.

General Education Foundation Programme (2017). Online Resources: http://www5.cuhk.edu.hk/oge/index.php/en/gef [Accessed on 22 April 2017].

Jordan, K. (2014). Initial Trends in Enrolment and Completion of Massive Open Online Courses. *International Review of Research in Open and Distance Learning*, Vol. 15, No. 1, pp. 134–160.

Li, M.; C. W. Lai & W. M. Szeto (2016, Dec). UGFN Animated – Flipped Classroom with Whiteboard Animations. Poster session presented at the Teaching and Learning Innovation Expo, The Chinese University of Hong Kong, Hong Kong.

Prince, M. (2004). Does Active Learning Work? A Review of the Research. *Journal of Engineering Education*, July 2004, pp. 223–231.

Sipress, J. M. & D. J. Voelker (2008). From Learning History to Doing History: Beyond the Coverage Model. In A. R. Regan; N. L. Gurung; L. Chick & A. Haynie (Eds.), *Exploring Signature Pedagogies: Approaches to Teaching Disciplinary Habits of Mind*. Sterling, VA: Stylus, pp. 19–35.

Sparkol VideoScribe (2015) Online Resources: http://www.sparkol.com/engage/how-scribe-videos-increase-your-students-learning-by-15/?_ga=1.25 6257608.254490627.1492913564 [Accessed on 22 April 2017].

Tsay, M. & M. Brady (2010). A case study of cooperative learning and communication pedagogy: Does working in teams make a difference? *Journal of the Scholarship of Teaching and Learning*, Vol. 10, No. 2, pp. 78–89.

Chapter 8

Revitalising the Past: Crafting a Digital Engagement Model to Innovate Humanities Curriculum

Sarah Midford and Rhiannon Evans

Introduction

This chapter contributes to the book *New Innovations in Teaching and Learning in Higher Education* as we demonstrate how an innovative digital curriculum can engage undergraduate arts students in historical studies through student-led learning. We are thus participating in ongoing research into the value of student-led learning (Prince, 2004; Tsay & Brady, 2010; Bean, 2011) and devising means by which entry-level students can be helped to design their own research projects. Our model uses popular representations of the past, along with digital tools, to improve student experiences of history and classics curricula through meaningful engagement with material usually branded as entertainment. In this chapter, new innovations in teaching and learning in higher education are teaching strategies that promote student-led learning through modern technologies and encourage students to participate in research that engages them in historical subject matter. Our model contrasts with traditional learning models that rely primarily on information transfer to the student and also with digital techniques that replace face-to-face teaching with pre-recorded lectures (a common feature of online or blended learning). We seek to provide high-quality digital resources for students and require them to seek out and critically evaluate digital sources that deal with the past and, eventually, to produce digital resources themselves.

Our innovative humanities curriculum employs a digital engagement model crafted by the authors to introduce students to historical subject matter through familiar access points such as television shows and films.

It provides easily accessible academic resources to students through the creation of podcasts, e-books (Midford & Evans, 2017; Midford, 2017), and vodcasts (YouTube, 2013), which supplement more traditional teaching materials. Rather than introducing students to the past through historical sources that are perceived as "foreign" and difficult to understand, our approach allows students to engage with familiar and popular modern texts as an entry point to their studies of the past. By starting their studies with popular texts that they have encountered in their everyday lives, and then moving on to unfamiliar primary source texts, students gain a sophisticated understanding of the past from a point of personal interest. To further engage our students, we harness input received from an international community interested in the same popular historical texts through social media channels and online learning platforms, including iTunes U (Rennie & Morrison, 2013). This creates relevant learning experiences and opportunities for students to reflect on popular receptions of history and develops their digital literacies within a pedagogical framework.

Teaching historical studies is complicated by our perception as instructors that we need to deliver a huge body of material to students to properly introduce them to the discipline. This is perhaps more apparent at La Trobe University, where it is increasingly common for our students to come from culturally diverse backgrounds. This means that shared historical knowledge cannot be assumed and must be taught through curriculum. Traditional information delivery can create the perception among students that there is a mountain of material to process, which can lead to disengagement along with feelings of being overwhelmed, or to a parroting of "facts", which demonstrates no analytical or research skills. Thankfully, students' preconceptions about the past, constructed by popular media, can provide common ground and a space where they can feel "equal" and confident discussing their understanding of a text based in the historical past. Building on this feeling of shared knowledge that is easily consumed and understood is at the core of our innovation. Most students are well aware that the historical fiction they see on television is not documentary, but it does provide a set of narratives that they already know or can easily acquire, dealing as it often does in historical clichés. Thus, our students experience another form of flipped learning, where they are effectively in control of the storyline and build on this knowledge as they analyse the text for historical veracity.

This chapter has four main sections. The first discusses the context in which our innovative curriculum was developed, and the second details the practice of our innovation so that the reader has the means to emulate it. The chapter then outlines how the development of our digital engagement model has positively affected our students' learning experience before considering the future of our innovative curriculum development. When reading this chapter, you should gain the following four insights:

1. engaging students in digital spaces requires the development and utilisation of tailor-made and carefully curated online resources;

2. the student learning experience becomes more engaging and meaningful when students can study what is familiar and relevant to them, and when they have opportunities to customise their learning experience;

3. a digital curriculum should prepare students to continue their learning beyond the classroom, developing their digital literacies – in this case, this primarily means their ability to critically evaluate information found online;

4. popular culture can be usefully embedded into the curriculum – firstly to capture student interest, but secondly as a significant source in itself, representing one kind of response to history.

Section 1: Background

The digital engagement model was developed over a number of years, and its origins lie in the teaching of an ancient history subject "The Roman World" at La Trobe University, Melbourne, Australia. This subject was taught in multiple iterations, from entirely face-to-face to entirely online, as well as a blended version, between 2012 and 2016. The model described here has therefore developed over a five-year period and been utilised in other subjects along the way. Full implementation of the model is likely to require multiple teaching sessions, but elements of it can be applied as and where appropriate by teachers of historical and wider humanities subjects everywhere.

In 2012, universities throughout the world were focused on the relatively new phenomenon of massive online open courses or MOOCs (Jordan, 2014:134). Laura Pappano named 2012 as *The Year of the MOOC*" in the *New York Times* (2/11/2012). In the same year, wishing to participate in the MOOC phenomenon, to innovate pedagogy and to utilise the Internet to broaden their reach, La Trobe University began to experiment with the online open access platform iTunes U. Lectures from subjects taught across the university were uploaded to the platform. These were enthusiastically downloaded by people wanting to learn from across the globe. Lectures by the authors were uploaded weekly and attracted a vast, worldwide group of learners, with the audience growing from under 100,000 in 2012 to over two million in 2015 (75% located outside of Australia). In the same year, Rhiannon Evans was named by Apple as one of the top 20 instructors in the world on iTunes U, the only instructor outside of the United States to feature on this honour roll. After the success of the iTunes U lectures on the ancient world, Apple Australia approached the authors to develop resources for the centenary of the Australian First World War Gallipoli landing in 2015. The Gallipoli podcasts were used as the backbone for the fully online second-year subject "Gallipoli: From the Trojan War to the Great War".

To capitalise on the popularity of their lectures, the two authors turned their attention to designing the first "for-credit" subject to be offered through the iTunes U platform. The idea was to capture a fraction of the loyal audience and tempt them to further their interests in the subject matter by taking an accredited subject. The hope was that, if a small number of the MOOC participants were interested in further education, we could use this opportunity to develop online curriculum that effectively engaged students and expanded our reach beyond traditional university catchment areas. MOOCs had and continue to have very low completion rates: Jordan (2014) ascertained that a 5% completion rate is typical. To mitigate this trend, the curriculum for the authors' online subject was designed to provide students with the most engaging learning experience possible.

The strategies employed were largely successful, and 50% of students completed and passed the subject. However, due to a lack of marketing, the pilot iTunes U subject did not attract nearly enough students to compare with MOOC enrolments and the for-credit subject was not run through iTunes U again. The experiment clearly demonstrated that success with open access educational resources did not automatically translate to fee-paying enrolment. However, the pilot project taught the authors a considerable amount about developing quality online curriculum, and after its completion, we shifted our efforts to the development of engaging online subjects within the university's Bachelor of Arts that employed our digital engagement model.

Having pulled back from MOOC-like environments, the university has become increasingly focused on the development of online and blended curricula, but also on student success and retention. Online curricula are a priority because they facilitate subjects being offered to La Trobe University students on all its campuses in regional and metropolitan Victoria, as well those in New South Wales and overseas. However, the university's success and retention objectives are difficult to achieve in combination with the push toward online and blended learning because online subjects have traditionally experienced low completion rates and poorer student performance than face-to-face subjects (Atchley *et al.*, 2013). To address student attrition and maximise student success, the authors created a suite of resources designed to increase student participation and engagement in an exclusively online learning environment.

Furthermore, many of La Trobe's culturally diverse students have limited opportunities to encounter historical studies in their education prior to university entry and have almost no previous experience of ancient world studies before undertaking our subjects. Despite a lack of previous academic exposure to the past, there is a great deal of interest in history among students who are familiar with popular representations of the past in historical novels, film, television drama, documentaries, and video games. These representations are enticing, but often anachronistic, paradoxically making the past simultaneously more palatable (e.g., the ancient Romans have nuclear families) and exotic (e.g., the Romans wear scanty clothes and hold orgies). Thus, when faced with primary historical sources – those written by ancient authors – many students are challenged by the alien aspects of the past. As well as the differences in literary genres and historical writing, they encounter complex political systems, ethnocentrism, slavery, arena sports, rampant imperialism, pederasty and paganism; and, because they are now encountering the direct thoughts of the ancients, rather than a textbook with commentary, they must nego-tiate all of these features in their "raw" unmediated state. Our model makes a virtue of students' limited experience of historical studies by requiring them to use digital tools to interrogate and evaluate popular representations of the past in order to gain a greater understanding of what is "wrong" with these screen versions. In the process, they attain insight into what is knowable (and unknowable) about the past, and how to access and evaluate that knowledge.

Section 2: Practice

2a. A General Introduction to the Innovative Practice

Our pedagogical innovation has achieved higher student engagement, retention, and progression in our subjects. This is because our teaching makes historical subject matter more accessible and therefore caters to students from a broad range of cultural backgrounds and across great geographical distances. The creation and incorporation of digital resources has enabled us to make our subjects available to students studying online on five of La Trobe's metropolitan and regional campuses spread across the more than the 237,000-km² state of Victoria. There is also the poten-tial to open them up more broadly to students studying on our inter-state and overseas campuses, as well as students studying at other universities looking for a broader range of online electives.

To fit in with the university's drive to online and blended curriculum, the authors developed two fully online and one blended subject (listed respectively, below) using the digital engagement model. This model was developed by the authors to guide their curriculum innovations. It culti-vates students' digital literacies so that their engagement is maximised, and this leads to improvements in student success and retention. This follows Leu (2000:746), who broadens the definition of literacy for the digital age to include: *"literacy skills necessary for individuals, groups, and societies to access the best information in the shortest time to identify and solve the most important problems and then communicate this information"*. We have now embedded our model into two further history-based subjects at second-year level: "Gallipoli: From the Trojan War to the Great War" (online) and "Gladiators and Emperors" (blended). The digital engagement components for these subjects were considerably easier to develop. Although still time-consuming, curriculum created within the model runs more smoothly first time around than that adapted from traditional face-to-face mode.

The digital engagement model is a significant contribution to innovative teaching and learning practice. As represented in Figure 1, it comprises three parts:

1. the creation of digital materials – these are materials developed by the instructors (podcasts, video/OneButton lectures, curated presentations);

2. the development of digital literacies – this occurs in stages: students navigate the instructors' online materials, they retrieve and evaluate internet sources, they create their own digital materials;

3. flexibility of customisable curriculum – this should be flexible for both instructor and student: for the lecturer, materials can be moved around and repurposed; for the student, choice is provided, both in terms of area of focus and asynchronous learning.

Its three components work together so that students can feel confident learning historical subject matter in an online environment and therefore remain engaged and achieve better results. The innovation of this model is that it facilitates students entering our subjects with little knowledge of the subject matter and rudimentary digital literacy to succeed by enhancing their abilities to analyse historical sources using sophisticated digital tools. This works to reverse the prevalence of low completion rates and low student success rates in online education.

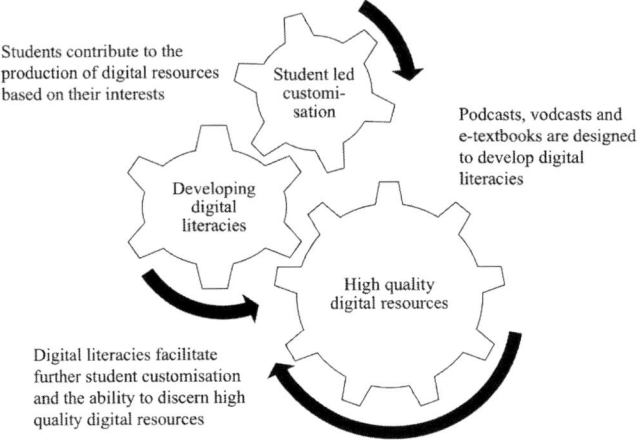

Figure 1: The digital engagement model.

The model builds on the team's "digital literacies framework", which was designed with asynchronous learning in mind. Central to the framework is the facilitation of student learning beyond the classroom, using online resources and peer-to-peer interaction (essential for preventing feelings of isolation that may increase when accessing learning materials online). Figure 2 demonstrates the cyclical nature of the framework, which reflects the cyclical nature of lifelong learning. The framework was designed to equip students with a broad skill set for navigating web-based content that can be employed across their studies and extended into the students' everyday lives.

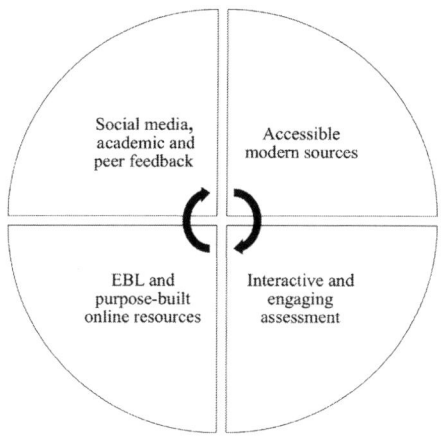

Figure 2: The digital literacies framework.

Students start with familiar representations of the past and move on to unfamiliar primary source texts through enquiry-based learning (EBL) tasks in the classroom and online (Aditomo *et al.*, 2013). The lessons are structured in accordance with research that demonstrates that student interest is engaged when they become personally involved in a process and when what they are learning has relevance to their life beyond university (Gee, 2005; Kuh, 2016). The modern text meaningfully engages students in the curriculum, which improves student success. The framework supports students to actively participate in their learning by bringing resources into the physical or virtual classroom, rather than passively consuming content provided to them by their lecturer (see Brown & Adler, 2008). Well supported social media use and engagement is encouraged so that aspects of the students' lives from outside the classroom also become part of their learning experience.

2b. The Curriculum – The Digital Engagement Model

(i) Digital resources

Essential to the digital engagement model is the creation of high-quality digital resources to use within an innovative online curriculum.

This allows students to investigate the past through the lens of modern historical representations. In each subject that employs the model, traditional lectures have been replaced with short podcasts (5–20 minutes), while easily accessible online academic resources, including e-books and vodcasts, have been created to supplement student learning. The creation and incorporation of digital resources in our subjects has enabled us to make them available online to all La Trobe University campuses, and also to a worldwide audience through open access platforms.

Rather than simply a "voice over a PowerPoint" approach, our podcasts and vodcasts are produced as engaging interviews with an expert or discussions between two specialists. The interviewer acts as a stand-in for the student, a questioner who is not (yet) an expert. Because our subjects often deal with an alien past – for example, the ancient Romans were pagans who lived in an extremely hierarchical and militaristic society – the interviewer demands an explanation of how the unfamiliar functioned. The interviews have a less rigid format than a lecture and are therefore more dynamic and engaging. Their availability online makes them more flexible than a timetabled lecture and their shorter length makes them more convenient to listen to in one sitting. The interview technique also prevents the podcast from becoming a barrage of information from the specialist, as the interviewer punctuates the recording and gives the student forewarning of the upcoming subject matter. Discussions between two experts take this technique further, as they allow students to view scholarly debate in action and are pointed towards the important recognition that multiple interpretations of the same evidence are possible. The format is more suited to intermediate- and advanced-level students within the undergraduate programme.

We also create other online content, most significantly e-textbooks, which are integrated with the curriculum of the subject, and which incorporate relevant podcasts or vodcasts and other multimedia resources, such as interactive glossaries, adaptable timelines, web links, and 3D reconstructions of monuments or urban areas. Our students are able to access our resources online or download them to their computers and/or devices to use offline. They can download the e-books, podcasts, and vodcasts onto mobile devices to listen to them on the go, adding an additional level of flexibility. This flexibility gives the student the power to decide when and how best they learn, allowing them to work at their own pace and revise sections of the course at their leisure (Read, 2005). When students listen to podcasts in a stationary environment, the ability for students to pause and review the content results in more comprehensive lecture notes (Evans, 2008; Gosper *et al.*, 2007). The combination of podcasts and note-taking results in significantly better student success rates (McKinney *et al.*, 2009). This then leads to better student note-making because their agency in the listening process allows them to pause and reflect, and therefore work towards deeper understanding of the concepts outlined in podcasts. This approach aligns with McLoughlin and Lee's (2010:28) argument that, in this digital age, "*students want an active learning experience that is social, participatory and supported by rich media*".

When designing digital resources, the authors ensure that as much material as possible is made open access. This practice stems from the authors' MOOC beginnings, and our open access resources include e-books, podcasts, and vodcasts. The development of innovative and engaging digital resources requires a large time commitment from teaching staff in the first instance. The creation of online resources requires the collection of the same material as a traditional lecture, but adds an additional layer of writing and recording (and sometimes rerecording) to the process. The creation of e-books and other online content is labour intensive, and some of the technical aspects of resource creation, such as virtual reality modelling, require particular expertise and, often, financial support.

(ii) Building digital literacies

The second component of the digital engagement model mitigates feelings of being overwhelmed by the sheer quantity of digital resources through the development of students' digital literacies. In all subjects, but particularly those offered online, the authors have observed a challenge for students, who are increasingly less capable of filtering sources found on the Internet. Students now have access to unlimited content via the Internet. While there are many positives to this (e.g., obscure historical works need no longer be accessed in only a few libraries), there are also negatives for students who cannot evaluate content judiciously. In a world where access to information is unlimited, students are no longer limited to material held by their institutional libraries and archives. Instead of providing access to resources, it has become more important for universities to train students to navigate and interpret what they see, hear, and read within *and* beyond their institution (see Schmar-Dobler, 2003). When the university library was the only repository of primary sources and scholarly analysis for students, they could be reasonably confident that anything accessed there would be scholarly. This is no longer the case. We address this issue by walking students through the stages needed to "filter" reliable and unreliable sources online.

In order to develop digital literacies, students start with reliable online material (the digital materials discussed in subsection (i) above); they are then asked to research further, in the first instance with some guidance, in order to find relevant sources that address a particular issue. The goal is that over time they become confident users of web-based content, gaining digital literacy and being able to distinguish between reliable, fully-referenced content and material that may be biased, badly-written, or unscholarly opinion.

In 2016, the digital engagement model was used in a new second-year subject Gladiators and Emperors. In this subject, students read ancient sources and also engage directly with a current podcast series "Emperors of Rome" (to which Rhiannon Evans is a primary contributor) as well as with its worldwide audience via social media, such as the enthusiastic contributors to the podcast Facebook page. Students are thus able to critique social media comments in class from a position of greater familiarity with primary sources.

Coaching students through this interaction is another way of teaching them to distinguish between scholarly and non-scholarly argument, developing their digital literacies. Although the commentators on social media have listened to the podcasts, they have not usually read the ancient sources, which are set texts for the students. Student are therefore able to give more informed comments and suggest further evidence or readings. In this way, students often recognise the value of primary sources and their confidence is boosted by their increased ability to analyse the past, thus enabling them to develop and demonstrate their digital literacies.

(iii) Student-led customisation

A degree of customisation allows students to personalise and control what and how they learn, and doing so sustains student curiosity and generates enthusiasm for further enquiry (McLoughlin & Lee, 2010; Dron, 2007). Johnson (2006:97–98) argues that choice is central to the 21st-century learning experience; that *"[l]earning is more efficient, effective, deep, and powerful with commitment and passion"*, and develops the capacity for students to make informed choices. In the context of our digital engagement model, the choice that comes from student customisation facilitates the autonomous development of digital literacies.

In their major assessment task, students should employ their newly acquired digital literacy skills to research the authenticity of a modern interpretation of historical events and investigate how and why changes from the historical record might have been made to narratives, characters, or settings. The modern text can be independently selected by the student or chosen from a selection made by the curriculum designer. In each case, the student is given some level of choice about what they will be studying during the subject, and this increases engagement.

This innovation works well at all levels of tertiary study: first-year students work on finding a small number of historical sources that inform the production of their chosen modern source. They also figure out the correct way to reference such sources and then critique the relevance of fellow students' research through a peer-review process. Upper-level students carry out more thorough investigations, demonstrating a sophisticated historical analysis of Hollywood movies and other modern cultural productions. Upper-level students also work together to synthesise their analysis of each primary source in a group project, which leads to a more complex understanding of the source, its context, and its value through collaboration.

By starting with familiar representations of antiquity and then moving on to "foreign" primary source texts, students develop both their classical and digital literacies, gaining a sophisticated understanding of the subject matter through enquiry-based learning (see Aditomo *et al.*, 2013). This means that students are encouraged to be active participants in their learning, contributing to it by bringing resources into the classroom. To facilitate active participation, the learning experience needs to be social, well supported, and involve an aspect of students' lives outside the classroom (Brown & Adler, 2008). In all cases, students are excited to use accessible texts as an entry point to historical study and to learn about anachronism and changes in social attitudes. They are then able to critically evaluate modern historical texts in a way not previously available to them, and this is a skill they can take with them after completing their degrees.

2c. Organisation of the Practice

Through the digital engagement model we are teaching students to apply theories recently developed in the emerging discipline of classical reception studies (Martindale, 2013). Reception studies seeks to better understand texts by examining both their original context of production and the context in which they are being read, in our case, in 21st-century Australia. Although classical reception studies is at the cutting edge of the classics discipline, it is currently better represented in academic research than in teaching, so its use with students is still rare: students are much more likely to be confined to studying only historical sources along with scholarly commentary, and then writing a traditional response to an essay question (Hardwick & Stray, 2011:4). Johnson (2013:8) emphasises the importance of teaching students the process of reception: "*Reception is more than matching sources or simply noting echoes of the past. Discussing the reception process is an important part of the pedagogy*". By encouraging students to look at both ancient sources and modern texts, our curriculum integrates this new theoretical model with established approaches to the study of the ancient world.

Our model is designed to broadly apply to historical subject matter from antiquity to modern historical contexts, and classical reception studies theory has been applied to the reception of historical texts from more recent time periods in "Gallipoli: From the Trojan War to the Great War". Although the historical period is relatively recent, the methodology is applied in a similar fashion to the same pedagogical ends and with similar success.

2d. Preparation

We use a variety of fairly simple technological resources to create our learning materials and encourage our students to make use of new digital tools in some of their assessment pieces. Any or all of these tools could be used in humanities subjects, and it should be noted that we began by simply putting our lectures online (via iTunes U) and worked gradually to use the tools and produce the resources listed here.

The simplest and earliest tool used is a handheld Zoom recorder, which allows us to record high-quality audio lectures. The Zoom recorder provides better quality recording than the university's on-location, automatic recording. It should be noted, however, that recorded lectures intended for live audiences are not the most engaging content delivery method online. The Zoom recorder can also be used to record student discussions, which can be uploaded to the LMS as a resource for students to access later. This is particularly useful for discussions held after a film screening, so that immediate responses to the film can be recorded.

Interview-style podcasts are recorded in a soundproof studio with two condenser microphones and a Zoom H5 recorder. They are then professionally edited down to circa 20-minutes in length with the Adobe Audition program (although any audio editing program would suffice). Editing might not be necessary or desirable, depending on the extent of pre-planning and the brevity of the interviewer and interviewee. In our case, we pre-plan by writing a set of questions and issues to be covered between the expert and the interviewer. We then conduct a scholarly, but informal, question-and-answer session, which often becomes conversational. Because these conversations can occasionally deviate from subject-relevant content, editing is desirable. In addition, this gives the editor the opportunity to rearrange the material if a topic arises out of logical order. The shaped, but conversational, nature of the podcasts makes them more engaging to students, but this does require more time commitment than a formal lecture-style delivery, which might be read from a script. The recordings are re-editable and reusable, and so can be seen as an investment in developing a library of teaching resources. We have used them in this way, particularly the podcasts dealing with historical background. It is important to bear this in mind when recording and to leave out references to semester dates, events, and subject-specific material that will confuse those listening in later years.

La Trobe University has recently introduced One Button Studios, devised by Penn State University (One Button Studio, 2016). These are simple to use and valuable for delivering subject content. This method avoids the "depersonalisation" that can occur when information is delivered with a disembodied voice over PowerPoint or a computer screen recording. Like the podcasts and vodcasts described above, this technology is flexible: recordings can be of whatever length the material demands. However, a limit is imposed if using the free version of Vimeo or YouTube to make videos available to students. In the case of Vimeo, there is a maximum upload of 500 MB per week. This amounts to around 15–18 minutes of recording time and also demands planning ahead: only one recording can be uploaded every seven days. YouTube limits free users to 15-minute video uploads, but permits multiple uploads in a week.

When conducting online seminars, the authors use Zoom (the online meetings program, not to be confused with Zoom microphones). There is a free version of this software, although an institutional licence has the advantage of allowing more participants to meet for longer periods. Zoom allows students to attend a virtual class and participate in an academic facilitated discussion with their fellow students. Discussion facilitators can share their computer screen to deliver visual subject material, display PowerPoint presentations, run through LMS instructions, and share web-based material. The program does not run fast enough to share video content through the screen-share function (but may do so with more high-quality Internet provision).

We also train students to use online tools and software that develop their digital skillsets. In Gallipoli: From the Trojan War to the Great War, students produce a WordPress website that features analysis of primary and secondary source materials, as part of a group assessment. The open access CMS allows students to experiment with web design. Moreover, the assessment provides them with an open access website for prospective employers to view that demonstrates each student's ability to work in a team, communicate using written expression, and analyse complex historical material. In Gladiators and Emperors, students produce a multimedia Microsoft Sway presentation as part of a group assessment. The assignment requires students to work together to find and create images, video, voiceover, and text, which they add to their Sway to answer an assessment question. The software is relatively easy to use; it optimises for different interfaces (i.e., computers/tablets/smart phones); and it generates a URL, rather than a large file. It is easy to share with other students and staff via e-mail or on the LMS, and can also be added to the student's CV to demonstrate the skills acquired from the task.

Section 3: The Outcome

3a. Student Perspective

Students have commented on the interactivity of the authors' online curriculum and praised it for the quality of its delivery when compared with other online experiences they have had. One student commented on a subject that employs our digital engagement model:

> "The unit was much more interactive than I was expecting, have previously done an online unit through OUA [Open Universities Australia]/ Macquarie [University]. I found the podcasts interesting and easy to listen to. Their length and change of speakers throughout made it easier to listen to than just a recorded lecture."

The structure of the online curriculum has been praised, and students have recognised that this contributes to their experience: *"Overall this subject exceeded my expectations and I believe a lot of that comes from the structuring and development done by Sarah"* and *"I truly believe that the teachers had put in a lot of effort into this subject. I am content with the structure of this subject".* When asked *"What aspects contributed most to your learning?",* a typical response was *"The clarity of the lectures and down-loadable recordings".* Another student commented on the flexibility of and ease of access to the material provided: *"I don't use a computer at uni so iTunes [the podcasts] was better for listening to lectures between classes and while I was travelling on public transport".* The students' appreciation of the flexibility our model provides is exemplified in this student comment: *"The online aspect of the subject was the best. It allowed me to watch a lecture whenever I wanted, and to be in complete control of my own learning".*

Student feedback further demonstrates the success of the digital engagement model from a student perspective. Student satisfaction with The Roman World is consistently above the faculty and university average of 3.94/5 and 3.78/5 (on a Likert scale): overall satisfaction has risen from 4.1 to 4.53/5 between 2012 and 2016. Moreover, consistent innovation has considerably increased retention, from 84% to 90%. Gladiators and Emperors is a new subject, first run in semester 2, 2016 (evaluations and success rates are not yet available). Retention for the subject was high, at 91%. In 2015, over 65% of students enrolled in Gallipoli: From the Trojan War to the Great War received an A or B grade (70%+). These results are a testament to student engagement. The subject was offered again in 2016, with a 30% rise in enrolment.

3b. Teacher Perspective

(i) Digital engagement

The instructors have learned four key points when developing their digital engagement model, which are:

1. it is easier to design online curriculum from scratch than to customise existing traditional curriculum to an online environment;

2. it takes a significant time commitment to develop online resources (often more time than it takes to develop traditional teaching resources). Although one benefit of online resources is that they can often be reused in later iterations of the subject, they do not eliminate the need for curriculum revision;

3. the nature of online teaching requires different staffing arrangements to traditional teaching. We organise our curriculum to have less face to face time, but this does not mean teachers are spending less time "with" students. It is important to factor the time it takes to reply to comments on the subject forums and to reply to student e-mails into the teaching schedule (especially when casual staff are involved in teaching). Ideally, for every hour allotted to online virtual classroom teaching there would also be an hour assigned to forum engagement and answering student queries;

4. when teaching in an online space, more time needs to be invested in formally teaching digital literacies to students. Because students are operating in an entirely online environment, we have an obligation to help them navigate this space and better understand what is helpful to their studies and what is a distraction.

(ii). Reception studies

The use of screen and other modern adaptations of historical narratives need not be "an additional extra" or reserved for postgraduate research. These resources have often been viewed (particularly by classicists) as unscholarly and therefore irrelevant or an annoying distraction from "real" history. Two key points to take from using these modern sources are that:

1. embedding these sources at the heart of students' learning makes it much easier for us as teachers to engage students in the first instance;

2. teachers must be flexible; as students may bring in a wide variety of supporting evidence, the teaching staff have less control over the material that may enter the classroom. However, this is usually a positive factor and exciting for both teachers and students.

All these innovations work together to produce a carefully scaffolded curriculum that revitalises the past for humanities students.

Section 4. Moving Forward

The digital engagement model started with a single subject but now incorporates two others and more to come. By employing principles of open access and building on our experience delivering MOOCs, the authors seek, eventually, to make their model scalable so that larger online cohorts can experience quality digital curriculum.

Two projects are currently underway that seek to explore new ways of engaging students effectively through digital tools. The first is a virtual reality project that will allow students to "walk through" 3D reconstructions of ancient Rome, better understanding the ancient city, its architecture, and landscape. The second is the development of an augmented reality mobile phone app that gamifies historical content through a quest narrative. These projects further the authors' aim to revitalise the past for their students and employ digital resources in their curriculum.

In 2017, a new subject, "History of Histories", will trial a version of the digital engagement model with third-year students. Upper-level students will require less scaffolding than those who have previously been taught using this model and will be required to create some of the digital resources themselves. This subject is a first step to disseminating the model more broadly across our school, as it is co-taught across university departments. After further scholarship of learning and teaching presentations and publications, we anticipate that the model will be adopted by other colleagues throughout the university and possibly beyond.

Conclusion

This chapter has presented several ways in which humanities curricula can be enhanced using innovative digital tools, classroom tasks, and assessment. The key innovations involve the creation of high-quality digital resources, the co-option of texts from popular culture as access points to the past, and the provision of choice to encourage student engagement. These innovations work together in the authors' digital engagement model. It should be noted that mirroring this model need not involve every element of it; for example, a simple move towards recording conversations between an expert and non-expert on a specific topic, then uploading to a university-provided learning management system would be a relatively low resource and workload entrée into improving student engagement and digital literacies.

By developing coherent and imaginative resources for student learning, and pairing them with the implementation of research-led approaches to learning and teaching, we have seen a marked improvement in student success. Over a sustained period, our digital engagement model has revitalised the past for students, who enthusiastically engage in our curriculum, and this has led to improved student satisfaction and retention in our subjects.

About the Authors

Sarah Midford is a lecturer in interdisciplinary studies in the School of Humanities and Social Sciences at La Trobe University. She has received two university and an Australian national teaching award for outstanding contributions to student learning. She can be contacted at this e-mail: s.midford@latrobe.edu.au

Rhiannon Evans is senior lecturer in Classics and Ancient History at La Trobe University, Melbourne. She was recently awarded an Australian Federal Government Citation for Outstanding Contributions to Student Learning for her work in digital engagement. She can be contacted at this e-mail: r.evans@latrobe.edu.au

Bibliography

Aditomo, A.; P. Goodyear; A. Bliuc & R.A. Ellis (2013). Inquiry-based learning in higher education: principal forms, educational objectives, and disciplinary variations. *Studies in Higher Education*, Vol. 38, No. 9, pp. 1239–1258.

Atchley, W.; G. Wingenbach & C. Akers (2013). Comparison of Course Completion and Student Performance through Online and Traditional Courses. *The International Review of Research in Open Learning and Distributed Learning*, Vol. 14, No. 4.

Bean, J. C. (2011). *Engaging Ideas: The Professor's Guide to Integrating Writing, Critical Thinking, and Active Learning in the Classroom* (2nd ed.). San Francisco: John Wiley & Sons.

Brown, J. S. & R. P. Adler (2008). Minds on fire: Open Education, the Long Tail, and Learning 2.0. *EDUCAUSE Review*, Vol. 43, No. 1, pp. 16–32.

Dron, J. (2007). Designing the undesignable: Social software and control. *Educational Technology & Society*, Vol. 10, No. 3, pp. 60–71.

Evans, C. (2008). The Effectiveness of m-Learning in the form of Podcast Revision Lectures in Higher Education. *Computers & Education*, Vol. 50, pp. 491–498.

Evans, R. (2014-). Emperors of Rome Podcast Series

https://itunes.apple.com/au/podcast/emperors-of-rome/id850148806?mt=2, [Accessed on 27 April 2017].

Gee, J. P. (2005). *What Video Games Have to Teach Us about Learning and Literacy*. New York: Palgrave Macmillan.

Gosper, M.; M. McNeill; K. Woo; R. Phillips; G. Preston & D. Green (2007). *Web-based lecture recording technologies: do students learn from them?* Paper presented at Educause Australasia.

Hardwick, L & C. Stray (2011). Introduction: Making Connections. In L. Hardwick & C. Stray (Eds.), *A Companion to Classical Receptions*. Oxford: Blackwell, pp. 1–9.

Institute for Writing and Rhetoric, Dartmouth University, http://writing-speech.dartmouth.edu/teaching/first-year-writing-pedagogies-methods-design/useful-links [Accessed on 22 April 2017].

Johnson, J. A, (2006). Beyond the Learning Paradigm: Customizing Learning in American Higher Education: 10 Bellwether Principles for Transforming American Higher Education. *Community College Journal of Research and Practice*, Vol. 30, No. 2, pp. 97–116.

Johnson, M. (2013). Classical Reception Studies: Some Pedagogical Approaches. *Classicum*, Vol. 39, No. 2, pp. 6–14.

Jordan, K. (2014). Initial Trends in Enrolment and Completion of Massive Open Online Courses. *International Review of Research in Open and Distance Learning*, Vol. 15, No. 1, pp. 134–160.

Kuh, G. D. (2016). Making Learning Meaningful: Engaging Students in Ways That Matter to Them. *New Directions for Teaching and Learning*, Vol. 145, pp. 49–56.

La Trobe University (2015) Gallipoli and the Great War Podcast Series https://itunes.apple.com/au/podcast/gallipoli-and-the-great-war/id967167107?mt=2, [Accessed on 27 April 2017].

Leu, D. J. Jr. (2000). Literacy and technology: Deictic consequences for literacy education in an information age. In M. L. Kamil; P. B. Mosenthal; P. D. Pearson & R. Barr (Eds.), *Handbook of Reading Research*, Vol. 3, pp. 743–770.

Martindale, C. (2013). Reception—a new humanism? Receptivity, pedagogy, the transhistorical. *Classical Receptions Journal*, Vol. 5, No. 2, pp. 169–183.

McKinney, D.; J. L. Dyck & E. S. Luber (2009). iTunes University and the classroom: Can podcasts replace Professors? *Computers & Education*, No. 52, pp. 617–632.

McLoughlin, C. & M. J. W. Lee (2010). Personalised and self-regulated learning in the Web 2.0 era: International exemplars of innovative pedagogy using social software. *Australasian Journal of Educational Technology*, Vol. 26, No. 1, pp. 28–43.

Midford, S. (2017). *Gallipoli Anzacs and the Great War*. Melbourne, La Trobe University eBureau.

Midford, S. & R. Evans (2017). *Caesar's Triumphs over Gaul and Rome*. Melbourne, La Trobe University eBureau.

One Button Studio. (2016). Pennsylvania, Pennsylvania State University, http://onebutton.psu.edu/ [Accessed on 11 April 2017].

Prince, M. (2004). Does Active Learning Work? A Review of the Research. *Journal of Engineering Education*, July 2004, pp. 223–231.

Read, B. (2005). Lectures on the Go. *The Chronicle of Higher Education*, 28 October 2005.

Rennie, F. & T. Morrison (2013). *E-Learning and Social Networking Handbook: Resources for Higher Education*. New York: Routledge.

Schmar-Dobler, E. (2003). Reading on the Internet: the link between literacy and technology. *Journal of Adolescent & Adult Literacy*, Vol. 47, No. 1, pp. 80–85.

Tsay, M. & M. Brady (2010). A case study of cooperative learning and communication pedagogy: Does working in teams make a difference? *Journal of the Scholarship of Teaching and Learning*, Vol. 10, No. 2, June, pp. 78–89.

YouTube, 'Roman Politics and Poetry: Cicero and Catullus', https://www.youtube.com/watch?v=-1-C5mbV9Lk

Chapter 9

MOOC→ SPOC via F2F: It's a Flipped Hybrid, SPOC!

Willie McGuire

Introduction

This chapter contributes to the book *New Innovations in Teaching and Learning in Higher Education* by describing a pilot study using the Moodle 2 platform with a cohort of 30 graduate students on the Postgraduate Diploma in Education (PGDE) course at the University of Glasgow that qualifies them to become teachers of English at secondary school level. The course also functions as a preparation for progression to the degree of MEd (Professional Practice). In the chapter, I also focus on the recent shift in many higher education institutions from the use of massive open online courses (MOOCs) to the deployment of small private online courses (SPOCs). The course I teach is a hybrid course featuring face-to-face (f2f) activities combined with three online learning domains identified in the seminal work of Garrison and Anderson (2003): 1) teacher-student interaction (T-S); 2) its reverse, (S-T); and finally, 3) student-design interaction (S-D), in which the student interacts with the course design itself. Reading the chapter, you will take away three insights:

1. the process of converting the strengths of a MOOC into the smaller format of a SPOC;

2. the improvements gained when placing the student at the centre of the learning, while using e-learning as a support mechanism;

3. some ideas on how you might use aspects of the process described in your own teaching to improve the quality of student learning.

The chapter is structured in four main sections. In section 1, I present the background for my particular work with student-centred e-learning using SPOC as a flipped hybrid. In section 2, I present my practice in detail. In section 3, I show some of the student feedback as I discuss the outcome of my SPOC innovation. Section 4 brings the chapter to its conclusion by looking forward.

Section 1: The Background

Even in the pre-MOOC era, according to Anderson (2004), online learning is still very much in a fluid and changing state. While at the same time, change at the level of the school curriculum, too, is seismic, thus necessitating a recalibration in our pedagogies to utilise the opportunities afforded to us by digital technology. MOOC popularity reached its zenith in 2012, the "year of the MOOC", and while still popular today in 2016, their early massiveness and openness have been repositioned, or *"cross-fertilised"*, according to Dillenbourg *et al.* (2014:6), into something smaller, more compact, and private – the SPOC – while still sharing some of the design characteristics of their former iterations but, importantly, according to Baggaley (2014), SPOCs may well prove to be qualitatively different from previous forms of online education.

This SPOC takes up that very point and attempts to humanise the learning environment again. The shift from MOOC to SPOC began when Harvard indicated a move in this direction in 2013 according to Conway (2013), perhaps as part of a need to eliminate the learned dependence on the expert as coined by Downes (2012). Additionally, knowledge of disciplinary concepts in a course is fundamentally defined by the personalised contexts that individuals bring with them (Hickey, 2013). The final driver of this MOOC-SPOC transition stemmed from the idea of Fox (2013) that if MOOCs are used as a supplement to classroom teaching rather than being viewed a replacement for it, they can increase instructor leverage, student throughput, student mastery, and student engagement, and so my SPOC was used as means of testing the design characteristics for future work (the MEd) (Combefis *et al.*, 2011), and collaboration was placed front and centre *via* the centrality of teamwork and collaboration, as opposed to the focus being on the technology itself (Dillenbourg *et al.*, 2014:7).

Section 2: The Practice

The aim of this project was to create a SPOC, the term coined by Fox *et al.* (2014). This SPOC was based on a pre-existing MOOC created several years ago. The key idea was to use the strengths of both main MOOC forms: the xMOOC and the cMOOC. The xMOOC is based on behaviourist principles within which transmission is the main engine of delivery *via* resources placed online, and so xMOOCs are, essentially, traditional courses converted to the online format, but with little or no change in actual delivery method to take advantage of the affordances of the new medium, although with a rich resource base. However, the cMOOC is based on the constructivist principle of putting the student at the centre of the learning by encouraging them to construct their own knowledge as opposed to simply receiving it, for example, through enquiry-led practices within a flipped structure as Couglan (2013) asserts that SPOCs (often) follow the flipped classroom model – hence the title of this chapter. So, the main intention in this project was to hybridise the strengths of both MOOC forms to create a SPOC with an x support system, but with c depth. Additionally, the intention was also to incorporate scope for the inquiry-led/collaborative components within a flipped structure, which describes the process of creating this structure.

In terms of design, the course lasts 18 weeks, with each week containing three parts: contextualisation, acclimatisation, and implementation, although the overall pattern is nonlinear-sequential and so the actual order in which topics appear may not necessarily be the order in which students work on them. The following cross section may create a clearer insight into the student experience/perspective:

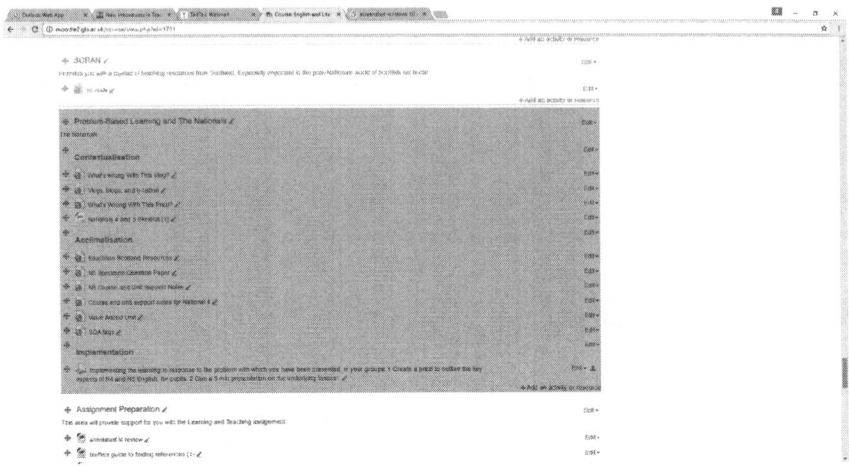

Figure 1: Students' perspectives of the course.

Figure 1 shows an exploded view of one topic from the full range of 42 topics. It is split into three distinct sections: contextualisation, acclimatisation, and implementation. The contextualisation section here provides the context of the learning and materials to be analysed in order to develop understanding of that topic on a straightforward, basic level, and so students are asked to read and comment on either a vlog or a Prezi presentation. This allows for rapid assimilation of the broad principles of the composition of the National 4 and 5 courses that the students will later teach to secondary school pupils once qualified. The acclimatisation section is more onerous and demands the reading of a wider body of policy materials, although some of this level of demand is offset by the fact that the students work on this in groups and disseminate the materials between them. The final stage of implementation is where the really deep learning occurs, as students have to combine the materials from the first two stages and reconstitute it into a different form, in this case a Prezi, which will also aid them in their roles as teachers of English when they qualify. It is also during this stage that the learning deepens yet again, as the role of the lecturer is to question, challenge, support, contradict, develop, synthesise, and, ultimately, to advise the groups on their end products, which then become the core learning materials for the next session, thus fitting with the suggestion of Fox *et al.* (2014), who believed that their SPOC was "helping to teach the teachers". This is also a key aim of my SPOC, as it is being used to both educate prospective teachers of English in the current condition of the subject and also prepare them for future practices in a digital age and to avoid the "transition shock" identified by Muller-Fohrbrodt *et al.* (1978).

This is the first SPOC to be created at the University of Glasgow. It is, essentially, a live trial, during which the existing f2f PGDE English course is gradually flipped to become a new form, which will then be implemented fully next session. Following this, the MEd 5-credit SPOC (see Moving Forward) will be implemented in session 17–18. A key aim was to improve on student learning experiences and outputs through a rethinking of the key pedagogies deployed on the course and to integrate more fully the theoretical course with its practical output: teaching practice. The axis of responsibility then was shifted more towards the student.

A more traditional structure might have looked something like this, where we would begin with a teacher-led presentation introducing the key dimensions of National 4 and 5 English, which would then be followed by a class/group discussion of the underlying issues. Finally, there would be an activity to develop a deeper awareness of any implications for teaching practice. Within the new format, the differences become apparent very quickly. First six groups of five would be formed. This would be followed by individual viewing of the Prezi and vlog materials as well as Power-Point of the skeletal structure of two school-level courses that students would be expected to teach upon qualifying National 4 and 5 English. Following this, the groups would meet to give their initial reactions to the vlog/Prezi materials, followed by further/deeper exploration of the topic using the acclimatisation materials. The next stage is for the groups to further collaborate to produce their own Prezis to highlight the key issues affecting the teaching of both National 4 and 5 English, after which the groups would present their work collaboratively in class to the wider audience. At this stage, the group presentations are then critiqued by peers/teacher, while at the same point in time the teacher moderates discussions and summarises the main points and clarifies the deeper implications for practice that students often omitted in the traditional approach. At the final stage, the Prezis are posted to Moodle, thus co-creating materials for the next session and further deepening the relationship between teacher, student, and online resourcing.

What are the advantages of this model? There is a range of advantages to this approach; for example, students have to work cooperatively to solve a problem, although they also have space for individual contemplation of their own responses to the online materials. This shift in the axis of responsibility creates deeper, more meaningful learning with greater retention, as they really remember the issues. Indeed, this is evident from their own teaching practice experiences and from the observations of their teacher mentors in schools. In addition to this, students have to engage actively with the materials and with their own learning as they have to "micro teach" their Prezis to the class, thus preparing them more effectively for teaching placements and creating a more effective bridge between the worlds of theory and practice as well as developing situative learning skills, (Lave & Wenger, 1991; Hickey, 2013) by encouraging students to bring their own experiences to bear on pedagogic problems prior to teaching practice in an attempt to offset the phenomenon of transition shock identified earlier. One unexpected outcome, however, was that the increase in student responsibility lowered the teacher focus that was a feature of the former practice, making the act of teaching more enjoyable.

How then would this innovation be replicated? To make this process more accessible, it is perhaps better to present it in phases. Phase 1 concerns familiarisation. It takes time to think about the kind of *product* you want at the *end* of the planning process. On which form of MOOC, if any, are you going to *model* your SPOC? What is the *purpose* and *audience* of the SPOC? Because this will condition its form. What are the key differences between MOOCs and SPOCs? Do some reading, too, around the various iterations of the MOOC to determine their affordances, such as little online courses (LOOCs) or corporate online courses (COOCs).

Phase two focuses on planning, and so you have to decide *what* you want to do and *how* you want to present it. In this case study, for example, the format of: *contextualisation, acclimatisation,* and *implementation* was used. Once you have determined how you wish to structure the materials, then you can draw up a *plan* showing the start, middle, and end stages.

The next stage in the initiative is its development. One key lesson learned from the experience of producing this SPOC was that the creation of a SPOC in parallel with the delivery of an existing course allowed for micro and macro changes based on ongoing feedback from students.

Finally, in the editing phase, it is prudent to open each week's slot only when you are *certain* that you are content with the product. Additionally, you need to consider the *balance* of teaching methodologies: visual, auditory, kinaesthetic, individual work, group work, and paired activities, and then manage the *interaction/social aspects* in a realistic manner.

Section 3: The Outcome

Formal formative student feedback was taken at three stages in each of the two semesters: close to the beginning, middle, and end (just prior to school placements, when students are at their most anxious). The formal feedback took the form of a peer questionnaire to determine the broad levels of dis/satisfaction with the progress of the course so that it could be fine-tuned quickly, and levels of satisfaction were extremely high, as can be seen from the comments below:

- "Flipping (I'll never get used to that word!) sounded mad at the start, but it's a brilliant idea; I'm using it next term with my senior school pupils."
- "The microteaching meant that I had to put into actual practice what I'd learned in theory."
- "I liked the opportunities to work with different people and in different ways and group sizes."
- "Having to read materials online and then discuss them with others and then to begin a class with a short presentation was something I'd, literally, never done before, but it left time in class to really explore the issues."
- "My school mentor has said on a number of occasions now that I seem to be unusually familiar with the workings of the National 5 and Higher English courses. I put this down to 'Mr. SPOC's' method!"

Figure 2: Feedback on the progress of this course.

Section 4: Moving Forward

The next step in the development of this SPOC initiative would be to learn the lessons from the implementation of this course in order to influence the design of two other courses, a pre-existing one and an entirely new one. The first of these courses is the MEd (Professional Practice) for which I am programme leader. While this course is mainly online, its current focus is on individual activities as opposed to group activities and the production of group artefacts. Also, the f2f elements, while few in number (three throughout the eight-month course), could be improved considerably by the application of at least a degree of flipping prior to the three f2f weekend meetings. The second course that could benefit from the experience of this project, is to apply the lessons learned to a new tranche of SPOCs that will act as showcases for each of the four courses that would constitute a new masters in assessment literacy to be offered by the University of Glasgow from 2018. Within this structure, each SPOC would contribute 5 credits for each course (of 20 credits in total) from the overall credits required to complete the degree, thus following the advice of Dillenbourg *et al.* (2014:11), who advocate the accreditation of such courses using the LOOC structure described by Chauhan (2014) as a way offering a free trial to preview the course and as a means of attracting potential learners.

Conclusion

What are the lessons learned? Course development is as much about trial and error as it is about effective forward planning, because sometimes we simply do not know what will work until we actually try it, and then, later, adapt it. Indeed, the concept of enhanced iterations is an important one in this field, as the changes required to transfer the learning weighting from lecturer in the real world to artefact in the digital world takes time. The impact on the curriculum architect must also be considered, as there is little doubt that this flipped model places much of the workload at the front end of teaching, paradoxically, perhaps to make the later teaching process less onerous and certainly more enjoyable. Indeed, the process of working more intimately with students to probe the deeper layers of meaning and their implications for professional practice is one of the most beneficial aspects of the project.

About the Author

Willie McGuire is a senior lecturer in the School of Education at the University of Glasgow and a senior fellow of the Higher Education Academy. His most recent innovative work has focused on the scholarship of learning and teaching in relation to the advancement of the purposeful deployment of student-centric approaches of e-learning to improve the quality of teaching and learning. He can be contacted on this e-mail: william.mcguire@glasgow.ac.uk

Bibliography

Anderson, T. (2004). *Towards a Theory of Online Learning Ch 2 from Theory and Practice of Online Learning*. Athabasca University, pp 35–60.

Baggaley, J. (2014). MOOC Postscript. *Distance Education*, Vol. 35, No. 1, pp. 126–132.

Chauhan, A. (2014). Massive Open Online Courses (MOOCs): Emerging Trends in Assessment and Accreditation. *Digital Education Review*, No. 25, June 2014. Online Resource: http://greav.ub.edu/der/ [Accessed on 5 June 2017].

Combefis, S.; A. Bibal & P. Van Roy (2011). *Recasting a Traditional Course into a MOOC by Means of a SPOC*. Proceedings of the European MOOCs Stakeholders Summit, pp. 205-208.

Conway, M. R. (2013). *HarvardX's new fall offerings to include two SPOCs*. Online Resource http://www.thecrimson.com/article/2013/6/21/new-edx-fall-2013 [Accessed on 5 June 2017].

Couglan, S. (2013). *Harvard Plans to Boldly Go With 'Spocs'*. Online Resource: http://etcjournal.com/2013/09/26/spocs-are-mooc-game-changers/ [Accessed on 30 September 2016].

Dillenbourg, P.; A. Fox; C, Kirchner; J. Mitchell & M. Wirsing (2014). Massive Open Online Courses: *Current State and Perspectives*. Dagstuhl Perspectives Workshop 14112.

Downes, S. (2012). *The Rise of MOOCs*. Online Resource: www.halfanhour. blogspot.ca/2012/04/rise-of-moocs.html [Accessed on 5 June 2017].

Fox, A. (2013). From MOOCs to SPOCs. *Communications of the ACM*, Vol. 56, No. 12, pp. 38–40.

Fox, A.; D. A. Patterson; R. Ilson; S. Joseph; K. Walcott-Justice & R. Wiliams (2014). Software Engineering Curriculum Technology Transfer: *Lessons learned from MOOCs to SPOCs*. Technical report no UCB/EECS-2014-17.

Online Resource: www.eecs.berkeley.edu/Pubs/TechRpts/2014/EECS-2014-17.html [Accessed on 5 June 2017].

Garrison, D. R. & T. Anderson (2003). *E-Learning in the 21st Century*. Falmer: Routledge.

Hickey, D. (2013, October 2). xMOOC, cMOOC, DOCC or BOOC: What's in a name? [Weblog post]. Online Resource: http://remediatingassessment.blogspot.com/2013/10/xmooc-cmooc-docc-or-booc-whats-in-name.html

Lave, J & E. Wenger (1991). *Situated Learning: Limited Peripheral Participation*. Cambridge: Cambridge University Press.

Müller-Fohrbrodt, G.; Cloetta, B. & Dann, H.D. (1978). *Der Praxisschock bei jungen Lehrern* [The transition shock in beginning teachers]. Stuttgart: Klett-Cotta.

Chapter 10

Whiteboard Animation: An Innovative Teaching and Learning Tool for Flipped Classrooms

Ming Li, Chi Wai Lai and Wai Man Szeto

Introduction

This chapter contributes to the book *New Innovations in Teaching and Learning in Higher Education* as we discuss how to flip a classroom with a non-traditional tool that facilitates discussions with students in interactive tutorials. In the chapter, we define innovations in teaching and learning as practices that, to our knowledge, have not been used in flipped classrooms. More specifically, the tool that we developed is a set of *whiteboard animations*, which are videos that mimic teaching on a whiteboard with a cartoon style. We see our tool, whiteboard animations, as different from recorded lecture videos. While the latter are relatively straightforward in production and are typically employed in flipped classrooms with a low budget, the former may demand more resources yet have the potential of being more elaborate and fanciful. To this date, recorded lecture is the major video format for flipped classrooms. However, our practice shows that using whiteboard animations may be more efficient in engaging students to learn.

When reading this chapter, you will gain the following three insights:

1. you will learn how to design the theme and content of a whiteboard animation;

2. you will learn how to produce such an animation from a technical point of view;

3. you will gain insight into how these animations can be used to facilitate discussions in a live classroom.

This chapter is divided into four main sections. In section 1, we present the motivation for creating whiteboard animations as a new learning tool for flipped classrooms instead of using traditional materials such as textbooks, lecture notes, or recorded lecture videos. We will see that this was driven by the practical needs that we saw from our teaching experience. In section 2, we describe in detail how we produced whiteboard animations that were tailor-made for our curriculum (Figure 1). In particular, we describe the workflow of the production, which includes how we designed the themes and contents of the animations (storyboard and whole-picture design) and how we implemented the ideas (animation production, voice-over production, and post-production). In section 3, we present the outcome of the project from the perspectives of both students and teachers. In particular, we discuss to what extent our tool enables students to learn more efficiently. In section 4, we discuss how this project can be extended to other courses, as well as activities other than in-class discussions.

Section 1: The Background

"What is the best way to learn?" is probably the single most important question in education. Traditionally, educators employ the teacher-centred model, where typically a teacher takes the major role in a classroom and knowledge is imparted by the teacher to the students in the form of a lecture. Aided by technological advancement, the *flipped classroom*, a student-centred model that is arguably more effective in teaching and learning, has become more and more popular as a classroom practice in recent years (Bergmann & Sams, 2012). In flipped classrooms, a student takes a more active role in the learning process and the teacher plays the role of a facilitator who motivates and guides the students to learn. While textbook knowledge is disseminated in-class by the teachers in the traditional model, in a flipped classroom materials such as lecture notes and lecture videos are posted online so that the students can engage themselves in course content before class, in the hope that teachers can foster active learning during the class time and hence the students can learn more productively.

With studies (Bishop & Verleger, 2013) suggesting the superiority of the new model over the traditional one, the popularity of the flipped classroom has increased steadily in Hong Kong over the past few years. Practitioners are everywhere. The Chinese University of Hong Kong (CUHK) organises seminars for teachers who practise flipped classroom to share their experience from time to time. At the same time, institutional advancement in e-learning is one of the major directions for development at CUHK. The construction of micro-modules to support flipped classroom is widely promoted and funding starting from 2015 has been secured. Our project described in this chapter was supported by "Micro-Module Courseware Development Grant 2015-2016" from CUHK. It has funded the production of a set of four whiteboard animations that are tailor-made for the needs of a course that we teach, UGFN1000 *In Dialogue with Nature* (UGFN). The goal of the project is to enhance the group discussions for students in the interactive tutorials of the course.

UGFN aims at engaging year one and two university students in exploring the world of science and knowledge. It employs the flipped classroom model. Every week, the students are required to read a selected text at home, followed by attending a tutorial session in the following week to discuss a variety of questions, ranging from the ones that require basic understanding of the selected text to more challenging extended follow-up questions (the details of the curriculum are given in section 2b). Despite the fact that students usually find the questions interesting and inspiring, our experience suggests that there is room for improvement. More specifically, to answer some of the extended questions, students may have to master concepts or ideas *beyond the text*. As a concrete example, one selected text was *DNA: The Secret of Life* (Watson & Berry, 2003), in which James Watson held the belief that a complete understanding of life can be achieved solely with the laws of physics and chemistry (albeit exquisitely organised ones) without the introduction of mysterious concepts such as vitalism (the doctrine that the processes of life are explained in terms of non-physical elements such as an immaterial soul). When students were challenged with the question of whether they held the same belief or not, some disagreed with Watson. A *frequently given* argument was that identical twins may have different personalities despite having identical DNA sequences. While Watson's (2003) belief may not be true, the students' answer above is certainly based on a misunderstanding of how DNA affects our behaviours.

It was the lack of knowledge or the misunderstanding of concepts of the kind discussed above that rendered discussions in tutorial sessions less productive than it could have been. However, note that the knowledge required (in this case how gene expression is affected by environmental factors) is not provided in Watson's text. Hence, somehow, we needed to bridge the knowledge gap between what can be learned from the text and what is required for an in-depth discussion. We usually improvised an explanation for how information stored in DNA is transformed into observable features of the biological organisms and what role the environment plays in this transformation. Whereas the impromptu explanation enabled the students to come up with a more satisfactory response, valuable time for discussion on other questions was sacrificed. The urge to fully utilise the time for discussions in the tutorial sessions emerged from such experience. Driven by the practical need discussed above, we proposed a *second flip* for our classrooms. The goal is to transform explanations of all such missing or misunderstood concepts frequently found in students into a form that they can study at home so that they are well equipped with the prerequisite knowledge for the in-class discussion on *specific issues*. To accomplish this, we adopted the form of whiteboard animation. The reason is threefold: First, we needed to create our own materials because existing ones were unfit for our task. Existing textbooks, for instance, are commonly either too advanced for general education or too superficial to offer information that helps analysis of specific issues relevant to UGFN. Second, Udo *et al.* (2004) showed that non-science major students, such as humanities and social science students, are anxious to study general education science courses. Similar findings were reported by Hoi *et al.* (2016) that non-science major students studying UGFN have higher science anxiety in general. Hence, it would be desirable to craft our materials in a relaxing and entertaining form. Third, research showed that people actually learn better with whiteboard animations. Wiseman reported that performance on memory questions increased by as much as 15% when one switched from watching videos in recorded lecture form to whiteboard animation form (Sparkol VideoScribe, 2015). This demonstrates that whiteboard animation is indeed a promising means to engage students in better learning.

Section 2: The Practice

2a. A General Introduction to the Innovative Practice

This practice has innovatively used an alternative tool for flipped class-rooms in UGFN. Instead of commonly practised short lecture recordings in flipped classroom teaching, it uses short whiteboard animations to enrich students' learning experience. It makes students pay more attention, and therefore understand the prerequisite knowledge better before tutorial classes, hence improves teaching and learning in classes. This animated storytelling approach can be effectively applied to nearly any subject and facilitates information delivery in a more engaging fashion.

Short whiteboard animations are tailor-made to focus on the learning needs and difficulties of students. High-quality whiteboard animations with step-by-step illustrations and voice-over narrations are hosted online (YouTube) for students' self-paced learning. They serve as good reference materials for detailed discussion and deeper reflection in interactive tutorial classes.

2b. The Curriculum

General education has played an important role in the undergraduate curriculum at CUHK ever since the foundation of the university. In 2012, a four-year curriculum replaced the former three-year curriculum, which jumpstarted two new general education courses for all undergraduates. The two courses, UGFN and UGFH1000 *In Dialogue with Humanity* (UGFH) are taught in the General Education Foundation Programme (GEFP), a common core programme targeted at year one and two university students from all major disciplines. The two courses are compulsory. The aim of the two general education courses is to engage the students in exploring the world of science and knowledge, as well as reflecting on what it means to have a good life and an ideal society, through the study of excerpts from mostly classic texts in science and humanity. The practice described in this chapter was employed in UGFN. The texts in this course include excerpts from Isaac Newton's *Principia*, Charles Darwin's *On the Origin of Species*, James Watson's *DNA: The Secret of Life*, Rachel Carson's *Silent Spring*, Joseph Needham's *The Shorter Science and Civilisation in China*, and Euclid's *Elements*. A full list of the excerpts is available on the website of UGFN (General Education Foundation Programme, 2017). All the excerpts are published in the coursebook *In Dialogue with Nature: Textbook for General Education Foundation Programme* (Wong *et al.*, 2016).

Each week, the students attend a 45-minute lecture given by the course teacher in which they are introduced to the background and the author of the text being studied that week, as well as the key ideas of the selected text. The students are then required to read the text at home, before they are engaged in a 105-minute tutorial session in the following week. Typically, there are 25 students a tutorial session. Within the tutorial session, the students are split into smaller groups, each with around four students. They will then participate in various activities guided by the teacher; the majority are discussion sessions where students will discuss a variety of questions with their groupmates, from the understanding of the text to more challenging questions, which are typically natural extensions of what is presented in the text.

2c. Organisation of the Practice

UGFN challenges students from all major disciplines to study science-related classic/core texts at home before attending the tutorial class in the following week to discuss and reflect on specific topics. In our experience, most students find this course challenging because of the lack of prerequisite knowledge and concepts, as well as encountering difficulties with the comprehension of abstract ideas from different texts. Most commonly, these issues are handled during class, which inevitably reduces the valuable time for discussion. Providing readily available supplementary resources may help, but sometimes it is difficult to find suitable materials on specific topics at the appropriate level of difficulty to engage all the students with a wide range of disciplinary backgrounds. In order to have more efficient and effective teaching and learning, we find it necessary to produce attractive supplementary materials tailor-made for UGFN. In order to do so, we have practised the use of tailor-made short whiteboard animations as an innovative tool for flipped classrooms in UGFN.

The first phase of the practice is the preparation and production of the tailor-made short whiteboard animations. We identified students' learning needs and difficulties, which become the focuses of the white-board animations being produced by the production team consisting of teachers, student helpers, and artists.

The second phase is the use of the whiteboard animations for flipped classroom in UGFN. The whole-pictures, URL addresses, and QR-codes of the whiteboard animations are provided to the students in the lecture. They are encouraged to watch the whiteboard animations at their own pace before the tutorial classes. In tutorial classes, when a specific topic is discussed, such as whether, as Watson said, life is just a matter of physics and chemistry, students are encouraged to refer to the whiteboard animations for discussion and reflection. We will show the whole-picture of the whiteboard animations in tutorial classes to aid their discussion when necessary. Feedback from students about this practice was collected by surveys after the classes.

2d. Preparation

A sophisticated short whiteboard animation requires highly produced audio and visual effects, while a basic one requires simple illustrations and straightforward narrations. Hence, the preparation and produc-tion works vary depending on the quality and length of the whiteboard animation, efficiency of communication among team members, and the resources available. These factors also affect the production time, varying from days to weeks. In our project, for instance, we produced four five-minute whiteboard animations in six months (which included three months of a teaching semester). In general, the preparation and produc-tion of a whiteboard animation includes the following steps:

+ storyboard design;

+ whole-picture design;

+ voice-over production;

+ animation production;

+ post-production.

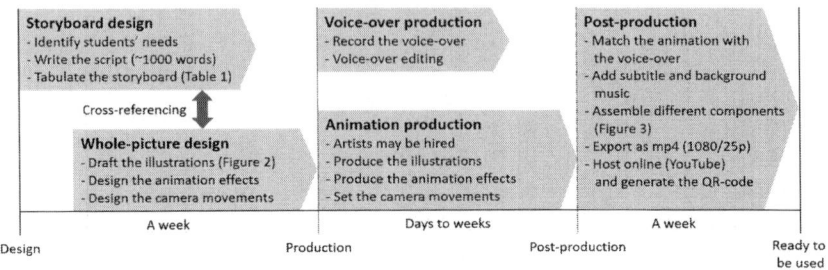

Figure 1: *The workflow for the preparation and production of whiteboard animation.*

Storyboard design

The goal of the production is to create tailor-made whiteboard animations as tools for effective teaching and learning in a flipped classroom. It is important to identify students' learning needs when studying the course. In the example discussed above, students often used identical twins having identical DNA sequences but different personalities as an example to argue against life being no more than physics and chemistry. This clearly demonstrates that students lack the knowledge of gene expression and its regulation affected by environmental factors. These are the learning needs that become the focus of the whiteboard animations. It is necessary to consider students' capabilities so as to define the level of difficulty and the duration of the whiteboard animation. This is particularly important for courses in which students come from different major disciplines. Using daily life examples to explain the scientific knowledge is highly recommended, since students reported that this can reduce their anxiety about learning science (Hoi *et al.*, 2016).

It is important to include really key concepts in short whiteboard animations. As a general guideline, a five-minute whiteboard animation is produced with a script of approximately 1,000 words. The script should include: (i) a statement or a question to be discussed, (ii) the explanation, clarification, and connection of concepts, (iii) examples in daily life, and (iv) a conclusion and/or a question to ponder. It is then incorporated into the storyboard together with the duration of each sentence (in second), description of the animation effects, and suggested illustrations, as demonstrated in Table 1. The storyboard is the blueprint of the whiteboard animation, which may take several full working days to complete. It allows efficient communication among teachers, student helpers, and/or artists.

Scene	Script sentence	Sec.	Animation	Illustration
1-1	What do you think about the saying "DNA determines you?"	5	Write "Does DNA determine you?" (with drawing hand)	-
1-2	DNA is regarded as the code of life	5	Draw DNA structure	
1-3	The biological information is hidden in the DNA sequence. Does it mean that DNA sequence determines you?	7	Write four lines of DNA sequence, colour fades from black to light grey (no drawing hand)	ATGTTCGCCGAC-CGTTGACTA CAAAGACATTG-GAACACTATA CATGAGCTGGAGTC-CTAGGCA CTTATTCGAGC-CGAGCTGGGC
2-1	Let's look at the following cases	4	Camera move to upper right corner	-
2-2	First, we are all developed from fertilized eggs. The cells divided thereafter have the same DNA sequence. If the hidden biological information is also the same…	10	Draw a cell, an arrow, 2 cells, an arrow, four cells, two arrows, and an embryoblast (no drawing hand)	
…	…			

Table 1: A sample of storyboard for whiteboard animation production.

Whole-picture design

The purpose of whole-picture design is to visualise the ideas in the storyboard. The style, sizes, and positions of all the illustrations in the storyboard should be designed so that they are integrated into a coherent whole-picture. The camera shots (camera panning and zooming) and animation effects (real-time drawing and movement of illustrations) should also be decided according to the storyboard. In fact, the storyboard and whole-picture should be cross-referenced and designed together. A few versions may be drafted and it may take several full days to generate a coherent final draft. The upper panel of Figure 2 shows the final draft of the whole-picture of one of our whiteboard animations.

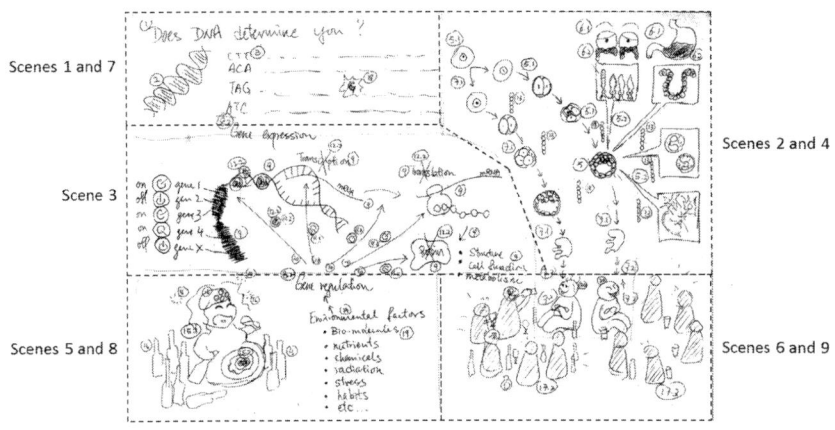

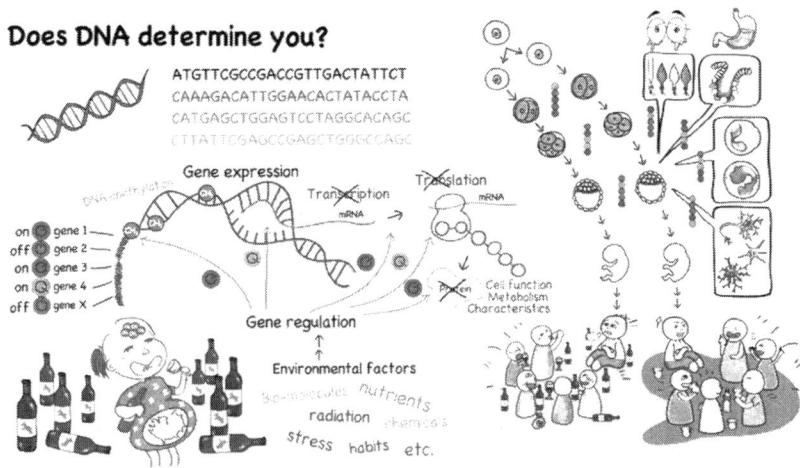

Figure 2: The final draft (upper) and published (lower) whole-picture of our whiteboard animation "Does DNA determine you?". The scenes of the storyboard are indicated in the draft.

Voice-over production

The quality of voice-over significantly influences how the students perceive the whiteboard animations. The style (such as enthusiastic, warm, youthful, friendly, deep, soft, strong, or sharp) of voice-over should be decided to match the purpose and content of the whiteboard animations. Although professional voice talents can be hired, teachers and student helpers can record the voice-overs for lower-budget productions. For the latter choice, it is important to note that fluency, style, energy level, and speaking volume of the entire voice-over should be kept consistent during the recording process. A recording studio and a studio-quality microphone (RØDE NT-USB) are needed to record high-quality voice-overs, which are then edited (Adobe Audition CC or CyberLink WaveEditor2) to produce the final voice-over products, preferably in MP3 format.

Animation production

This is the key step in the production workflow, which involves the production of illustrations and animation effects (VideoScribe) according to the storyboard and the whole-picture. The illustrations are better produced (Adobe Creative Illustrator) in SVG format so that the real-time drawing process of the illustrations can be shown. The opening frame can show the course title and the ending frame can show the reference list and the production information. Animation production is challenging for teachers who are not good at drawing. Although purchasing from an online image library may help, recruiting artists or student helpers who excel in drawing may be needed. If so, strong communication among the teachers, student helpers, or artists is crucial for efficient animation production. It is also important to note that sufficient time should be reserved for revising the animation several times. The entire animation production may vary from a few days to weeks depending on the quality of the whiteboard animation, communication efficiency among team members, and the resources available.

Post-production

This is the final step of animation production and includes audio-visual editing, subtitle editing, and background music editing. Audio-visual editing enables the animation elements (real-time drawings, animation effects, and camera panning) to match the narrated voice-over. The time frames of the animation elements are fine-adjusted (VideoScribe), which may take two to three full working days. The fine-adjusted animation, opening and ending frames, if any, voice-over, subtitles, and background music are then assembled (CyberLink PowerDirector13) to produce the whiteboard animation (MP4, 1080/25p) as described in Figure 3. It is hosted online (YouTube) and a QR-code is generated to allow easy access. It is noted that subtitles may not be imported in post-production. Instead, subtitles, especially more than one languages are provided, in SRT format can be uploaded to YouTube separately. A demonstration of one of our short whiteboard animations "Does DNA determine you?" can be found here: https://youtu.be/GFPf-rIjG2I [Accessed on 26 August 2017].

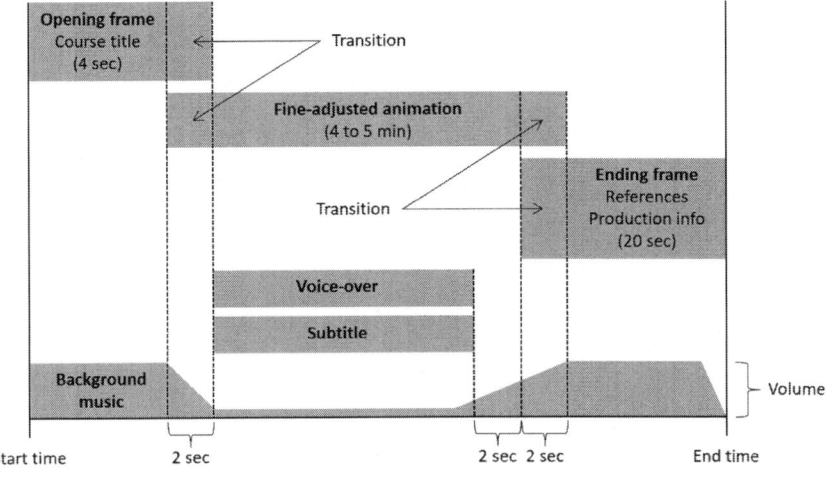

Figure 3: Framework for the assembly of different components of a whiteboard animation.

2e. Teacher Perspective – My Reflection

The use of short whiteboard animation is a key success factor in this practice which makes learning fun and enjoyable. In principle, whiteboard animations can be used for flipped classrooms in any course. They can be simple or sophisticated. A high-quality whiteboard animation is more attractive, but they require more substantial financial resources as well as more preparation time, manpower, and equipment. If financial support is limited, simple whiteboard animations can be produced with the help of student helpers. It should be noted that the production of whiteboard animations may be more demanding, compared to short lecture recordings, because it is a delicate process requiring considerable time and work to produce high-quality products.

In our project, we found that tailor-made five-minute whiteboard animations are useful and effective for flipped classrooms in UGFN. This innovative teaching and learning practice was presented at the Teaching and Learning Innovation Expo 2016 in CUHK (Li *et al.*, 2016). It was also reported in the newsletter of University General Education in CUHK (UGE News, 2017). Colleagues were thrilled by these whiteboard animations and they were interested to watch them. Some other UGFN teachers also adopted this practice for their own teachings. Our whiteboard animations are now available in all UGFN classes. Approximately 1,800 students per semester will benefit from these whiteboard animations. We are pleased to know that our colleagues and students find the whiteboard animations interesting and useful.

Section 3: The Outcome

3a. Student Perspective

We perceived that the whiteboard animations were well received by the students. A survey from over 300 students showed that more than 85% of students who watched the whiteboard animations agreed that whiteboard animations were more interesting than lecture recordings and that the whiteboard animations raised their interest in the issues discussed. Over 90% of students agreed that the whiteboard animations were helpful for understanding the texts, clarifying the concepts, and providing the prerequisite knowledge before tutorial classes. The effectiveness of the whiteboard animations is also described in students' comments:

> "The whiteboard animations are lovely and interesting";

> "The whiteboard animations explain the complicated ideas in a concrete way";

> "The whiteboard animations are clear. They are helpful for understanding and learning, especially for the students without studying biology [in high school]";

> "The expression and the explanation in the whiteboard animations are clear and concise. They bring up the questions for reflection".

This encouraging feedback indicated that the practice of flipping the classrooms using whiteboard animations successfully enriched students' learning experience. Students enjoyed watching whiteboard animations and gained the prerequisite knowledge and concepts for discussion in tutorial classes. The whiteboard animations improved students' preparation for the tutorial discussion and enhanced their motivation for studying the course.

3b. Teacher Perspective

During the tutorials, we observed that the tailor-made whiteboard animations had successfully helped students to gain the prerequisite knowledge for the specific topics to be discussed. We found that students who watched these whiteboard animations were more engaged in the discussion and were able to discuss weekly topics with confidence. For example, as mentioned in section 1, students discussed Watson's belief that a complete understanding of life can be given solely with the laws of physics and chemistry. Some students challenged this belief by wrongly arguing that identical twins may have different personalities despite having identical DNA sequences. In one case, a student, who probably had not watched our whiteboard animations on DNA, presented this faulty argument in class. It was immediately refuted by another student who used the example in the whiteboard animations to explain the correct understanding to the class. Correcting classmates' misunderstandings is only one of the examples showing how the students used the whiteboard animations for peer learning. During their discussion, students often referred to the examples in the animations to clarify their understanding and formulate their arguments. We also used the animations to connect the texts and the extended questions. For example, after the whole-picture in Figure 2 (lower) had been shown, the students promptly recalled the evidence supporting Watson's belief. Then, the discussion on Watson's belief, which is a significant extended question on the nature of life, could be substantiated by the correct understanding of the question. This certainly saved the time necessary for the teacher's one-way explanation and enabled students to fully utilise the tutorial class for discussion. Hence, the quality and depth of the discussion were improved.

Section 4: Moving Forward

With the encouraging results and the positive feedback from both students and teachers of UGFN, we will expand the flipped classrooms in UGFN by developing more whiteboard animations. These new whiteboard animations will provide the prerequisite knowledge not only for tutorial discussion but also for other activities including games and role play. Given that whiteboard animations can be effectively applied to nearly any subject, we are going to adopt this practice to flip the classrooms in another foundation course UGFH in CUHK (General Education Foundation Programme, 2017). We are pleased to receive another grant, "Micro-Module Courseware Development Grant 2016-2017", from CUHK to continue producing tailor-made whiteboard animations for flipped classrooms, not only in UGFN but also in UGFH, which equip students with the prerequisite knowledge for studying humanity classics. The whiteboard animations would engage students in reflecting on what it means to be an ideal society. This extended project is in fact in progress, with a teacher from UGFH joined for the extension. We foresee that the potential beneficiaries of the whiteboard animations will be more than 3,800 students in 150 UGFN and UGFH tutorial sessions per semester. Moreover, the whiteboard animations have the potential to be incorporated into the massive open online course (MOOC) for UGFN and UGFH in the future. The whiteboard animations could also be used for other courses teaching similar issues. In addition, the technical skills for whiteboard animation production can be adopted to produce whiteboard animations for other courses at CUHK.

Conclusion

In this chapter, we have introduced whiteboard animation as an innovative teaching and learning tool for flipped classrooms in UGFN. We have discussed how to design the theme and content of a whiteboard animation (storyboard design and whole-picture design), how to produce such a whiteboard animation (animation production, voice-over production, and post-production), and how whiteboard animations can be used to facilitate discussions in a live classroom. Our practice demonstrated that whiteboard animations successfully equipped the students with the prerequisite knowledge before tutorial classes, saved the time for the teacher's explanation, and enabled students to fully utilise the time for discussion.

Our whiteboard animations are tailor-made to suit the teaching and learning needs for UGFN, a common core course, which has students of diverse backgrounds. They enable step-by-step illustrations with voice-over narrations to explain abstruse and abstract concepts in a simple and entertaining form. Feedback from students indicated that whiteboard animations are more interesting and engaging than traditional lecture recordings. They are effective to help students to learn better. Indeed, whiteboard animation is a new innovation in teaching and learning in higher education. We hope that this chapter can promote the use of whiteboard animation, an alternative teaching and learning tool, in higher education so that not only students at CUHK but also those in other parts of the world can benefit from it and taste the fun.

About the Authors

Ming Li is a lecturer in the General Education Foundation Programme at The Chinese University of Hong Kong. He can be contacted at this e-mail: liming@cuhk.edu.hk

Chi Wai Lai is a lecturer in the General Education Foundation Programme at The Chinese University of Hong Kong. He can be contacted at this e-mail: cwlai@cuhk.edu.hk

Wai Man Szeto is a lecturer in the General Education Foundation Programme at The Chinese University of Hong Kong. He can be contacted at this e-mail: wmszeto@cuhk.edu.hk

Bibliography

Bergmann, J. & A. Sams (2012). *Flip Your Classroom: Reach Every Student in Every Class Every Day*. International Society for Technology in Education.

Bishop, J. L. & M. A. Verleger (2013). *The Flipped Classroom: A Survey of the Research*. 2013 ASEE Annual Conference & Exposition.

General Education Foundation Programme (2017). Online Resource: http://www5.cuhk.edu.hk/oge/index.php/en/gef [Accessed on 22 April 2017].

Hoi, W. H. S.; W. H. Wong & K. M. Pang (2016, Dec). *Confronting Science Anxiety through In Dialogue with Nature*. Poster session presented at the Teaching and Learning Innovation Expo, The Chinese University of Hong Kong, Hong Kong.

Sparkol VideoScribe (2015). Online Resource: http://www.sparkol.com/engage/how-scribe-videos-increase-your-students-learning-by-15/?_ga=1.25 6257608.254490627.1492913564 [Accessed on 22 April 2017].

Li, M.; C. W. Lai & W. M. Szeto (2016, Dec). *UGFN Animated – Flipped Classroom with Whiteboard Animations*. Poster session presented at the Teaching and Learning Innovation Expo, The Chinese University of Hong Kong, Hong Kong.

Udo, M. K.; G. P. Ramsey & J. V. Mallow (2004). Science Anxiety and Gender in Students Taking General Education Science Courses. *Journal of Science Education and Technology*, Vol. 13, No. 4, pp. 435–446.

UGE News (2017). Online Resource: http://cu-genews.com/2017/01/26/a-animations-apps/ [Accessed on 22 April 2017].

Watson, J. D. & A. Berry (2003). *DNA: The Secret of Life*. New York: Alfred A. Knopf.

Wong W. H.; C. W. Chan & W. M. Szeto (Eds.) (2016). *In Dialogue with Nature: Textbook for General Education Foundation Programme* (revised 2nd edition). Hong Kong: Office of University General Education.

Section 3: Technology for Learning

Chapter 11

Technology for Learning: Something Old, Something Borrowed, and Something New

Christopher Klopper, Amy Gillett and Ghada Salama

Introduction

For a number of years, the university sector has been learning to accommodate the "digital native" born of the "Net Generation" (Jones, Ramanau, Cross & Healing, 2010). This group is said to think and consume knowledge differently than previous generations. In some universities, this has led to calls for curricula and instructional delivery technologies to be reconceived. It has been observed that the technology is frequently adopted in response to a mandate for digitisation of learning, with little consideration given to the underlying learning objectives. At the same time, some institutions have been laggards in adopting new technologies by perpetuating traditional teaching practices. However, in today's rapidly changing environment, "business as usual" is not a viable option. Teaching and learning methods need to be reconfigured purposefully to embrace technologies for learning.

Numerous technologies for learning are already pervasive in higher education for a range of purposes. Blogs, for instance, have been used for students to record reflections on their learning experiences or to share their insights about the learning content with other students (Farmer, Yue & Brooks, 2008; Instone, 2005; Osman & Koh, 2013; West, Wright, Gabbitas & Graham, 2006). Wikis are commonly used for students to collaborate over the production and publication of course-related content (Klopper & Weir, 2015). Other technologies, such as mobile phones, social networking, and online gaming have also been deployed and have been shown to enhance learning outcomes. Of course, technology use in education is an old (established) phenomenon. Journey back to the 11th century when new technology was slate and chalk. Then the blackboard came along in the 19th century and was an exciting innovation at the time. Next came the whiteboard, to be replaced decades later by the digital whiteboard, a revolution at the time. Cloud technology came along and changed our practices but borrowed the same underlying principles and assumptions. What has changed over the past decade when we consider technology in education is the rate of change of technological innovation: An explosion of education technologies has created new opportunities for learners and instructors, while at the same time creating confusion over what technologies might be appropriate to adopt or, if warranted, to create.

In this chapter, we position technology for learning in the extent of literature; we borrow from the task-technology fit theory as an organiser for four new applications of technology:

+ learning management systems for professional education;

+ digital learning activities for student engagement;

+ Web 2.0 platform for English as a second language;

+ virtual reality integration into the classroom in higher education.

This sample of applications makes a useful contribution to the advancement of technology for learning in higher education by illustrating the need for fit for purpose and showing some of the key roles that technology can play to support learning and teaching.

Section 1: The Theory of Task-Technology Fit (TTF)

While technologies for learning are nothing new, the pace of innovation has accelerated dramatically in recent years. During this rapid change, there has been the propensity to adopt technology for its own sake, to be seen as trailblazers in a highly competitive market. The explosion of educational technology options has bolstered the possibilities for teachers and learners, but at the same time it requires discretion in selecting the right tools to support learning. According to task-technology fit (TTF) theory, for technology to have a positive impact on outcomes and satisfaction, the technology must fit with the tasks it seeks to support and the understandings and needs of those who use it (Rubin *et al.*, 2013). This theory suggests that the needs and understandings of the user must be explored. Further, TTF necessitates that there is an understanding of the functionality and characteristics of the technology. In order to have a successful outcome with technology adoption, instructors need to distinguish the goals for the task and the fit between the task and the technology (Sammel, Weir, and Klopper, 2013). The process for identifying the right technology for learning is represented in Figure 1.

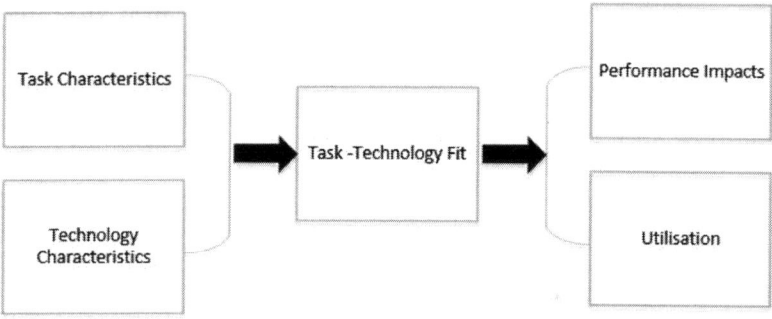

Figure 1: The process of technology-task fit theory (Goodhue & Thompson, 1995).

We demarcate task characteristics as the parameters of the envisaged learning activities that lead to learning design. The process involves breaking down the task into the sequence of parts that the students would need to accomplish. The technology characteristics can be understood as the features and benefits offered by the learning technology. When you bring together task characteristics and technology characteristics, the intersection results in the establishment of a technology-task fit.

Section 2: Technology for Learning Case Studies

This section of the anthology *New Innovations in Teaching and Learning in Higher Education* shares first-hand experiences of deploying technology for learning and explores the many roles that technology for learning can play. These include: technology for fostering a community among adult learners, technology as a facilitator for active learning, technology to support learning, and technology as an enabler of learning.

Technology for Fostering a Community among Adult Learners

Learning is at its heart a humanised activity that thrives on personal connection, purpose, and meaning. As such, learning communities are an effective way to foster closeness among learners in a programme of study. Such communities are more likely to share information, leading to peer-to-peer learning and sustained connection. Gillett and Hamori-Ota understood the value of a learning community and sought a way to foster one in short-term professional education programmes. Weighing the desired task characteristics against the characteristics of available technologies led them to design a learning management system (LMS) for professional education systems from the ground up. Matching the technology to the task should consider the age and stage of the learner. In designing the LMS, Gillett and Hamori-Ota (Chapter 12) decided to draw on andragogical assumptions versus pedagogical assumptions for the learning design. For instance, we know that when adult learners are active agents in the learning design and learning activities and are able to see the relevance and impact of the instruction, they are more engaged in the process. The technology they created enables learners to co-create content, to select materials of most interest to them, and to personalise their learning goals for the programme. To build an effective learning community takes time and ample opportunity to interact. Therefore, Gillett and Hamori-Ota designed the system to extend the experience of a short-term programme, offering access to the course portal two weeks before the face-to-face course and extending one year after the conclusion. The ExtendEd portal exemplifies TTF theory, where technology is used to support learning and not for technology's sake. The ExtendEd portal leverages technology to enhance the student experience and expands the possibilities of what would be possible in the traditional classroom.

Technology as a Facilitator for Active Learning

Drawing on TTF theory, Salama (Chapter 13) details her decision-making process in finding a solution to promote active learning and teaching in an introductory materials engineering course. She had been teaching this heavily laden theoretical course in the same manner for a number of years and had repeatedly observed high levels of student disengagement. She sought a way to engage her students and empower them to become active agents of their learning. Given that her students were tech-savvy millennials, she decided to consider how technology could be deployed. Together with the IT consultants at her university, she explored the task characteristics and technology characteristics to identify the right solution. Collectively, they settled on Socrative as a fit. Given that it was free, user-friendly software, Salama knew it would be a low-risk way to increase student engagement. After the initial trial, Salama received positive feedback from students and so she decided to adopt it permanently. This shows TTF theory in action: start with task characteristics and technology characteristics, consider how they intersect to provide the most effective solution to engage students, enhance performance, and promote active learning.

Technology to Support Learning

Van Rensburg and Nguyen (Chapter 14) report on the evaluation and assessment of the influences of a Web 2.0 technology and an LMS on an English as foreign language (EFL) course in Vietnam. Van Rensburg and Nguyen noticed a lack of motivation among EFL students and turned to technology to address this issue. They created a learning platform to support increased engagement and participation of students. The LMS transformed their students from passive recipients of knowledge to active learners, in charge of their learning process. For example, students were offered a range of articles to read through the LMS and could choose the ones of most interest. The discussion forum offered them a voice. Realistic video scenarios depicting EFL speakers successfully doing business in English showed them the benefits of mastering English and allowed them to imagine their own potential. They share students' reflection on the technology to support learning, the advantage of an LMS to motivate students, and confirm that the integration of Web 2.0 technologies has the potential to increase intrinsic motivation and lead to better learning outcomes.

Technology as an Enabler of Learning

Klopper and Burt (Chapter 15) detail their response to a teaching challenge of moving a traditionally face-to-face teaching course to a fully online offering. This was a geography curriculum course within a teacher education programme that included a number of fieldwork activities. These activities were broken down into their learning components and considered alongside viable technology characteristics that would create the same learning opportunity in an online course. The overlap resulted in a TTF, which led to the design of a "hands-on" virtual reality field excursion. This enabled online students to be placed in the field via virtual headsets and to interact with the learning experience – in other words, an analogous opportunity the on-campus students experienced. Once again, here, we see how technology has been used to enable learning and open new possibilities for teaching activities.

Conclusion

Promoting active learning is one of the biggest trends in higher education today. Students have an expectation to be co-creators of knowledge in the classroom, rather than passive vessels waiting to be filled with knowledge. The easy accessibility of information today has spelled the end of the centuries old "sage on the stage" archetype. In the knowledge economy, knowledge is the provenance of all and is accessible to all. To benefit from this understanding, we need to promote active learning and to re-think ways to share knowledge and then embrace appropriate technologies to support these goals.

About the Authors

Christopher Klopper is deputy dean (learning and teaching) for the Arts, Education and Law Group, Griffith University, Australia. He can be contacted at this e-mail: c.klopper@griffith.edu.au

Amy Gillett is the vice president of education at the William Davidson Institute, a centre at the University of Michigan dedicated to the emerging markets. She oversees about 40 professional education programmes per year around the world. She can be contacted at this e-mail: gilletta@ umich.edu

Ghada Salama is an instructional associate professor in the Chemical Engineering programme at Texas A&M University at Qatar. She can be contacted at this e-mail: ghada.salama@qatar.tamu.edu

Bibliography

Farmer, B.; A. Yue & C. Brooks (2008). Using blogging for higher order learning in large cohort university teaching: A case study. *Australasian Journal of Educational Technology*, Vol. 24, No. 2, pp. 123–136.

Goodhue, D. & R. L. Thompson (1995). Task-technology fit and individual performance. *MIS Quarterly*, Vol. 19, pp. 213–236.

Instone, L. (2005). Conversations beyond the classroom: Blogging in a professional development course. In *ASCILITE 2005: Balance, fidelity, mobility: Maintaining the momentum?*

Jones, C.; R. Ramanau; S. Cross & G. Healing (2010). Net generation or digital natives: is there a distinct new generation entering university? *Computers & Education*, Vol. 54, No. 3, pp. 722–732.

Klopper, C. & K. Weir (2015) Classrooms and chat rooms: Augmenting music education in initial teacher education. *Australian Journal of Music Education.* Vol. 1, pp. 45–54.

Rubin, B.; R. Fernandes & M. D. Avgerinou (2013). The effects of technology on the Community of Inquiry and satisfaction with online courses. *Internet and Higher Education*, Vol. 17, pp. 48–57.

Osman, G. & J. H. L. Koh (2013). Understanding management students' reflective practice through blogging. *The Internet and Higher Education*, Vol. 16, pp. 23–31.

Sammel, A.; K. Weir & C. Klopper (2014). The pedagogical implications of implementing new technologies to enhance student engagement and learning outcomes. *Creative Education*, Vol. 5, No. 2, pp. 104–113.

West, R. E.; G. Wright; B. Gabbitas & C. R. Graham (2006). Reflections from the introduction of Blogs and RSS Feeds into a preservice instructional technology course. *TechTrends*, Vol. 50, No. 4, pp. 54–60.

Chapter 12

A New Tool for Improving Learning in Professional Education Programmes

Amy Gillett and Virginia Hamori-Ota

Introduction

This chapter contributes to the book *New Innovations in Teaching and Learning in Higher Education* as we describe the development of a new tool to optimise delivery of short-term professional and executive education programmes. By reading this chapter, you will learn:

1. how to leverage technology to cultivate an engaged learning community;

2. how to use a "before-during-after framework" to maximise learning for participants in professional education programmes;

3. how adult learning theory assumptions can inform the design of new technologies aimed at professional education students.

In providing short-term education programmes, many institutions use a traditional learning management system (LMS) such as Blackboard. However, these systems were designed with the needs of teachers in mind and for traditional classroom settings driven by assumptions of pedagogy. Adult learning theories tell us that specific learning requirements should be taken into account when designing programmes for adults (Knowles, Holton & Swanson, 2014). This includes one's orientation to learning. Adult learners are interested in "immediacy of application", or how relevant and applicable the learning is to their real-world needs. Another assumption is that adult learners have a reservoir of experience and can draw on that experience as a resource for learning. This would imply that adult learners are well-positioned to co-create content in the classroom, as they can draw on their rich experience to share examples and resources. Adult learners are also self-directed. Therefore, they should be given the opportunity to make choices relevant to the course learning objectives and to have a role in setting their own learning goals.

In this chapter, we view innovation as a departure from the established mode of delivering professional education. Generally, professional education has been in face-to-face classrooms, with large quantities of information presented over the course of several days or weeks among strangers who assemble for a learning event. These participants come together for a short period of time – they do not have a full semester to build a learning community as traditional students do. Our point of inquiry began with the question: *"How can we re-think the learning experience in short-term professional programmes such that we create the same type of learning communities that typically take months to develop and nurture?"*

When reading this chapter, you will gain the following insights:

1. instructors value systems designed around the needs of the students, hence, learner-centric;

2. short-term professional programmes can be transformed into longer, more impactful experiences by adopting a "before-during-after framework";

3. students value the opportunity to engage with peers and instructors beyond the walls of the classroom and such engagement fosters a learning community and provides extra motivation for students to learn and share with their peers.

To maximise the impact of its short-term, in-person training programmes, the William Davidson Institute at the University of Michigan (WDI) leveraged new cloud-based technologies and drew on principles of adult learning and instructional design to create a new online portal.

This chapter is organised around four main sections. In the background section, we detail the pain point we were experiencing in delivering professional education programmes that led us to create a new technology. In the practice section, we explain how this technology works from the perspective of both the student and the instructor. The outcome section details the successful learning communities that have emerged as a result of deploying the technology. The moving forward section describes some of the next steps we are planning in improving the technology and broadening its usage. Finally, the chapter concludes by suggesting how other providers can leverage our experience and insights to improve their own professional education programmes.

Section 1: The Background

WDI offers short-term professional education programmes for managers. WDI's clients were increasingly interested in the return on investment (ROI) of training and development (Elkeles *et al.*, 2015). This reflects a trend of company leadership wanting to see the application and impact of training. In a Fortune 500 survey, 96% of executives stated that we should measure impact, making it the most important training metric. Yet, impact is measured 10% or less of the time (Phillips & Phillips, 2012).

Additionally, participants in professional education programmes are exposed to an abundance of information in a short period of time, often leaving them feeling overwhelmed. Furthermore, the Ebbinghaus forgetting curve shows that people will generally forget 70% of what they learned within 24 hours (Ebbinghaus, 1885). Of course, information that is forgotten cannot be applied back on the job. Further, once participants return to work, they prioritise immediate tasks. Therefore, application of the new learning – which may take time and careful consideration to implement – often sinks to the bottom of the priority list. As highlighted by Kirkpatrick's four-level training evaluation model, with no application on the job, there is no business impact – meaning WDI was largely not addressing the key metric of most value to clients (Kirkpatrick & Kirkpatrick, 2015).

Gillett and Hamori-Ota were frustrated by their inability to meet client and student needs. Furthermore, they found that a range of technologies – including e-mail, Twitter, WhatsApp, and Facebook groups – were being used in programmes. This patchwork approach meant that the programme information resided in multiple locations and not everyone had access to the same information. For example, sometimes instructors did not have access to the information that students had, such as when a Facebook group was created and did not include them. This led to a somewhat disjointed learning and teaching experience, and meant that the learning community had no single, centralised hub in which to gather information, interact, and share information.

In the face of these needs, Gillett and Hamori-Ota started investigating learning management systems (LMS). They could see that programmes such as Blackboard, Sakai, and Canvas were developed with a focus on the instructor and their own course organisation needs, as well as the need to communicate announcements and disseminate information to the students. The typical menu of items included rubrics designed for traditional undergraduate and graduate courses, with class rosters and categories such as "Gradebook", "Lecture Recordings", "Assignments", and "Syllabus".

The first generation LMS appears as a one-way communication tool from instructors to students, with the ability of students to access the information pertinent to their own standing in the course, such as assignments and grades. Threaded discussion boards often ended up as a collection of disjointed student comments, lacking instructor presence in the online environment (Creasman, 2012; Pekansky-Brock, 2013).

In 2015, Educause Learning Initiative published "The Next Generation Digital Learning Environment: A Report on the Research" (Brown *et al.*, 2015). The report underscored that the course-centric and instructor-centric nature of current solutions was bound to evolve toward putting learners at the centre of the activity in a more personalised and customisable fashion while continuing to handle administrative tasks. The report stated: *"What is clear is that the LMS has been highly successful in enabling the administration of learning but less so in enabling learning itself".*

Gillett and Hamori-Ota decided to collaborate on a system specifically designed to enhance learning in short-term professional education programmes. This new tool would follow the learner on their journey through the course, before, during, and after the face-to-face training. The LMS would consist of a simple homepage whose elements would follow students at every stage of their learning. Students would find exactly the content they needed on the page at every moment of the learning process. They decided to name this new portal "ExtendEd" because it extends the learning of a short-term programme to a much greater duration, allowing more time for a learning community to develop and flourish.

Section 2: The Practice

2a. A General Introduction to the Innovative Practice

As students log in from their computers or mobile devices at extended-portal.com, the portal draws on data behind the scenes, recognises the student and the stage they are at in their journey, and delivers personalised information accordingly. In this way, the student never has to search for the right information.

The ExtendEd portal is arranged around three key phases: before, during, and after. The "before" phase focuses students on getting to know their peers and instructors in the learning community. Participant and instructor bios and introductory videos allow them to discover who will be in their classroom and explore what their fellow students hope to gain from the programme and why their instructors are excited about teaching the programme. They become agents of their own learning as they input learning goals into the embedded goal-setting tool, the "Compact for Success". Students can also access materials such as articles, cases and videos, and a review of the course objectives. A chat room enables students to get the learning community started even before they meet in person. Here, they can interact with one another and programme instructors, post questions about the programme or reflections on their pre-readings, and respond to instructor prompts.

During training, the portal updates to highlight timely elements. For example, in the "Programme Work & Tasks" panel, the content for the day – including presentations and readings – appears in an expanded view, while the content for the other days is minimised. The chat room allows students to share key takeaways from the day as well as assets they may capture during the programme, such as links to breakout exercises they may have filmed during the training. On the final day of the training, the "Resource Room" appears on the portal. This section allows participants and instructors to crowdsource their learning by sharing recommended resources and information with each other. Again, this nurtures the learning community, as everyone in the room is encouraged to share and everyone is co-creating knowledge.

After the training, students and instructors continue to engage in the social features of the portal – sharing via the chat room and the "Resource

Room" – thereby sustaining the learning community and deepening their interaction with the content, reinforcing their learning, and encouraging each other to apply the content back on the job. Students also continue to track completion of the learning goals in the "Compact for Success", helping to ensure they are following through on their learning goals even when they are back to dealing with the daily demands of their jobs. To provide them with prompts for discussion and to reinforce what they learned, the system issues a series of automated reminders that we call "Memory Pings". Instructors can also see how learners are applying the content, providing them with valuable insight into the practicality of their course.

A few weeks after the programme concludes, the "Resource Room" should contain a rich library of crowdsourced articles and links. Instructors may post short videos elaborating on some of the course content to an embedded video viewing section, the "Screening Room". Participants end up with a smorgasbord of options to choose from to personalise their learning. In this way, the portal enables them to be agents of their own learning.

Not only do the resources that students have identified assist in peer-to-peer learning, they also create a repository of relevant content that can be used to populate the next offering of the programme. In this way, students are joining with instructors in co-curating the course and continuously improving it.

The following screenshot shows the "Participant Portal" in the "before" phase of a professional education programme on management offered in Riga, Latvia.

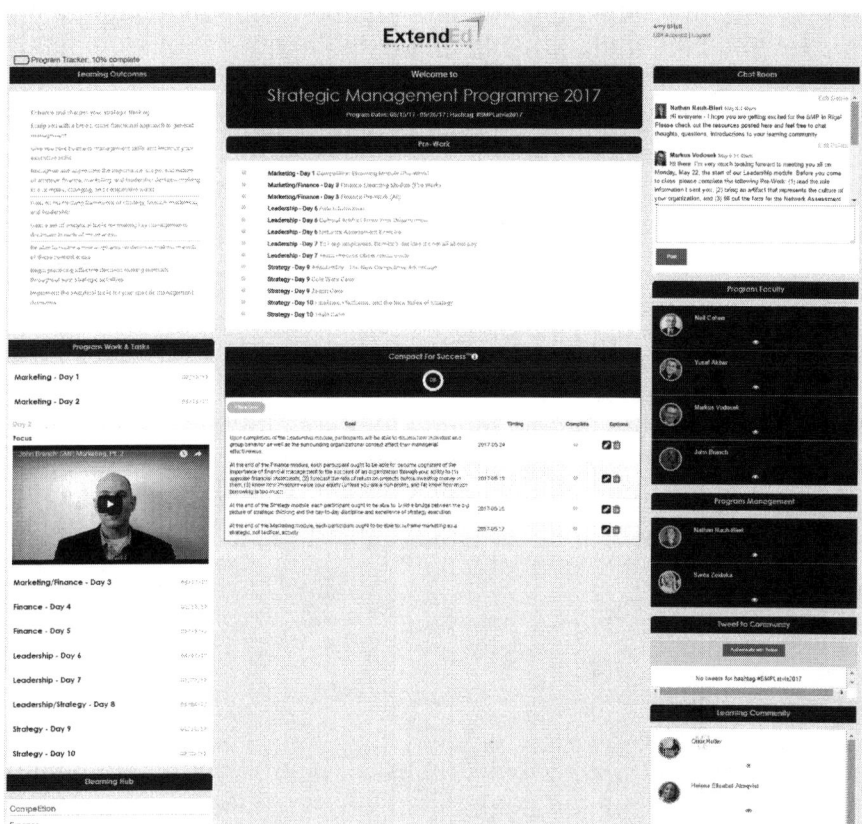

Figure 1: The view of the ExtendEd portal that participants see during one of WDI's professional education programmes.

2b. The Curriculum

The ExtendEd portal is a flexible, cloud-based system that adapts to any curriculum and subject matter. WDI uses the portal to support short-term executive education certificate programmes in management education, covering topics such as finance, marketing, human resource management, and non-profit management. Programmes range in duration from 2 to 10 days, with intensive days typically lasting from 9 a.m. to 5 p.m. Programmes require pre-engagement with materials prior to the face-to-face training. Post-engagement is not a formal requirement, but the portal offers several features to keep learners active post-programme. These include automated reminders of concepts taught during the programme, new materials uploaded to the portal by students and instructors, and opportunities for continued discussions in the chat room.

2c. Organisation of the Practice

The instructor's activities

The back end of the portal features an authoring tool so that instructors can easily upload and assign content, learning outcomes, and goals. Programme administrators are also on the back end of the system and can support the instructor in uploading the programme content. This content is then reflected on the front end of the portal, the "Participant Portal". Instructors organise their content in a user-friendly template that groups information according to whether it is delivered before, during, or after the programme. Being able to deliver content before and after the programme means they can spread the delivery of information over a much longer period, avoiding the "firehose of information" that often occurs in short-term programmes. This means that they need to spend some time beforehand deciding where each piece of content best fits in the "before-during-after framework".

For the "before" phase, instructors list the learning outcomes for the course. They also produce a short introductory video and upload it along with a bio and photo. Instructors create a lesson plan for each day that indicates the pre-work and a video introducing the day's content, the course materials, and the "Memory Pings" to be disseminated via e-mail and on the portal after the programme concludes. Instructors can add goals for students through the "Compact for Success".

As the programme approaches, instructors join students on the "Participant Portal". Thus, both students and instructors are part of the same virtual learning community. They can also send prompt questions to prepare students for the programme. Instructors also read through the student bios and their responses to the question: "What do you hope to gain from this programme?" In this way, instructors get to know the participants' background and expectations before the programme and can tailor their content. Instructors are encouraged to post welcome messages to the chat room.

During the programme, the instructors continue to post to the chat room, including asking students what their key takeaway was from the day.

After the programme, instructors can continue to communicate with the students via the chat room, including answering any questions, encouraging them to share examples of application of content, and reminding them to complete goals in their "Compact for Success". Instructors share articles and videos through the "Resource Room". They can also produce short follow-up videos exploring topics of interest that came up during class, which can then be posted to the "Screening Room".

The students' activities

Two weeks before the course begins, students receive instructions to log in to the portal and input their bio, upload a photo, and answer the question: "What do you hope to gain from this programme?" They can also review the content the instructors have uploaded to the portal, including pre-work. In this phase, students fill out their individual learning goals in the "Compact for Success". They can also post messages to the chat room. Students in some programmes complete preparatory e-learning modules on the portal. In the days before the programme kick-off, students view each other's bios, the instructor bios and videos, complete the pre-work posted to the portal, and view the videos showcasing the focus content for each day of the programme.

During the programme, students use the portal to access materials. They also watch a video of the instructor highlighting the focus of the next day's class so they know what to expect and are better prepared. Students remain active on the chat room and can use it to post links to resources or videos. For example, during one workshop a participant shot a video of her group doing a breakout exercise, and then she posted the link to the chat room. Following instructor prompts, students post their key takeaway from the day's class to the chat room.

After the programme concludes, students continue to use the chat room to discuss how they are applying their learning back on the job. Students continue to track the completion of the goals for the programme on the "Compact for Success". As they find articles and other assets that relate to the programme content, they can share these through the "Resource Room". Learning also continues through follow-up videos that instructors can upload to the "Screening Room". Students retain access to the portal for one year after they conclude the programme, allowing the learning community ample time to continue to network and share insights related to the programme.

2d. Preparation

The portal is still being developed and is only in use in programmes offered in partnership with WDI. We anticipate adding features and functionality so that other institutions can use the portal in the future.

Section 3: The Outcome

The introduction of the ExtendEd portal into WDI's executive education has resulted in the creation of a much stronger learning community. By bringing students and instructors together online before the start of the programme, the community starts to build before the face-to-face training begins. Students begin interacting with the content a week or two before the start of the programme– reading articles and case studies, watching short videos, and interacting via the chat room. They come to the programme with a solid understanding of the programme and with some familiarity of each other and their instructors. Instructors get to know the students and can tailor their content accordingly. Through the portal, they can see in real time what students are thinking about. This allows the learning community to blossom during the in-person training days, with everyone feeling more familiar with each other and thus more likely to share ideas and resources.

Once this learning community has been established, students and instructors have been able to sustain it by remaining on the portal. Their continued engagement after the programme means that students have the opportunity to deepen their learning, to apply what they learned back on the job, and to share this application with their fellow participants and instructors. Instructors appreciate being able to remind students of the key points in their lessons. They value the opportunity to stay in touch with participants after the programme and to see what students are thinking from their chats. These can give them unprecedented insight into which parts of their teaching is most useful and applicable back on the job. They can then use these learning analytics to adjust their content and improve their delivery in the next offering of the programme.

3a. Student Perspective

In four beta tests using the ExtendEd portal to support WDI's programmes, feedback has been positive, with students citing many benefits.

The portal establishes the learning community early on. According to one student:

> "The ExtendEd portal gave me chance to look forward to what we will have in the upcoming modules. I utilised this portal to find out who else will join this course and what lecturers we will have."

The portal frames the course beforehand, setting student expectations and allowing for greater preparedness:

> "I like pre-learning materials and videos. They help me understand concretely what the course is about."

The portal reinforces the learning after the face-to-face training, as a student explains:

> "After the course study this is great tool to recap what we learned and on what issues we need to keep focus on."

3b. Teacher Perspective

Instructor feedback cites many advantages to using the portal. These include:
- Creates and nurtures a strong and active learning community: Instructors like the fact that everyone gets to know each other before the programme starts. Professor Julie Felker commented:

"Relationship building didn't start on the first day of the workshop. It began a few weeks before. Therefore, there was a stronger sense of camaraderie going in which leads to a much more positive learning environment at the outset."

This learning community continues to build during the programme as participants and instructors interact through the chat room. It persists after the programme as they continue to chat and share materials through the "Resource Room". Professor Julie Felker stated:

"It is habit forming like other social media, which in the case of learning is a good thing! As a result, it seems much less like work. This is especially important since active participation, especially after the training ends, is voluntary."

- Enables customisation of content: By getting to know the participants in advance, instructors can tailor their content. Professor Linda Gasser said:

"The portal helped me to begin to relate to what might be student interests and needs so that I might think ahead about these and better address them."

- Enables learning to continue after the programme ends: Instructors appreciate that they can continue to chat with participants and share resources after the in-person training. According to Professor Gasser:

"The portal provides a space for participants to reflect upon content and share thoughts, ideas, reactions and application of content. This was especially helpful because it is sometimes after a class and once one relaxes a bit and content begins to get integrated that new ideas or questions surface that did not in the classroom and participants could share these when they occurred."

- Offers an effective way to reinforce content. Instructors praised the "Memory Pings" as useful. Professor Felker noted:

"Being able to 'ping' participants with reminders to put their learning to practice is an incredibly useful feature. Many participants leave

workshops with enthusiasm and good intentions, though back in the office, reality sets in and learning is set aside. The pings are a great way to help folks stay on course and think, 'Oh yes, I really need to get to that' or 'I can test out what I learned on this project I'm currently working on with my team.'"

- Provides an easy and user-friendly way to share materials. As Professor John Branch stated:

"It provided a one-stop shop for materials."

Professor Gasser has used other learning management systems in teaching college courses, including Blackboard and Sakai. She said:

"These are much bigger systems and require more time and learning and faculty involvement just to get started. This was simple to use and the results were fast. I liked the simplicity."

Section 4: Moving Forward

We anticipate deploying the ExtendEd portal to different types of professional education programmes, including medical and legal education. We will look into ways to increase student participation on the portal, such as what can be done to ensure students complete their bios and participate actively in the chat room. We hope to be able to document actual training transfer on the job (Carnes, 2015; Kohn, 2015; Pollock & Jefferson, 2013; Vehar & Mehta, 2014). We will also investigate ways to report this transfer to companies so that they can better understand how the knowledge gained from training is driving business impact.

We are considering adding quiz functionality so that students can be given a pre-quiz to prepare them for the course. Research indicates that such "priming" boosts retention (Brown *et al.*, 2014). The instructors would receive the results and could then tailor their content to the level of the participants.

We are thinking about enhancements to the "Compact for Success". These could include messaging students with reminders that a goal is coming as well as the ability for instructors to see what goals students have set.

Conclusion

Today's professional education students can best be served by a learning management system designed around the assumptions of adult learning theory. Adult learners need the opportunity to play a part in the design and development of their learning. Their learning is facilitated when they have the opportunity to tie it to real-world application. Adult learners are self-directed, and so allowing them the opportunity to personalise the programme through activities such as setting their own goals is important.

An effective LMS for professional education programmes should bring together students and instructors in a user-friendly, learner-centered environment. In such a community, students and instructors will share resources, ideas, and own learning together: The transmission of ideas will flow in all directions, versus the traditional flow from instructor to student. Active learning will flourish.

Coupled with systems like the ExtendEd portal, the "before-during-after framework" provides an effective way to organise learning in professional education programmes. Using simple technologies such as video cameras, assets can be created that can be presented before and after the face-to-face learning. This extends the learning process and helps students digest a lot of information presented in a short period of time. Furthermore, participants understand in advance that they are not "done" with a programme once the formal training ends: The conversation – including around application of content – can continue long after the last cup of coffee and pastry have been consumed.

About the Authors

Amy Gillett is the vice president of education at the William Davidson Institute, a centre at the University of Michigan dedicated to the emerging markets. She oversees about 40 professional education programmes per year around the world. She can be contacted at this e-mail: gilletta@ umich.edu

Virginia Hamori-Ota is an instructional design and programme development officer with the University of Michigan College of Engineering, Integrative Systems & Design, which offers hybrid master degree programmes. She can be contacted at: otav@umich.edu

Bibliography

Brandon Hall Group (2015). *LMS Trends 2015: Is It Time for Something Different?* Licensed for Distribution to Docebo.

Brown, P.; H. Roediger & M. McDaniel (2014). *Make it Stick: The Science of Successful Learning.* The Belknap Press of Harvard University Press.

Carnes, B. (2013). *Training Transfer Technologies.* Carnes and Associates Inc., White Paper.

Creasman, P. (2012). *Considerations in Online Course Design.* The IDEA Center, IDEA Paper #52.

Ebbinghaus, H. (1885). *Memory: A Contribution to Experimental Psychology.* Originally published by Teachers College, Columbia University, NY.

Brown, M.; J. Dehoney & N. Millichap (2015). *The Next Generation Digital Learning Environment: A Report on Research.* Educause Learning Initiative.

Elkeles, T.; P. Phillips & J. Phillips (2015). ROI Calculations for Technology-Based Learning. *Training & Development Magazine,* January.

Kirkpatrick, J. & W. Kirkpatrick (2015). *Build a Better Reaction Sheet: Tips from Jim and Wendy Kirkpatrick.* Kirkpatrick Partners, LLC.

Knowles, M.; E. Holton & R. Swanson (2014). *The Adult Learner: The Definitive Classic in Adult Education and Human Resource Development, Edition 8.* Taylor & Francis.

Kohn, A. (2015). Use it or Lose it. *Training & Development Magazine,* February.

Pecansky-Brock, M. (2013). *Best Practices for Teaching with Emerging Technologies.* New York: Routledge.

Phillips, J. & P. Phillips (2012). *Measuring ROI in Learning and Development.* American Society for Training & Development.

Pollock, R. & A. Jefferson (2013). *Ensuring Learning Transfer.* ASTD White Paper.

Vehar, J. & S. Mehta (2014). *Making Learning Stick.* Center for Creative Leadership, Webinar.

Socrative: A "Smart Clicker" for Teaching and Assessing Engineering Students

Ghada Salama

Introduction

This chapter contributes to the book *New Innovations in Teaching and Learning in Higher Education* by showing how I use software tech to engage engineering students in their learning. I approach innovation not as a revolutionary or dissonant change but rather as an incremental modification of an existing construct. An array of technologies exist that are designed for student assessment and management as well as effective classroom teaching. However, making best-practice choices amidst such abundance can be overwhelming without targeted guidance. One tool that has proven valuable in a college engineering course is a free online student response system (SRS) called Socrative. Students can quickly create an account on their laptops, tablets, or smart phones, allowing for semester-long interactive engagement with the classroom instructor. Four usages of SRS technology have been effective: being able to gauge concept recognition; determine level of comprehension of content; assess accumulative knowledge; and create competition between students. This chapter will expand on these applications and offer anecdotal evidence of Socrative's value. When reading this chapter, you will gain the following insights:

1. learn about the different types of assessments available in the Socrative software;

2. how to use Socrative during a lecture;

3. how SRS enhances both the student and the instructor experience.

The chapter has five main sections. The background section introduces you to the conditions that encouraged me to consider introducing Socrative software into my engineering course. This is furthered by explaining how I deployed Socrative in my lectures and, more importantly, how I applied it in the classroom. Then I will relate the benefits that Socrative has brought both to my students and to myself, which is followed by the presentation of the adaptability of this SRS in a range of other teaching areas. The chapter concludes by reinforcing the use of software technology for the teaching of engineering courses.

Section 1: The Background

Over the past three years, the university I have been working at, a branch campus of Texas A&M University in Qatar, has adopted an initiative around innovation that includes offering financial incentives to encourage adoption of software technology, invited guest lecturers to introduce different interactive teaching techniques, and introduced "teaching week" for faculty to showcase their innovations. Encouraged by the mandate of the university, I decided to look at the courses I teach; namely, Introduction to Materials (a third-year mandatory course), which is steeped in theoretical content and not representative of the typical problem-solving intensive engineering courses the students are accustomed to. As such, more time is spent in information transmission versus practical application with equation sets. This presented me with a challenge: how to maintain student attention and engagement?

Given the rapid advancement of technology, it would be an injustice not to experiment with innovative applications as we seek to teach and engage our students. Not far from what Dewey (1916) said: *"If we teach today as we taught yesterday, we rob our children of tomorrow"*. Millennials are accustomed to using personal digital assistance (PDA) in all aspects of their lives. One emerging technology that made its way into classrooms is the "smart clicker" – or student response system (SRS). These clickers have demonstrated a positive impact on student engagement (Terrion & Aceti, 2012; Blasco *et al.*, 2013). Students learn better when they actively participate, increasing their academic performance (Mayer & Wittrock, 2006; Awdeh *et al.*, 2014) and improving assessment scores (Knight &Wood, 2005). Nevertheless, clickers have enabled students to give immediate feedback to the instructor and do indeed enhance interaction in the classroom. Here, I share my experience in the application of Socrative in an engineering course.

I recognised that the Socrative smart clicker would certainly turn students' heads, if only for the novelty. And the price – free! – was precisely what is dreamed of in an academic budget. So, I was determined to give this new approach a try, and then assess student reaction. As it turned out, the students were intrigued. It allowed them to legitimately "play with" their smart phones, iPads, and other electronic gadgets (which now seem to be standard issue at birth). Responding to instructor questions was as natural as texting or tweeting or whatever the next digital communication fad may be. Also, competitive aspects of racing to an answer turned the classroom itself – for brief moments here and there – into a lot of fun. And the incentive to come to class with an anticipatory mindset was increased, to my appreciation.

Section 2: The Practice

Socrative is a free online SRS that I have used in my college engineering course. It has many advantages. First, this program is very simple to set up: It does not require any special knowledge of software applications or previous training. Indeed, no software has to be installed. Students merely need to be given access to the website. Best of all, it requires no hardware other than a student laptop, tablet, or mobile phone – which means that neither the instructor nor the institution has to purchase equipment to use the program. In brief, the teacher signs up for an account and Socrative sets up a virtual classroom that the instructor assigns a unique name and through which assignments can be administered. The account can be linked to Google Drive if a Gmail address is provided. This allows student responses to be sent directly and immediately to the instructor upon assignment completion. Or you could send the student responses to any e-mail address without prior set up. The Introduction to Materials Engineering course is a required 3-hour credit course for chemical engineering students, which is administered in their third year. This materials course, compared to all other engineering courses, is more theoretical based than the other courses that heavily depend on problem solving and design. So, I found the application of Socrative particularly useful due to the course content. In my classroom, I have used Socrative for: 1) quick question for concept recognition; 2) exit-ticket for lecture comprehension; 3) quizzes; and 4) generating competition. I will now give examples of how this was accomplished.

Quick Question

In my introduction to the engineering materials course, I was lecturing on the properties of crystal structures as well as the geometric configurations of the crystals themselves. This is a significant concept that lies at the heart of understanding the nature of materials. About half way through the lecture, before moving on to the next idea, I wanted to assess the comprehension of these foundational principles. To do so, while standing in front of the students at the lectern, I quickly input two questions into Socrative to get student responses. Those questions were as follows:

1. Silicon carbide does not have a crystalline structure: T/F?

2. We discussed four types of cubic structures. Give one example.

So, how did the process work? As soon as the students entered my classroom that day, I asked them to log into the virtual Socrative classroom in preparation for questions that I *might* ask during my lecture. That was the clue that they needed to pay attention. At the appropriate moment, I asked the students to access the virtual classroom on their electronic device and respond to the two questions. Note that for the first question, the students could simply click on either the true or false tab attached to that question. On the second short-answer question, the students had to type in an original response. After ending the quiz, the system then gives me three reporting options, the reports can either be downloaded or e-mailed to you. First, it can provide a detailed Excel spreadsheet that shows the class roster with a colour-coded, question-by-question breakdown of student responses; the percentage of correct answers; plus individual and class-average scores. The second option is the individual student reports, which provide a graded quiz for each student in the class and which the instructor can print and share with the students. Lastly, question-specific reports include data for each question in a quiz, including the number of correct answers per question; those with the most and fewest correct answers; and students' full answers to open-ended questions.

Exit Ticket

The second application I use is the "exit ticket" – which is a pre-packaged three-question quiz. The first one asks the students how well they understood the content of the lecture. It gives four options that they can select to describe their level of understanding, ranging from "totally got it" to "not at all". The second question is a free response that gives students an opportunity to state their main takeaway from the lesson. This is an important summary exercise that helps with information retention. The third is an instructor-composed wrap-up question to determine comprehension of a target concept. As with other Socrative quizzes, this activity ends when the instructor clicks "Finish" and selects the reporting form. After reviewing the reports, the teacher can determine how best to start the next lecture, whether to review a topic, or move on with a new topic.

Quizzes

The third application is the quiz, which I use for formative assessments in the course. This is an instructor-prepared activity in place before or after the lecture. As mentioned above, questions can be true/false, short answer, or multiple choice. True/False and multiple choice answers are immediately gradable by the program and do not require instructor perusal. Short answer responses can be made machine-readable, but students have to use exact terms/phrases and correct spelling. If there is any variation from the formula, then the instructor must go over the individual responses to provide a grade. Therefore, a short-answer approach might be better used on more traditional pencil-and-paper exams.

After choosing the quiz to be administered, there are additional options available for the instructor in terms of administering the questions, such as providing "instant feedback" – in which the student answers the questions given in order and cannot change their responses. They receive instant feedback after each response they give. The instructor monitors their progress on a live table, an example of which can be seen in Figure 1. Note that the left-most column is not displayed because the "names removed" option is selected. This is an option that the instructor can choose if the chart is to be made available to the class (for example, via a classroom projector). The column in blue shows percentage of completion

– allowing the instructor to determine whether students are finished or are still working on the questions. The remaining columns show question numbers, responses, and the percentage of correct answers. "Open Navigation" allows the student to go back and forth between questions and change responses while the instructor monitors their progress on a live table. The last option is "Teacher Paced", in which the instructor controls the flow of questions. Additional settings are also available, such as shuffling questions (this feature is not available when the teacher-paced mode is selected), shuffling answers, showing feedback to their responses (not available when in open navigation mode), and showing final score.

Progress	#1	#2	#3
100% ✓	B	Idaho	False
100% ✓	C	Idaho	True
100% ✓	C	Tennessee	False
100% ✓	C	Idaho	False
100% ✓	C	ID	True
100% ✓	C	ID	False
	83%	83%	67%

Figure 1: A sample of assessment results report (Socrative, 2016

Generating Competition

To infuse fun and to sustain engagement, I use the "Space Race" feature. Ahead of time, I prepare a mixture of questions covering the entire course. On the last class day, I divide the students into teams. I display the race course using the classroom projector and watch the excitement as team's race against each other to correctly answer the questions and win the race. This allows students to revise for the final exam in a fun and productive environment.

Section 3: The Outcome

I had taught this course previously in a traditional manner through lecturing and noticed that students were disengaged. This was mainly due to the high theoretical content of this particular course in comparison to most engineering courses that are more on the problem-solving side. I wanted to bring in an element of technology, which is what millennials are practically born with, and at the same time make it interactive to keep them on their toes. From the students' side, after introducing Socrative, I noticed how students would come to class showing more enthusiasm and I also observed an improvement in their performance. On my side, this method did lessen the amount of time I spent on correcting the assessments. It also gave me an insight into which topics students were struggling with that I needed to go over again for the next class meeting, and not at the end of semester when it was too late. Overall, I have found Socrative to be very beneficial in my teaching experience, whether it be to gauge the students' learning and identify misconceptions through the "exit tickets" and "quick question" or when used as a formative assessment tool in quizzes.

However, there are some limitations to using technology in the classroom. First, you do have to spend time and energy creating the assessments; and naturally there is a learning curve to all technology. Second, if you have a pre-planned electronic assignment, you are put in the position of "teaching to the test". If student questions and participation take your lecture in an unexpected direction, then you may have to abandon the quiz – but such is the nature of education. And perhaps we have all had to deal with technological breakdown – when the Internet connection goes down or a site gets caught in an error loop. Under such circumstances, students may have to refresh their page or re-do the quiz entirely – which results in a regrettable "black-eye moment" for the instructor.

On the other hand, going paperless in my assessments – and especially not having to do the grading – was a bonus. The program does all the grading for you and e-mails a detailed report, including a general analysis of each question as well as of each student's work. And if you do need to print it for a student or for any other reason, there is that option. In brief, this aspect of the program saves me a lot of time. The test of any new innovation in teaching is whether the idea has a positive effect on students and educators – without undue impact on time and learning.

3a. Student Perspective

When I conducted an end of year survey, the feedback I received from the students was positive and encouraging. Here are a sample of the comments received on the application of this SRS. In terms of usage, I received positive responses such as *"It is easy to use"*, and another student said: *"It is convenient because there is no need for pen or pencil"*. Other students liked the fact that they received instantaneous responses to their assessment, commenting: *"Socrative keeps us on our toes and tells us our mark right away"*. Another student commented *"Instant results"*, and another comment I received was: *"I like it because it tells you if you answered the question right or wrong"*. The end of year review that I do is in the form of a race among the students that Socrative sets up; the students always enjoy that class: *"The race we had was so fun"*. The positive responses to Socrative seem to be universal: It is efficient, enjoyable, and adds a bit of zest to the classroom experience.

Section 4: Moving Forward

In general, Socrative is part of a trend toward interactive learning models. A totally prepared online course checks the box for using technology in the classroom. But even with spectacular bells and whistles, a totally electronic classroom is simply a paperless version of the workbook approach – students individually interacting with a text. Having an educator in the classroom, working directly with students, answering questions while looking the students in the eyes is still an unbeatable combination. However, an intentional pause in the flow of a lecture, to briefly check for understanding, is an ideal condition for an electronic intervention.

If a program such as Socrative were to be used to teach a same course over a period of years, it would be possible to build up a question/assignment bank that could be accessed at any time during a class. The instructor would be aware before beginning the lecture that any of three or four quiz sets might be appropriate for the day's topic. Thus, in an instant, the teacher could instruct students to log in, take a quick quiz that fits an immediate need, and then continue with the class in a smooth transition, re-teaching as necessary or moving on to new material. The in-flow quiz also has the added bonus of reinforcing facts and concepts without a rote (and often mind-numbing) rehash. It also allows both students and the instructor to hit the classroom reset button, to clear the mental cache, and prepare to resume with a fresh perspective. And perhaps this method of interaction could suggest other modes of delivery, such as a surprise in-class video that leads to a Socrative quiz. Or even a clever way of introducing a guest lecturer. The key is in breaking up the class hour into instructional segments and then checking for understanding as often as possible to ensure that learning is taking place.

Conclusion

Students today are attuned to technology and are not only prepared to use it in the classroom but see it as a modern-day expectation. Socrative is a simple online SRS that brings technology into the classroom in a non-intrusive manner and helps to engage students in the learning process. It has proven valuable in a collegiate setting with students of chemical engineering, and it likely has an application throughout the spectrum of academic studies.

About the Author

Ghada Salama is an instructional associate professor in the Chemical Engineering programme at Texas A&M University at Qatar. She can be contacted at this e-mail: ghada.salama@qatar.tamu.edu

Bibliography

Awdeh, M.; A. Mueen; B. Zafar & U. Manzour (2014). Using Socrative and smart phones for the support of collaborative learning. *International Journal on Integration Technology in education*. Vol. 3, No. 4, pp. 18–24.

Blasco-Arcas, L.; I. Buil; B. Hernández-Ortega & F. Sese (2013). Using clickers in class. The role of interactivity, active collaborative learning and engagement in learning performance. *Computers & Education*, Vol. 62, No. 3, pp. 102–110.

Dewey, J. (1916). *Democracy and education: An introduction to the philosophy of education*. NY: Free press.

Eberly Center for Teaching Excellence and Educational Innovation. What is the difference between formative and summative assessment (2015), Online

Resource: http://www.cmu.edu/teaching/assessment/basics/formative-summative.html [Accessed on 2 December 2016].

Knight, J. & W. Wood (2005). Teaching more by lecturing less. *Cell Biology Education*, Vol. 4, No. 4, pp. 298–310.

Mayer, R. & M. Wittrock (2006). Problem solving. In P. A. Alexander & P. H. Winne (Eds.), *Handbook of Educational Psychology*, pp. 287–304.

Socrative User Guide (2016). Online Resource: https://www.socrative.com/materials/SocrativeUserGuide.pdf [Accessed on 24 September 2016].

Terrion, J. & V. Aceti (2012). Perceptions of the effects of clicker technology on student learning and engagement: a study of freshmen chemistry students. *Research in Learning Technology*. Vol. 20, pp. 1–11.

Chapter 14

The Influence of Web 2.0 on EFL-Students' Motivation and Autonomous Learning Behaviour

Henriette van Rensburg and Nguyen Van Han

Introduction

This chapter contributes to the book *New Innovations in Teaching and Learning in Higher Education* by discussing how a Web 2.0 learning management system (LMS) affects students' motivation and autonomous learning behaviour. Our study uses qualitative interview data from eight undergraduate students taking part in a 12-week English as a Foreign Language (EFL) course at a tertiary college in Vietnam. Since the innovation of Web 2.0, worldwide online communication has been a growing phenomenon. Through this technology, EFL students have acquired numerous opportunities to express ideas, advance their involvement in learning activities, and affirm their confidence in virtual interaction. Such advantages help create a learning environment which motivates students to learn English, leading to the advancement of autonomous learning behaviour. Because most students prefer using the Internet and computers, Web 2.0 can influence interactive communication of students and also have impact on the learning environment. According to Discovery Education (2017:1): *"Web 2.0 is about revolutionary new ways of creating, collaborating, editing and sharing user-generated content online. It is also about ease of use. There is no need to download, and teachers and students can master many of these tools in minutes. Technology has never been easier or more accessible to all."*

The use of LMS can affect language learning of students through Web 2.0 technologies like instant messaging, discussion boards, and blog posts that initiate interaction. In the context of Vietnam, where broadband Internet has recently gained popularity due to more affordable prices, there are still limitations to the application of Web 2.0 in EFL language acquisition. However, as we show in our chapter, there are some benefits. When reading this chapter, you will gain the following:

1. an insight into Vietnamese EFL students' reflection on their use of a Web 2.0 LMS;

2. the advantage of LMS for educational purposes to motivate students;

3. confirm that intrinsic motivation is an important element for the process of enhancing autonomous learning behaviour.

We have structured our chapter in four sections. In the first section, we present the background to our innovative practice. In section 2, the progress of our practice is mentioned. Section 3 discusses the outcome of this study, and section 4 outlines the advancement of our innovative practice.

Section 1: The Background

Learner Autonomy and Motivation in EFL Education

According to Brown (2001), learner autonomy is affirmed as a goal connected to motivation. Many researchers argue that this goal extends to material selection and task motivation (Balçıkanlı, 2010; Nunan, 1997). As observed by Dornyei (2001), the objective of teaching students a foreign language is to instil the legitimacy of the production of language in different social groups. That includes inside and outside learning environments, which points to the primacy of autonomy. As stated by Garcia and Pintrich (1996), autonomy is connected to the motivational elements compared to performance. As such, the primary focus of autonomy seemed to prioritise intrinsic objective assessment, role value, and self-efficacy. A strong link between motivation and autonomy can be perceived in the theory of self-determination (Deci & Ryan, 1985) into intrinsic motivation. Self-determination theory (STD) argues for the existence of natural positive tendencies that motivate individuals to behave in specific, healthy ways. The creators of the theory, Deci and Ryan (1985), support the notion of the intrinsic nature of such tendencies. The developed framework illustrates that conditions which support intrinsic motivation enhance and stimulate learner autonomy so that students are able to engage in creative activities and improve overall performance. Deci and Ryan (1985) further emphasise that intrinsically motivated students study for their own sake in order to gain experience and pleasure. In addition, these students do not study because of external pressure or promise of reward, which results in fostering an interest in learning and confidence in the student's own capacities and attributes. Therefore, intrinsic motivation is more desirable in language education.

As emphasised in the seminal research by Deci and Ryan (1985), intrinsic motivation helps students to learn effectively, and this form of motivation is promoted when students have self-determination and control themselves. The approach advocates for the learners to promote efficient learning while focusing on the achievement of the theory that deals with the students applying intrinsic motivation, as well as depending on the performance of autonomy support or informational conditions. Through these conditions, intrinsic motivation should be promoted. The primary argument, according to the theory of Ryan and Deci (1985), leads to the consideration of the issue that self-determination attracts intrinsic motivation. Self-determination focuses on trends of causality by which the learner internalises the behaviours and can therefore be seen as related to the capacity of autonomy.

Gardner (2000) prioritises intrinsic motivation by arguing that it is more lucrative and efficient because it originates from the student's intrinsic or internal motivation to engage with language and culture. Gardner (2000) also affirms that intrinsic motivation has a stronger prediction as far as successful approach of learner autonomy in the field of foreign language learning.

Benefits of Online Technology in Students' Motivation

Several researchers have noted that using computer-assisted language learning (CALL) or computer-mediated communication (CMC) was advantageous to the EFL students, who claimed that their motivation in learning increased (Ortega, 2009). Various studies have been conducted to examine the benefits of using asynchronous and synchronous CMC in foreign language learning (Liu & Chen, 2007; Tudini, 2003). Through asynchronous CMC, learners are permitted to delay responding to questions, which would suggest a keen construction of grammar (Hudson & Bruckman, 2002). A major objective of synchronous CMC meant for L2 learning demands communicating with native speakers who would consider the importance of oral communication as far as language interaction was concerned. Based on the personal interactions of learners, social networking, as well as text-messaging, have been embraced as an opportunity to explore behavioural learning and decision-making. According to Campbell (2004), adapting social networking patterns that are already used for the surrounding of EFL contains a natural stage that motivates learners.

A comparison of the use of LMS within EFL studies tells us that it is influenced by intrinsic motivation (Eken, 2003; Secules, Herron & Tomasello, 1992). Lee (2009) confirms that LMS would be more efficient in maintaining the focus of learners on different tasks at hand than the traditional textbook approach. In addition, Erwin (2001) emphasises that LMS is simpler to access and further admits that most of the keywords and sentence patterns have been made easier for learners to understand in an effective way, thus increasing students' motivation.

Section 2: The Practice

This chapter reflects only on preliminary findings of a larger research project aiming to explore the effects of CALL on learner autonomy and how students' learning strategies, motivation, and attitudes can change through CALL. The students were asked to complete a questionnaire as the pre-test and post-test. The first phase of the larger project was to investigate the components of learner autonomy that Vietnamese college students perceive. The questionnaire with 50 Likert scale items was developed through SurveyMonkey, and 300 students were invited to respond to this survey. As a result, the factor analysis and internal consistency tests from this sample generated three components of learner autonomy. One of these was *motivation by using technology in education*. Taking this into consideration, the study was designed to illustrate how the students' use of technology in education improved their motivation to develop their learner autonomy. A Web 2.0 LMS was designed and 50 students were invited to learn English, face to face, in class with LMS during a 12-week course. On completion of the course, 15 students were invited to take part in a semi-structured interview, and 8 of them were randomly selected to join the interview. The transcribed results of the audio-recorded interviews were coded to protect the anonymity of the interviewees, with each being assigned a code (e.g., "Student 1", "Student 2", etc.).

The LMS was a collaborative and user-friendly platform that was a customised design developed by teachers at the college and approved for integration into the curriculum by the college authority in Vietnam. The LMS was based on the core content of the current textbook of the syllabus used in the institution, namely *Starter TOEIC* (Test of English for International Communication) (Taylor & Malarcher, 2013). The reason for this choice was that it aligned with the existing curriculum, and it was necessary to implement innovative teaching methods in order to motivate students to achieve better results. Therefore, the level of English competency of students could meet the requirements of corporate recruiters.

The focus of the EFL lessons was student-centered in order to enhance students' sense of responsibility and ability to set learning goals, plan, implement, and evaluate their learning. Both teachers and students were expected to use English for their classroom interactions, such as asking questions for clarification, giving explanations, and providing feedback during the lessons. They were also encouraged to access and explore information in English. It was expected that language proficiency would develop through the English lessons: improvement in vocabulary, grammar, and the four macro skills of listening, speaking, reading, and writing. During the lessons, the teachers played the role of facilitators to support the learning process, especially for language preparation and assessment. Content including authentic websites, videos, and pictures that were used for scaffolding and stimulating the students' learning interests.

Regarding the theoretical framework for LMS and lesson design, Schwienhorst (2003) outlined three approaches to enhance motivation to foster learner autonomy in the technology learning environment: 1) individual-cognitive approach, 2) social-interactive approach, and 3) experimental-participatory approach. In our design we adapted principles consistent with Schwienhorst's (2003) three approaches to enhance motivation and Dang and Robertson's (2010) theoretical framework for the online learning space. These principles are:

+ interactions between students and teachers in and out of classes need facilitating;

+ team learning brings better outcomes than solo learning;

+ structured exercises, challenging discussions, team projects, and peer critiques can enhance learning engagement;

+ proper and timely feedback is important for learning development;

+ time management is a critical skill for both students and professionals;

+ higher expectations need to be negotiated;

+ diversifying course delivery is necessary, and different talents are expected (Dang & Robertson, 2010:9).

The "Home" page of the Vietnamese college's LMS course contained different activities for students to choose to interact with the content, instructors, and classmates, as shown in Figure 1.

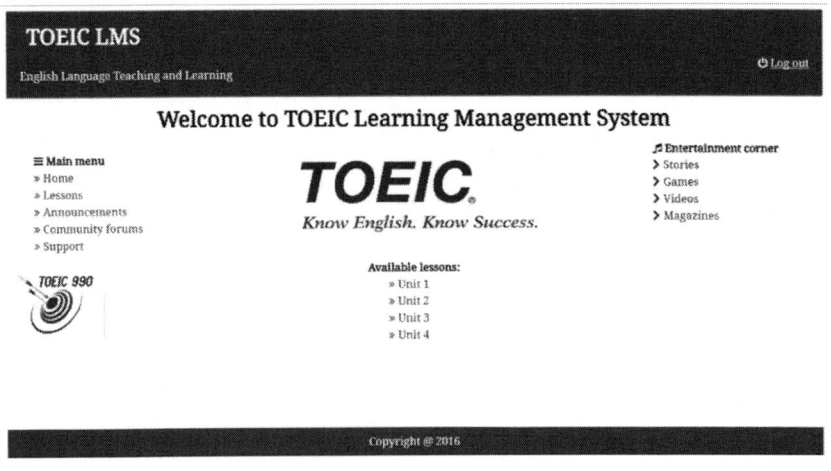

Figure 1: LMS course home page.

According to the college curriculum policy, second-year students need to study the first four units of the textbook. These four units were designed and covered different topics regarding business themes. For each unit, the students were responsible for practicing English skills such as listening, reading, speaking, and grammar. The sample activities are shown below.

Regarding the *speaking activities*, students were presented with various questions to discuss. They then needed to discuss these questions with their peers using headphones in the laboratories to express their ideas and points of view with respect to issues raised in each question. Some of questions are illustrated in Figure 2, below.

Conversation topics

1. Self-employment is more stimulating than working for a large organization?
2. Companies become more efficient as they grow in size.
3. It is impossible for young people to find a good job to day without the help from someone.

PART VII

Figure 2: Conversation topics.

Aside from the speaking activities in the lessons, students were also required to work in groups of three or four to choose one topic from a list of 10 topics for which careful preparation was required in order to make a meaningful presentation. Each group took turns to give a presentation every week. Participants were required to use the Internet to search for relevant information and select video clips and hyperlinks that were useful to support their presentations. Computer-based materials also encouraged learners to use cognitive strategies and apply metacognitive awareness in language learning. Computer-based instructional materials and web-based materials for language learning can provide students with a variety of authentic and pedagogical materials that may have a positive influence on learner autonomy. In addition, the ability to work outside the classroom without a teacher's presence is necessary for the development of learner autonomy.

With regard to the *reading activities*, students read the text and answered the questions by clicking the answers they believed were correct. If their responses were incorrect, they received an audible indication that they needed to choose again. An explanation also appeared in order to help them understand, as depicted in Figure 3, below. Independent action, decision-making, and freedom of choice will stimulate learner autonomy development.

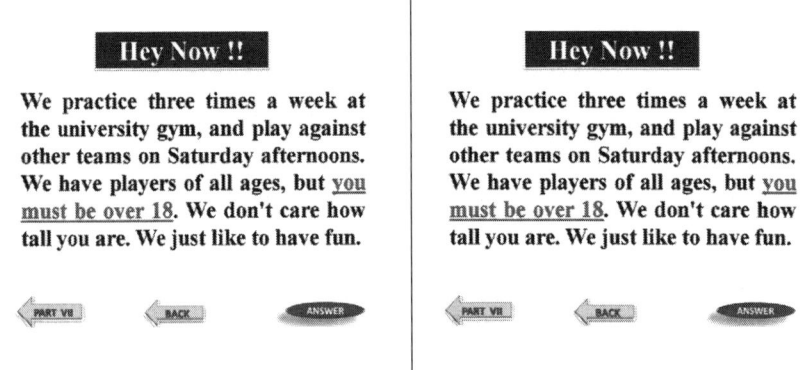

Figure 3: Reading activities.

In the *vocabulary activities*, students learned vocabulary with sounds and through the presentation of images with definitions. The LMS course also included automatic speech recognition (ASR) technology for vocabulary practice. Students' voices were recorded and scored to provide students with feedback concerning the accuracy of their pronunciation. Figure 4 below illustrates an example of a representative vocabulary activity and the ASR tool. These activities helped students to become more involved in learning, which is considered as a fundamental factor for improving autonomy.

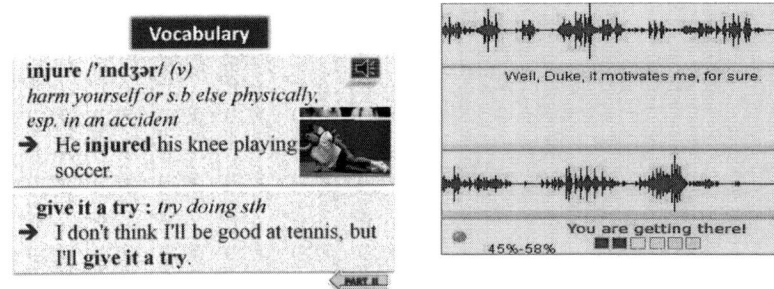

Figure 4: Vocabulary activities.

Aside from the main content in the curriculum, students had access to the other supporting materials that promoted engagement with the coursework. For example, the entertainment corner was linked with the EFL websites. Students could play games with crossword puzzles that had six levels, from level 1 (the easiest) to level 6 (the most difficult). In this part, students were asked to click on the number to see the clues or they could type directly in the crossword cells. When students did not know the answer, they could click on the "Hint" button for clues. Students could also learn about vocabulary and grammar by reviewing testing contributions from others around the world and most of quizzes were in the form of multiple-choice, flashcards and matching. In addition, videos were available that helped learners to get exposure to language used in real-world environments, and practice pronunciation by listening and repeating daily uploaded sentences to recognise not only new words, but also useful expressions as illustrated in Figure 5.

Figure 5: Extra activities.

Section 3: The Outcome

The major theme emerging from the interviews with the treatment group members was the motivational aspects of language learning. Learning English with this customised LMS has made students feel more motivated to develop their language competence. Although their specific individual motivational reasons for learning English as a foreign language differed, most of them had intrinsic motivation, and according to self-determination theory, students with this kind of motivation would maximise their learner autonomy. Three students explained that they studied English because of their interest and success in language learning. For example, Student 2 and Student 8 stated that the activities in the LMS were interesting compared to the previous class, where they had been taught with traditional teaching methods. As a result, they felt keen to learn English and made a decision to learn some sentences to improve their speaking. Student 2 said:

> "The learning activities with CALL are interesting. Each activity is designed in a unique way and I do not get bored. That is the reason why I feel motivated to get engaged in learning English. Especially, I love reading articles online for relaxation. In the past, we just looked at the text book and listened to the teacher. I could not imagine how English was used in the real life. Every day I learn some short sentences to practice with my friends."

Similarly, regarding the question about the motivation to study English, Student 3 and Student 5 both expressed a strong interest in learning. They explained that the discussion and exchange of ideas in the forums raised their desire to use English effectively so that they could communicate with everyone confidently. As Student 3 explained:

> "I feel motivated to join the forum for discussing as it helps me communicate with other people. I think there is the general need to learn English in an increasingly globalised business world where it has become a de facto lingua franca."

Success in learning a foreign language was what motivated students 4 and 6. These students wanted to study English to master it well and conquer the challenges in life. Student 4 stated:

> "I found it a bit difficul to learn English and therefore I used to have the idea of stopping learning it. However, you know what, getting exposure to LMS helps me change my mind and I think learning a language is not that tough at all. I need to take part in the activities designed with technology so that I can become my habit to get rid of the fear of learning English that I used to have."

It can be inferred that these students were intrinsically motivated because they learned English for its inherent satisfaction. According to Ushioda (1996), this is a good condition for fostering learner autonomy because intrinsic motivation is conducive to learner autonomy.

In contrast, Students 1 and 7 said that they had not known the real purposes of learning English as they thought it was the curriculum policy; therefore, they and their classmates attended the English classes because it was a compulsory subject. However, exposure to authentic content through watching the video clips has changed their minds. They made a decision to learn English and put effort into it, and they were motivated to be actively engaged in the learning process in order to work in a professional working environment. These students learned English for its instrumental value and this reason can be considered as extrinsic motivation. As Student 1 responded:

> *"When watching, the conversation taking place in the real company, I feel really motivated as the characters who speak English fluently in that video are top employers. I wish someday I could speak English like that, but now I think I have to try more to reach that goal."*

Section 4: Moving Forward

The LMS employed in the study was chosen to direct students' attention to a local CMC environment for idea exchanges and negotiations. Also, the students' online behaviours increased in a holistic and quantitative manner; students did significantly better on the post-test than the pre-test in regard to motivation of learning English ($F=56.85$, $df=1,94$, $p<0.001$). In other words, LMS activities basically modified students' online habits quantitatively. From the activities, there was a clear indication that the online habits of the students were more focused, especially in terms of social and academic factors. The online processes are most likely related to social and academic purposes. From this study, it is clear that students who became intrinsically motivated took on more responsibility for their English language learning. This condition is a characteristic of learner autonomy as it is described in EFL learning.

Intrinsic motivation helps learners to identify with their learning goals and as such gives a clear indication of how learner motivation solves the issue of autonomy. Aside from this, once the learners are motivated to focus on their goals, they can easily link their ability to interpret learner autonomy and would therefore concentrate on the development of the same skills for evaluation of reflective self-management learning. On the other hand, intrinsic motivation considers self-interest to be an important factor that leads to self-determination. The results from this study suggest that when there is an increase in the use of intrinsic motivation, there are higher possibilities that LMS would influence this situation.

From this outcome, it is clear that intrinsic motivation is used for a short-term period, but it is quite sustainable, especially to the learners, who are meant to transform from being dependent on their teachers to learning on their own as independent learners.

Conclusion

According to the findings, the students who take English as their second language in Vietnam confirm that intrinsic motivation is an important element for the process of learner autonomy. As mentioned in self-determination theory, intrinsic motivation assists students in the development of autonomous learning behaviours. Further reports collected from different regions that use English as their second language have affirmed that intrinsic motivation is self-built. For instance, studies conducted by Kim (2007) in Korea as well as He (2009) in China suggest that in most countries, including the USA, English is used as a second language. From the studies, significant roles of intrinsic motivation tend to support autonomy in learning. Therefore, the finding for EFL students in relation to the self-determination approach supports the theory.

The study has some limitations. First, the interview concerning the data collection was voluntary, meaning that only individuals who opted to express their opinions were considered. Second, the study only reports on the information that was collected from the eight interviewees, from a total of fifteen individuals who were evaluated. As such, other opinions were not represented.

This chapter began with the benefits that the application of technology in EFL education could bring to the development of learner autonomy. It went on to discuss self-determination theory in order to demonstrate the relationships of intrinsic and extrinsic motivation for learner autonomy capacity development. The data collected from the interviews revealed the differences in the Vietnamese local students' motivation from the impact of activities in an online context. In addition, it discussed the influence of EFL on motivating students' intrinsic motivation, which contributed to fostering learner autonomy. These findings have suggested that EFL educators need to take advantage of customised LMSs for specific educational purposes to motivate students so that they can become engaged in learning activities.

About the Authors

Henriette van Rensburg, PhD, is an associate professor (special education) in the Faculty of Business, Education, Law and Arts at the Toowoomba campus of the University of Southern Queensland, Australia. She can be contacted at this e-mail: vanrensb@usq.edu.au

Nguyen Van Han is a teacher of English at the College of Finance and Customs in Vietnam. He has completed a MED TESOL and MLAD (Research) and is currently doing his PhD in education at University of Southern Queensland. He can be contacted at this e-mail: nguyenvan-hantesol@gmail.com

Bibliography

Balçıkanlı, C. (2010). Learner Autonomy in Language Learning: Student Teachers' Beliefs. *Australian Journal of Teacher Education*, Vol. 35, No. 1, pp. 90–101.

Brown, H. D. (2001). *Teaching by principles*, 2nd Ed. New York: Longman.

Campbell, A. P. (2004). Using LiveJournal for authentic communication in EFL classes. *The Internet TESL Journal*, Vol. 10, No. 9, pp. 35–46.

Dang, T. T. & M. Robertson (2010). *Pedagogical lessons from students' participation in Web 2.0. TESOL in Context*, Vol. 20, No. 2, pp. 5–26.

Deci, E. L. & R. M. Ryan (1985). *Intrinsic Motivation and Self Determination in Human Behaviour*. New York, NY: Plenum Press.

Discovery Education (2017). Online resource: http://web2014.discoveryeducation.com/web20tools.cfm [Accessed on 16 March 2017].

Dornyei, Z. (2001). *Teaching and researching motivation*. Harlow, England: Longman.

Dornyei, Z. (2003). Attitudes, orientations, and motivations in language learning: Advances in theory, research, and applications. *Language Learning*, Vol. 53, No.1, pp. 3–32.

Eken, A. N. (2003). 'You've got mail': a film workshop. *ELT Journal*, Vol. 57, No. 1, pp. 51–59.

Erwin. T. (2001). Language acquisition in the classroom: The role of digital video. *Computer Assisted Language Learning*, Vol. 14, No. 3, pp. 305–319.

Garcia, T. & P. R. Pintrich (1996). The effects of autonomy on motivation and performance in the college classroom. *Contemporary Educational Psychology*, Vol. 21, No. 3, pp. 477–486.

Gardner, H. (2000). *Multiple Intelligences: The Theory in Practice.* (Second Edition). Alexandria, VA: ASCD.

He, Y. C. J. (2009). *Self-determination among adult Chinese English language learners: The relationship among perceived autonomy support, intrinsic motivation and engagement.* University of Southern California, USA.

Hudson, J. M. & A. S. Bruckman (2002). IRC Francais: The creation of an Internet-based SLA community. *Computer Assisted Language Learning,* Vol. 15, No. 2, pp. 109–134.

Kim, H. Y. (2007). *Studying the 'second foreign language' in Korea: Choice, self-determination, and motivational orientations.* PhD Thesis, University of Hawaii, Honolulu, USA.

Lee, W. (2009). Making English lessons engaging through video materials supported with advance organisers and prediction activities. *TESL Reporter,* Vol. 42, No. 2, pp. 57–74.

Liu, G. & A. S. Chen (2007). A taxonomy of Internet-based technologies integrated in language curricula. *British Journal of Educational Technology,* Vol. 38, No. 5, pp. 934–938.

Nunan, D. (1997). Designing and adapting materials to encourage learner autonomy. In P. Benson & P. Voller. (Eds.), *Autonomy and independence in language learning,* Longman: London, pp. 192–203.

Ortega, L. (2009). Interaction and attention to form in L2 text-based computer-mediated communication. In A. Mackey & C. Polio (Eds.), *Multiple perspectives on interaction in SLA: Research in honor of Susan M. Gass,* New York: Routledge, pp. 226–253.

Scharle, Á. & A. Szabó (2000). *Learner autonomy: A guide to developing learner responsibility.* Cambridge: Cambridge University Press.

Secules, T.; C. Herron & M. Tomasello (1992). The effect of video context on foreign language learning. *The Modern Language Journal,* Vol. 76, No. 4, pp. 481–490.

Schwienhorst, K. (2003). Neither here nor there? Learner autonomy and intercultural factors in CALL environments. In D. Palfreyman & R. Smith (Eds), Learner autonomy across cultures: language education perspectives, New York: Palgrave Macmillan, pp. 164–179

Taylor, A. & C. Malarcher (2013). *Starter TOEIC.* Ho Chi Minh City: Nha Xuat Ban Tre.

Tudini, V. (2003). Using native speakers in chat. *Language Learning and Technology,* Vol. 7, No. 3, pp. 141–159.

Ushioda, E. (1996). *Learner Autonomy 5: The Role of Motivation.* Dublin: Authentik.

Chapter 15

Virtual Reality in the Classroom and the Mandate to Bring Edutainment to Adult Learners

Christopher Klopper and Malcolm Burt

Introduction

This chapter contributes to the book *New Innovations in Teaching and Learning in Higher Education* by showing how we incorporate cutting-edge technology into mainstream programs of study in higher education. The chapter details the deployment of virtual reality in higher education and illustrates how the principles of andragogy, or adult learning theory, are closely aligned with the practice. This chapter appropriates the definition of virtual reality (VR) as a technology that provides participants with *"a head-mounted display that allows them to see a digital world, matching the video image to the movement of the guest's head"* (Younger, 2016:532) and the utility of andragogy as the art and science of adult learning (Kearsley, 2010). We contend that designing and delivering VR learning experiences founded in adult learning theory not only appeals to the adult learner but also ensures active participation in the learning process and the motivation for learners to imbibe information, rather than just simply memorise. When reading this chapter, you will gain:

1. guidance to produce an educational VR learning experience;

2. insight into the application of a VR learning experience in initial teacher education; and

3. motivation to bring edutainment to digital natives.

This chapter is arranged in four sections. In section 1, we provide the background to the innovative practice by positioning our work within contemporary literature. We progress the practice in section 2 by providing an in-depth account of the initiative. The outcome of this innovation is narrated in section 3 utilising the student voice, which segues into section 4 outlining how the innovative practice can be advanced.

Section 1: The Background

The arrival of digital natives – or those born of the net generation – into the higher education sector has received much attention over recent years (Jones *et al.*, 2010). There has been much speculation that this group of students thinks and processes information differently from previous generations. In some instances, higher education providers have called for curricula and instructional delivery technologies to be revitalised (Klopper & Weir, 2015) with the intention of transforming the higher education of today into the 21st century, user-centred, on-demand, engaging, technology-centric activity that it has not been for much of its existence. As such, contemporary higher education has the obligation to enrich student learning experiences through the advanced deployment of high-tech digital technologies.

VR is one digital technology gaining traction as a teaching tool that allows students to be immersed in a learning experience and to evoke an empathetic response from *"the feeling of being there"* (Morie, 2006:6). The application of VR in higher education learning experiences has been broad and includes work in the field of neuroscience (Verschure, 2011); the health sciences (Banerjee, 2007; Tarr & Warren, 2002); architecture and engineering (Sala, 2016), including testing virtual models of bridges prior to construction (Sampaio & Martins, 2014); fire safety evacuation simulations (Rüppel & Schatz, 2011); orientation exercises for underground coal miners (Grabowski & Jankowski, 2015); the manipulation of data results from oil extraction engineering (Hui *et al.*, 2012) displaying complex database visualisation; and assembling virtual molecules of water (Sala, 2016). More specifically, VR has also been employed specifically in geography education with the use of 360-degree photos and videos, accessing heritage sites via Google Expeditions (Defanti, 2016) and visiting the Amazon rainforest as well as *"provincial parks virtually"* and exploring other locations using Google Earth (Lisichenko, 2015:160).

Section 2: The Practice

The NMC Horizon Report 2017 Higher Education proposes that *"online, mobile, and blended learning are foregone conclusions. If institutions do not already have robust strategies for integrating these now pervasive approaches, then they simply will not survive"* (Adams Becker *et al.*, 2017:2). In our own institution, Griffith University, Australia, the process of putting into action a comprehensive VR schedule for online course offerings (Griffith Online) is already in place, and digital technologies as a normalised practice for all teaching staff across the gamut of programmes of study is being embraced. The Griffith 2020 vision has laid the blueprint by promoting key domains for all programmes of study to employ. The key domains include: flexibility in delivery and progression of study, engagement of students through enhanced learning and teaching innovations, stronger and closer industry connections, digital reformation, and intensifying employability skill development. Collectively, these domains have resulted in a revision of programme offerings across the university and the opportunity for teaching staff to revise the content of a course, the curriculum design, and most importantly how they teach. This has seen a number of innovations being implemented and a growing keenness from teaching staff to experiment, whether that be with modes of delivery, technology-enabled teaching activities, gamification for learning, VR, or augmented reality. In this way, these emerging learning experiences come to resemble digitally enriched entertainment more so than traditional pedagogical practices, creating a hybridity of technology-enabled teaching possibilities that can be identified as *edutainment*. Edutainment can be defined as *"teaching through forms of entertainment, such as computer games or television shows"* (Collins, 2011:165). One such example is the deployment of a VR excursion via a custom VR video played on the student's own phone or tablet inserted into branded Google Cardboard headsets within a course that prepares initial teacher education students to teach history and geography in the primary phase of schooling in Australia.

2a. An Introduction to VR in the Classroom

The VR learning experience was designed to give students the opportunity to participate in the observation of water management in a local environment through a custom-made "hands-on" VR field excursion. Specifically, the students:

- + viewed six locations filmed as 360-degree static video setups that were edited together as a single video with crossfades between locations and included audio from the locales;

- + heard information via voiceover about the landforms they were seeing and what they should be looking for;

- + addressed a set of questions posed by the lesson planner without ever leaving their lecture seats or homes;

- + experienced a location intimately through the VR experience.

The deployment of a VR excursion differs from traditional pedagogical practices in several areas, which makes it an intriguing possibility to explore further. These differences include but are not limited to:

- + *authenticity* – students are able to visit locations virtually and engage in co-curricular learning experiences by simply putting on a headset, thereby allowing them to experience simulations of reality that can replicate authentic real-world circumstances and theoretically can elicit the same emotional and learning responses (Marquis, 2012) in the brain as actually doing the real activity;

- + *student engagement* – the hidden agenda of games and play is to teach, illustrating the use of technology-enabled teaching possibilities (edutainment) and enhancing engagement and interest, which closely aligns with the assumptions of andragogy;

- + *creativity and innovative thinking* – students not only intimately explore locations and answer questions about the locations relevant to the course in much the same way as if they were present, they are also exposed to an entirely new way of exploring and co-constructing knowledge by being immersed in any location around the world (and potentially off it!).

2b. The Curriculum

Each generation of student is said to have their own unique traits to consider, and adult learners – those learners 25 years of age and older – are no exception. In fact, their life experience, established habits, and empowered mindsets can work for, and against, any teaching and learning strategy. According to Knowles (1980, 1984) adult learning theory maintains that the adult learner has specific learning requirements and that these specific learning requirements should be taken into consideration when designing and deploying learning and teaching approaches and strategies. Knowles (1984) progresses adult learning theory through the maintenance of four principles:

+ *Principle 1* maintains that an adult learner must play a part in the learning design and development of their learning experience. Adult learners should play an integral part of the development and implementation of the curriculum, as well as the evaluation process. Notwithstanding any professional accreditation stipulation, ensuring that the adult learner's voice is heard affords this and provides the opportunity to design materials and activities based upon the needs and wants of the adult learner;

+ *Principle 2* advocates for the adult learner to gather experience through instruction and activities. Rather than offering a task that relies on recall of information, providing the adult learner the opportunity to go "out and explore" the subject matter ensures active participatory learning;

+ *Principle 3* supports the notion that the adult learner must be able to make an explicit connection between the subject matter and real-world benefits and applications. If the adult learner is unable to make this connection, it is highly likely that the learner will disengage with the subject matter;

+ *Principle 4* cultivates the subject matter in a problem-centred way so that the adult learner can delve into specific tasks that enable them to interact and engage with the information through repetition and experience, and not through teacher-dominated declarative learning. Figure 1 presents the above principles in a simplified form.

2c. Organisation of the Practice

There are multiple elements that contribute to creating a VR learning experience (Pine & James, 1998; Grigorovici, 2001:2; Oculus.com, 2016; Campbell, 2008; Collins & O'Brien, 2011). It is said that attendance to these elements has the potential to inform a subjective response from users. The elements are:

- *advance description* – this refers to the way the experience is promoted before being experienced;

- *hardware experience* – this demarcates anything physical required for the VR experience to be undertaken. This might include headsets, hand controllers, headphones, and more. It also includes the responsiveness of positional tracking and whether virtual elements respond naturally (i.e., if users turn their head, the expected video immediately appears);

- *rules of edutainment* – relates to narrative trajectories that are coupled with the traditional elements of entertainment, including a stated objective and the means to achieve it, and as many elements as possible of the "hero's journey" (Campbell, 2008), which is a series of specific plot points evident in nearly all popular major Western entertainment vehicles, to provide a satisfying resolution for the user;

- *audio/video experience* – this refers to the technical quality of the vision and sound and also to clarity, frequency, and fidelity of audio, spatial positioning, and refresh rates, colour and brightness intensity, and resolution of the video.

The application of adult learning theory principles combined with the pivotal elements to VR learning experiences, as per our experience, is presented in Figure 1.

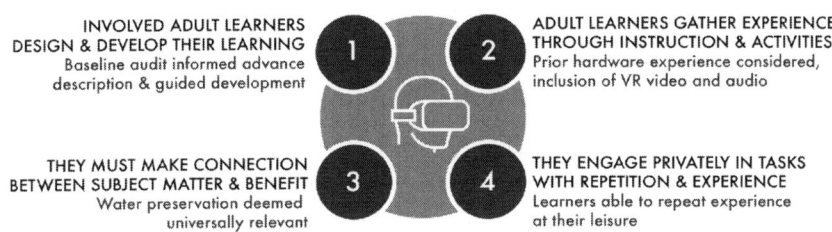

INVOLVED ADULT LEARNERS
DESIGN & DEVELOP THEIR LEARNING
Baseline audit informed advance
description & guided development

ADULT LEARNERS GATHER EXPERIENCE
THROUGH INSTRUCTION & ACTIVITIES
Prior hardware experience considered,
inclusion of VR video and audio

THEY MUST MAKE CONNECTION
BETWEEN SUBJECT MATTER & BENEFIT
Water preservation deemed
universally relevant

THEY ENGAGE PRIVATELY IN TASKS
WITH REPETITION & EXPERIENCE
Learners able to repeat experience
at their leisure

Figure 1: Application of adult learning theory to VR learning experiences.

2d. Preparations

The preparation of the virtual learning experience required the staging, filming, and editing of the VR video. This consisted of gaining a thorough understanding of the real-world field trip, including specific locations and details about the specific educational outcomes. Then, each location in the field trip was filmed as a 360-degree video using two VR cameras placed back to back. Additional sound was also captured with an audio recorder at each of these locations. The VR footage was then stitched together in a proprietary program (http://www.kolor.com/autopano-video). After the stitching had occurred, the VR footage was exported and then edited as normal with crossfades in Adobe Premiere (http://www.adobe.com/products/premiere.html). The additional audio recordings and pre-recorded voiceover were also added at this point. The video was then exported as a VR video with metadata identifying it as VR video injected by Adobe Premiere and uploaded to YouTube, nominated as VR content.

The students in the classroom were provided with Google Cardboard headsets. The students accessed the VR video on YouTube on their phones and then selected the Google Cardboard icon, after which they placed their devices in the headsets to view the content. In the absence of Google Cardboard headsets, students could view the VR video as a 360-degree video in their browsers via YouTube.

Section 3: The Outcome

At the commencement of the course, the academic teaching team introduced the mandatory learning activities and requirements for the course. This afforded the class of adult learners the opportunity to discuss their expectations, concerns, and ideals they had for the course. Evaluation and assessment dominated these initial discussions, since the course was part of a graduate initial teacher education programme and as such the adult learners had already completed a disciplinary-focused undergraduate programme of study, and so they were well aware of their own assessment ideals and needs. However, the teaching team was able to navigate discussions towards the planning of the students' learning activities and experiences. In order to plan sufficiently for the inclusion of the VR learning experience, a baseline audit of prior experience with, and understanding of, VR was undertaken through a focus group interview. Student 1 exclaimed: *"Um not much really all I know is it's used in games and stuff and you feel like you're in the area that the game is"*. Student 2 shared: *"I know it's an emerging technology and I've had an experience with it previously at the natural history museum in London"*, and Student 5 claiming: *"I don't know a lot besides it's quite a new technology I think that's used in gaming and it's also being introduced into roller coasters"*.

The customer adage "expectations drive experience" (Pieters *et al.*, 1995) is also true in the teaching sphere. From the interviews, it was understood that these students had little knowledge of the application and needed guided assistance. The fieldwork excursion was designed as a simple application that made use of the most basic and affordable VR delivery tool on the market, Google Cardboard. The experience was not designed to be comparable to high-end VR experiences such as those achievable with Oculus Rift or HTC Vive headsets, which are both tethered and require powerful computers to function. Rather it was the students' own phones that would be providing the processing power to deliver the VR experience. Immersion was promised, but in a limited fashion.

What matters most with adult learners is not the end result but rather the experience that is gathered through the journey of instruction and interrelated and connected learning and teaching activities. This was achieved through careful consideration of the students' prior learning. A requirement of the professional accrediting body for teachers in Australia mandates that students have a minimum of six courses in their first teaching area and four courses in their second. This course prepares initial teacher education students to teach history and geography curriculum areas in the primary phase of schooling in Australia, so the demarcation of requisite knowledge could be safely assumed as sufficient by the learners' entry into the programme of study. This is an important point for designing learning experiences for adult learners, as assumptions can be made and projected for the development of subsequent learning experiences. However, the timing of the virtual learning experience in relation to the planned schedule of learning across the trimester was crucial and considered. The students needed to have acquired sufficient pedagogical content knowledge (Schulman, 1987) prior to engaging with the field excursion: *"I actually liked the exploring bit of it and not having somebody there. I thought it was more... I don't know.... I just felt like I was exploring"* (Student 7).

Adult learners are most interested in learning topics and subject matter that have immediate relevance and impact to their job, personal life, or future profession. Living in Australia, a country known for its hot, harsh, and arid landscape, water consumption and preservation is of concern. By placing the VR learning experience within an environmental landscape linked to water management, it not only transported the students outside of the classroom but placed them in the very landscape that required their consideration and action. Placing students in an environment necessitates the learning design to provide prompts and cues for learning to occur and experiences to be engaged with. The approach was twofold in provision: voiceovers to guide the learning activities and sound bites of the naturally occurring fauna to authenticate the learning experience. The voiceovers corresponded with the provided workbook that required learners to document what they were seeing, hearing, or experiencing in order to document the field excursion for elaboration at a later point in time.

Image 1: Students exploring the VR experience in class.

The VR learning experience posed the following problem: What is the impact of water and water flow in natural and man-made waterways? This placed the adult learner at the heart of the problem rather than providing content-oriented subject material.

> *"I think I was shocked when I first arrived in the field! There were so many things happening. I wasn't taking it in but then as it went on I was concentrating more on what I was seeing instead of listening to what they were saying. I needed to solve the problem."* (Student 3).

> *"I loved the 360-degrees part of it so we could look up down and felt like I was in the place and maybe if we stood up and we walked instead of sitting I'd feel like it would have been more that we were like there and we could look around."* (Student 5).

During the student focus group discussion, the following three key themes emerged:

- *personalised learning* – and the opportunity to undertake the learning experience at a time that is managed by the student and not restricted by the timetable – *"It personalises the situation"* (Student 2) and *"it enhances your experience because you feel like it's through your own eyes"* (Student 4);

- *broader range and deeper learning opportunities* – which previously would have been considered prohibitive, *"Allows us to experience things we would otherwise never ever be exposed to"* (Student 1);

- *captivating and a novel approach to learning* – *"It must be nice for you to teach in a different way and for us to learn in a different way"* (Student 6).

Section 4: Moving Forward

As with any rapidly evolving technology, developers need to stay abreast of *"updated content delivery model approaches"*, and to continue *"identifying key issues and applying appropriate changes"* (Lisichenko, 2015:161). Building on the findings of the fieldwork excursion, further applications of VR learning experiences in our university are occurring in:

+ financial planning courses, where case scenarios have been filmed as role plays, and students engage as either the financial planner or the client. The intention of the learning activity is for students to identity environmental cues as triggers that may impact a consultation (empathy);

+ office field trips that offer students in situ experience of a modern best-practice financial planning office (immersion);

+ international law, where students gain a sense of the gravity of legal decisions that manifest in incarceration in a prison cell through placing the student inside a prison cell (empathy);

+ deploying filmed case scenarios of stressful workplace situations for business students to gain a sense of work place challenges and calls on the students to deepen their professional identity (empathy, immersion).

Conclusion

VR technology creates a convincing simulation of reality and can trigger both immersion and empathy, which is capable of disrupting the boundaries of traditional education. With this in mind, we predict that the student experience of this course and teaching in the course will yield greater levels of satisfaction than previous iterations of the course. This in turn will be evident in the depth of understanding displayed by students in the assessments evaluated during the course. While it cannot be assumed that the VR excursion could be the sole arbiter of high levels of course achievement, it was anticipated that the opportunity for students to learn in different ways within this course would contribute to higher scores overall.

A learning environment that promotes the development of creativity, innovativeness, and capability for self-directed learning will undoubtedly have a strong flavour of adult learning theory, rather than one of teacher-dominated declarative learning. Students who are active agents in the construction and acquisition of their knowledge, rather than passive recipients of that knowledge from teachers, will achieve greater learning outcomes and realise the relevance and impact to their own lives. The deployment of a VR excursion actively placed the student in the learning environment, promoting ownership of the learning and responsibility for active learning. In an age where change is the only constant, exploiting digital technologies such as VR for learning has the potential to engage, enhance, and deepen the learning experience for all students. This small yet significant innovation has provided impetus for teaching staff to extend their teaching repertoire to include andragogical prospects to engage students in a university course through a novel and captivating manner.

About the Authors

Christopher Klopper is deputy dean (learning and teaching) for the Arts, Education and Law Group, Griffith University, Australia. He can be contacted at this e-mail: c.klopper@griffith.edu.au

Malcolm Burt is a senior educational media producer at Griffith University, Australia. He is also undertaking a PhD that seeks to define the ultimate virtual reality experience. He can be contacted at this e-mail: m.burt@griffith.edu.au

Bibliography

Adams Becker, S.; M. Cummins; A. Davis; A. Freeman; C. Hall Giesinger & V. Ananthanarayanan (2017). NMC Horizon Report: 2017 Higher Education Edition. Austin, Texas: The New Media Consortium.

Banerjee, P. (2007). Virtual Reality Simulations. *Anesthesiology clinics*, Vol. 25, No. 2, pp. 337–348.

Campbell, J. (2008). *The hero with a thousand faces*. New World Library: Novato.

Christou, C. (2010). Virtual Reality in Education. In A. Tzanavari & N. Tsapatsoulis (Eds.), *Affective, Interactive and Cognitive Methods for E-Learning Design: Creating an Optimal Education Experience*, PA: Hershey, pp. 228–243.

Collins, J. W. & N. P. O' Brien (2011). *The Greenwood Dictionary of Education*. Online resource: http://ebookcentral.proquest.com.ezp01.library.qut.edu.au/lib/qut/detail.action?docID=729876. [Accessed on 27 April 2017].

Defanti, A. (2016). Using augmented and virtual reality to bring your geography classes to life. Interaction, Vol. 44, No. 3, pp. 43–46.

Economist (2016). *The difference between virtual and augmented reality*. Online resource: http://www.economist.com/blogs/economistexplains/2016/04/economistexplains-8 [Accessed on 27 April 2017].

Grigorovici, D. (2001). Affectively Engaged: Affect and Arousal Routes of Entertainment Virtual Reality. In *Proceedings of the Seventh International Conference on Virtual Systems and Multimedia* (VSMM '01), p. 634.

Hui, L.; Z. Yunmin & D. Yuhong (2012). The Research of Oil Extraction Engineering Based on Virtual Reality. *AASRI Procedia*, Vol. 1, pp. 189–195.

Lisichenko, R. (2015). Issues surrounding the use of virtual reality in geographic education. *The Geography Teacher*, Vol. 12, No.4, pp. 159–166.

Marquis, J. (2012). *Building social skills and literacy through gaming*. Online resource: http://www.onlineuniversities.com/blog/2012/04/building-social-skills-and-literacy-through-gaming/ [Accessed on 28 April 2017].

Morie, J. F. (2006). Virtual reality, immersion and the unforgettable experience. In A. J. Woods; N. A. Dodgson; J. O. Merritt; M. T. Bolas & I. E. McDowall (Eds.), *Stereoscopic Displays and Virtual Reality Systems XIII*.

Oblinger, D. (2012). *Game Changers: Education and Information Technologies*. Louiseville, CO: Educause.

Oculus.com (2016). *Introduction to Best Practices*: Online resource: https://developer3.oculus.com/documentation/intro-vr/latest/concepts/bp_intro/ [Accessed on 27 April 2017].

Pieters, R.; K. Koelemeijer & H. Roest (1995). Assimilation processes in service satisfaction formation. *International Journal of Service Industry Management*, Vol. 6, No. 3, pp. 17–33.

Pine, B. J. & H. G. James (1998). Welcome to the experience economy. *Harvard Business Review*, Vol. 76, pp. 97–105.

Rauschnabel, P. A.; A. Brem & Y. Ro (2015). *Augmented Reality Smart Glasses: Definition, Conceptual Insights, and Managerial Importance*. The University of Michigan-Dearborn, College of Business.

Rüppel, U. & K. Schatz (2011). Designing a BIM-based serious game for fire safety evacuation simulations. *Advanced Engineering Informatics*, Vol. 25, No. 4, pp. 600–611.

Sala, N. (2016). Virtual reality education: Overview across different disciplines. In D. Choi; A. Dailey-Herbert & J. Estes (Eds.), *Emerging tools and applications of virtual reality in education*. Hershey: IGI Global.

Sampaio, A. Z. & O. P. Martins (2014). The application of virtual reality technology in the construction of bridges: The cantilever and incremental launching methods. *Automation in Construction*, Vol. 37, pp. 58–67.

Shulman, L. S. (1987). Knowledge and teaching: Foundations of the new reform. *Harvard Educational Review*, Vol. 57, pp, 1–22.

Tarr, M. J. & W. H. Warren (2002). Virtual reality in behavioral neuroscience and beyond. *Nature Neuroscience*, Vol. 5, pp. 1089–1092.

Verschure, P. F. (2011). Neuroscience, virtual reality and neurorehabilitation: Brain repair as a validation of brain theory. In *Annual International Conference of the IEEE Engineering in Medicine and Biology Society*, pp. 2254–2257.

Younger, D. (2016). *Theme Park Design and the Art of Themed Entertainment*. United States: Inklingwood Press.

Section 4: Simulation

Chapter 16

Stimulating Critical Thinking Through Simulation

Amanda Louw, Christopher Dawson, Amanda Andrews and
Bernie St. Aubyn

Introduction to Critical Thinking and Simulation

As well as passing on factual knowledge, higher education needs to prepare students to fulfil all sorts of active professional roles. In addition to a thoroughly developed repertoire of specific skills, such real-life roles frequently demand further abilities – to engage effectively alongside others in existing practices whilst thinking critically about them, to make quick decisions under pressure, and to build collective learning from shared experiences. These higher-order cognitive abilities cannot be effectively developed in lectures and tutorials, but require hands-on experience. The increasing use of simulations has resulted partly from the arrival of new technologies that make these strategies more practical to use in professional training contexts. The need for their much wider application is made evident by a range of general social and theoretical changes that have taken place over the last century and that are now placing ever more urgent pressures on the whole field of higher education worldwide.

The impact of these changes on teaching practices can be brought out by considering the various literatures drawn together by Schatzki (2012:13–14) as *"practice theory"*. Philosophers influenced by Heidegger or Wittgenstein, sociologists and anthropologists such as Bourdieu and Giddens, as well as other writers in fields such as psychology all emphasise three common themes regarding human practices that Schatzki (2012) identifies:

+ Practices are social in the sense that they involve many individuals behaving in an organised manner together;

+ Individual actions, and even our very thoughts, are coloured by and depend on the practices we participate in;

- We are so thoroughly immersed in our practices that it makes no sense to think of individuals as separate subjects trying to understand an objective world.

While these ideas are far from new, their direct application to classroom practice in higher education has yet to be completely followed through. We cannot think of ourselves as trying to educate each student in isolation, and, from the student's point of view, the input from any one teacher means little until it is brought into a collaborative practical context.

The need to address the embedding of learning in a practical context has long been recognised (Bonwell & Eison, 1991; Gallo, 1994), and simulations are one tool that has been used to try to get students actively engaged together in their learning. Hopwood *et al.* (2016) aim to provide what they call a "socio-material" theoretical underpinning specifically for this use of simulation in adult education. They identify the importance of setting up physical circumstances that allow for multiple interpretations, where learning arises from what *emerges* as a result of many people participating together. This kind of learning cannot take place in lectures, tutorials, traditional fully guided group projects, essays, or online quizzes. It requires the challenge of genuine decisions, with consequences, that the participants must make together, and the freedom to explore unanticipated approaches and negotiate collective responsibility.

In this kind of simulated situation, there is a need for critical thinking to emerge. When there is no one right answer and a pressing problem must be faced in a group, everyone's ideas tend to be welcomed and critically discussed. From Brookfield's (2012) extensive study of critical thinking in adult students, he was able to identify five frequently repeated themes:

- "critical thinking is a social learning process";

- "it is important for teachers to model the process for students";

- "critical thinking is best understood when grounded in very specific events or experiences";

- critical thinking is triggered by "having to deal with an unexpected event";

- "learning critical thinking needs to be incrementally sequenced".

The chapters in this section of the anthology explore a whole spectrum of ways in which students can be confronted with the kinds of unexpected events from which critical thinking can emerge and how the learning processes involved can be modelled and structured. Given the importance of critical thinking in education, educators should be developing teaching methods that foster this ability.

A nurse's approach to critical thinking is believed to affect the accuracy of the nursing assessment with a direct link to patient care and outcomes (Paans *et al.*, 2012). It is believed that using simulation can simultaneously provide the students with an opportunity for training and promote their critical thinking skills. Simulation has been part of nursing education practice and has appeared in the past 40 years (Nehring & Lashley, 2009). It aims to replace and amplify real experiences with guided ones, which are often immersive in nature. These experiences evoke or replicate substantial aspects of the real word in a fully interactive fashion. The underpinning literature values the benefits of this technique, which include enhanced problem solving and decision-making skills, enhanced interpersonal and communication skills (with a positive effect on team working), and enhanced technical and functional expertise (Moyer, 2016). Simulation-based learning can be the way to develop health professionals' knowledge, skills, and attitudes whilst protecting patients from unnecessary risk (Lateef, 2010).

It is not surprising, given the nature of the nursing role, that this teaching technique is well documented as a successful method of nurse education (Adib-Hajbaghery & Sharifi, 2016). In Chapter 17, Andrews and St. Aubyn demonstrate this in relation to the skill of record-keeping in nursing. Record-keeping is an essential aspect of nursing practice; however, it is not always afforded the time and inclusion in essential nursing care that it requires. They illustrate how, by using a low-fidelity (low-cost, minimal resources) simulation strategy, the importance of accurate record-keeping can be instilled in the clinical practice and in the attitudes of nursing students.

An example of a high-fidelity simulation strategy is offered by Louw in Chapter 18 on inter-professional simulation training, involving the medical imaging, emergency medical care, nursing, and medical professions. With the use of sophisticated artificial patient simulators in a highly authentic setting, and supported by knowledge and skills embedded in the long-term memory of medical imaging students, she illustrates how, without the explicit involvement of the facilitator, students come to insights such as the importance of the specific roles of healthcare team members, and the need for prioritisation and multi-level communication.

Although simulation techniques have been most often described in the healthcare education literature, Lateef (2010) describes simulation as a technique for practice and learning that can be applied to many different disciplines, and, in higher education, simulations are being used in various educational courses to reach a variety of learning outcomes. In addition to the applications already highlighted, Dawson describes in Chapter 19 the use of a political hierarchical structure to stimulate creative thinking and the use of the English language among students from diverse language backgrounds. The political and business interactions simulated in that course were not even directly relevant to the material being taught but were chosen purely because they allowed students to engage in the kinds of interaction that would stimulate their full creative involvement in the process of developing the language skills they required.

Together, these three chapters illustrate the role of simulation training in terms of its capabilities to incorporate real-world situations and familiar concepts in unfamiliar or stress-laden contexts to enhance students' critical thinking proficiencies in a variety of educational settings. We demonstrate that simulation training is not, as might be inferred from the available literature, applicable only to health sciences education, but that it is also a valuable teaching strategy in language education. Furthermore, simulation strategies can be tailored to pursue specific learning outcomes that target higher cognitive skills such as critical thinking, teamwork, and multi-level communication. Simulations in education are not necessarily resource bound and can be conducted either in high-fidelity settings, which are highly effective but restrictive in terms of the resources needed, or in low-fidelity settings, which are less costly and therefore more easily achievable but can be somewhat less authentic. The achievement of learning outcomes is, however, similar in both high- and low-fidelity settings (Hoadley, 2009).

This section of three chapters aims to demonstrate the use of simulation practices to stimulate critical thinking that is both effective and transferable to the wider educational landscape. The authors in this section come from a range of professional backgrounds but have in common their use of simulation practices to improve their students' learning experiences and develop their critical thinking and other higher-order cognitive skills as they become proficient in their chosen fields. In all three cases, students were presented with a challenging situation: the pressure of justifying oneself in a courtroom, the need to prioritise patient care, and the task of creating an original project with minimal guidance. The learning outcomes targeted in each of the three cases forced the students to work together collaboratively and creatively and to apply previously acquired knowledge and skills in a novel setting. This resulted in vivid social learning experiences that produced new knowledge through the full engagement of all the students.

About the Authors

Dr Amanda Louw is an educator in the Department of Medical Imaging and Radiation Sciences, Faculty of Health Sciences, University of Johannesburg, South Africa. She can be contacted at this e-mail: amandal@ uj.ac.za

Dr Chris Dawson is a lecturer in English language at Lugano University (*Università della Svizzera italiana*) and adjunct professor of philosophy at Franklin University, Switzerland. He can be contacted at this e-mail: dawsonc@usi.ch

Amanda Andrews is a senior teaching fellow in nursing at the School of Professional Practice at Birmingham City University and is a qualified registered nurse. She can be contacted at this e-mail: amanda.andrews@ bcu.ac.uk

Bernie St. Aubyn is a senior lecturer in nursing at Birmingham City University and has also worked as a registered nurse, registered midwife, and a registered health visitor. She can be contacted at this e-mail: bernie. st.aubyn@bcu.ac.uk

Bibliography

Adib-Hajbaghery, M. & N. Sharifi (2016). Effect of simulation training on the development of nurses and nursing students' critical thinking: A systematic literature review. *Nurse Education Today*, Vol. 50, pp. 17–24.

Bonwell, C. C. & J. A. Eison (1991). *Active Learning: Creating excitement in the classroom*. Washington DC: Association for the Study of Higher Education ERIC Clearinghouse on Higher Education.

Brookfield, S. D. (2012). *Teaching for Critical Thinking: Tools and techniques to help students question their assumptions*. San Francisco: Jossey-Bass.

Gallo, D. (1994). Educating for Empathy, Reason and Imagination. In K. S. Walters (Ed.) *Re-Thinking Reason: New perspectives in critical thinking*. Albany: State University of New York Press.

Hoadley, T. A. (2009). Learning advanced cardiac life support: a comparison study of the effects of low- and high-fidelity simulation. *Nursing Education Perspectives*, Vol. 30, pp. 91–95.

Hopwood, N.; D. Rooney; D. Boud & M. Kelly (2016). Simulation in Higher Education: A sociomaterial view. *Educational Philosophy and Theory*, Vol. 48, No. 2, pp. 165–178.

Lateef, F. (2010). Simulation-based learning: Just like the real thing. *Journal of Emergencies, Trauma, and Shock*, Vol. 3, No. 4, pp. 348–352.

Moyer, S. M. (2016). Large group simulation: Using combined teaching strategies to connect classroom and clinical learning. *Teaching and Learning in Nursing*, Vol. 11, No. 2, pp. 67–73.

Nehring, W. M. & F. R. Lashley (2009). Nursing simulation: A review of the last 40 years. *Simulation & Gaming*, Vol. 40, No. 4, pp. 528–552.

Paans, W.; W. Sermeus; R. M. B. Nieweg; W. P. Krijnen & C. P. van der Schans (2012). Do knowledge, knowledge sources and reasoning skills affect the accuracy of nursing diagnoses? a randomised study. *BMC Nursing*, Vol. 11, Article 11.

Schatzki, T. R. (2012). A Primer on Practices. In J. Higgs; R. Barnett; S. Billett; M. Hutchings & F. Trede (Eds.), *Practice-based education: perspectives and strategies*, Rotterdam: Sense, pp. 13–26.

Sinclair, B & K. Ferguson (2009). Integrating simulated teaching/learning strategies in undergraduate nursing education. *International Journal of Nursing Education Scholarship*, Vol. 6, pp 1–11.

Chapter 17

Court-Proofing Professional Records – An Innovative Simulation Teaching Resource

Amanda Andrews and Bernie St. Aubyn

Introduction

This chapter contributes to the book *New Innovations in Teaching and Learning in Higher Education* as it outlines an innovative simulation teaching resource used to educate student nurses about record-keeping. Record-keeping skills are essential in order to produce court-proof professional records. Court-proof records promote communication between professionals, demonstrate that evidence-based practice had been used, and provide robust evidence to defend the care provided. They would be written in a clear and logical fashion acceptable to the legal profession. Many health professionals report that they have never been formally taught how to write records. It is not surprising then that more than 66% of practitioners report inconsistencies in their report writing. Most say that they have learned "on the job", and 61% say that reading other workers' records has been a significant influence (St. Aubyn & Andrews, 2012). Policies on record-keeping are not considered particularly helpful and include general statements on the requirement to be accurate, relevant, and concise. These are viewed as meaningless without the use of practical examples (St. Aubyn & Andrews, 2012).

In an ideal world, no healthcare practitioner should have to go to court, but when this happens it can be a daunting and stressful experience. In any court environment, the only tangible evidence a practitioner has to defend their practice is their records. Record-keeping can be seen as a "dry" topic and readily lends itself to innovation in order to deliver this topic in a memorable and engaging way. The simulation of the high-risk and problematic area of a courtroom setting focuses students as to the importance of their records and the consequences if they fail to maintain them properly. A major benefit of simulation is that it provides an active learning environment, whereby students are free to make mistakes and learn from them (Durham & Alden, 2008).

Professional nurse education in the United Kingdom (UK) takes place within higher education institutes (HEIs) and is validated by the Nursing and Midwifery Council (NMC). Nurses are trained to a graduate level and need to be able to care for patients with evermore complex needs within cost-constrained, continuously evolving healthcare settings. Healthcare is delivered in a litigious environment, and nurses are increasingly being held to account for the standards of their records (Andrews & St. Aubyn, 2015). Poor records are often reflective of poor practice, and this link is often exploited in cases of legal proceedings, professional accountability, and patient complaints to the detriment of the nurse in the witness box.

Nurse training is a three-year programme, and the topic of record-keeping is threaded through the course. In year one, the principles of good record-keeping are taught and linked to the NMC code (2015). The session outlined in this chapter is part of the year-two programme. This session takes place after students have experienced hands-on patient care and have had a chance to write and use patients' records. In year three, before the students qualify and become registered nurses, there is a consolidation record-keeping session. Reading the chapter, you will gain at least three important insights:

1. the challenges faced by nurse educators in their bid to prepare student for the ever-changing diverse role of the nurse;

2. the relevant learning theories underpinning the didactic behaviourist approach versus a simulation constructivist approach to learning;

3. the courtroom simulation approach used to facilitate student nurses to write court-proof records.

We have structured our chapter in four main sections. In section one, we present the background for our use of simulation in our teaching and learning. Section two presents the simulation in use. In section three, we present and discuss the outcomes of our innovative teaching and learning practice. And in section four, we very briefly touch upon our way forward from here.

Section 1: The Background

Graduate nurses now need to achieve a higher level of skills, competencies, and attitudes in order to meet the demands of contemporary nursing practice, clinical reasoning, and decision-making (Lambie, 2015). Unfortunately, current undergraduate nursing curricula have attracted criticism for failing to adequately prepare nurses for the continually changing demands of healthcare services (Moyer, 2016). This could be attributed to the fast-paced changes within healthcare settings and clinical practice and the failure of educational institutions to keep up with it. Graduates will be better equipped to respond to the changing face of nursing by having the qualities of "graduateness" (Stacey *et al.*, 2012). These are outlined as the ability to research, analyse and present information coherently. The impetus to continue learning and its application to a wide range of subjects is also a mark of a graduate (Stacey *et al.*, 2012). This resonates with the more recent work of Moyer (2016), who considers how students use their knowledge to think critically and problem-solve in the clinical setting. These are essential elements in the provision of safe and competent patient care. The courtroom simulation session enhances the student's ability to deal with information coherently, problem-solve, and apply the principles of record-keeping in a safe learning environment – the hallmarks of a graduate.

There is a global call for change in professional education to ensure the application of evidence-based theoretical learning is relevant to the clinical context (Duff *et al.*, 2014). This requires educators to shift from teacher-centred, lecturer-focused programmes to a student-centred active learning approach (Moyer, 2016). Student-centred strategies for educational change not only have the dual purpose of being cost-effective and efficient, they also create students who have the required critical thinking and decision-making skills (Della Ratta, 2015). Moreover, adopting these strategies has a positive impact on student engagement, leading to higher levels of student retention (Zepke *et al.*, 2006). Traditional teacher-dependent methods are criticised as being inadequate. In particular, they are seen to fall short in terms of developing advanced thinking skills that can effectively incorporate theory into practice and trigger positive innovation (Oztuk *et al.*, 2008). The courtroom simulation affords the students the opportunity to practice and develop the high-level critical skills needed to enable them to deliver safe and competent patient care.

The literature contrasts these two diametric methodologies under the broad headings of behaviourist and constructivist approaches (Johnson *et al.*, 2009; Horsfall *et al.*, 2012; Sadler, 2012).

In nurse education, the behaviourist approach has the benefit of giving structure to both the educational process and the students' experiences. It has traditionally been favoured in HEIs because it works for the large group numbers and is a cost-effective way of giving large amounts of information to the most students. The focus on the achievement of learning outcomes and clinical competencies ensures that students are fit for professional practice (Mackintosh-Franklin, 2016). However, the constructivist approach, where the educator is attempting to change the students' worldview or thinking, encourages students to interact and share their own experiences and knowledge (JISC, 2016). This pedagogy has implications for the nature of knowledge. Information is not a fixed construct, and as such the delivery of knowledge can no longer be linear from educator to student. Knowledge is increasingly both socially and personally constructed and as such needs to reflect authentic real-life situations and experiences. The courtroom simulation is constructivist *by design* to engage the students within an emotionally charged situation – a situated approach to learning that promotes learning within an authentic context. The use of a situated approach has been proven to be very relevant in courses leading to a professional qualification such as nursing (JISC, 2016).

Proponents of student-centred learning such as Hockings (2009) explore the potential for it to replace the more traditional pedagogies, and Allan (2010) suggests that a paradigm shift in nursing pedagogy is essential. Students need to be placed at the centre of the educational process, enabling them to move from passive recipients of knowledge to fuller engagement in the educational process, through the development of autonomy, empowerment, and skills for lifelong learning (Duff *et al.*, 2014).

Simulation provides real-life interactive experiences (Moyer, 2016). It encourages active participation from the students and allows them to construct knowledge, develop skills, and explore their own assumptions and feelings in a safe environment (Sinclair & Ferguson, 2009). Seropian (2003) states that simulation mimics reality and that the learning is further enhanced when the simulation seems realistic.

Section 2: The Practice

Our simulation provides an opportunity for students to observe and/or participate in a courtroom scenario in a safe and protected environment. Before the simulation session takes place, the students are reminded of the principles of record-keeping taught in year one and asked to remember the key points. They are then asked to look at a set of notes in groups of five and highlight the areas that demonstrate poor record-keeping. The students are given time to do this exercise but are not forewarned as to what comes next. They are recalled by a gavel being banged and welcomed to the "coroner's court". The "coroner" outlines the rules and behaviour expected within the court. The students will be randomly selected to stand up, introduce themselves to the "barrister", and be prepared to answer questions relating to the records they have already reviewed. They are reminded that they should not "perjure" themselves and that they will be held in "contempt of court" if their behaviour falls short of the standard expected of a professional in this situation. This all helps to enhance the authenticity of the experience as well as raising the tension, thereby prompting their engagement. The students stand up in a "witness box" and answer questions posed in a manner akin to a court-room setting. The rest of the students in the session are asked to observe their colleague in the witness box and give constructive feedback about the witness' demeanour and ability to defend their record. The barrister and coroner remain in role and are required to modify their approach and questions in relation to the student's ability and/or answers. The facilitators thus "model the process" for the students and set the tone for the interactions. There is "timeout" built in the process to allow all participants in the courtroom to ask contemporaneous questions and clarify any issues (e.g., if a student perjures themselves by fabricating information or demonstrates unprofessional behaviour). The appropriate use of humour throughout the process enhances the interaction (e.g., the "faultometer" – a buzzer that is pressed when the student is blatantly lying!).

The whole structure of this simulation aims to produce nurses who are critical thinkers. Brookfield (2012) identified five themes in his study of critical thinking in adult students. Critical thinking is a social learning process, and this is demonstrated by the simulation taking place within a group of students where they are all participants in the learning. It is important for teachers to model the process for the students, and this is done organically by the facilitators in the simulation by assuming and maintaining their different roles. Brookfield (2012) postulates that critical thinking is best understood when grounded in very specific events. The novelty of the courtroom setting is a memorable and specific event in the students' training programme. It is thought that critical thinking is triggered by having to deal with an unexpected event. In this simulation, the students' focus is switched abruptly from a classroom exercise to a mock-up court within one session! Finally, the process of critical thinking should be incrementally sequenced. Record-keeping is threaded throughout the three-year nursing training programme in a logical staged approach to embed the knowledge.

Preparation

- If possible, a courtroom setting to include a witness box. A desk and chair would suffice.

- A gavel and sound block.

- A copy of the patient's records for participating students to defend. These include common errors noted by the NMC (e.g., failure to identify the patient correctly).

- A copy of the NMC Code (2015) and suggested witness questions relating to the patient's record.

The time for each simulation would be approximately 10 minutes per witness, with eight witnesses being questioned in the simulated courtroom in relation to the records. This leaves 40 minutes for debriefing and feedback (Total: two-hour session).

Role	Descriptor
Witness	The witness/nurse will be required to familiarise themselves with the scenario and the notes provided. After being sworn-in, they will answer questions to the best of their ability from the notes, remembering that they are under oath.
Barrister	The barrister will put relevant questions to the witness to clarify the information included in the records.
Coroner/Judge in charge of the court proceedings	The coroner/judge will keep order and add to the gravitas of the proceedings.
Members of the public	The members of the public observe and give constructive feedback.

Table 1: Roles of participants.

Section 3: The Outcome

Simulation allows students to experience how much easier it is to rebut allegations when supported by well-written, factual, court-proof records and is resonant of the need for them to be able to analyse and present information coherently. However, the process can be costly, and this could pose a barrier to its implementation. Sharpnack and Madigan (2012) describe an approach called low-fidelity simulation. The resources involved are cost-effective, requiring a limited amount of faculty resources, but the students are still engaged in a real-life situation. This helps the students to transfer their learning smoothly into practice (Moyer, 2016).

After the simulation, time is factored in for the students to have the opportunity to:

- reflect on and practice the skills required to produce "court-proof" records. They will then be able to write records that are defendable in court and appreciate the importance of applying the principles of good record-keeping.

- identify poor practice and experience first-hand how records are dealt with in court within the legal process. They will then be aware of the consequences of producing poor records and take remedial action to improve the standard of their own records.

· discuss the feelings and emotions they experienced. This debriefing facilitates consolidation of their learning and enhances their reflective practice skills.

Points for Consideration

Ensure the environment is safe and allows for students to feel able to make mistakes without undue ridicule and destructive criticism. This simulation should promote students' confidence and adopt a positive approach with constructive feedback.

The students learn the importance of keeping records in accordance with taught principles and adherence to professional codes.

Student-Focused Outcomes

The simulation engages and focuses the students in a very interactive way. Using Kirkpatrick's (2006) four level evaluation model, step one considers how well the students like the learning process. The feedback from the students is consistently good and this is supported by positive comments on the university's social media sites. For example,

"Really enjoyed the record-keeping session within the module – very informative and interactive – makes you think."

"These sessions were both scary and instructive – I will really pay attention to numbers, names, dates and times in my records from now on!"

Step two of the evaluation model looks at the extent to which the learners gain knowledge and skills. This is tested in the summative assessment associated with the model that requires the students to construct a plan of care adhering to the taught principles of record-keeping. However, despite being able to academically assess their learning, it is hard to definitively evaluate the outcome of this simulation from the students' perspective in terms of how they apply these record-keeping skills in clinical practice. Step three looks at whether there were any behavioural changes as a result of the learning. This behavioural change would manifest itself within the students' clinical placement and definitive evaluation would require joint audits/research with the governance departments of our NHS partner organisations. Step four considers the tangible results of the learning process. This would be evidenced by an overall improvement in the standard of record-keeping in the nursing profession. Strategically a measure of this would be a reduction in the number of nurses being removed by the NMC from the nursing register due to poor record-keeping.

Section 4: Moving Forward

Our record-keeping campaign does not end here! In line with advancing technology, there is a need for the creation of an online interactive resource. The resource will be aimed at healthcare partners as part of the mandatory training for all staff. There is also a place for the production of an individual learning resource/app for use in the clinical setting.

Conclusion

The philosophy of our court-proofing professional records simulated teaching resource is coterminous with the prevailing Birmingham City University teaching and learning strategy. This advocates a move away from traditional didactic teaching to a more customised method of learning to accommodate the documented trends of learning styles across different generations (McCrindle & Wolfinger, 2010). It also resonates with the global call for change in professional education to sacrifice the "sacred cow" (Duff et al., 2014) in educational practice and examine new strategies to promote independent lifelong learning, critical reasoning, and critical questioning, essential qualities of graduate nurses.

About the Authors

Amanda Andrews is a senior teaching fellow in nursing at the School of Professional Practice at Birmingham City University and is a qualified registered nurse. She can be contacted at this e-mail: amanda.andrews@bcu.ac.uk

Bernie St. Aubyn is a senior lecturer in nursing at Birmingham City University and has also worked as a registered nurse, registered midwife, and a registered health visitor. She can be contacted at this e-mail: bernie. st.aubyn@bcu.ac.uk

Bibliography

Allen, S. (2010). The revolution of nursing pedagogy: a transformational process. *Teach. Learn. Nurse*, Vol. 5, pp. 33–38.

Andrews, A. & B. St. Aubyn, (2015) When you choose nursing, you also choose the law. *Journal of General Practice Nursing*, Vol. 1, No. 4, pp. 56–58

Brookfield, S. D. (2012). *Teaching for Critical Thinking: Tools and techniques to help Students question their assumptions*. San Francisco: Jossey-Bass.

Della Ratta, C. B. (2015). Flipping the classroom with team based learning in undergraduate nursing education. *Nurse Educator*, Vol. 4, No. 2, pp. 71–74.

Duff, B.; G. Gardner & S. Osborne (2014). An integrated educational model for continuing nurse education. *Nurse Education Today*. Vol. 34, pp. 104–111.

Durham, C.F. & K. R. Alden (2008). Enhancing patient safety in nursing education through patient simulation. Online Resource: http://www.ncbi. nlm.nih.gov/books/NBK2628/ [Accessed 12 May 2017].

Hockings, C. (2009). Researching the students that student-centred learning cannot reach. *British Educational Research Journal*, Vol. 35, No. 1, pp. 83–98.

Horsfall, J.; M. Cleary, M & G. E. Hunt (2012). Developing a pedagogy for nursing teaching-learning. *Nurse Education Today*, Vol. 32, No. 8, pp. 930–933.

JISC (2016). Curriculum design and support for online learning. Online Resource: https://www.jisc.ac.uk/guides/curriculum-design-and-support-for-online-learning/behaviourist-approaches [Accessed 12 May 2017].

Johnson, A.; R. Kimball; B. Melendez; L. Myers; K. Rhea & B. Travis (2009). Breaking with tradition: preparing faculty in a student-centred or problem solving environment. *Primus*, Vol. 19, No. 2, pp. 146–160.

Kirkpatrick, D. & J. Kirkpatrick (2006). Evaluating *Training Programs: The Four Levels*, (3rd Ed.). San Francisco: Berrett-Koehler Publishers, Inc.

Lambie, A.; K. Schwend & A. Scholl (2015). Utilisation of the Nursing Process to Foster Clinical Reasoning during a Simulated Experience. Online Resource: http://journals.sagepub.com/doi/10.1177/2158244015617516 [Accessed 12 May 2017].

Mackintosh-Franklin, C. (2016). Pedagogical principles underpinning undergraduate Nurse Education in the UK: A review. *Nurse Education Today*, Vol. 40, pp. 118–122.

McCrindle, M. & E. Wolfinger (2010). *The ABC of XYZ: Understanding the Global Generations*. Sydney: University of New South Wales Press.

Moyer, S. M. (2016). Large group simulation: Using combined teaching strategies to connect classroom and critical learning. *Teaching and Learning in Nursing*, Vol. 11, pp. 67–73.

Nursing & Midwifery Council (2015) *The Code*. Online Resource: https://www.nmc.org.uk/standards/code/read-the-code-online/ [Accessed on 12 May 2017].

Oztuk, C.; G. K. Muslu & A. Dicle (2008). A comparison of problem based and traditional education on nursing students' critical thinking dispositions. *Nurse Education Today*, Vol. 28, pp. 627–632.

Sadler, I. (2012). The Challenges for new academics in adopting student-centred approaches to teaching. *Student Higher Education*, Vol. 37, No. 6, pp. 731–745.

Seropian, M. A. (2003). General concepts in full scale simulation: Getting started. *Anesthesia & Analgesia*, Vol 97, pp. 1695–1705.

Sharpnack, P. A. & E. A. Madigan (2012). Using low fidelity simulation with sophomore nursing students in the baccalaureate nursing programme. *Nursing Education Perspectives*, Vol. 33, No. 4, pp. 264–268.

Sinclair, B. & K. Ferguson (2009). Integrating simulated teaching/learning strategies in undergraduate nursing education. *International Journal of Nursing Education Scholarship*, Vol. 6, pp. 1–11.

Stacey, G.; J. McGarry; A. Aubeeluck; H. Bull; C. Simpson; F. Sheppard & S. Thompson (2014). An integrated educational model for graduate entry nursing curriculum design. *Nurse Education Today*, Vol. 34, pp. 145–149.

St. Aubyn, B. & A. Andrews (2012). *Documentation in Developing Healthcare through simulation* (Aldridge and Wanless Eds). London: Sage.

Zepke, N; L. Leach & T. Prebble (2006). Being Learner-centred: One Way To Improve Student Retention? *The Student Higher Education*, Vol. 31, No. 5, pp. 587–600.

Chapter 18

High-Fidelity Simulation-Based Training in Radiography

Amanda Louw

Introduction

This chapter contributes to the book *New Innovations in Teaching and Learning in Higher Education* as I introduce high-fidelity simulation-based training (SBT) of radiography students as a complementary teaching strategy to the pedagogical toolkit of educators. I define high-fidelity SBT in a health education context as the use of highly realistic, but artificial, representations of real-world clinical scenarios to achieve specific educational outcomes by means of experiential learning. The simulation experience (SimX) used to collect data for this chapter entailed a fully equipped casualty department in a hospital with high-fidelity patient simulators, a full staff complement, a family member, functional heart rate monitors, and appropriate additional sound effects. The combination of all these components provided an authentic clinical setting fit for experiential learning, which is the process whereby students learn and create new knowledge by linking new experiences to existing knowledge and understanding through the deliberate practice of reflection (Kolb, 2015).

SBT as an experiential learning approach allows students to acquire clinical skills that encompass procedural skills, underlying basic knowledge, and clinical reasoning as well as communication skills through deliberate practice, by making mistakes, repeating actions, and learning from the process without the risk of harming real-life patients (Al-Elq, 2010; Berndt, 2010; Michels *et al.*, 2012; Friederichs *et al.*, 2014). The benefits of deliberate practice as a key component of achieving learning outcomes in the health sciences is extensively documented, and SBT is widely used in medicine and nursing education to complement traditional teaching and to make the transition from classroom to clinical practice as smooth and effective as possible (Ericsson, 2004; Rosen, 2008; McGaghie *et al.*, 2010; Berragan, 2011; Buckley & Gordon, 2011; Friederichs *et al.*, 2014).

High-fidelity SBT in the radiography domain is however a relatively novel concept, judged by the scarcity of literature on its specific applications for undergraduate radiography students. As result, the work described here was based mostly on personal experience of what could work, combined with a good dose of creativity and guided by literature from the nursing and medical domains. The focus of this chapter is an interprofessional simulation scenario that was specifically designed to stimulate higher-order skills such as critical thinking, multilevel communication, teamwork, and prioritisation in a stress-loaded multi-case scenario. When reading this chapter, you will gain the following three insights:

1) the planning and preparation implicit to a high-fidelity SimX;

2) enactment of the SimX;

3) the importance of a debriefing session to guide reflection and consolidate the learning that took place (often subconsciously) during the SimX (Konia & Yao, 2013).

The chapter is subdivided into three main sections. In the first section, the conventional educational strategies mostly used in teaching radiography students, together with the shortcomings thereof, are outlined. In section 2, the planning and enactment stages of the SimX are discussed, while section 3 concludes with a reflection on the debriefing session and the four themes that emerged from it.

Section 1: The Background

In undergraduate diagnostic radiography training, learning outcomes entail the application of knowledge about routine radiographic procedures on uninjured persons who can follow instructions and achieve and maintain specific positions to real-life scenarios with injured patients. These injured patients often pose communication challenges and may present with unique physical complications to be solved in order to obtain X-ray images that allow accurate interpretation and subsequent effective patient management and care.

At the University of Johannesburg (UJ) in South Africa, conventional textbook teaching and learning in terms of the clinical skills required of radiographers is supplemented with various approaches such as role play, digital radiographic practice programmes, and the use of skeletons and a full body articulating phantom, broadly a mannequin with a skeleton inside and human tissue density surrounding it. These techniques all contribute to layered learning (Colding, n.d.) through the embedding of knowledge and understanding from diverse angles and at different levels. The variety of approaches accommodates students' differing preferences in terms of the visual, auditory, reading, writing, and kinaesthetic modalities of learning and is essential to enhance their academic and clinical performance (Murphy *et al.*, 2004). Whether used in isolation or combined, these techniques fail however to present students with the problem-solving opportunities in authentic real-life settings that they need to become mentally prepared and skilful in problem solving to function effectively and efficiently in stressful non-routine casualty, trauma, and ward settings.

Students are enrolled in a system of work-integrated learning (WIL) (CHE, 2011), which entails them rotating through academic blocks at university and clinical blocks in hospitals. During their clinical blocks, they engage in X-ray imaging that has the potential to damage human tissue (Goodman, 2010), and it is therefore ethically imperative that they are suitably prepared to image patients with minimal risk and optimal benefit. Harm to patients as a by-product of experiential training can only be justified once measures to minimise the risk thereto are in place (Ziv *et al.*, 2006). In terms of training through a WIL arrangement, this entails sufficient opportunity to practice clinical skills and professional competence prior to engaging with patients in real clinical settings.

The potential to address the void in the learning experience of radiography students and bridge the gap between academic learning and real-life clinical application in problem-posing scenarios, presented itself in 2014 with the inauguration of a modern simulation laboratory complex that included authentic trauma and ward settings equipped with high-fidelity simulation props, manikins, and sophisticated patient simulators in the Faculty of Health Sciences at UJ. It became possible to devise SimXs to promote the progressive achievement of specific learning outcomes indicated by the undergraduate curriculum without subjecting real-life patients to possible mistakes made as a result of experiential learning.

Previously, students would be taught specific procedures in an academic context, but the clinical application thereof largely depended on the case-mix presentation encountered at hospitals during the students' clinical blocks. As hospitals do not always offer the same services in terms of trauma, orthopaedic surgery, oncology, etc., the clinical presentation of patients did not necessarily expose all students to all aspects of the curriculum, resulting in non-standardised learning experiences for students, which could, in some instances, impact negatively on patient management.

From the bioethical perspectives of *first do no harm* and *justice* (referring to the distribution of resources, risks, and benefits), such a situation leads to a number of ethical dilemmas in healthcare education. Firstly, it negates the moral obligation of educators to provide their students with the best possible learning experiences (Ziv *et al.*, 2006) to ensure that they become fit for practice, referring to radiography students' ability to provide optimal patient imaging and care. Secondly, it implies that some students might get less comprehensive exposure to clinical cases with resultant diminished opportunity to become clinically proficient, introducing the dimension of inequity and discrimination into the educational programme. Lastly, both these dilemmas may result in a lessened ability to provide optimum imaging and care to the comprehensive patient cohort. By introducing SBT as a complementary didactic strategy to the training toolkit of radiography educators locally at UJ and globally to all radiography training institutions, the reliance on vulnerable patients as training commodities can however be greatly reduced while the future radiography workforce can be trained in an ethically enhanced manner, displaying an awareness of socially accountable pedagogy.

Section 2: The Practice

The availability of authentic simulation facilities at UJ offered novel and unfamiliar possibilities of learning enhancement. Initially, the various prospects were explored and the best ways of utilising the different facets of the facility to bridge the gap between theoretical teaching and the application of knowledge and understanding to solve problems were identified. With these lessons learnt, attention recently turned to interprofessional SBT with the focus on casualty, trauma, and ward-based patients presented in high-fidelity settings to engage students in authentic clinical surroundings with as many of its associated challenges as is possible.

2a. A General Introduction to the Innovative Practice

Inter-professional training is vital due to the need for effective health-care teams (Gough *et al.*, 2012), and especially in trauma scenarios, radiography often has a central role in the effective early management of patients (Brown *et al.*, 2016). Apart from achieving clinical competence with regard to specific skills, interprofessional trauma training also stimulates and enhances professional competence, which is defined as the full range of everyday activities in a radiographer's life, such as interaction with the public and health team colleagues, critical thinking, judgement, and reflection. Recent research indicates that it also improves perceptions of the roles and responsibilities of other members of the healthcare team, even after only limited exposure, and that students feel more prepared to face major trauma situations once they have been involved in multidisciplinary trauma simulations (Alinier *et al.*, 2014). In addition, students also appear to have clearer perceptions of their own roles once they are exposed to multidisciplinary training. The combination of all these outcomes thus suggests an enhanced readiness for clinical practice (Brown *et al.*, 2016).

2b. The Curriculum

In order to enhance all-round professional competence, scenarios are created to expose students to the following learning elements:

- patients with different injuries and/or diseases that necessitate the adaptation of routine textbook teaching to accommodate the limitations of each patient while still obtaining X-ray images of high diagnostic value. Such scenarios require students to develop competencies such as problem identification, analysis, and decision-making;

- patients in casualty, trauma, and ward settings that imply the need for effective interprofessional demeanour, communication, and teamwork skills;

+ settings where students need to function without supervision as part of the medical team responsible for the care of a patient. These scenarios require students to venture into even higher cognitive levels such as critical thinking, judgement, prioritisation, and management.

The additional goal with the SimX, which is the focus of this chapter, was to obtain students' perceptions after their first participation in an interprofessional high-fidelity simulation experience that involved chest, elbow, and suspected non-accidental trauma.

2c. Organisation of the Practice

In line with literature, which indicates the need for a pre-SimX refresher lecture on the educational content earmarked for the SimX (Koo *et al.*, 2014; Piette *et al.*, 2015), students were given various opportunities to revise and master the prerequisite knowledge and skills. This strategy is based on the cognitive load theory (van Merriënboer & Sweller, 2011), which indicates that a person's working memory has limited capacity when dealing with new information but no known limits when dealing with information stored in long-term memory. For problem-solving scenarios that involve advanced cognitive resources, it is thus important to prepare students sufficiently by ensuring that an extensive knowledge base is stored in their long-term memory to be available for easy retrieval and application, thus enabling their working memory to be concerned with solving problems and learning in the process (Fraser *et al.*, 2015).

The build-up to the actual SimX was a three-step process, commencing weeks before the exercise. Four weeks prior, knowledge and skills concerning chest and elbow imaging were revised and new knowledge about suspected non-accidental trauma pertaining to paediatric patients was introduced in a class context, supporting synchronous learning. Three weeks prior, allowing for asynchronous learning, students received a tutorial guide through BlackBoard, indicating relevant reading and video material in preparation for small group forum discussions in separate cubicles.

The forum discussions, which are valuable platforms for social learning, took place one week prior to the SimX. Students were presented with worksheets consisting of questions and problems based on the

BlackBoard material, which were further aided and stimulated by a range of X-ray images posted onto large monitors in each cubicle. The purpose was to test knowledge and initiate group discussions while the facilitator rotated through the cubicles to assist and guide thought processes. Students were encouraged to use their textbooks and electronic devices with the available Wi-Fi to assist them in answering the questions and debating the problems.

Towards the end of such a session, students are always invited to step up to the control room and give feedback via the general communication system on sets of questions and problems, while the facilitator guides the feedback and ensures that answers are correct. During the first session of this kind, students are often hesitant to volunteer, intimidated by the possibility that they may err in front of their classmates, but as the facilitator guides them in a supportive manner, the feedback component soon becomes a favourite part of the tutorial and one that students compete for.

Forum discussions are limited to a 45-minute period and 10 groups of five students can comfortably be accommodated in the cubicle venue. Time must be managed well, but as students get used to this tutorial format, surprisingly much learning takes place in the limited time frame. As result of the tutorial, the three weeks' preparation time, and the range of learning opportunities that facilitated knowledge scaffolding, the students were considered ready for the actual SimX.

Five days prior to the SimX, 10 students volunteered (on a rotational basis) to participate in the experience. They were invited to the simulation complex where they familiarised themselves with the specific setting resembling a casualty department in a small hospital. They received a scenario sheet (Box 1) that listed the roles they had to fulfil as well as the fictitious location of the planned scenario, the equipment and accessories available, and the time frame for the different components of the SimX. They also received an aim and objectives indicator (Box 2) for the SimX. Pre-briefing is done to stimulate long-term memory and minimise stress and anxiety on SimX day that may negatively affect learning. For this scenario, four groupings were required: four critical observers, two nurses, one family member, and three student radiographers. The students decided among themselves who would fulfil which roles and had time to think about the challenges the specific setting might pose.

On the day of the SimX, the groups were separated from each other into different venues. The four critical observers went to the casualty setting where they were positioned in the four corners of the venue so as not to intrude on the activities. Each received an observer guide (Box 3) to focus their observations and allow them to take the lead during the reflective session at the end of the SimX. The two nurses also went to the casualty setting, where they were introduced to the "medical doctor" of the day, a role played by one of the emergency medical care educators. The family member went to an ambulance simulation area, where he met the child patient, Baby Amee (SimBabyTM), and a paramedic student. The three student radiographers waited in the reception area of a fictitious X-ray department together with a mobile X-ray unit.

To enhance the authenticity of the SimX, one of the nurses phoned the X-ray department from casualty and requested chest and elbow imaging to be done in the casualty department. To maintain the element of impromptu critical thinking and problem solving, the X-ray request form (Box 4) for the 38-week-pregnant adult female patient with respiratory distress symptoms, Mrs Bebee (SimMom®), was handed to the student radiographers only once they arrived with the mobile unit in the casualty department. The pregnant status of the patient introduced a problem, as the general rule is to avoid X-ray imaging of pregnant patients. However, the students decided to proceed with the request.

Halfway through the imaging procedure, the facilitator signalled the ambulance setting, and the paramedic student wheeled a crying baby in, followed by a distressed father figure. The dynamics changed instantly with the paramedic handing the case over to a nurse, the baby's condition deteriorating, the nurse calling on the doctor who was busy attending to another patient, and the father being in the way of everyone. After a quick clinical examination, the doctor ordered an immediate chest X-ray on Baby Amee (Box 5). This facet introduced a dilemma to the student radiographers and necessitated the need for prioritisation, as both patients were simultaneously in need of urgent imaging that would determine their immediate management. At first, they proceeded with Mrs Bebee, but as they were increasingly pressured to image Baby Amee, they eventually left the adult's elbow imaging incomplete and started with the baby.

While busy with baby Amee, the chest image of Mrs Bebee was

projected on a screen and indicated the presence of a tension pneumo-thorax, a potentially fatal condition if not managed immediately. This challenged the students to apply their image interpretation knowledge, make a judgement decision, and communicate their finding to the doctor. In response, the doctor decompressed Mrs Bebee's chest and immediately requested a post-decompression follow-up chest X-ray.

By this time, some of Mrs Bebee's elbow images and Baby Amee's chest image were displayed. The students firstly recognised an elbow frac-ture for Mrs Bebee and thereafter several rib fractures for the baby. The picture archiving and communication system (PACS) employed in the hospital recognised and displayed images of the baby's lower extremi-ties that were done 10 days earlier. These images demonstrated peculiar injuries that usually relate to non-accidental trauma in children and chal-lenged the students to correlate the current injuries with the previous injuries, come to a conclusion, make a judgement decision, and commu-nicate their finding to the doctor in charge. Mrs Bebee's follow-up chest imaging was subsequently performed, and the final image displayed a successfully decompressed chest.

The student radiographers tidied up and left the casualty department 20 minutes after they first responded to the telephone call – a realistic time frame for a similar real-life setting. Once the sound effects of the heart rate monitors were muted and the stress-laden ambience settled down, all 10 students resumed their real-life student radiographer capaci-ties and gathered to discuss the X-ray images and how they had been interpreted. This was done specifically for the benefit of the "critical observers" and "father", who were not in close vicinity when the imaging team and "nurses" viewed and interpreted the images during the scenario.

One of the objectives of high-fidelity SBT is to provide students in healthcare with problem-solving opportunities in stressful, non-routine, and highly authentic real-life settings to allow them to become mentally prepared and skilful in problem solving in similar real-life situations. For this scenario, fidelity was enhanced by the presence and active involve-ment of a doctor, paramedic, two nurses, and a family member, among patient simulators, as well as the audible sounds of heart rate monitors and a telephone. The female patient simulator was visibly breathing and made vocal sounds from time to time. Even before the baby simulator entered the casualty department, her crying was audible (a cell phone in the baby's nappy played a YouTube video of a crying baby) and once inside, her crying was never-ending. The crying sounds combined with the visible breathing movements of the baby, the constant interference of the father, the interaction between the doctor, nurses, and student radiographers, and the intermittently ringing phone elevated the scenario to real-life.

Despite the added cognitive load that the multi-case scenario presented, the imaging team performed well. Radiographic procedures were executed to an acceptable level by the three students. They realised that even though imaging is contraindicated on pregnant patients, the patient was in her third trimester which rendered ionising radiation to the foetus less damaging and that the patient's respiratory distress symptoms justified imaging. They appeared flustered when the baby arrived and they were needed in two places at the same time, and during the debriefing session they admitted that they had never before been in a multi-case situation where they had to prioritise between patients. After initial hesitance, they did leave the adult and attended to the baby's chest X-ray, which appeared to be crucial at the time.

Both the radiographers and the nurses immediately recognised the tension-pneumothorax and its life-threatening impact on the adult patient's chest image and immediately brought it to the attention of the doctor, thus being cognisant of their ethical responsibility in terms of beneficence towards the patient and effective teamwork towards patient management. The two groups also recognised the fractures on the baby's chest image and realised, once they correlated it with previous images, that the injuries are indicative of non-accidental trauma (child abuse). They reported their notion to the doctor in charge, again being ethically responsible and committed to a team effort regarding optimal patient care. Both groups furthermore recognised the signs of a fracture in the adult patient's elbow and also communicated that to the doctor.

Scenario sheet 6/3/17 (Box 1)
Roles to be filled by 2nd year diagnostic radiography students (DIPO1Y1):
- 3 x 2nd year radiography students;
- 2 x nurses;
- 1 x family member;
- 4 x critical observers.

Scenario setting:
- casualty unit in a hospital in the Free State;
- 3 am on a Sunday morning;
- 2 patients in need of imaging;
- no radiologist available.

Equipment and accessories:
- mobile CR x-ray unit;
- 1 x 18x24 CR cassette;
- 1 x 24x30 CR cassette;
- 2 x 35x43 CR cassettes;
- 2 x full lead rubber aprons;
- 1 x lead rubber strip;
- sponges;
- anatomical lead letters;
- images done two weeks ago on one of the patients are available.

Image presentation:
- all images are in digital format and will be displayed when indicated.

SimX schedule:
- 10:30: SimX team receives request forms and learning outcomes;
- 10:40: SimX start;
- 10:40-11:00: Radiography students perform the requested imaging and nurses and family member take up their roles. Four observers are positioned each in a corner to observe the happenings and take notes for discussion during the reflection session;
- 11:00-11:20: Image interpretation session;
- 11:20-11:50: Critical reflection;
- 11:50 12:05: SimX feedback.

Figure 1: Scenario sheet (Box 1).

Aims & objectives indicator (Box 2)

This tutorial aims to introduce you to the imaging of patients in a casualty/trauma context with regard to chest and elbow requests.

The objectives are:

- to familiarize you with the casualty/trauma context;

- to allow you the opportunity to become familiar with protocols in a Casualty department;

- to allow you the opportunity to communicate with other members of the health care team on a professional level;

- to allow you to apply your knowledge of radiation safe protocols;

- to prompt you to be aware of the bioethical principles and how they are integrated into everyday imaging;

- to allow you the opportunity to critically assess the given scenario, make appropriate decisions, and adapt routine text book projections to suit the condition and presentation of the patient;

- to allow you to apply your image interpretation knowledge in a setting devoid of radiologists;

- to introduce you to the practice of critical reflection in order to consolidate the learning that took place through the tutorial.

Assessment of the knowledge, skills and attitudes implicit to this tutorial will firstly be on a formative basis and thereafter by means of written tests, OSCEs and practical assessments in the clinical practice setting.

Figure 2: Aims and objectives indicators (Box 2).

Observers' guide (Box 3)

Your role in the SimX is of the utmost importance, as it is envisaged that you will be leading the reflective session – in other words, you will prompt discussions on the happenings by making either a positive or a negative statement, where after all 10 members of the team will join in the discussion. You thus have to be alert to all that is happening during the scenario. It might be helpful to take some concise notes.

The following SimX objectives should guide you in your observations:

Appropriate adaptation of routine text book projections: cases 1 & 2

Radiographic technique: cases 1 & 2

Professional communication: cases 1 & 2

Radiation safety protocols: cases 1 & 2

Image evaluation: cases 1 & 2

Image interpretation: cases 1 & 2

Awareness and management of ethical responsibilities: cases 1 & 2

All over professional competence:

Additional notes:

Many thanks for your contribution!

Figure 3: Observer's guide (Box 3).

Mrs Bebee X-ray request (Box 4)   *Baby Amee X-ray request (Box 5)*

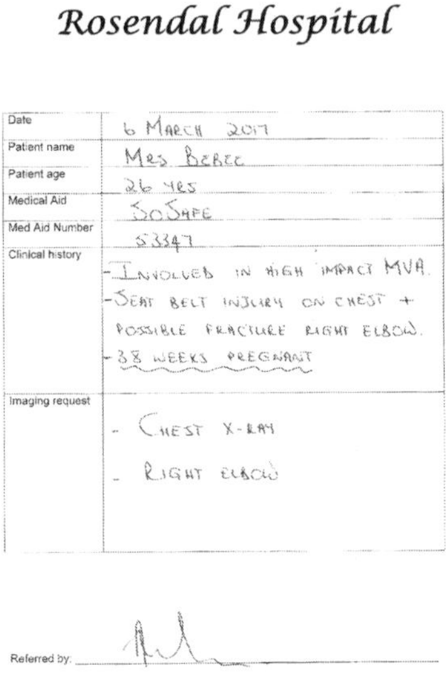

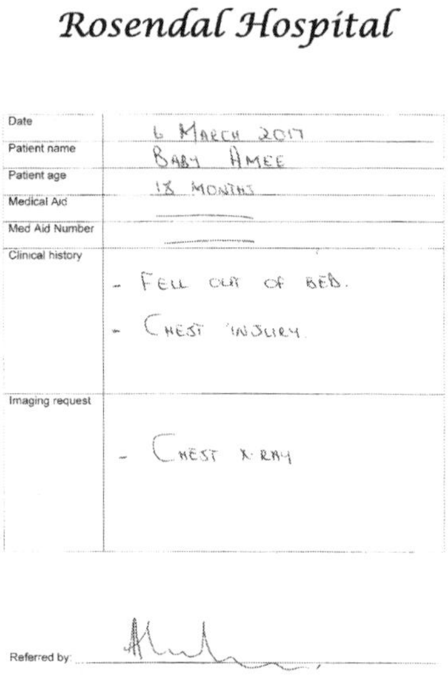

Rosendal Hospital   Rosendal Hospital

Date	6 MARCH 2017
Patient name	MRS BEBEE
Patient age	26 YRS
Medical Aid	SOSAFE
Med Aid Number	53347
Clinical history	-INVOLVED IN HIGH IMPACT MVA. -SEAT BELT INJURY ON CHEST + POSSIBLE FRACTURE RIGHT ELBOW. -38 WEEKS PREGNANT
Imaging request	- CHEST X-RAY - RIGHT ELBOW

Referred by: _____

Date	6 MARCH 2017
Patient name	BABY AMEE
Patient age	18 MONTHS
Medical Aid	
Med Aid Number	
Clinical history	- FELL OUT OF BED. - CHEST INJURY
Imaging request	- CHEST X-RAY

Referred by: _____

Figure 4: X-ray request (Box 4).   *Figure 5: X-ray request (Box 5).*

Needs in Sim Complex, 6/3/17, 09:45 – 12:00. (Box 6)

Venues:

Casualty room + X-ray room + Ambulance room

Manikins:

- 1 patient simulator (SimMom°), female, 26 yrs, 38 weeks pregnant, moulaged to resemble chest & rib injuries (both right & left), + elbow injury. No spinal injuries. Breathing and voice please;
- 1 intercostal drain – to be inserted to decompress tension pneumothorax;
- 1 pediatric patient, 18 months old (SimBaby™) moulaged to resemble (S)NAT. Fresh chest bruises/injuries + signs of old cigarette bud burns on body and various bruises. Breathing and crying please;
- 2 additional patients, on respirators/drips/monitors – these are just to add to the cognitive load, especially in terms of sound effects.

Equipment –

- mobile x-ray unit;
- cassettes – 35x43 & 24x30;
- lead rubber apron;
- image projector;
- electrical extension cord;
- 12 chairs for debriefing session.

Actors –

- 1 Doctor;
- 1 Paramedic.

Figure 6: Needs in sim complex (Box 6).

2d. Preparation

SimXs need ample preparation:

- firstly, to decide what knowledge, skills, and attitudes of the syllabus to target;

- thereafter, choices must be made with regard to scenario selection and design, as the SimX should be aligned with the curriculum and its overall learning objectives;

- the scenario "script", including all its elements, must be formulated;

- preparatory knowledge transfer concerning revision, new knowledge, electronic learning opportunities and tutorials must be planned;

- all supporting documentation must be formulated;

- digital X-ray images applicable to the scenario must be sourced and prepared;

- the debriefing stage must be planned; and

- the simulation laboratory and requirements for the day must be booked (Box 6).

The simulation laboratory complex that was utilised for the SimX consists of various venues of which four were used for this particular experience. The preparatory forum discussions were conducted in a room that consists of a master venue with ten separate student cubicles, each with its own desk surface, five chairs, and a large high-resolution monitor. An eleventh cubicle is equipped as a control room with a public address system, closed-circuit television monitors, and a computer, from where the facilitator can post X-ray images or relevant digital material on the student cubicle monitors, view the students in their cubicles and communicate with them through an individual or general communication system.

The second venue was altered to fit the setting of a casualty department. It is equipped with paediatric cribs, child and adult patient beds, fully functioning patient monitors, oxygen, and suction apparatus. Three patient simulators, resembling an adult male (SimMan 3G®), a pregnant female (SimMom®), and an adolescent, each with a range of realistic simulation functions, filled the beds. The pregnant female was made up (moulaged) to have a bleeding laceration on her chin and severe bruises on her chest and right elbow. Equipment to project pre-selected digital X-ray images in a large format is also available. A third venue served the setting of an X-ray department equipped with a telephone, computer radiography (CR) mobile X-ray unit, CR cassettes, lead rubber aprons, immobilisation sponges, and anatomical letters. The fourth venue authentically resembled an ambulance and was occupied by an 18-month-old patient simulator (SimBabyTM), moulaged to have various cigarette burns and bruises all over her body.

Section 3: The Outcome

The debriefing process that followed immediately after the SimX allowed the students to verbalise and analyse their thought processes and actions during the simulation. This reflective practice is vital because it develops new insights and shapes future performance as a result of the lessons learnt through the experience (Kolb, 2015). Debriefing is also an ideal mode of formative assessment whereby the facilitator can shape students' knowledge, skills, and attitudes by providing constructive feedback. It furthermore encourages the development of students' professional identity, as the learning conversations provide the opportunity for social interaction on professional matters (Rudolph et al., 2008).

3a. Student Perspective

As this was the first interprofessional SimX I developed, I was interested in the true and novel reactions of the students on the exercise. Therefore, in order to prevent bias resulting from my own expectations that were shaped by literature, I asked the critical observers to lead the debriefing process, using the SimX objectives listed in the observers' guide (Box 3). Initially, they were unsure and hesitant and stuck to comments on the basic radiographic skills, but as everyone relaxed, they pointed out higher-order mistakes and successes, such as prioritisation and communication, to which the three student radiographers reacted spontaneously. Of interest is that the radiographers did not try to justify their reactions but rather explained their thought processes. As all 10 participants were student radiographers, they related well to the explanations and all took part in the enthusiastic discussions that followed. From the debriefing session, which lasted 30 minutes, four definitive themes emerged: prioritisation, communication, healthcare team roles, and situational and mental preparedness.

Prioritisation

When an observer commented that the radiographers did not immediately adhere to the request for the baby's chest imaging but proceeded with the adult's less serious elbow imaging, the responses were:

+ *"I was not sure if we could, if we could not, as I have never been in that situation before."*

+ *"I thought we would look incompetent, running all over ..."*

These thoughts opened the floor, and all 10 students voiced their opinions, focusing on different aspects of prioritisation. It became clear that none of them had been put into a position before where they had to make decisions about which patient to attend to first. In this respect, the SimX was successful, as it sensitised the students to the advanced cognitive function of prioritisation:

+ *"... now I know the importance of decision-making ... I will think about a decision ... what should be done first."*

Communication

Two observers commended the radiographers for their calm communication with the nurses, doctor, and baby's father, but the radiographers spontaneously admitted that they neglected to communicate with their patients:

+ *"... the communication, we do like, forget ..."*

+ *"... you just think, you don't explain to the patient ..."*

The discussion that followed suggested that the concept of professional communication with other healthcare colleagues is embedded in the long-term memory of the students and therefore happened automatically, while the practice of patient communication, which is vital for instruction, to obtain information, and to transfer empathy and care, was less embedded and thus neglected when the cognitive stress load increased.

Healthcare team roles

The two students who acted as nurses spontaneously stated that they realised for the first time under how much pressure nurses and doctors in a casualty setting are under, as they are continuously responsible for the well-being of the patients, while radiographers only provide a service during a short encounter.

+ *"This scenario made me appreciate other people's professions ... the nurses have a lot on their shoulders ..."*

+ *"... the doctor ... with them also there is a lot of stress, ... new patient, patient after patient."*

Other students' comments echoed these sentiments and the general consensus was that all are healthcare workers and therefore should join forces for the well-being of the patient:

+ *"Next time ... when the doctor is busy with the patient I will think to give her the lead apron to carry on with her work – this is something I was never thinking of before."*

The multiprofessional dimension of the SimX thus constituted an interprofessional awareness and the realisation that everyone who attends to a patient, despite having different foci, is part of the healthcare team and should be respected for his/her role and expertise.

+ *"In practice, a lot of the time you go by yourself (to perform imaging) ... This (SimX) actually taught you to work with more radiographers, with the nurses, with the doctor.... under that specific pressure, you know, you can't just stand by yourself, you need to put trust in other people."*

Reflecting specifically on radiographer performance during the SimX, the students realised that they would have been more efficient as an imaging team if they decided beforehand on specific responsibilities for each person:

+ *"... if you have three people then you can say, hold on, somebody must take care of sterilising, making sure everyone wears gloves ..."*

The concluding remark of the in-depth discussion on teamwork, pertaining to both the imaging team and the general healthcare team, was:

+ *"If everybody does their job well, then everything will go well ... focus on what YOU have to do ... just make sure you do your thing well ..."*

Situational and mental preparedness

The value of the SimX in terms of future situational and mental preparedness emerged as follows:

+ *"Just the fact that we had a situation with one patient versus the next would help us. Like now, we kind of learnt what to do. We've seen what – like – most people (in the team) think about it."*

+ *"These things happen for real. If you are not used to such scenarios, you always gonna be chilled .... The reality is we need patients like this to prepare you mentally."*

+ *"I've learnt to calm down, be focused and prioritise."*

+ *"... leave the emotions outside. Relax, so that you can also think what you are doing."*

+ *"... apply our knowledge, what we have learnt in school, to real life – this is what I have learnt."*

These comments about future preparedness indicate that the students have interconnected the problems they have encountered during the SimX with their responses towards it; they analysed it through open discussion in a safe space with those who were involved, and they came to relevant and valid conclusions and wisdoms that will affect their future actions in real-life scenarios positively.

3b. Teacher Perspective

This interprofessional high-fidelity SBT strategy incorporated various pedagogical theories and approaches and entailed much planning and coordination. The outcome was however worth all the effort and energy, as it yielded positive results and some unexpected successes.

My concern that those who did not participate as student radiographers might not benefit optimally from the SimX was proven invalid by the lively and participatory discussions during the debriefing session. Reflecting in a team context and analysing the various actions and future alternatives provided all participants with enhanced insights that they would not have acquired otherwise.

- *"I loved the realistic vibe of the situation. I enjoyed being exposed to new situations. I enjoyed that we were able to provide feedback and learn other people's thoughts."*

- *"I must say the actual SimX was extremely fantastic. Sometimes it is more interesting to put things into practice and live in the moment."*

- *"I have benefited tremendously on this SimX; it was such an eye opener – an insight of the real world in our chosen profession."*

Of note was the effect of the smaller, more personal context of the SimX on student performance. Three students, known to be quiet and subdued in a class context, emerged as a confident leader, actor, and communicator, respectively, and contributed much to the learning that took place. These characteristics might never have materialised in the conventional class context, and I consider it as an unexpected SimX outcome and one to be further explored to assist in realising the hidden potential of all students.

Another unforeseen and most significant achievement of the SimX and subsequent reflective debriefing process is the fact that it also addressed the "hidden curriculum" of all education – that of the awakening and development of a professional identity, attitude, and sense of responsibility among the students.

As an educator, this training intervention reminded me again that students, when given explicit guidance in various formats to scaffold supportive knowledge and skills and embed it into their long-term memory, will create their own knowledge once they have the opportunity to reflect, analyse, and make sense of their actions and attitudes.

Section 4: Moving Forward

The SimX discussed in this chapter was video recorded with the aim of using it for further research and educational purposes. Firstly, as only 10 students out of a class of 80 could, for logistical reasons, participate in the SimX, I aim to screen the video for the rest of the class and allow them to also reflect, albeit indirectly, on the performance of the SimX team members. The objectives are twofold:

- to explore whether the students who were not directly involved in the SimX identify the same themes during their discussions; and

- to correlate knowledge retention between the two cohorts at similar time intervals after direct or indirect involvement with the simulation.

The results of these objectives will indicate whether videos of SimXs can be used as BlackBoard postings to enhance problem-solving abilities and stimulate critical thinking in students. The incorporation of the nursing, medical, and paramedical disciplines into a radiographic SimX was novel to both the students and I (the facilitator). However, the outcomes in terms of professional awareness and the need for general healthcare team cohesion suggest, and even insist, that similar interprofessional SimXs should be pursued and taken to an advanced level. Although the past SimX involved the dimensions of other disciplines, it was only of benefit to the radiography cohort. Future interprofessional simulation scenarios will be created with the full involvement of actual nursing and para-medic students to ensure the learning that emerges through the reflective debriefing process benefits all traditional healthcare students at UJ.

Conclusion

All the individual components of the teaching and learning strategy described in this chapter are well known and widely used. The specific combination and in particular the extensive application of the cognitive load theory afford it the status of a new and innovative approach to radi-ography education at the University of Johannesburg in South Africa. Through the preceding scaffolding of knowledge by means of various modes over an extended time period, and catering for different learning preferences, the learning outcomes (i.e., awareness and enhancement of critical thinking, multilevel communication, teamwork, and prioritisation) were achieved.

The concluding debriefing session offered students the opportunity to create their own knowledge and expertise through the process of reflection, and the social interaction with classmates and the educator on serious professional matters saw the emergence of a professional identity previously indistinct in undergraduate radiography students:

+ *"I learnt that being a medical professional is a steep road because you need to deal with pressure and still do a good job and working as a team is important as in the end we all save lives."*

Whereas SBT was initially introduced as a complementary teaching strategy, the various outcomes of this SimX constitute it an *essential* strategy in the pedagogical toolkit of all radiography educators, even more so because students enjoy learning through it:

+ *"What I enjoyed is that everything was so realistic and it made us aware of the pressure that comes with casualty situations. It was a great learning experience."*

About the Author

Dr Amanda Louw is an educator in the Department of Medical Imaging and Radiation Sciences, Faculty of Health Sciences, University of Johannesburg, South Africa. She can be contacted at this e-mail: amandal@uj.ac.za

Bibliography

Al-Elq, A. H. (2010). Simulation-based teaching and learning. *Journal of Family and Community Medicine*, Vol. 17, No. 1, pp. 35–40.

Alinier, G.; C. Harwood; P. Harwood; S. Montague; E. Huish & K. Ruparelia (2014). Immersive clinical simulation in undergraduate health care interprofessional education: Knowledge and perceptions. *Clinical Simulation in Nursing*, Vol. 10, No. 4, pp. 205–216.

Berndt, J. (2010). The ethics of simulated nursing clinical experiences. *Teaching and Learning in Nursing*, Vol. 5, pp. 160–163.

Berragan, L. (2011). Simulation: An effective pedagogical approach for nursing? *Nurse Education Today*, Vol. 31, pp. 660–663.

Brown, C. W.; M. Howard & J. Morse (2016). The use of trauma interprofessional simulated education (TIPSE) to enhance role awareness in the emergency department setting. *Journal of Interprofessional Care*, Vol. 30, No. 3, pp. 388–390.

Buckley, T. & C. Gordon (2011). The effectiveness of high fidelity simulation on medical-surgical registered nurses' ability to recognise and respond to clinical emergencies. *Nurse Education Today*, Vol. 31, pp. 716–721.

CHE (Council on Higher Education) (2011). Work Integrated Learning: Good Practice Guide. Online Resource: http://www.che.ac.za/sites/default/files/publications/Higher_Education_Monitor_12.pdf [Accessed on 21 March 2017].

Colding, H. D. (n.d.). Integrating a layered curriculum to facilitate differentiated instruction. Online Resource: http://www.ascd.org/ascd-express/vol3/324-colding.aspx [Accessed on 21 March 2017].

Ericsson, K. A. (2004). Deliberate practice and the acquisition and maintenance of expert performance in medicine and related domains. *Academic Medicine*, Vol. 79, No. 10, pp. S70–S81.

Friederichs, H.; A. Weissenstein; S. Ligges; D. Moller; J. C. Becker & B. Marschall (2014). Combining simulated patients and simulators: pilot study of hybrid simulation in teaching cardiac auscultation. *Advances in Physiology Education*, Vol. 38, No. 4, pp. 343–347.

Fraser, K. L.; P. Ayers & J. Sweller (2015). Cognitive load theory for the design of medical simulations. *Simulation in Healthcare*, Vol. 10, No. 5, pp. 295–307.

Goodman, T. R. (2010). Ionising radiation effects and their risk to humans. Online Resource: http://www.imagewisely.org/~/media/ImageWisely-Files/Imaging-Physicians/IW-Goodman-Ionizing-Radiation-Effects.pdf [Accessed on 6 May 2017].

Gough, S.; M. Hellaby; N. Jones & R. MacKinnon (2012). A review of undergraduate interprofessional simulation-based education (IPSE). *Collegian*, Vol. 19, No. 3, pp. 153–170.

Kolb, D. A. (2015). *Experiential Learning. Experience as the Source of Learning and development* (2nd ed.). New Jersey: Pearson Education, Inc.

Konia, M. & A. Yao (2013). Simulation – a new educational paradigm? *The Journal of Biomedical Research*, Vol. 27, No. 2, pp. 75–80.

Koo, L.; C. Layson-Wolf; N. Brandt; M. Hammersla; S. Idzik; P. T. Rocafort; D. Tran; R. G. Wilkerson & B. Windemuth (2014). Qualitative evaluation of a standardized patient clinical simulation for nurse practitioner and pharmacy students. *Nurse Education in Practice*, Vol. 14, pp. 740–746.

McGaghie, W. C.; S. B. Issenberg; E. R. Petrusa & R. J. Scalese (2010). A critical review of simulation based medical education research: 2003-2009. *Medical Education*, Vol. 44, pp. 50–63.

Michels, M. E. J.; D. E. Evans & G. A. Blok (2012). What is a clinical skill? Searching for order in chaos through a modified Delphi process. *Medical Teacher*, Vol. 34, pp. e573–e581.

Murphy, R. J.; S. A. Gray; S. R. Straja & M. C. Bogert (2004). Student learning preferences and teaching implications. *Journal of Dental Education*, Vol. 68, No.8, pp. 859–866.

Piette, A.; F. Muchirahondo; W. Mangezi; A. Iversen; F. Cowan; M. Dube; H. Grant-Peterkin; R. Araya & M. Abas (2015). Simulation-based learning in psychiatry for undergraduates at the University of Zimbabwe Medical School. *BioMed Central Medical Education*, Vol. 15, No. 23, pp. 1–8.

Rosen, K. R. (2008). The history of medical simulation. *Journal of Critical Care*, Vol. 23, pp. 157–66.

Rudolph, J. W.; R. Simon; D. B. Raemer & W. J. Eppich (2008). Debriefing as formative assessment: Closing performance gaps in medical education. *Academic Emergency Medicine*, Vol. 15, pp. 1010–1016.

Van Merriënboer, J. J. G. & J. Sweller (2010). Cognitive load theory in health professional education: design principles and strategies. *Medical Education*, Vol. 44, pp. 85–93.

Ziv, A.; P. R. Wolpe; S. D. Small & S. Glick (2006). Simulation-based medical education: An ethical imperative. *Simulation in Healthcare*, Vol. 1, No. 4, pp. 252–256.

Chapter 19

A Political Solution to Stimulate Creative Group Work in a Large Class

Christopher Dawson

Introduction

This chapter contributes to the book New Innovations in Teaching and Learning in Higher Education because it describes an innovative teaching structure used successfully in one particular class to stimulate students' creativity, learning, and personal development. The class in question is a second-year undergraduate English language course at the *Università della Svizzera italiana* (Lugano University) called *Inglese settoriale*, compulsory for all students in the faculty of communication sciences (which also offers a degree programme in Italian literature). The students are also learning either French or German, and there are parallel courses for those languages. Although this is a foreign language course, I do not translate the name into English because "Sectorial English" means little, and other alternatives would lose the parallel with the other languages. The "sector" to which the course is specific is not sharply defined, as the students are divided between 90% whose focus is communication – and whose interests and ambitions typically involve sport or fashion journalism, marketing, advertising, or event organising – and 10% who are studying Italian literature and tend to have no interest in any of those other fields. By reading this chapter, you will gain insights into:

1. the challenges presented by trying to stimulate students' individual and collaborative creativity in a large compulsory university class;

2. a structure that has proved successful in tackling those challenges;

3. a critical reflection on the results produced and, then, how the same techniques might be applied elsewhere.

Section 1: The Background

When I was first employed to teach the course (in 2008), I was asked to teach a business English course, but I subsequently moved it closer to the students' real needs by using authentic materials regarding marketing, journalism, and communication. At that time, it was a C1-level language course on the Common European Framework of Reference for Languages (CEFR) (Council of Europe, 2001), and students took a final exam that tested their language ability at that level for internal credits as part of their degree course.

The course was changed as a result of changes to the university's Master's programme. A new rule was introduced that all applicants for Master's courses, including internal applicants, must have an internationally recognised C1 English certificate. This requirement created the need to offer an optional course to prepare students for the Cambridge Advanced English exam, and when that course was introduced, the internal requirement for a C1 exam was dropped. The *Inglese settoriale* course, however, also represents a step between the first-year programme (in which students reach B2 on the CEFR) and a final semester course in culture and writing. Consequently, the course continued, but without a specific aim in terms of language level. It was also made compulsory for all students, where previously students could be exempted if they had a C1 certificate.

I was asked to deliver a course to a class of around 150 students ranging in ability from pre-B2 to proficiency, where the aim was to encourage students to put their language skills into practice in real and realistic contexts, with an emphasis on communication but also including enough stimulation for students of literature. While I had long been a proponent and practitioner of student-centred learning, on this occasion I really had no choice but to invent a new kind of structure. I drew on well-known group work techniques that are widely used in English language teaching, such as the use of a group scribe (Hadfield 1992:124). I was fully expecting considerable resistance on the part of the students, especially those who had not been expecting to be obliged to take an English language course because they already had perfectly good English. In considering how to give value to those students, I took up Packer and Goicoechea's (2000) application of ontological hermeneutics to learning, making use of the idea that learning depends on building identity within a community. I gave the course for the first time in the fall of 2014, and again in the fall semester of 2015 and 2016. There have been small changes across the three sessions of the course, but the essential structure has remained the same, so my description will refer to the course in its final form, as I taught it in 2016.

Section 2: The Practice

2a. A General Introduction – The Course and Its Syllabus

The course involves four main projects, two of which take place in class and two outside of class time. This is done because there are some students who are obliged to do the course but cannot be physically present in class, for a variety of reasons. The assessment structure is very flexible, offering students a choice between a variety of optional elements. A summary is given in Table 1.

PROJECTS		FINAL INTERVIEW	
Project name	*Points available*	*Project quality*	*Presentation performance*
Media monitoring	15	50% of grade awarded for one chosen project, using a rubric.	20% of grade awarded for language use and fluency in an individual interview.
Book report	15		
Debating	15		
Group projects	15		
Occasional activities	10		
30% of grade awarded before the final interview. Any score of 30 or over (out of the possible maximum of 70 points) gets the full 30%, allowing students to choose where to focus their energies.			

Table 1: A summary of the assessment structure of the course.

There is a media monitoring project that takes place entirely out of class and involves writing three reports on a current story in the global press. The other out-of-class project involves choosing a non-fiction book and writing a report about its content, author, and context (extending the notion of self-selected reading in Nation (2014) and Krashen & Mason (2015)). That project can also involve giving a 3-minute presentation about the book to the class. One of the two class sessions each week is devoted to debating skills, and three debates are held during the semester, with systematic work on rhetoric and public speaking in preparation for them. After working on contemporary relevant debates from the US election and from the Oxford Union, the students themselves were invited to suggest and then vote for the motions they wanted to debate. Their preferred topics tended to be either philosophical or flippant: the main debates in 2016 were about "It is important to be irresponsible when you're young" and "Life is empty and meaningless". The part of the course that is the focus of this chapter constitutes the fourth project, also accounting for one 90-minute class session each week, in which students work in groups to develop and complete projects of their own design.

2b. How the Group Work is Organised

The principal aim of the group work is to give students plentiful realistic speaking practice in English. Owing to their experiences on other courses, students tend to be resistant to group work, and there are some well-known problems such as "free riding" and "the sucker effect" (Davies 2009). It is difficult to get people to share the workload evenly, and preventing groups from speaking in Italian, a language they all share, is another challenge. I chose two basic strategies to tackle these problems: structure and freedom. The structure works to make the groups operate effectively without direct supervision, but it also provides a stimulating simulation of political and business interactions. Motivation comes from the freedom of an open-ended task. Students know how much time they have and are simply asked to work together to accomplish something real in that time that they can be proud of.

At the start of the semester, I ask all the students to briefly introduce themselves in writing to the class in a discussion forum on the Moodle platform. They have to mention their hobbies, interests, enthusiasms, and passions. I use what they say to sort them into eight or nine groups of like-minded people. Meanwhile we spend a class session reading and discussing a draft constitution for the political body that the class will become (see

Table 2). This also provides an initial reading and speaking task. Students get the opportunity to propose changes. The structure outlined here is, in a sense, a double simulation: it simulates a political structure, most notably in its superficial reference to constitutionalism, but it is a much closer simulation of the everyday practice of conducting and recording business meetings. The political constitutionalism takes advantage of the diversity of the students, turning what might otherwise be a barrier to effective group work into a strength, while the business skills are likely to be of direct practical relevance once the students graduate.

CONSITUTION of "NO BOUNDARIES"

1 The members of the 'No Boundaries' group (hereinafter referred to as 'the state') shall be all currently matriculated students of USI (*Università della Svizzera italiana*) in their 2nd year or above enrolled on the 'Inglese settoriale 2015' Moodle platform.

2 The language of all communication and interaction whatsoever relating to the organisation, discussion, decision making and implementation of the affairs of the state and its groups shall at all times be English, whether that communication happens inside or outside the classroom or the platform.

3 The facilitator is, and shall remain, Chris Dawson. Within the limits of his ability and power he will implement all final decisions duly submitted to him by the Head of State.

4 The members of each group are to be established in September and will remain unaltered.

5 Each group always includes a President, a Vice-president, a Secretary and a Monitor (together referred to as the Leaders of the group), and a maximum total of fifteen members.

6 Every week there is a new President, Vice-president, Secretary and Monitor, who will be appointed by the facilitator and communicated through the platform.

7 The groups will meet all together in class on a Thursday afternoon. At the same time, the Presidents from each group will all meet together as a Presidential Council. The presidents will start in the council, and there agree when to convene together and when to meet with their groups.

9 The Presidential Council has the same structure as the other groups, with its own President, Vice-president, Secretary and Monitor (each of whom is also President of another group). The President of the Presidential Council is the Head of State (who will be a different person every week).

10 The President is responsible for:

a) Finalizing all decisions of the group

b) Delegating individuals within the group to carry out any actions the group may decide to undertake

c) Ensuring that actions that the group previously delegated to its members have been duly completed or are making appropriate progress, and, if not, re-assigning them as necessary

d) Taking the group's collective opinions and decisions up to the next level. In the case of most groups, this means speaking on behalf of the group in the Presidential Council. In the case of the Head of State, this means taking the whole State's decisions to the facilitator or to the relevant authority (University authorities, City Council, national parliaments, United Nations, etc., as appropriate); all such communications must be posted in their entirety on the platform for the whole community to see

e) Taking the decisions and action points from the Presidential Council back to the group and delegating them to individuals as appropriate

f) Working with the Secretary to set the agenda for each meeting.

11 The Vice-president is responsible for:

a) Organizing any additional group meetings and ensuring that all members (if possible) can and (so far as possible) do attend them, as well as keeping non-participating members involved online and consulting them whenever possible

b) Chairing the meetings, keeping the group to the agenda, ensuring that all business is completed within the time available and that everyone contributes to the group

c) Mediating to resolve any disputes that arise within the group to the satisfaction of all concerned

d) Ensuring that all group and constitutional rules are kept to

e) Organising group members to shift the furniture as quickly and efficiently as possible in preparation for the meeting.

12 The Secretary is responsible for:

a) Working with the President to set the agenda for the meetings, writing up the agenda, ensuring that it is complete, and circulating it to all members of the group in advance of the meeting

b) Taking notes during the meeting and writing up the minutes afterwards to provide a permanent record of what was said and agreed, and, where appropriate, who said what. Minutes must include all action points that are agreed on, with the individuals delegated to carry them out and the deadlines for completing them.

c) Circulating the minutes from the previous meeting at the beginning of each meeting, and drawing attention to the action points they contain for review by the group.

13 The Monitor is responsible for:

a) Listening to all the transactions in the meeting and noticing what languages are used at all times.

b) Encouraging all members of the group to continue to make the effort to speak only in English, even and especially when they get excited or try to explain something difficult.

c) Writing a short report after the meeting about the languages used, stating the circumstances under which individuals felt the need to use languages other than English, and giving credit for successful use of English under difficult circumstances. The report will be posted to the same forum as the minutes.

14 Whenever possible, group decisions should be unanimous, and discussions should be continued where possible until everyone agrees. When an urgent decision is needed and agreement is not reached quickly, or if agreement cannot be reached at all and the group agree to differ, the President should take a vote. In the event of a tied vote, the decision of the President is final and binding on all members of the group.

15 Groups may undertake any projects they collectively choose and design; they are only required to choose a name, mission statement and logo (or representative image), to carry out any actions delegated to them, and to write a Wiki together on the platform. The Wiki text should include an account of the group's experience of the democratic processes of the state, and may also include anything else that the group collectively considers to be of interest or relevance. Everyone in the group can write contributions and edit the Wiki at any time. It is the duty of all group members, whenever anyone does not approve of any text in the Wiki for any reason to remove it and to replace it with something better.

16 Groups are free to make and change their own internal rules. Constitutional change is possible only by the agreement of the entire state. This requires an initial unanimous agreement in the Council of Presidents, which each President must then take back to his or her own group for further discussion. If each group unanimously approves a proposal, or suggests modifications and gives provisional approval, and a further discussion in a subsequent week's Council of Presidents again produces unanimous approval of a single agreed text for the change, then the change comes into force.

Table 2: The constitution.

When the groups meet, they hold a simulation of a business meeting. Four members of the group have named roles: a president, a chair, a secretary, and a monitor. The presidents from each of the groups sit together at first in a council of presidents. That council has the same structure: one of them is the head of state, and then there is a presidential chair, presidential secretary, and presidential monitor (each of whom is also president of one of the groups). The head of state confers with me at the start of class, and I give them specific objectives to achieve. In the first class, the objectives are to discuss and ratify the proposed modifications to the constitution and to select a name for each of the groups. If modifications are proposed to the constitution, I implement them as much as I possibly can: the only non-negotiable element is that the language of all interactions within and between the groups must at all times be English.

The chair in each group is responsible for leading the meeting and making sure that everyone gets an equal opportunity to speak. The secretary takes minutes (I give them a template for this) and posts them afterwards in a group Moodle forum, along with an agenda for the next meeting. The monitor reports back on the group's success in speaking English and notes when people had to look words up or were tempted to use other languages. The roles rotate each week so that everyone gets the chance to play all the roles within the group during the semester, and everyone gets a turn in the presidential council.

The first tasks for the groups are to choose a name, design a logo, and then draw up a mission statement or slogan. This allows them to spend some time getting to know each other and establishing a collective identity before they start to design the project. Around the third week of group work, the head of state passes round the message that each group needs to take on a project, involving as much real-life activity as possible, and state an outcome that they will achieve by the end of the semester. No further instructions are given – the choice of projects is left as open as it can possibly be, which the students find extremely challenging. They are merely encouraged to make good use of the time available, to use their English together, and to "do something as real as possible". The only way they can deal with such an instruction is to make use of the identity they have been constructing together, to get creative, and to listen to one another.

During the meetings, I circulate among the groups, helping them when necessary and noting down how well each person performs the various roles. Towards the end, many groups start to produce English text and I go through it with them before they use it in public. These group meetings take up one of the two weekly classes through the semester. After about ten weeks, the groups present what they've been doing – in a variety of ways, depending on the nature of their projects.

Some students prefer not to get involved with the groups, and the course structure offers them the opportunity to make that decision. The groups usually start with 15 members and end up with an average of 10. The group projects are a popular part of the course, and students keep coming to class (attendance is not required) as their projects build up. At the end of the semester, points are awarded for attending class in the last couple of weeks in order to ensure that there is a large audience for all of the presentations.

2c. Preparations

Apart from writing the draft constitution itself, my principal input on this project consists of establishing the roles within the groups each week. It is crucial to the success of the course that I am lucky enough to be teaching in a room with moveable furniture. The room contains 11 rows of tables, with five three-seater tables in each row. Before the group classes, I re-arrange them (usually with students' help) so that each group has four tables pushed together to form a boardroom table, with six seats along each side and one or two at each end. There is one boardroom table for each group and an extra one for the presidents' council, and they are spaced as far apart as the room will allow so that noise interference is kept to a minimum and so that I can circulate freely among the tables.

Each week the secretary from each group posts minutes of their meeting by Sunday night, and on Monday morning I can look at the minutes to see what happened in all of the meetings. I correct the English in the meeting minutes, and print them out to circulate at the next meeting, adorned with the group's logo and mission statement. I then decide on the roles within each group for the next week and publish the list on the platform (with all of the logos and mission statements on display). I also then print out place markers with logos for each named role with the individual's name and job title, and arrange them smartly on the tables to make the scenario look as business-like as possible.

Most students probably do not care about these details, but there are always some who love to see their name printed smartly next to the word "President". I believe the groups' visual identity makes a major contribution to the success of the projects and of the students' interaction.

Section 3. The Outcome

3a. Teacher Perspective

One of the principal aims of the course is to awaken students' creativity and encourage them to use their language skills for practical purposes. So far, for this course, students have created a wide variety of stimulating and original projects, as listed in Table 3.

EXHIBITIONS
* A poster exhibition about the theme of madness across different art forms.
* An annotated photo gallery of differing concepts of women's beauty around the world.
* An exhibition on the theme of love in *Macbeth, Hamlet, Romeo and Juliet,* and *A Midsummer Night's Dream,* with original artwork and live performances of brief excerpts.

FILMS
* A documentary film about musical styles around the world.
* A comedy film with sketches intercut with demonstrations of traditional dance styles from around the world.
* A film of interviews with students from around the world, presented with statistics about students' backgrounds.
* A film about student life in Lugano.
* A film about different world cuisines, including the preparation of dishes identified by students as typical of their home countries.

BOOKS AND MAGAZINES

- A recipe book for students.
- Glossy magazines containing:
  - reviews of students' favourite films and books;
  - articles about current affairs and issues of general interest;
  - articles of local interest.
- Travel advice in the form of:
  - a booklet about 10 destinations around the world;
  - a live performance of a scene in a travel agent's office;
  - a website showing where famous films were set and shot;
  - an Internet blog with interactive forum;
- A complete marketing campaign for an imaginary event, including a website, magazine, Facebook page, flyers, and a TV ad.

PRESENTATIONS

- A website and social network discussion platform about cultural diversity and minority rights, presented with a moving compilation film and a stirring call to action.
- A presentation about diets and cookery around the world.
- Market research on a series of potential tech products.
- A detailed lecture on the process of brewing beer, featuring an app for rating craft beers and an interview with a local microbrewery (and samples).

SOCIAL ACTIVITY

- An awareness-raising social network campaign about poverty around the world.
- Involvement in the redistribution of waste food from local supermarkets to the poor, with a presentation of relevant facts and figures.
- A winter sports weekend, complete with promotional video and interviews with real-life ice hockey stars.

Table 3: Student projects.

In terms of language learning, since the course no longer measures achievement on the accepted scales, I no longer have any objective basis on which to claim demonstrable success. However, I have two relevant observations. First, the step from B2 to C1 can only be made with extensive practice of productive language skills and oral interaction; this was always a challenge with a more traditional course, since it is not possible while following a coursebook or even working with comprehension of authentic materials to push everyone in a large group to actually spend time speaking and expressing themselves. With this group work, everyone does exactly that.

Secondly, I have been struck by the students' language improvement. I had been testing students orally at C1 level for several years previously, and I have also taught many of the students on this course in their first year, prior to their joining the course, and tested them in an oral exam. I notice a very significant increase in students' speaking confidence and spoken competence in English, both with regard to the level students previously achieved on the more traditional course and with regard to the same students' level of ability earlier in the year. This impression is entirely informal and there are no comparable rubrics on which to check its true extent.

3b. Student Perspective

Feedback for the course from the first two sessions was mixed. In the first session, there were one or two very negative comments, which perhaps resulted from the changes to the regulations that made the course obligatory. There was also an issue with the structure of the course itself, which was too complicated and not sufficiently clear. There were no such strong comments in the second session, but a number of students did still offer some constructive criticism about the course structure, the details of the assessment system, and the way it was presented. By the third session, few verbatim comments were offered along with the feedback scores beyond mentioning the group work under "positive aspects of the course". There, students said that they appreciated "the interaction", "the opportunity to discuss in class", "the opportunity to explore personal interests", and "the freedom of choice carrying forward projects freely and spontaneously". The overall average student rating of the course (out of 10) went from 6.82 in 2014 (11th of 12 comparable courses assessed) to 7.53 in 2015 (5th of 12), and 7.87 in 2016 (3rd of 12).

Nevertheless, in all sessions, a majority of the students were very positive about the course. This showed up in their questionnaire responses, but those who gave positive evaluations did not write much in the way of commentary beyond saying that they really appreciated the group work.

A few said that they had learned a lot from the course, while others (especially in the 2014 version) did not feel they had learned much. I believe this latter group may be divided into those who did not perceive how much they actually were learning because they missed the frontal grammar lessons that they were used to (in which their language skills will not necessarily have improved more quickly) and those who did not put much effort into the course because they did not understand the purpose of it and, consequently, learned little. This is borne out by contradictory feedback comments to the effect that the workload of the course was both too high and too low.

Informally, a number of students have talked to me about the course, saying how much they appreciated having direct control over what happened and how it pushed them to work and learn autonomously. They have also felt free to offer criticism of the details, which has been very helpful. Some of the warmest appreciation of the course I have heard should be disregarded because it was offered during the final exam interviews in which students were being assessed on how much effort they had put into the course.

Section 4. Moving Forward

This course will now change again, as there is a new pressure to prepare students for third-year courses in communication, in research techniques, and in linguistics that are now to be taught in English. This will require a different approach and may make it impractical to continue with such an extensive and open group work component, even though there is enthusiasm from the university authorities for it to continue because it has gained a reputation for being motivating.

I have also replicated a similar structure elsewhere (at a different institution, Franklin University Switzerland), with a much smaller group, for an advanced academic writing course. Four sections of that course have now run, with an average of 12 students in each class. The course is organised around the topic of business ethics, and I set it up in such a way that students work together in groups to co-author a book on that subject, writing one chapter each. The political structure described here was replicated to the extent that sub-groups were established and then held regular business meeting simulations: in this case, they were essentially publishing meetings. Each group had to plan, research, revise, edit, and then physically produce a book. I used the same rotation of roles, in that a different member of the group would be president, chair, and secretary each week. Disputes inevitably arose about roles, deadlines, and responsibilities, which were always smoothly, efficiently, and amicably resolved through this mechanism.

Although this kind of structure will certainly not be suitable for courses in which a large quantity of specific content input needs to be taught and learned, the key features can certainly potentially be replicated in any course whose objective is to develop real professional or technical skills in which students need to develop their judgement, creative thinking, and interpersonal collaboration. There are some basic steps that are necessary in order to employ this kind of technique, some pitfalls to avoid, and some more detailed features that were specific to my actual circumstances. In general, learner autonomy and spoken interaction can be increased by using a structure of this kind to organise groups, with rotating positions of power, that collectively have real control of the course.

The first step is to set up the groups. Care is needed at this stage, as the participants will have to work closely together for a long period. In my experience, the dangers to be avoided at this point include:

- putting students together who are too different and share no common interests;

- putting all the strong students in one group and all the weaker students in another group;

- making the groups too big or too small. Eight to ten participants is a good number.

Secondly, everyone needs to invest emotionally in the group identity, so it is vital to devote class time early on to setting this up. Activities are needed that encourage free thinking about issues the students actually care about, which can lead them to choose group elements such as a name, title, slogan, or logo together. If students perceive this as too artificial or as being imposed on them, there is a risk that some members of the group will lose interest and the others will then feel they are doing too much of the work.

The third step is to set up the roles. The larger the class, the more formal the structure that is needed; a written constitution, explicitly rati-fied by all groups and individuals, allowed a class of 150 to know what to expect and to become sufficiently motivated for all groups to produce a worthwhile project and useful interactions.

+ The role of secretary is perhaps the most important, allowing each of the students in rotation to take responsibility for recording the interaction by writing minutes (which can also be graded).

+ The role of chair is useful for co-ordinating discussions and can also be assessed, providing that students know that a group that interacts effectively, equitably, and productively will earn points for its chairperson, while a group that squabbles, allows one person to dominate, falls quiet too quickly, or gives up and falls apart will not.

+ The role of monitor is useful in the specific context of foreign language learning, especially because it offers an opportunity to report on the specific language difficulties people encounter.

+ The role of president is useful to allow the group to arrive at clear, quick decisions when they disagree, and in a large class a council of presidents can also be a mechanism for guiding the class as a whole without direct interference.

The final stage is to keep the interactions going and lead them to a useful conclusion. This is done partly by setting up the space in a professional way; partly by circulating, monitoring, and helping the groups; and partly by feeding guidance to the council of presidents via the head of state. In each lesson, there is an objective that the council of presidents needs to achieve – a decision to be taken, deadlines to the fixed, etc. – which they feed back to the teacher about at the end of the class period, after having discussed it between the presidents, taken it back to the groups, and then discussed it centrally again.

Conclusion

The principal barrier to using large class simulations in university teaching is the need to deliver specific content to the students. It is a method that can be applied in practical classes where students need to develop academic, critical, or linguistic skills. Theoretical input needs to take place separately. Nevertheless, group work is increasingly prevalent in higher education situations, and students often quickly become resistant to it as a result of predictable bad experiences. A structure of the kind described here can, under the right circumstances, help to ensure that group members buy into a shared project and participate in it equally.

About the Author

Chris Dawson is a lecturer in English language at Lugano University (*Università della Svizzera italiana*) and adjunct professor of philosophy at Franklin University Switzerland. He can be contacted at this e-mail: dawsonc@usi.ch

Bibliography

Council of Europe (2001). *Common European Framework of Reference for Languages: Learning, teaching, assessment*. Cambridge: Cambridge University Press.

Davies, W. M. (2009). Groupwork as a form of assessment: common problems and recommended solutions. *Higher Education*, Vol. 58, No. 4, pp. 563–584.

Hadfield, J. (1992). *Classroom Dynamics*. Oxford: Oxford University Press.

Krashen, S. & B. Mason (2015). Can Second Language Acquirers Reach High Levels of Proficiency Through Self-Selected Reading? An Attempt to Confirm Nation's (2014) Results. *The International Journal of Foreign Language Teaching*, Vol. 10, No. 2, pp. 10–19.

Nation, P. (2014). How much input do you need to learn the most frequent 9,000 words? *Reading in a Foreign Language*, Vol. 26, No. 2, pp. 1–16.

Packer, M. J. & J. Goicoechea (2000). Sociocultural and Constructivist Theories of Learning: Ontology, not just epistemology. *Educational Psychologist*, Vol. 35, No. 4, pp. 227–241.

Section 5: Effective Transformation

Chapter 20

Changing Frames of Reference through Effective Transformation

Daniel Cermak-Sassenrath, Nancy H. Hensel, Kirsten Jack
and Jeff Lewis

Introduction to Effective Transformation

Transformational learning was described by Mezirow (1997) as a process of change that transforms learners' frame of reference. Frames of reference are described as the assumptions we hold that enable us to understand our experiences. As Mezirow (1996:162) suggests, *"learning is understood as the process of using a prior interpretation to construe or revise interpretation of the meaning of one's experience to guide future actions"*. Behaviours, perspectives, and assumptions might change as a consequence of this revision (Cranton, 1992). The ability to change one's assumptions about the world leads us to more reliable and critical beliefs rather than those we might have inherited uncritically from others.

A recent driver for the introduction of a transformative model is the globalisation of education and the adoption of a holistic approach that includes many education designs and strategies (Selander, 2008). To remain responsive to future challenges, students need to be able to synthesise the proliferation of information available through new technologies and objectively evaluate the credibility and reliability of the information. The interaction of focus, synthesis, and creativity can lead to new innovations and knowledge. Potential changes within higher education communities require people to engage in dialogue and work collaboratively.

Pink (2005:1) suggests, *"The future belongs to a very different kind of person with a very different kind of mind – creators and empathizers, pattern recognisers, and meaning makers"*. The future that Pink envisions relies on six senses or attributes: design, story, symphony, empathy, play, and meaning. We suggest that transformatory methods are well suited to supporting the development of such minds.

One motif in our chapters is the idea that the practices we discuss facilitate learning *about* learning for students and for educators. While learning skills and acquiring knowledge are the foreground activity and aim, we see the essential outcome to be the understanding of the learning process by the people involved in it. This involves students and educators identifying structures and patterns, practices and activities, and perspectives and approaches. Participants become able to make informed choices and gain reflective distance.

The chapters build upon an understanding of learning that identifies several common themes that relate to the transformative method. These include, learner autonomy, a collaborative approach to learning, individualised and developmental learning, and challenging prior assumptions.

Learner Autonomy

Learner autonomy can be described as the capacity of the individual to take control of their own learning. First defined by Holec (1979) in the field of language learning, autonomous learners are able to set their own learning goals, reflect on and evaluate their learning, and have a clear motivation to learn. As Holec (1979) suggests, learner autonomy can be viewed as a means to an end, when the student learns what it is they need to know, or as the end itself, the way in which they learn to become autonomous learners. Reinders (2010:52) describes a mindset required for learner autonomy, one that views learning as *"an active process of discovery"*. Adopting this particular mindset might be difficult for some students, who might be more familiar with the idea of teacher-centred learning, in which educators hold the knowledge which they then impart to the student. Indeed, students might feel that teachers are not doing their job if they do not adopt this role. Therefore, students need support to develop into independent learners. This would include ownership of learning material and resources, the design of curricula, and individual assignments that "fit" the learner.

Collaborative Approaches to Learning

A collaborative approach to learning values all contributions, with no one being perceived as having "greater" knowledge than anyone else. The educator might have more subject-specific knowledge, but students bring other things to the learning environment such as life skills and experiences, and thoughts and knowledge gained from prior learning. Working together in this way develops the students' team working and leadership skills. Perspectives are not only challenged by the educator but by other students in the group, and in doing this, students learn how to critically analyse each other's work and thoughts in a safe environment. Similarly, educators have their pre-conceived ideas challenged and they are reminded of what it is like to be a student, of the challenges and anxieties that emerge through close, open, and honest collaboration. This approach encourages students and educators to support and empathise with one another. These are important qualities that might be taken by students into the work environment upon leaving the university.

Individualised and Developmental Learning

While some students may learn more easily through listening, others engage through reading or discussion (Kolb, 1984), and this can further be influenced by gender (Belenky *et al.*, 1986). A variety of learning styles can be incorporated into active, experiential learning. Engaging students in active learning can also recognise individual strengths and weaknesses and value the individuality of each student. Cultural and gender differences in learning and knowing are also accommodated in the active learning process. Developing an understanding of various styles of learning and knowing that are grounded in culture and gender is an important life skill. Learning inevitably takes into account and builds on individuals' prior knowledge, experiences, values, habits, needs, and emotions; this recognition emphasises the importance and relevance of individualised learning design. Students have suggested that this process of development is important for them in preparation for their future prospects and the development of work skills (HEA, 2013).

Challenging Prior Assumptions

Central to transformative learning theory is the need to engage in the critical reflection and questioning of prior assumptions (Mezirow, 2000). This might be an uncomfortable experience, although developing a questioning approach progresses the learning process. On various levels, students and educators find their existing positions confronted rather than complemented by the learning experience. Such differences between expectation and experience provide ample motivation, opportunity, and a need to learn. The chapters that follow share different ways in which the authors have supported transformative learning. Each considers the themes described above; they all engage learners in perspective transformation of various kinds.

In Chapter 21, Kirsten Jack and Jeff Lewis discuss how they offered a choice of reflective expression that removed traditional restrictions of text-based documentation, thereby supporting the development of student creativity and promotion of individualised learning. Allowing students to utilise arts as methods of expression, they lifted restrictions of traditional writing and in doing so encouraged a more honest and open reflection on practice.

In Chapter 22, Nancy H. Hensel describes the ways in which course-based research can be transformative for students by engaging them during the first two years of the programme. Students learn how to challenge assumptions and existing knowledge through collaborative research that introduces them to the production and construction of knowledge. The process of becoming a researcher or scholar also involves learning how to become an autonomous learner and to have a level of control over one's personal learning process, particularly important for low-income and first-generation students.

Chapter 23 describes hands-on experiences with material construction made over several years in a "making" workshop series and observes tangible effects for the learning process. From the basis of these experiences and observations and a dialectical constructivist position, Daniel Cermak-Sassenrath proposes and sketches a model that identifies three kinds of learning transfers within and between subject domains and abstraction levels, and locates them on a continuum of material and cognitive construction. The hypothesis is that physical making and conceptual thinking can happen together, inspire each other, and build on each other.

About the Authors

Daniel Cermak-Sassenrath is associate professor at the ITU, Copenhagen, and member of the Center for Computer Games Research (game. itu.dk). He can be contacted at this e-mail: mail@dace.de

Nancy H. Hensel is president of the New American Colleges & Universities. She previously served as executive officer for the Council on Undergraduate Research. She can be reached at: nhensel@newamericancolleges.org

Kirsten Jack is reader in learning and teaching development at Manchester Metropolitan University, England, United Kingdom. She can be contacted at this e-mail: k.jack@mmu.ac.uk

Jeffrey Lewis is principal lecturer in dental technology at Cardiff Metropolitan University, Wales, United Kingdom. He can be contacted at this e-mail: jlewis@cardiffmet.ac.uk

Bibliography

Belenky, M. F.; B. M. Clinchy; N. R. Goldberger & J. M. Tarule (1986). *Women's Ways of Knowing.* New York: Basic Books.

Cranton, P. (1992). *Working with adult learners.* Toronto, Ontario: Wall & Emerson.

Higher Education Academy (2013). *Learning Journeys: Student experiences in further and higher education in Scotland.* Edinburgh: HEA Press.

Holec, H. (1979). *Autonomy in foreign language learning.* Oxford: Pergamon Press for the Council of Europe.

Kolb, D. A. (1984). *Experiential Learning: Experience as the source of learning and development.* Vol. 1. Englewood Cliffs, NJ: Prentice Hall.

Mezirow, J. (1996). Contemporary Paradigms of Learning. *Adult Education Quarterly,* Vol. 46, pp. 158–172.

Mezirow, J. (1997). Transformative learning: Theory to practice. In P. Cranton (Ed.), *New directions for adult and continuing education: Transformative learning in action: Insights from practice.* San Francisco, CA: Jossey-Bass, pp. 5–12.

Mezirow, J. (2000). Learning to think like an adult. In J. Mezirow & Associates (Eds.), *Learning as Transformation: Critical Perspectives on a Theory in Progress.* San Francisco, California: Jossey-Bass, pp. 3–33.

Pink, D. H. (2005). *A whole new mind: Moving from the information age to the conceptual age.* New York: Riverhead.

Reinders, H. (2010). Towards a Classroom Pedagogy for Learner Autonomy: A Framework of Independent Language Learning Skills. *Australian Journal of Teacher Education*, Vol. 35, No. 5, pp. 40–55.

Selander S. (2008). Designs of Learning and the formation of transformation of knowledge in an era of globalization. *Studies in Philosophy and Education*, Vol. 27, No. 4, pp. 267–281.

Chapter 21

Creative Reflection: Thoughts from Two Vocational Programmes

Kirsten Jack and Jeffrey Lewis

Introduction

This chapter contributes to the book *New Innovations in Teaching and Learning in Higher Education* as it showcases the use of art-based approaches to reflective practice from students on two vocational programmes. We define innovation as something that encourages learning in a different way and makes a difference to our students' learning experiences. We take a well-known approach, that of reflective learning, and adopt a different method by using drawing, collage, photography, and creative writing. Traditionally, our students have written their reflections on practice often as part of formal portfolio development. Our innovation offers students a more creative way to work, one that affords them freedom and an opportunity to engage in creative thinking. Given that they are enrolled on vocational programmes, the ability to think creatively is a great asset to their future work as professionals in the workplace (Chan, 2013).

Reflective practice is described by Taylor (2000:3) as *"the throwing back of thoughts and memories, in cognitive acts such as thinking, contemplation, meditation and any other form of attentive consideration, in order to make sense of them, and to make contextually appropriate changes if they are required"*. This style of development is helpful for students on vocational programmes because it supports learning through practical experiences. Not only does this lead to the development of helpful practical knowledge, it also serves as a means of self-awareness development and self-monitoring. By reading this chapter, you will gain the following three insights:

1. Ways in which reflective practice can be undertaken in a creative

way (e.g., through drawing, collage, photography, and creative writing);

2. The student and educator perspectives on the value of creative reflective activities;

3. Tips for adopting creative approaches to reflective practice that might be applied in your own teaching.

This chapter has four main sections. In the first section, we will outline the background to this innovation in terms of our student groups and the need for them to engage in reflective practice as part of their programmes. In the second section, we discuss our innovation including some practical guidance for those wanting to adopt a similar way of working in their own academic context. In section 3, we discuss the outcome of our innovation, presenting views from both our students and ourselves. We present examples of our students' work to show how the innovation was brought to life in the two different contexts of nursing and dental technology. In section 4, we suggest how this innovation can be widened out to other aspects of education.

Section 1: The Background

The idea for this innovation was developed to support undergraduate students to engage in reflective practice, specifically students enrolled on two vocational programmes: BSc (Hons) Adult Nursing and FdSc Dental Technology. Nursing programmes often attract mature students, and applications might be through non-traditional routes, so rather than A levels, students apply with equivalent qualifications or through accreditation for prior learning. The nursing student population often comprises applicants who have engaged in other work (e.g., care support work) before applying to become a qualified nurse. The dental technology student population is taken from a creative and usually artistic group who, like the nurses, often access higher education through non-traditional routes. Both groups must engage in experiential learning in order to qualify in their chosen profession (NMC, 2010; GDC, 2013). Indeed, there are similarities across both programmes in that students cannot learn all they need to know through empirical ways of knowing and learning, and experience plays a large part in personal and professional development. However, over the years, we have identified reluctance on the part of many of our students, on both programmes, to engage with reflective learning. This led us to consider the need to offer alternative methods to engage them in this process.

Traditionally, students on the two programmes, Adult Nursing and Dental Technology, had the singular option of writing reflective pieces using templates based on a reflective cycle, either online or by hand, and these have proven to be unpopular methods. Coward (2012) reports that student nurses are suffering from reflection overkill, viewing it as just another tick-box exercise to be completed. Students complain that reflective templates are dry and impersonal and do not add to learning, becoming just another chore to complete in order to qualify as a nurse. Dental Technology students view completion of the reflective templates as non-essential or irrelevant to their work. Indeed, a large amount of Dental Technology students regularly fail to complete the e-portfolio, which includes the reflective pieces, or complete it inadequately. Many have not had any experience of writing academically and have not had exposure to reflection as an activity. Despite this process being intro-duced in the first year, reluctance continues throughout the programme. However, both Nursing and Dental Technology students do (whether they realise it or not) go through the reflective process regularly as part of their day-to-day roles. For example, student nurses reflect in prac-tice as they are discussing their work with their educators, particularly when completing their assessment paperwork. Reviewing, discussing, and reflecting on performance should be a natural part of this ongoing assessment. For Dental Technology students, their work involves the development of complex and bespoke artefacts, such as crowns and dentures for demanding customers (dentists and patients) which need to mimic all the characteristics of natural teeth and their supporting oral structures. So, the process of continual self-critique enables them to improve their work. It was hoped that this creative method of reflection would add value as an engaging process, with the option of using another media rather than traditional writing for these students, as reported by McBain *et al.* (2015). Learning from experience can help students make sense of events and reach different understandings of what has happened in their professional lives (Jasper, 2013). It also helps contextualise what they have done, how they did it, and how their learning might affect their decision-making in future scenarios.

The overarching aim of this innovation was to offer students a creative choice of method when engaging in reflective practice. It was hoped that this would encourage students to engage more meaningfully in this style of learning, which would have a positive impact on their professional development. The innovation is commensurate with the drive at both universities, towards the development of a more inclusive curriculum, one which appeals to different styles of learner.

Section 2: The Practice

2a. General Introduction to the Innovation

During the latter part of the third year of both programmes, we introduced alternative ways of reflecting on practice to two cohorts of students (one group from Nursing and one from Dental Technology). Nursing students undertake reflective activity on a formal basis at the end of each block of clinical placement, twice a year at six-monthly intervals. However, they are encouraged to reflect on their practice regularly throughout the programme in order to gain new insight and learn from their ongoing experiences. The Dental Technology cohort are asked to reflect on learning in the workplace throughout the three years as an ongoing year-long process and record this in Mahara® – their e-portfolio. Traditionally, the reflective templates used by both programmes have consisted of a series of headings under which students write about issues from practice and what they have learned through their experiences (for example, see Gibbs' reflective cycle, 1998; Dreyfus' skills acquisition model, 1986). The reflective templates support the students' development and make up a portfolio of evidence of achievement.

2b. The Curriculum

The BSc (Hons) Nursing is a three-year full-time programme leading to the award of the degree and registration with the Nursing & Midwifery Council, the regulator for nurses and midwives in the United Kingdom (UK). Fifty percent of nursing undergraduate programme hours are spent in a clinical practice setting, which includes placements across a range of acute and community settings, for example, in a hospital or home environment. Students are supported in the clinical environment by a named assessor who supports and guides the learner during their clinical practice weeks.

The FdSc in Dental Technology is a three-year part-time programme. Students are enrolled on a reduced attendance model and visit the campus 4–6 times per academic year, with much of the delivery via weekly web-based videoconferencing meetings. Within the programme, there is the requirement to complete work-based learning modules and professional practice modules. Students are employed in dental laboratories either based within a healthcare trust or at an independent/commercial company. Within the laboratories, "mentors" are nominated and are required to be dental technicians registered with the GDC to support the student and liaise regularly with the university.

Students on both programmes are asked to reflect on their practical activities as part of their ongoing professional development.

2c. Organisation of the Practice

We began by presenting the reflective cycles already known to the students on both programmes in pictorial form to remind them of the essential process. However, rather than asking for written reflective pieces, we suggested that our students choose a different way to reflect – one that was meaningful to them and that could portray their thoughts and feelings most effectively. We offered suggestions, which could be (but were not restricted to) one of the following: a reflective poem, a collage or picture, a creative story, a sculpture, a film, or a podcast. In keeping with the autonomous feel of our request, we provided little guidance, apart from revisiting the reflective cycle with our students. We wanted to move away from a prescriptive way of working, believing that offering choice might support students' development as autonomous practitioners, an important consideration due to the nature of the work they would be completing upon qualification. On their return to university after a placement period, the students shared their reflections in the new format. This was on a one-to-one basis in a personal tutorial lasting approximately 30 minutes.

This method differs in that it enables students to choose how they want to engage in experiential learning and encourages them to consider how they learn best. Indeed, many students' experiences of higher education involve a certain amount of passivity, in that they are told what they need to know and are given little choice as to how they learn it. Enabling students to take control of their learning can greatly support their ability to learn from experiences (Kolb & Kolb, 2005). Encouraging the use of non-traditional methods in experiential learning supports mental characteristics such as imagination and creativity, two important aspects of professional education (Carter, 1985).

Many students are very keen to experience freedom to learn in a way that is personal to them. However, students were concerned about the standard of their reflection, for example, the quality of their poem, story, or piece of art. This led to reluctance on the part of some students, and as educators it was important to value all pieces and remain non-judgemental. Engagement was helped by reassuring the students that it is the *process* of the reflective experience that is important, not the end product.

2d. Preparation

When preparing to introduce a new way of working, timing is important. Choosing a time when students are not under pressure to complete other work or make deadlines can be helpful so that they can give the innovation more attention. Students can become too focused on the product, and this can take away from the valuable act of reflecting on their practice. Having some preparatory notes can be useful for students so that they can feel supported when choosing how they might like to reflect. For example, having some guidance on how to make a podcast can be helpful so that students can focus on their reflection rather than the practicalities of the actual method itself. For the Nursing cohort, having the resource http://www.caringwords.mmu.ac.uk was helpful. This website is an online poetry community and was successful in whetting the appetites of some of the nursing students who chose this method of creative reflection. Students felt encouraged when they saw creative work completed previously by their peers. We wanted to move away from the formulaic reflective templates, although we were still keen for the students to keep in mind the reflective cycle, to support their thinking. Therefore, we developed diagrammatic materials of the most common reflective cycles in order to support the students through this process.

Section 3: The Outcome

3a. Student Perspective

Encouraging arts-based approaches has led to a more meaningful learning experience for our students. This is because they have been given a freedom to be creative, and using their own choice of method has led to students developing confidence in their abilities as autonomous learners. The ability to be an independent learner is important, as students graduate and become professionals responsible for their ongoing development. Being offered a choice has resulted in more students completing reflective pieces. Previously, entries were missing, leading to gaps in the portfolios and an inadequate portrayal of the students' learning trajectory. The students described creative methods as being more "fun" and less of a "tick-box" exercise, gaining more meaning to their work in the process.

An example of the students' work is presented below. The first is a reflective poem written by a second-year Nursing student that relates to the development of her confidence on an accident and emergency placement (Example 1). The second is a piece of graphic art created by a Dental Technology student and relates to the fear experienced by him when using high-speed mechanical equipment (Example 2). In the Nursing example, there is a description of a situational fear, and in the Dental Technology example, there is concern about a potentially dangerous piece of equipment. The equipment is described as a "beasty", and using metaphorical language is helpful to convey the power of the emotion felt during that time.

Example 1: "A&E":

Once upon a time there was a student nurse
Who found herself in A&E
Full of self-doubt and fear
But ready to give it everything she knew
Walking down the corridor one day
She found herself throwing all her fear away
Rising to the challenge that had just been set upon her
She saw life holding on before her

Try as she might the life slipped away
Away from the chaos and madness
Peace and calm filled the room
Machines that once beeped
And voices that once shouted
Slowly became silent
That instance the student nurse's life changed
She learnt that nothing could hold her back

Example 2: Taming the beasty.

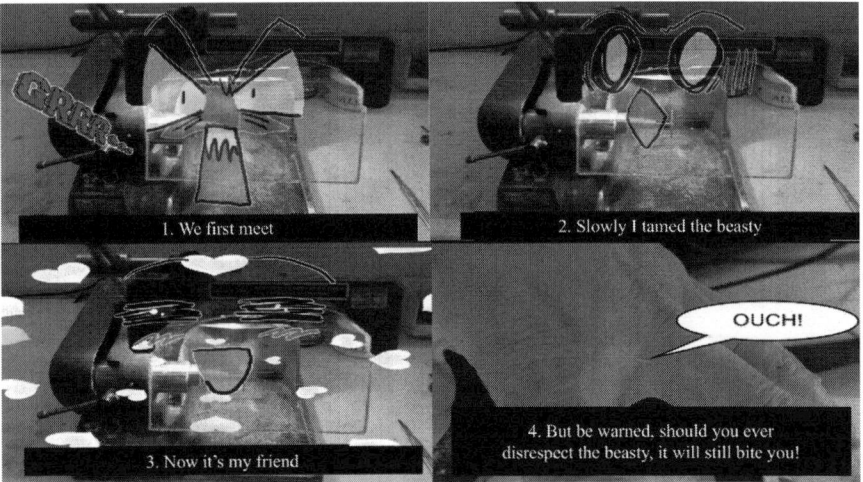

3b. Educator Perspectives

Using creative methods is helpful to us as educators, since students were more honest about how they feel about practice in comparison to traditional methods of reflective writing. Students are revealing more about their experiences using their own choice of method. Indeed, in using arts, a means of reflection has been shown to facilitate the description of emotion in ways that the traditional reflective pieces cannot (for example, see Jack, 2012). This leads to a greater understanding of the students' personal and professional needs, meaning that we can tailor our pastoral support for them more adequately. This creative practice is helpful because it reminds us of how it was to *be* a student, reminding us of anxieties and the trepidation we felt, a state that we have not experienced for many years. The honest accounts of practice allow us access into the students' lifeworld, and we learn not only about their needs but about our capacity to meet them.

Section 4: Moving Forward

Moving forward, we would like to widen this innovation out to other aspects of education, for example, as a means of module evaluation. Haiku, (short, non-rhyming Japanese poetry) has been used as a way for nurses to write about clinical or educational experiences (see Biley & Champney-Smith, 2003) and provides a succinct but thoughtful way for students to feed back their thoughts on modules and courses. As the arts enable a more honest reflection on events, this could prove an excellent way to gain candid feedback from students about their thoughts and feelings on the educational experience.

We plan to introduce students to experts in the field (e.g., poets, artists, and creative writers) as part of timetabled activities. In doing this, we can work across faculties, utilising the expertise of colleagues to inform our curricula and sharing ideas and learning. This might be facilitated by our student ambassadors, thus developing their skills and expertise in this area. The innovation will be promoted in other faculties in order to support students in other disciplines to reflect more creatively in their personal and professional lives.

Conclusion

In this chapter, we have discussed an innovative way of supporting students on two vocational programmes to reflect on their practical experiences. We have outlined the practicalities of this approach so that the reader can adapt this method to their own teaching practice. We have outlined both our own and our students' views on this style of reflection and the advantages gained over more traditional methods of experiential learning. Ultimately, using creative approaches to reflection leads to more honest and open accounts of practice. This has advantages on both sides of the student/educator relationship in terms of growth and development.

Further, ways in which the arts can be brought into other aspects of our students' experiences should be sought, as this medium develops creative thinking, an essential aspect of professional development.

About the Authors

Kirsten Jack is reader in learning and teaching development at Manchester Metropolitan University, England, United Kingdom. She can be contacted at this e-mail: k.jack@mmu.ac.uk

Jeffrey Lewis is principal lecturer in dental technology at Cardiff Metropolitan University, Wales, United Kingdom. He can be contacted at this e-mail: jlewis@cardiffmet.ac.uk

Bibliography

Biley, F. C. & J. Champney-Smith (2003). Attempting to say something without saying it…: writing haiku in health care education. *Medical Humanities*, Vol. 29, pp. 39–42.

Carter, R. (1985). A taxonomy of objectives for professional education. *Studies in Higher Education*, Vol. 10, No. 2, pp. 135–149.

Chan, Z. C. Y. (2013). A systematic review of creative thinking/creativity in nursing education. *Nurse Education Today*, Vol. 33, No. 11, pp. 1382–1387.

Coward, M. (2011). Does the use of reflective models restrict critical thinking and therefore learning in nurse education? What have we done? *Nurse Education Today*, Vol. 31, No. 8, pp. 883–886.

Dreyfus, H. L. (1986). *Mind over machine: The power of human intuition and expertise in the era of the computer.* New York: Free Press.

General Dental Council (2013). *Standards for the dental team.* London: GDC.

Gibbs, G. (1988). *Learning by Doing: A guide to teaching and learning methods.* Oxford: Further Education Unit.

Jack, K. (2012). Putting the words 'I am sad', just doesn't quite cut it sometimes!: The use of art to promote emotional awareness in nursing students. *Nurse Education Today*, Vol. 32, No. 7, pp. 811–817.

Jasper, M. (2013). *Beginning Reflective Practice.* Hampshire: Cengage.

Kolb, A. Y. & D. A. Kolb (2005). Learning styles and learning spaces: Enhancing experiential learning in higher education. *Academy of Management Learning and Education*, Vol. 4, No. 2, pp. 193–212.

McBain, L.; S. Donnelly; J. Hilder; C. O'Leary & E. McKinlay (2015). I wanted to communicate my feelings freely: a descriptive study of creative responses to enhance reflection in palliative medicine education. *Bio Med Central Medical Education,*15:180.

NMC (2010). *Standards for Pre-Registration Nurse Education.* London: NMC.

Taylor, B. J. (2000). *Reflective Practice: A guide for Nurses and Midwives.* Buckingham: OU Press.

Chapter 22

Course-Based Undergraduate Research for Student Success and Equity

Nancy H. Hensel

Introduction

This chapter contributes to the book *New Innovations in Teaching and Learning in Higher Education* as it describes the way to bring the well-documented benefits of undergraduate research to all students by incorporating research into first- and second-year courses in all disciplines. The chapter provides a definition of course-based research and examples of how research activities are incorporated into the first two years of college. In addition to examples of practice at two-year community colleges and four-year undergraduate colleges, the chapter addresses: (1) why course-based research is important for educational equity; (2) the challenges of course-based research; (3) appropriate expectations for research in the first two years; (4) how to design appropriate course-based research experiences for first- and second-year students; and (5) how to provide group rather than individual mentoring. Particularly important about this chapter is that disciplines other than the sciences will be addressed. Far fewer professors in the social sciences and humanities incorporate collaborative research into introductory first- and second-year courses. In this chapter, the use of the word research is inclusive of scholarship and creative activity. Course-based research is defined in this chapter by the following criteria:

+ research is embedded into the course curriculum;

+ all students engage in the research project;

+ the students work collaboratively on the project;

+ the research project introduces students to the research methodology of the discipline;

+ the outcome of the work is initially unknown. The student outcomes of the work are communicated in some manner.

There is great interest in American higher education, as well as internationally, in expanding opportunities for students to engage in authentic undergraduate research. While nearly every undergraduate college in the United States offers students opportunities to do research, it is the sciences rather than social sciences and humanities that more commonly engage students in research. Usually research is offered to students in the junior and senior years and is typically available to only a few students who will work closely with a professor either in the summer or during the academic year in what is commonly known as the "apprentice model". The apprentice model is too costly to provide research opportunities for all students. Research that is embedded in a course, especially courses required for every student, addresses the issue of how to expand undergraduate research to all students. It also addresses issues of educational equity because it makes undergraduate research benefits available to students who must work while attending classes during the academic year and in the summer. Undergraduate research prepares two-year community college students for transfer to four-year undergraduate colleges and graduate school. It is also widely accepted that the skills developed through undergraduate research help to prepare students for their future careers. Course-based undergraduate research equalises the opportunities for all students. When reading this chapter, you will gain the following three insights:

1. you will understand the educational equity rationale for course-based research;

2. you will realise that challenges to undergraduate research in the first two years can be overcome;

3. you will become familiar with appropriate expectations and project design for course-based research and gain insights regarding group mentoring of course-based research students.

I have structured the chapter in four sections. It begins with a brief historical overview of the development of undergraduate research, including a summary of the benefits of undergraduate research. It is followed by a discussion of why course-based research is an educational equity issue. The challenges of course-based research are identified, and appropriate expectations for students, project design, and mentoring are also discussed. The chapter ends with examples of successful programmes and suggestions for course-based research in several disciplines.

Section I: Background

Undergraduate research is not a new pedagogy. It actually has its roots in the "Humboldtian ideals", when Wilhelm von Humboldt suggested in 1810 that the *"pursuit of knowledge through original research and the partnership of student and professor"* is a central purpose of the university (as cited in Zupanc, 2012:6). Many prominent scientists, including Nobel Prize winners, attribute their interest in science to their undergraduate research experiences. The California Institute of Technology (Caltech) may be the first institution to engage undergraduates in research. In 1920, the chemistry professor Arthur Noyes (Pauling, 1958) identified the most promising Caltech students and engaged them in laboratory research. Two of his students, Edwin McMillan and Linus Pauling, published their work in 1927 in the Journal of the American Chemical Society. McMillan and Pauling later went on to receive Nobel Prizes in 1951 and 1954, respectively. In a more recent example (Merkel, 2001), the Massachusetts Institute of Technology (MIT) has involved undergraduate students in research since 1969, when Professor Margaret MacVicar founded the Undergraduate Research Opportunity Program (UROP). United States colleges and universities often engaged students in research earlier than 1969 without formal programmes like UROP. For example, Phillip A. Stone (2010), who won a Nobel Prize in 1993, commented about his undergraduate experiences at Union College in 1966, *"Undergraduate research was my first taste of laboratory life. The experiments did not work, but I was addicted"*. Carl Wieman, who received a Nobel Prize in Physics in 2001, said in his Nobel biographical statement that he was not a particularly good student in his first year of college but found success when he became deeply engaged in research and worked closely with a professor at MIT.

Undergraduate research became more institutionalised when the Council on Undergraduate Research (CUR) was founded in 1978 by ten chemists to promote undergraduate research at private liberal arts colleges. CUR has now grown to 10,000 individual members and 750 institutional members from private and public institutions including research universities, liberal arts colleges, and two-year community colleges. It also covers nearly every discipline. As undergraduate research programmes have expanded to almost every four-year undergraduate campus in the United States, funding support for undergraduate research has also grown. In the early 1980s, the National Science Foundation began providing support for students to participate in research with faculty through its Research Experiences for Undergraduates (REU) programme. Other federal agencies, such as the National Institutes of Health, also provide support for undergraduate research. Private Foundations such as the Research Corporation for Advancing Science, the Camille and Henry Dreyfus Foundation, and the American Chemical Society Petroleum Research Fund also began funding undergraduate research.

As programmes like UROP were developed on many more campuses across the United States and federal support expanded, a body of research investigating the benefits of undergraduate research was also growing. Many researchers (Nagda *et al.*, 1998; Lopatto, 2003, 2010; Seymour *et al.*, 2004; Russell *et al.*, 2007; Hunter *et al.*, 2007; Harrison *et al.*, 2011) have described the benefits to students when they participate in an undergraduate research experience as:

+ learning a topic in depth;

+ learning to work independently;

+ tolerance for obstacles faced in the research process;

+ transformation of the student/teacher relationship;

+ developing critical thinking and problem-solving skills;

+ developing self-confidence;

+ clarification of career goals;

+ improving oral and written skills.

As the benefits of undergraduate research received wider recognition, other reports emerged calling for new approaches to higher education that engaged students more actively in the learning process. The late

Ernest Boyer, president of The Carnegie Foundation for the Advancement of Teaching, suggested in a 1998 report that research universities should make research-based learning the standard and that inquiry-based learning should be introduced in the freshman year. Other reports by the American Association for the Advancement of Science (AAAS, 2009), the President's Council of Advisors on Science and Technology (PCAST) (2012), National Academies of Science, Engineering Medicine (2015), and Gentile *et al.* (2017) called for more active learning pedagogies and undergraduate research for college science students. Science has been at the forefront of the development of undergraduate research; however, other disciplines are taking notice and beginning to develop programmes for undergraduate research. In 2009, George Kuh identified undergraduate research as one of ten "high impact practices" that emerged from an analysis of data collected through the National Survey of Student Engagement. Inclusion of high impact practices in the undergraduate experience has become a major effort on the part of American colleges and universities.

Institutions of higher education of all types are implementing a number of creative approaches to facilitate innovation, problem-solving, and discovery. They see undergraduate research as a critical vehicle for achieving these objectives. Undergraduate research can be a powerful pedagogical tool that should be made available to all students. Students will benefit from an early introduction to research. They will be more prepared to develop high-quality, significant senior projects because they have already incorporated knowledge of research methodology into their way of thinking, and they will be better prepared for graduate school and their future careers.

Section 2: The Practice

2a. A General Introduction – Course-Based Research for Educational Equity

Making the benefits of undergraduate research available to all students is an issue of educational equity. In their 2013 report *Separate and Unequal: How Higher Education Reinforces the Intergenerational Reproduction of White Racial Privilege*, Carnevale and Strohl suggest that while access to higher education has significantly improved in the past several years, the educational experiences of white students are vastly different from the experiences of African-American and Hispanic students, who are more likely to attend open access two-year community colleges or four-year undergraduate institutions. Expenditures on instruction at highly selective institutions are two to five times greater than at open access colleges. Undergraduate research is more available to students who attend institutions with robust instructional expenditures. Such institutions are likely to provide opportunities for students to work one-on-one with a professor on a research project. Access for all students is a first step to educational equity, but pedagogy must also change. Traditional instructional practices do not always recognise the differing needs of students as campus demographics change. Many instructional practices, including the apprentice model for undergraduate research, are based on assumptions that do not necessarily apply to underrepresented students. Pedagogical changes to embed research experiences in the curriculum are needed in order to address educational equity for all students and expand the benefits of undergraduate research to everyone.

Students who participate in summer research projects or have the opportunity to work closely with a professor in the apprentice model are more likely to receive the benefits of undergraduate research than students who do not have the opportunity for such experiences. Students who need to work during the academic year or in the summer have difficulty finding time to engage in out-of-class or summer research. In addition, first-generation college students may be less aware of the possibilities of research and the advantages it can provide. Embedding research experiences into courses, particularly in the first two years, can address these concerns for educational equity.

Undergraduate research increases retention and degree completion for all students, but it is especially important for underrepresented students. In an early groundbreaking study, Nagda *et al.* (1998) conducted a comparison study of students admitted to the minority scholars programme who participated in undergraduate research and those who did not participate in research. They found that the randomly selected undergraduate research students were more likely to stay at the university and complete their degree than the non-research students.

Bangera and Brownell (2014) suggested that in addition to financial constraints, first-generation students may not be aware of the opportunities and benefits of research. They also may not understand the culture of research and how to initiate interactions with faculty outside of the classroom. According to Pyles and Levy (2009) at East Tennessee State University, early exposure to research and scholarship can "demystify" research for students who may be intimidated by the idea of research. They further state that early research experiences help students to define their interests and see themselves as potential researchers and scholars. Because of these barriers, Bangera and Brownell believe that the inequities in undergraduate research can be addressed through course-based research.

Several reports (AAAS, 2009; PCAST, 2012; National Academies, 2015; Gentile *et al.*, 2017) have called for universities to replace standard laboratory courses with discovery-based research courses and make research opportunities available for more students. The recent report from the National Academies of Science, Engineering, and Medicine (2015:7) found that:

- course-based research can provide many benefits for students from first year to senior year and also to underrepresented students;

- many faculty members are not familiar with course-based research or are not aware of local and national models that already exist;

- well-designed course-based research projects use many of the "best practices" identified by pedagogical research.

Despite these calls for making research experiences available to more students, a review of recent publications on inquiry-based exercises (Beck *et al.*, 2014) found that there was a greater emphasis on guided-inquiry rather than open-ended inquiry or research-based approaches. In addition, they found that research seemed to be included more in upper-level courses than in introductory courses.

Embedding research into a course introduces students to the possibilities of research and its benefits. It also reduces the time and financial constraints of participation in research. Course-based research can create a research community that encourages more student-faculty interaction to support student retention and degree completion. Some institutions have found ways to provide research opportunities for more students. For example, St. Edward's University (Hart, 2016) has embedded a research experience into all twelve sections of the introductory biology course. As a Hispanic-serving institution, they see the inclusion of research in courses as a way to increase educational equity. Pepperdine University has included research experiences in first-year seminar courses (Carr *et al.*, 2013). Montana State University (www.montana.edu) has designed a core curriculum that includes opportunities for research at several points. As a public institution with about 15,000 students, it is significant that Montana State has been committed to providing research experiences for all students for over 20 years and has found a way to meet the challenges of course-based research.

2b. The Curriculum – Challenges of Course-Based Research

Many professors are hesitant to engage first- and second-year students in undergraduate research because they feel students do not know enough to conduct research in the discipline. They also worry about how much time it will take to develop legitimate research activities for first- and second-year students. Many are also concerned about how they can mentor a whole class of students doing research.

While implementing course-based research is not easy, having a supportive network engaged in the same goal will make implementation more manageable. There are both logistical and attitudinal challenges in developing a successful course-based research programme. The logistical challenges of time, curricular design, identification of projects, and tools can be supported by a collaborative network. One of the major barriers Lopatto and colleagues (2012) found to the implementation of course-based research was the lack of colleague support. Course-based research is more likely to be successful when it fits within the curriculum of the department or college. In a survey, Lopatto and his colleagues found that an introductory workshop on how to develop and implement course-based research was critical for its success. They further found that creating a community of practice network was important for those embarking on this curricular change. The network provided support for troubleshooting, sharing of information about pedagogy and use of resources, technical support, and access to the expertise of others in the network. Planning course-based research activities takes more time than traditional classroom instruction and it also requires more knowledge of pedagogy for successful projects. An advantage of a research network and standardised methods and equipment is that small, short-term course projects can be placed in the context of larger-term data sets and large, possibly national, projects. There are also cost issues to be considered in course-based research. Successfully replicable course-based science research projects must use materials that are inexpensive, readily available, and straightforward to train students to use. Social science and humanities course-based research must consider access to resources such as library and archival materials and human subjects.

Brownell and Tanner (2012) suggested that in addition to lack of training, time, and incentives as barriers to pedagogical change, a scientist's professional identity as a researcher rather than as a teacher might be a hidden barrier. A collaborative network can also encourage and support faculty identity as teacher/scholars. Professors need to reframe their concept of undergraduate research from the apprentice model to a concept that includes working with a whole class and seeing research as a developmental process. When professors think of research, they often think of their own senior thesis or dissertation. Research experiences for first- and second-year students need to be appropriate for their skill level but also use authentic research methodology. The research process in any discipline can be broken down into steps and specific activities. Some of the steps in a research process can be introduced to students in their first-year courses. When considering course-based research, professors often remember the close interaction they had with their research mentor and they wonder how they can duplicate that experience for all the students in their course-based research class. They cannot duplicate the apprentice model experience, but they can find ways of adapting individual mentoring to group mentoring by changing their concept to go beyond individual student mentoring and include whole-class mentoring.

These are legitimate concerns; however, many professors have successfully embedded authentic research activities into first- and second-year courses. Those who have successfully integrated research into their courses have realised that learning to be a researcher is a developmental process, and they see their role as both a teacher of research and a collaborator in research activities. Their goal is to teach students to think in a particular discipline and to understand the research methodology of the discipline.

They also understand the role they play in developing future researchers and scholars as well as preparing students for professional careers.

2c. Organisation of the Practice – Appropriate Expectations for Course-Based Research

The Council on Undergraduate Research (www.cur.org) developed a definition of undergraduate research that is accepted by most universities and scholars: *"Undergraduate research (including scholarship and creative activity) is an inquiry or investigation by an undergraduate in collaboration with a faculty mentor that makes an original intellectual or creative contribution to the discipline".*

Implicit in the CUR definition are four elements considered necessary for undergraduate research: mentorship, acceptability, originality, and dissemination. These elements should also be present in course-based research, though perhaps the expectations for first- and second-year students will differ from more advanced students. The implementation of the four elements will also be different in course-based research from the apprentice model.

Mentorship implies a collaborative relationship between the student and the faculty mentor. Professors are supportive of the student's development as a researcher by ensuring that the student is intellectually engaged in the research or scholarly project. In course-based research, mentoring means creating a supportive classroom environment that encourages each student to ask questions and raise issues that are of concern to him or her. The professor will mentor the class as a group rather than the one-on-one mentoring that is typical of the apprentice model.

As professors consider developing course-based research, they may ask what constitutes "authentic" or acceptable research for first- and second-year students as well as non-majors. Spell and colleagues (2014) conducted a national survey to determine definitions of authentic research experiences in laboratory classes. They found that faculty tended to emphasise either the scientific process or the discovery of new data. Spell *et al.* (2014) concluded that both goals reflect authentic science teaching because they reflect what scientists do in their own labs. Spell *et al.* (2014:108) further suggested that the two approaches do not need to be exclusive and that a *"well-mentored research lab should strive to develop future scientists while generating new data"*. Beckman and Hensel (2009) suggest that process versus product is actually a continuum and that process might be more appropriate for the beginning stages of undergraduate research and preparation for an eventual product outcome. Course-based research may place more emphasis on process in introductory courses while still providing research experiences that mirror what researchers do and that may eventually lead to a new discovery. Students, according to Rowland et al. (2016:17), can engage in *"projects that produce 'novel results' that contribute to existing research"*, suggesting that students can experience what scientists do and how they do it. The discussion about what constitutes authenticity has occurred more frequently in science literature but authenticity is also important in the social sciences, humanities, and arts. Students, even in the first two years, should be learning the research methodology of their discipline.

Originality is the most challenging aspect of the CUR definition, and it is even more challenging in course-based research. Many feel that undergraduates cannot make original discoveries or contributions. Students are more engaged in the research process, however, when they are pursuing the unknown, and there is nothing like the excitement of an original discovery to encourage students to further efforts. Undergraduates can make original discoveries, and small discoveries are made in course-based research. For example, in Gita Bangera's (2014) genomics course at Bellevue Community College, students are discovering new bacteria as they sequence and analyse bacterial strains of wheat. Banger's students are experiencing the thrill of discovery even though it is small, and they are developing a better understanding of research. Senior-level students are more prepared to make original discoveries when they have had an early course-based research experience. Early research experiences in humanities and social sciences may encourage students to continue their involvement in undergraduate research with the possibility of a new discovery. For example, humanities student Cynthia Dretel (2010) from Moravian College visited the United States Holocaust Museum and discovered Polish musical puppet plays about the nativity story written in concentration camps. Apparently, little to no scholarly work had been done on these puppet plays. Dretel learned Polish in order to translate and analyse these pieces to show their historical importance and how the symbols were code for life in the concentration camps. She then developed new arrangements of the plays that were performed on campus as part of her honours thesis and later in churches in Poland. Originality should not be the primary objective of course-based research, but it is an added benefit when it occurs.

Finally, it is desirable that undergraduate research projects have a tangible product that can be shared with peers, faculty, and perhaps a larger audience. Students might present at the National Conference on Undergraduate Research or regional or national disciplinary conferences. Dissemination encourages attention to quality and adherence to deadlines. It also gives students an opportunity to receive feedback and respond to questions. Dissemination builds confidence and communication skills that will be valuable in students' professional activities.

2d. Preparation – Designing Appropriate Experiences for Course-Based Research

There are several factors to take into consideration when designing course-based research activities for first- and second-year students. Some are obvious, but others may not be. First, one must consider the developmental level of the students. Most of the students will be recently out of high school. Only a few students will have had minimal exposure to research prior to entering college. Engaging in research may sound overwhelming to students and they may be intimidated by the prospect. Thinking of themselves as researchers or scholars is not yet part of their self-identity. Also, they may not have had much experience with asking questions and challenging ideas and assumptions. A research project will be most successful if the research question is of personal interest to the students. What have they wondered about that might relate to the topic of the course? For example, students in a chemistry class at a Hispanic-serving institution wondered what made peppers that are an important part of Mexican foods hot. They analysed the chemical structure of the peppers and found the answer to their question. Beginning with what students are curious about provides a level of comfort with the idea of research and builds confidence that they can become researchers and scholars.

Second, the research project must be one that can be completed within a semester. It is possible that the project is a long-term project and the students are only contributing a small part to the total project, but that small part needs to be completed in the semester and students need to see the results of their work.

Availability of resources is a third consideration. In science courses the students are not likely to have access to expensive equipment or know how to use it. Inexpensive and easy-to-use equipment will work best for beginning science students. Humanities students may need access to library materials and archives. Social science students may need access to human subjects, and if so, they may also be required to submit their projects to their campus Institutional Review Board to assure ethical treatment of human subjects. They may also need to learn how to use basic statistical programs.

By reviewing the literature on course-based research, Corwin Auchincloss and colleagues (2014) identified five dimensions of laboratory learning experiences: (1) use of science practices; (2) discovery; (3) broader relevance or importance; (4) collaboration; and (5) iteration. While Corwin Auchincloss studied science course-based research, social sciences and humanities students should also use the practices of their discipline, and discovery should be a goal of a project that has relevance outside the classroom. Collaboration is an important part of research for beginning students, as it creates a small but supportive community. Cynthia Brame (n.d.), assistant director of The Center for Teaching at Vanderbilt University, also reviewed several course-based research projects and identified additional common elements:

+ well-defined problems – if the project is going to generate new knowledge, it is important that the research question is clear;

+ important but not "hot" topics – course-based research proceeds at a slower pace because the students are beginners learning the research process, so the project needs to accommodate a slower pace;

+ common tools, different problems – students can use similar techniques for different projects and this has the advantage of lower resource use but also encouraging peer teaching.

Appropriate course-based experiences teach students the research methodology of the discipline by engaging them in real research to address a real question. The project should be completed within a semester and should develop data or new information that can be shared with peers and others at the end of the course.

2e. Mentoring Students in Course-Based Classes

As we think about mentoring experiences in course-based research, we first need to ask what do students need from mentoring in the apprentice model and what do they gain from such experiences? Students who participate in the apprentice model of undergraduate research develop strong and often lifelong relationships with their professor/mentor. They not only learn how to become competent researchers or scholars, they also learn how to present and publish their work, about various career possibilities, and how to be successful as a researcher for government, industry, non-profit organisations, or in a professorial career. What are the elements from apprentice model mentoring that can be adapted to group mentoring? Packard (2016:12–18) has identified three factors that are important to persistence in degree completion and should be part of the mentoring process: capacity, interest, and belongingness. Students need to see themselves as learners and have a sense of self-efficacy. Course-based research or scholarship that is carefully planned and takes into consideration students' developmental level can build confidence and students' sense of their own capacity. Achieving success in the beginning steps of a project encourages students to take the next perhaps more difficult step. Effective, constructive, and timely feedback develops the capacity for further learning. Students will more actively engage in their own learning when they have a personal interest in the topic and they will be more likely to persist because of their interest if the project becomes more challenging. Course-based research can be especially effective in developing a sense of belonging because all of the students in the class will be working on the same project. As the students and the professor engage in the investigation together, they are developing connections to each other, sharing the excitement and challenges of the research, and becoming a community of scholars.

What are mentoring strategies that can be specifically applied to group mentoring? Creating an open classroom where student ideas and opinions are encouraged and valued is the first priority. This is, of course, a strategy that applies to every class but is especially important in a course-based research class so that students will feel they can make a meaningful contribution when they may initially feel intimidated by the idea of research. Asking students at the beginning of the class what questions they have about the topic or what they are curious about lets students know that their questions and ideas are valued. During the semester, professors can make students more comfortable with the idea of research if they anticipate the process or academic culture questions that some first-generation students might be too shy or embarrassed to ask and raise them in class. What is a discipline, what is a network and why is it important, what is a syllabus, and what is the purpose of office hours might be examples of questions students might feel uncomfortable asking. An explanation of a liberal arts education could also be helpful to some students as they try to understand their college experiences. Students can be encouraged to bring their own experiences to the research process. Their cultural perspective might add depth to the research project or even suggest a research question. Their work experience might also contribute to the research project. Valuing students' perspectives, even those experiences that do not directly relate to the project, encourages a sense of belonging. Professors can share their own learning experiences as well. Understanding the successes and challenges that a professor faced as a student or even as a professor will encourage students to persist in their own work. A professor, for example, may want to share with students a copy of an article that will be accepted for publication if the comments by the editor are addressed. Letting students get an inside view of the editing process will help them see the importance of rewrites in their own papers and reassure them about their progress as a learner. It is especially important to share experiences that were not initially successful, as students need to know that sometimes failure is part of the learning process and especially the research process.

Mentoring a class is somewhat similar to building a positive and productive team in the workplace. The team is the professor and students enrolled in the class, and the classroom is the workplace. Teams function best when the team leader, in this case the professor, communicates in positive ways with the team members. Learning a little about each student/team member such as career interests, co-curricular activities, or work experience can help to create a more personal relationship between student and professor. Everyone wants to be appreciated, and positive comments about individual student work and the group's work provides encouragement and helps to build confidence and capacity. Implementing transparent teaching, where the professor explains why she is using a particular pedagogical strategy and then asks students to comment on its effectiveness, also builds a sense of belonging and capacity. A willingness to listen to student ideas and provide feedback when needed also encourages students and builds a sense of belonging. Making the assumption that all students in the class are responsible and will contribute to the success of the project demonstrates trust in the students and respect for their work.

A 2014 Gallup poll (Ray & Kafka, 2014:3) on mentoring found that feeling supported and having deep learning experiences during college is important to the long-term outcomes after college. Three elements were linked to long-term success for college graduates related to emotional support: (1) feeling that they had a professor that made them excited about learning; (2) that the professor cared about them as a person; and (3) that they had a mentor who encouraged them to pursue their goals and dreams.

It is possible to mentor a class of students by continually acknowledging that all students have the capacity to learn, encouraging questions and discussion, listening, showing interest in each individual, asking questions about goals and plans, and providing information that can help students feel a part of the class as well as the university.

Section 3: Outcomes

While the literature on the assessment of course-based research is in its early stages, there are several studies that support the advantages of course-based research. In a comparison of course-based research and apprentice-based research in an upper division life science laboratory curriculum, Shapiro and colleagues (2015) found similar gains for students who participated in course-based research and apprentice-based research. They further found that the achievement gap between the highest-performing students and other students was reduced. Brownell et al. (2015) integrated research experiences into high-enrolment introductory biology classes and, using open-ended written prompts, found that students gained in their understanding of what it means to think like a scientist, and the course examinations indicated gains in the ability to analyse and interpret data. A large study involving over 100 institutions, across all sectors with differing approaches, found that students made learning gains in course-based research (Shaffer *et al.*, 2014). Current assessment studies support the viability and benefits of course-based research for undergraduate students.

To date, the studies of course-based research have primarily focused on science courses. There are few studies of embedding undergraduate research into humanities and social science courses. John Ishiyama (2002), in an early study at Truman State University, found that when humanities and social science students participated in collaborative research, they were more able to think analytically and logically, put ideas together, and learn on their own. When more humanities and social science courses are designed to embed research in the curriculum, it is highly likely that the results will be similar to those identified by Ishiyama and in the sciences.

Section 4: Moving Forward

While each discipline has a different approach to research, there are some commonalities that can be included in first- and second-year course-based research for all disciplines. Courses in the first two years can include development of three foundational skills: observing, questioning, and connecting.

4a. Observing

John Stilgoe (1998), Harvard professor and author of *Outside Lies Magic: Regaining History and Awareness in Everyday Places*, advocates for what he calls "acute observation". Stilgoe takes his students on walks around Harvard and encourages them to notice things in the environment that they might not have paid attention to before. He believes that observing is another way of knowing and can lead to discovery and a better understanding of what is happening around us. Noticing the dates, for example, on fire hydrants introduced the idea of the shift of iron founding from Worcester to Pittsburgh and suggested the question, "Why did this happen?" Observation is a necessary skill for scientists, historians, sociologists, health professionals, writers, actors, artists, and many other professions. Amy Herman (2016), author of *Visual Intelligence*, trains policemen, doctors, and business people to be better observers because she believes it will make them more effective in their work. Herman takes her students to an art museum and, as they look at paintings, she asks them to describe as many details as they can see and then to describe the "who, what, when, and where" of the painting and to avoid making assumptions and subjective comments. In addition to teaching observation skills, she is also emphasising the use of evidence when students describe what they see. First-year students can learn how to be acute observers and there are many ways that professors can include observation in their courses. Professors can take students for a walk around the campus and then discuss what they saw when they return to the classroom. Students can be encouraged to observe their environment and note the changes that occur each day. Is there a new bird nest in a tree? Did a neighbour paint their front door? Has a restaurant added a new organic item on the menu posted in the window? Students can be asked to sit in a coffee shop or other similar environment and write down objectively what they see. They can be encouraged to visit and observe new places in their city or state. Students can look at magazines, newspapers, and photographs and be invited to objectively describe what they see. Observation is the foundation of the research process. Research begins with observation and a sense of curiosity. In 1854, Louis Pasteur said, *"chance favors only the prepared mind"*, and a prepared mind results, in part, from developing strong observation skills. In his 1957 book *The Art of Scientific Investigation*, Beveridge suggests that observation is an active rather than passive mental process. New understandings, discoveries, and innovations are developed from careful observations of one's environment. It is important for deep learning that students develop prepared minds and actively engage in the mental process of observing. When they do, they will become more curious and ask more questions.

4b. Questioning

The ability to frame a researchable question is a fundamental skill for undergraduate research. Asking questions has not always been encouraged in K-12 education, and students will need assistance in learning how to ask good questions. Matthew Bowker (2010:127), assistant professor at Medaille College, suggests that teaching students how to ask questions is a valuable pedagogical objective. He uses a question-centered pedagogy in his courses that he believes helps students to *"understand how the answers we have come to accept are connected, contingent, and contextual, how they rely on, imply, and beg additional questions"*. Questioning suggests that there is an unknown, and it is curiosity about the unknown that drives research. Questioning involves speculation and imagining possibilities. Students' initial questions may be the kind where it is easy to find the answer. For example, googling "what are the demographic changes in New York City" can bring up many objective answers. Students need to learn to ask questions that are probing, encourage analysis, speculation, and creative thinking. Warren Berger (2014:8), author of *A More Beautiful Question*, defines the type of question that we want our students to ask as *"an ambitious yet actionable question that can begin to shift the way we perceive or think about something- and that might act as a catalyst to bring about change"*. Students need to develop analytical, reflective, and open-ended questions that ask *why, what if,* and *how* rather than *what*. This type of question encourages critical and creative thinking that can challenge current assumptions or dig deeper into a topic. When framing questions, students can be encouraged to think about the hidden assumptions or bias in the question. What perspective does the question reflect? How would someone else from a different discipline, a different gender, culture or country frame the same question? In developing research questions, students will need assistance in finding an appropriate level for the questions. Initial questions are often too broad to be able to clearly seek information or too narrow to expand ideas and creativity. Bowker opens each class by saying that they will begin with answers and end with questions. Taking such an approach encourages students to question assumed knowledge and can further develop their curiosity about a topic. The ability to ask actionable questions is a skill that will serve students well in their studies and throughout their life. Asking good questions can be the basis for good decision-making. Successful actions are more likely when the decision-maker can be confident that the right questions have been articulated and considered.

4c. Connecting

Observations and questions become more useful when connections can be made between various ideas, concepts, and pieces of knowledge. Breakthrough discoveries are more likely to occur when the researcher or scholar is able to take what might seem like disparate pieces of information and connect them to develop a new idea, concept, or product. In higher education, professors hope that their students will make connections among the subjects they are studying. Making connections, however, is not something that comes naturally to everyone but is a skill that can be developed. Campuses that intentionally integrate the curriculum to make connections across disciplines are fostering integrative thinking and connectivity in their students. The e-portfolios that many campuses use can also foster integrative thinking when the rubrics ask students to reflect on the connections they are able to make across their courses. Individual faculty can also support and encourage connectivity in their courses. Frequent references to what students are learning in another class can help students see how knowledge develops and is connected. In a history class, for example, the professor might discuss the impact of discovering the cause of malaria on the successful completion of the Panama Canal or the impact of the Russian launching of Sputnik on American education. Asking students at the end of a class session to write down one idea that connects to something they discussed in another class can help them make connections. Professors can describe for students the connections they might make between their own discipline and other information they might encounter. How is an article in the daily newspaper, for example, connected to the current research project of the class? Connecting classroom learning to outside events can add relevance to the research project and help in sustaining and expanding student interest.

Experiences outside one's discipline or normal activities can also lead to new connections. Faculty can encourage students to read outside their discipline, to listen to new kinds of music, to see movies they would not ordinarily watch, and then ask if they were able to make any connections to their own area of study. The Israeli conductor Itay Talgum, in his 2009 TED talk, shares videos of several conductors with different styles of conducting and then provides an analysis of each style. He does not make a direct connection for the audience but one cannot watch the TED talk and not make the connection between conducting, teaching, and leadership. Talgum made the connection between music and business and is now a business consultant. Seeing how other people make connections in their professions can give students insights that will enhance their own ability to make connections. Making connections requires an open and prepared mind. Connections are the result of acute observations and the questions that might follow.

In addition to observing, questioning, and connecting, first- and second-year students can also develop information literacy and library skills that will help them in all of their courses to learn how to use evidence in drawing conclusions and making decisions and how to apply the research methodology of a discipline.

4d. Information Literacy and Library skills

The Association of College and Research Libraries (ACRL) released a new framework for higher education information literacy in January 2016. The document reflects both changes in widespread availability of information and the increased role that students have in generating new knowledge through undergraduate research and scholarship. The ACRL (2016:3) defines information literacy as:

> *"the set of integrated abilities encompassing the reflective discovery of information, the understanding of how information is produced and valued, and the use of information in creating new knowledge and participating ethically in communities of learning."*

As undergraduates learn how new information is produced and disseminated, they also need to learn how to determine the authority of the information and to understand that different information may have a different source of authority. Expert authority gives credibility to the information, but personal experience can sometimes provide authority as well. An important objective for information literacy in the first two years of college is the ability to recognise what information is credible and what information is not reliable and may, in fact, be a hoax. Nina Clements (2016:14–16), a librarian, and Laura Guertin, professor of geology at Penn State-Brandywine, focused on scientific and information literacy in a beginning course for geology majors and a course for non-majors. The overarching goal for both courses was to allow students to understand, communicate examples, and make informed decisions relating to big ideas and fundamental concepts of Earth/ocean science. Students were introduced to criteria that can be used to determine if an information source is credible by asking a series of questions about currency of the information, reliability, authority, and the purpose or point of view of the source. The questions, aptly known as the CRAP test, are a beginning step for developing an understanding of information authority. Guertins' and Clements' students learned to ask these questions to identify unreliable sources.

A literature review is a beginning step for many research projects. As students develop a literature review, they learn the difference between primary and secondary sources, what peer review means, and how to locate and identify the sources they need for their project. In addition, they learn the importance of attribution and how to cite a variety of sources. Learning to look at the bibliographies and references of their sources will help them identify the experts in the area they are studying. Students will undoubtedly begin to see how information is built through the cross-pollination of scholars and may begin to feel they are joining a community of scholars. The development of the literature review will also help students to see the kinds of questions scholars are asking, how one project leads to another question, and assist them in framing their own research question. By reading journal articles and other publications, students can begin to see how to organise information, synthesise their ideas, and draw appropriate conclusions. Knowing how to take full advantage of all of a library's resources and understanding the value of information literacy will reap many benefits as students progress through their college experience as well as when they enter their profession.

4e. Using Evidence

Developing strong information literacy skills and learning how to identify credible, reliable sources is an important part of learning how to use evidence. It is always important for students to understand the necessity of credible evidence, but it is especially important in an age of misinformation and mistruths. Learning how to use evidence in making decisions, drawing conclusions, and formulating ideas is an important life skill as well as a necessary element in maintaining a healthy democracy. Evidence is the use of concrete facts to support a claim. Learning how to verify a claim can be challenging. One would think that using evidence in decision-making would be a best practice in many professions, and yet in a Harvard Business Review article Pfeffer and Sutton (2006:1) report that only 15% of the decisions physicians make are based on evidence. Most of the other decisions are based on outdated knowledge from medical school, traditions, patterns developed from experience, and information from vendors. Giving students skills to verify information by using reliable evidence should be a part of every undergraduate research experience. Always asking the question, "what is the evidence to support your conclusion" is a beginning step to assist students to incorporate the use of evidence into their thinking process. Students can learn to analyse information and evaluate it.

As students read articles for their literature review, the first step is to see who is making the claim and consider if they have the recognised expertise to make such a claim. Then they can learn to analyse the source to determine what it is that the authors are claiming, consider the facts the authors use to support their claim, and ask if the facts presented are relevant to the claim. To evaluate the credibility of information, students can ask if there is other evidence to support the information or if it is new information, is there previous information that would lead to the claim the authors are making now. Students can also ask about any assumptions of the claim and are those assumptions based on a particular point of view or school of thinking? Class discussions of articles that can pass the credibility test and those that cannot will help students to internalise the skill of questioning the evidentiary base of information. Evidence, of course, is different for different disciplines. In the sciences and social sciences, the quality of the experiment or survey can be questioned, while in literary analysis the text is the source of evidence. Strategies for learning to question the evidence and make a determination of its credibility are similar, however, for all disciplines.

4f. Applying Research Methodology

Each discipline has its own research methodology, and it is important for students to learn the methodology of the discipline they are studying. The fundamentals of observing, questioning, and connecting are common to all disciplines but may be developed in different ways in the sciences, social sciences, humanities, and arts. It is possible and desirable to analyse the discipline's methodology and design a developmental sequence specific to the discipline.

For example, Gita Bangera (2014) has integrated research into the genomics course she teaches, with the students learning how to do the sequencing and analysis of a bacterial strain of wheat. In addition to the laboratory work, students do a literature review prior to the lab work, participate in a once-a-week journal club where they write a summary of related articles, and at the end of the course they develop and present a poster. Bangera has identified the key components of graduate-level research and adapted them for her beginning students.

Kevin Ostoyich (2015), a history professor at Valparaiso University, engages his students in solving mysteries as a way of introducing students to the process of historical research that he sees as basically unravelling a mystery. Students first explore a mystery in their own family and then the class collaboratively solves the hypothetical murder of their professor. Students learn how to ferret out clues to the murder in the library and the archives while also learning how to use primary and secondary sources. They begin to understand that the study of history involves analysis and interpretation of information obtained from many sources, including archival documents, newspapers, oral interviews, eyewitness accounts, and other sources. At the conclusion of the class, students develop a narrative that describes the mystery and its solution. Students also learn that history is a collaborative project, as historians work with librarians, archivists, news reporters, and the community to tell the story. Ostoyich has identified the basic elements of historical research and incorporated them into activities that engage students. His students are learning to think like historians, how to gather and analyse information, and how to use evidence in drawing conclusions.

When Mary Isbell (2016), University of New Haven, teaches the introduction to the English major course, she asks students to collaborate to create a digital edition of a text from the public domain. Students read the text on *project gutenberg* and she and the students work together to decide what sort of context is needed to make sense of the text. They divide up responsibilities to create the notes. The students are learning about literary scholarship as well as learning other skills such as analysis, library skills, and collaboration.

The Howard Hughes Medical Institute (HHMI) Science Alliance Education Phage Hunters Advancing Genomics and Evolutionary Science (SEA-PHAGES) project has been incorporated into several course-based projects for first- or second-year students (Caruso *et al.*, 2009; Jordan *et al.*, 2014). These projects provide authentic research experiences for students, and their work leads to new discoveries that add to a national database. The Caruso project is especially significant because it engaged non-majors in research. Russell *et al.* (2015) developed an integrated course-embedded research experience (ICURE) that brought several classes and levels of instruction together to engage students in a longitudinal study of biodiversity. The inclusive research project had a goal of documenting biological changes in the local environment and creating a longitudinal biodiversity database. Other models have included collaborating across multiple sections of a course (Kowalski *et al.*, 2016), engaging students in designing a research question (Jacob, 2012), and partnering with a national research lab (Harvey *et al.*, 2014).

Conclusion

Incorporating research into first- and second-year courses allows students to gain the benefits of research by learning to become good observers, frame actionable questions, explain and defend their ideas, develop tolerance for uncertainty, use evidence, and work collaboratively. The inclusion of course-based research in first- and second-year introductory courses is an issue of equity and social justice. Course-based research that is authentic and accessible can provide every student with the intellectual benefits of undergraduate research. Students who are careful observers know how to ask actionable questions, make connections, use evidence, and tolerate ambiguity will become the kinds of citizens we need for a healthy and sustainable future. Our communities will benefit when every graduate can apply their research skills and knowledge to the important questions in their professional and community lives.

About the Author

Nancy H. Hensel is president of the New American Colleges & Universities. She previously served as executive officer for the Council on Undergraduate Research. She can be reached at: nhensel@newamericancolleges.org

Bibliography

American Association for the Advancement of Science (2009). *Vision and Change in Undergraduate Biology Education: A Call to Action.* Washington, DC: American Association for the Advancement of Science.

Association of College and Research Libraries. (2016). *Framework for Information Literacy for Higher Education.* Online Resource: http://www.ala.org/acrl/standards/ilframework [Accessed on 21 April 2017].

Bangera, G. & S. E. Brownell (2014). Course-Based Undergraduate Research Experiences Can Make Scientific Research More Inclusive. *CBE Life Sci Educ,* Vol. 13, No. 4, pp. 602–606.

Beck, C.; A. Butler & K. Burke da Silva (2014). Promoting Inquiry-Based Teaching in Laboratory Courses: Are We Meeting the Grade? *CBE Life Sci Educ,* Vol. 13, pp. 444–452.

Beckman M. & N. Hensel (2009). Making the Explicit the Implicit: Defining Undergraduate Research. *CUR Quarterly,* Vol. 29, No. 4, pp. 40–44.

Berger, W. (2014). *A More Beautiful Question: The Power of Inquiry to Spark Breakthrough Ideas.* New York: Bloomsbury Publishing Plc.

Beveridge, W. I. B. (1957). *The Art of Scientific Investigation.* New York: Vintage Books.

Bowker, M. H. (2010). Teaching Students to Ask Questions Instead of Answering Them. Online Resource: https://ctal.udel.edu/files/.../bowker-2010-teaching-students-to-ask-questions-16echtl [Accessed on 15 April 2018].

Boyer E. L. (1998). *Reinventing undergraduate education: A blueprint for America's research universities.* Stony Brook, NY: Stony Brook University.

Brame, C. (n.d.). Incorporating Research into Science Courses. Center for Teaching, Vanderbilt University. Online Resource: https://cft.vanderbilt.edu/guides-sub-page/incorporating-research-into-credit-bearing-science-courses [Accessed on 22 December 2016].

Brownell S. E. & K. D. Tanner (2012). Barriers to Faculty Pedagogical Change: Lack of Training, Time, Incentives, and...Tensions with Professional Identity. *CBE Life Sci. Educ,* Vol. 11, No. 4, pp. 339–346.

Brownell S. E.; D. S. Hekmat-Scafe; V. Singla; P. Chandler-Seawell; J. E. Conklin Iman; S. L. Eddy; T. Stearns & M. S. Cyert (2015). A High-Enrollment Course-Based Undergraduate Research Experience Improves Student Conceptions of Scientific Thinking and Ability to Interpret Data. *CBE Life Sci. Educ,* Vol. 14, No. 2, pp. 1–14.

Carnevale, A. P. & J. Strohl (2013). *Separate and Unequal: How Higher Education Reinforces the Intergenerational Reproduction of White Racial Privilege.* Online Resource: https://cew.georgetown.edu/wpcontent/uploads/2014/11/SeparateUnequal.FR_.pdf [Accessed on 13 April 2017].

Carr K. S.; S. D. Davis; S. Erbe; C. M. Fulmer; L. B. Kats & M. U. Teetzel (2013). Developing First-Year Students as Scholars. *CUR Quarterly,* Vol. 33, No. 4, pp. 8–15.

Caruso, S. M.; J. Sandoz & J. Jelsey (2009). Non-STEM Undergraduates Become Enthusiastic Phage Hunters. *CBE Life Sci Educ,* Vol. 8, No. 2, pp. 278–282.

Clements, N. & L. Guertin (2016). Science literacy meets information literacy. *College & Research Library News.* Vol. 77, No. 1, pp. 14–16.

Corwin Auchincloss, L.; S. L. Laursen; J. L. Branchaw; K. Eagan; M. Graham; D. L. Hanauer; G. Lawrie: M. McLinn; N. Pelaez; S. Rowland; M. Towns; N. M. Trautmann; P. Varna Nelson; T. J. Westom & E.L. Dolan (2014). Assessment of Course-Based Undergraduate Research Experiences: A Meeting Report. *CBE Life Sci Educ,* Vol. 13, No. 1, pp. 29–40.

Dretal, C. (2010). *Cynthia Dretel.* Online Resource: https://www.moravian.edu/academics/undergraduate-research/honors/dretel [Accessed on 30 March 2017].

Gentile, J.; K. Brenner & A. Stephens, (Eds.) (2017). *Undergraduate Research Experiences for STEM Students: Successes, Challenges, and Opportunities.* Washington, DC: The National Academies Press.

Harrington, M. (1962). *The Other America: Poverty in the United States.* New York: Macmillan Publishers.

Harrison M.; D. Dunbar; L. Ratmansky; K. Boyd & D. Lopatto (2011). Classroom-Based Science Research at the Introductory Level: Changes in Career Choice and Attitude. *CBE Life Sci Educ,* Vol. 10, pp. 279–286.

Hart, E. (2016). Personal communication. 30 September 2016.

Harvey, P. A.; C. Wall; S. W. Luckeu; S. Langer & L. A. Leinwand (2014). The Python Project: A Unique Model for Extending Research Opportunities to Undergraduate Students. *CBE life Sci Educ,* Vol. 13, no. 4, pp. 698–710.

Herman, A. E. (2016). *Visual Intelligence: Sharpen Your Perception, Change Your Life.* New York: Houghton, Mifflin, Harcourt Publishing Company.

Hunter A. B.; S. Laursen & E. Seymour (2007). Becoming a scientist: the role of undergraduate research in students' cognitive, personal, and professional development. *Sci Educ.* Vol. 91, No. 1, pp. 36–74.

Isbell, M. (2016). Personal communication. 28 January 2016.

Ishiyama, J. (2002). Does Early Participation in Undergraduate Research Benefit Social Science and Humanities Students? *College Student Journal,* Vol. 36, No.3, pp. 380–387.

Jacob, N. (2012). Investigating Arabia Mountain: A Molecular Approach. *Science,* Vol. 335, pp. 1588–1589.

Jordan, T. C.; S. H. Burnett; S. Carson; S. M. Caruso & K. Clase et. al. (2014). A Broadly Implementable Research Course in Phage Discovery and Genomics for First-Year Undergraduate Students. *BIOS,* Vol. 5, No. 1, Online Resource: http://digitalcommons.wustl.edu/cgi/viewcontent. cgi?article=3797&context=open_access_pubs [Accessed on 30 June 2017].

Kowalski J. R.; G. C. Hoops & R. J. Johnson (2016). Implementation of a Collaborative Series for Classroom-Based Undergraduate Research Experiences Spanning Chemical Biology, Biochemistry, and Neurobiology. *CBE Life Sci Educ,* Vol. 15, No. 4. Online Resource: https://www.ncbi.nlm. nih.gov/pubmed/27810870 [Accessed on 10 March 2017].

Kuh, G. D. (2008). *High-Impact Educational Practices: What They Are, Who Has Access to Them, and Why They Matter.* Washington, D. C.: Association of American Colleges and Universities.

Laursen, S.; A. B. Hunter; E. Seymour; H. Thiry & G. Melton (2010). *Undergraduate Research in the Sciences: Engaging Students in Real Science.* San Francisco: John Wiley & Sons.

Lopatto D. (2003). The Essential Features of Undergraduate Research. *CUR Quarterly,* Vol. 23, No. 3, pp. 139–142.

Lopatto, D. (2010). *Science in Solution: The Impact of Undergraduate Research on Student Learning.* Washington, DC: Council on Undergraduate Research and Research Corporation for Science Advancement.

Lopatto D.; C, Hauser; C. J. Jones; D. Paetkau & V. Chandrasekaran *et al.* (2012). A Central Support System Can Facilitate Implementation and Sustainability of a Classroom-Based Undergraduate Research Experience (CURE) in Genomics. *CBE Life Sci Educ,* Vol. 13 No. 4, pp. 711–723.

McMillan, E. & L. Pauling (1927). An X-ray study of the alloys of lead and thallium. *Journal of American Chemical Society,* Vol. 49, No. 3, pp. 666–669. Online Resource: pubs.acs.org/toc/jacsat/49/3 [Accessed on 10 April 2017].

Merkel, C. A. (2001). *Undergraduate research at six universities: A pilot study for the Association of American Universities.* Pasadena, CA: California Institute of Technology.

Montana State University (2017). *Core 2.0 Courses* Online Resource: www.montana.edu/core2/approved_courses.html [Accessed 17 April 2017].

Nagda B. A.; S. R. Gregerman; J. Jonides; W. von Hippel & J. S. Lerner (1998). Undergraduate Student-Faculty Research Partnerships Affect Student Retention. *The Review of Higher Education,* Vol. 22, No. 10, pp. 55–72.

National Academies of Sciences, Engineering, and Medicine (2015). *Integrating Discovery-Based Research into the Undergraduate Curriculum.* Report of a Convocation. Washington, DC: The National Academies Press.

Ostoyich, K. (2016). *Personal Communication.* 6 February 2016.

Packard, B. W-L. (2016). *Successful STEM Mentoring Initiatives for Underrepresented Students: A Research-Based Guide for Faculty and Administrators.* Sterling, CA: Stylus Publishing, Inc.

Pasteur, L. (1854). Lecture, University of Lille (7 December 1854).

Pauling, L. (1958). *Arthur Amos Noyes: A Biographical Memoir.* Washington, DC: National Academy of Sciences. Online Resource: www.nasonline.org/publications/biographical-memoirs/memoir.../noyes-arthur-a.pdf [Accessed on 10 April 2017].

PCAST: President's Council on Advisors on Science and Technology (2012). *Engage to Excel: Producing One Million Additional College Graduates with Degrees in Science, Technology, Engineering and Mathematics.* Washington, DC: U.S. Government Office of Science and Technology. Online Resource: www.whitehouse.gov/sites/defaulty/files/microsites/ostp/pcast-engage-to-excell-final_2-15-12.pdf [Accessed on 20 December 2016].

Pfeffer, J. & R. I. Sutton (2006). Evidence-Based Management. *Harvard Business Review.* January. Online Resource: https://hbr.org/2006/01/evidence-based-management [Accessed on 20 April 2017].

Pyles, R. A. & F. Levy (2009). Opening the Door to early Student Involvement in Scholarly Activity: Coordinating Efforts and Providing Financial Support. In M. K. Boyd & J. L. Wesemann (Eds.), *Broadening Participation in Undergraduate Research: Fostering Excellence and Enhancing the Impact.* Washington DC: Council on Undergraduate Research, pp. 134–139.

Ray, J. & S. Kafka (2014). Live in College Matters for Life After College. Washington, D.C.: Gallup (6 May 2014).

Rowland, S.; R. Pedwell; G. Lawrie; J. Lovie-Toon & Y. Hung (2016). Do We Need to Design Course-Based Undergraduate Research Experiences for Authenticity? *CBE Life Sci Educ.,* Vol. 15, No. 4, Online Resource: https://www.ncbi.nlm.nih.gov/pmc/articles/PMC5132376/ [Accessed on 30 June 2017).

Russel, S. H.; M. P. Hancock & J. McCullough (2007). Benefits of undergraduate research experiences. *Science,* Vol. 316, No. 5824, pp. 548–559.

Russell J. E.; A. R. D'Costa; C. Runck; D. W. Barnes; A. L. Barrera; J. Hurst-Kennedy; E. B. Sudduth; E. Ll. Quinlan & M. Schlueter (2015). Bridging the Undergraduate Curriculum Using an Integrated Course-Embedded Undergraduate Research Experience (ICURE). *CBE Life Sci Educ,* Vol. 14, No. 1, ar4.

Seymour E; A-B. Hunter; S. L. Laursen & T. DeAntoni (2004). Establishing the benefits of research experiences for undergraduates in the sciences: First findings from a three-year study. *Science,* 88, 493–534.

Shaffer, C. D.; C. J. Alvarez; A. E. Bednarski; D. Dunbar & A. L. Goodman *et al.* (2014). A Course-Based Research Experience: How Benefits Change with Increased Investment in Instructional Time. *CBE Life Sci Educ,* Vol. 13, No. 1, pp. 111–130.

Shapiro C.; J. Moberg-Parker; S. Toma; C. Avon; H. Zimmerman; E. A. Roth-Johnson; S. P. Hancock; M. Levis-Fitzgerald & E. R. Sanders (2015). Comparing the Impact of Course-Based and Apprentice-Based Research Experiences in a Life Science Laboratory Curriculum. *Journal of Microbiology and Biology Education,* Vol. 16, pp. 186–197.

Spell R. M.; J. A. Guinan & K. R. Miller (2014). Redefining Authentic Research Experience in Introductory Biology Laboratories and Barriers to Their Implementation. *CBE Life Sci Educ,* Vol. 13, No. 1, pp. 102–110.

Sharp, Phillip A. Communication on the occasion of the Library of Congress celebration of the joining of the Council on Undergraduate Research and the National Conference on Undergraduate Research, 27 October 2010.

Stilgoe, J. R. (1998). *Outside Lies Magic: Regaining History and Awareness in Everyday Places.* New York: Walker and Company.

Stone, P. A. (2010). Communication with Council on Undergraduate Research, Washington, DC October.

Talgum, I. (2009). Itay Talgum: Lead the great conductors. TED Talk. Online Resource: https://www.ted.com/.../itay_talgam_lead_like_the_great_conduc [Accessed on 24 April 2017].

Wieman, C. E. (2001). *Carl E. Wieman – Biographical.* Online Resource: https://www.nobelprize.org/nobel_prizes/physics/laureates/2001/wieman-bio.html [Accessed on 4 April 2017].

Zupanc, G. K. H. (2012). Undergraduate Research and Inquiry-Based Learning: The Revitalization of the Humboltian Ideals. Bioscience Education Vol. 19, No. 1, p. 6, Online Resource: http://www.tandfonline.com/doi/full/10.11120/beej.2012.19000011?scroll=top&needAccess=true [Accessed on 6 April 2017].

Chapter 23

From Material Construction to Cognitive Construction – On the Roles of the Artefact in the Learning Process

Daniel Cermak-Sassenrath

Introduction

This chapter contributes to the book *New Innovations in Teaching and Learning in Higher Education* when it investigates the connection between material construction and cognitive construction from a dialectical constructivist position. It starts from the hypothesis that physical making and conceptual thinking can happen together, inspire each other, and build on each other. I define material construction as the creation of all kinds of artefacts, from software applications such as games (e.g., Habel & Hope, forthcoming) to websites, films, electronic gadgets, and woodworking. The material activity itself is seen as exemplary (the question of language as material construction (e.g., see Mercer, 2002; Baker, 1999) is ignored for the moment). No position is taken with regard to technology use, but it is noted that many features that need to be painstakingly implemented in digital media are often implicitly available in material interaction (such as real-time and multi-user interaction, haptic or tactile properties). Reading this chapter, you will gain the following three insights:

1) Material construction has several tangible benefits for the learning process;

2) Material construction and cognition construction are essentially related and connected;

3) Three kinds of learning transfers within and between subject domains and abstraction levels can be identified and located on a continuum of material and cognitive construction.

The text is structured into several sections: First, a constructivist approach to learning based on a phenomenological view is motivated and sketched. This approach proposes a continuum between bodily and mental activity. Practical, hands-on observations made over several years in a making workshop series identify bottom-up, tangible effects that the material construction of artefacts can exhibit with regard to the learning process. From the conceptual basis and practical observations, a model is proposed that links material and cognitive construction and identifies three specific kinds of transfers that can happen within and across those domains.

Section I: Background

From a phenomenological position, a person's interaction with the world is the reality that person has access to and creates. This view invites or even necessitates a dialectical constructivist approach to learning: Understanding is not directly transmitted from one person to another (e.g., taught), but it is constructed by individuals based on their interactions in various situations over time with other people and objects. Such a constructivist approach highlights the situatedness and bodily locatedness of cognitive activities (Kolb, 1984): Learning happens *in correspondence with* locations, people (Mercer, 2002), and materials. The learning environment not only contains the learner, the material, and other people, in the same way that a box contains marbles, the environment *participates* in the cognitive process and situates it in a social context (Schunk, 2012). Piaget observes a direct link between "*rich environments that allow for [learners'] active exploration and hands-on activities*" and the "*active construction of knowledge*" (Schunk, 2012:239; see Mercer, 2002:149). Verbeek (n.d.:3; cf. Ehrmann, 1968:55, 56) develops as the "*central idea*" of his well-known phenomenological study the idea of "*the mutual constitution of subject and object, or of humans and their world*": People are located in their environments, and they are the places they experience and the locations of their existence (Verbeek, n.d); and the world is only what it is through human action and interpretation (Verbeek, n.d.). Thus, a constructivist approach to teaching aims to create learning situations in which learners construct knowledge based on challenges, tensions, and contradictions in the interactions with other people and the world. It is widely acknowledged (e.g., by Vos *et al.*, 2001) that learner engagement, knowledge acquisition, recall, and application benefit when the learners' existing knowledge, skills, and interests are taken into account and built upon.

How can material objects and body movement initiate or facilitate cognitive processes and help learners' understanding? A radical constructivist position on learning posits that to literally make something is the only way to genuinely understand it (Glasersfeld, 1984). Milne (2007) describes that the importance and effectiveness of construction in learning was recently recognised in the area of digital media and institutionalised teaching.

Damşa (2014:252) posits that artefacts can assume a central position in learning when they are used instrumentally to create other artefacts, embody past learning activities, and are *"shared, articulated, and extended by shared efforts and by mobilizing collective cognitive resources"*. For objects to become catalysts of understanding, however, they require *"some form of productive interaction"*; that is, *"communicative encounters between collaborating individuals"* centred on creating a *"shared understanding of concepts and ideas"*, turning ideas and concepts *"into knowledge objects"*, and the progressive development and iteration of such objects Damşa (2014:273). The following section discusses how the construction of artefacts can exhibit such qualities.

The idea that people's activities and experiences are located, situated, and mediated by their material bodies, and do not happen in an empty space by abstract agents, has been applied and investigated with regard to cognitive processes in many areas and domains such as mathematics, neuroscience, cognitive and social psychology, linguistics, and performing arts (Lindgren & Johnson-Glenberg, 2013); Verbeek, (2005) enquires into the role of artefacts in our Western technological culture.

Section 2: Practice

2a. A General Introduction to the Innovative Practice

This section describes hands-on experiences with material construction made over several years in a Making workshop series, and observes tangible effects for the learning process.

2b. The Curriculum

This chapter is based on observations made in the *BreakIT* workshop series at the IT University of Copenhagen (ITU). *BreakIT* is a hands-on, practical workshop series about electronics, mechanics, interfaces, and dangerous things. Workshops are offered monthly during the (taught) semester, for a total of six to eight workshops per year. A different practical project is built in each workshop. The projects differ considerably in their difficulty, scope, and materials; participants may explore, search, assemble, model, experiment, take apart, shape, manufacture, test, discuss, perform, and play. However, each project has to involve an *artefact* that can be built or made or fixed, and which people *want to have* (an overview of past projects is available online at dace.de/breakit. html). The workshop series is extracurricular and not (in the author's estimate) conceived of by the facilitators or perceived by the participants as an educational event.

The time frame for each project is one afternoon; workshops usually start at 2 p.m. and finish when people go home (occasionally projects are offered as two-part workshops (e.g., building microscopes from webcams), or several workshops are connected (e.g., amp building and CMOS audio hacking; PCB etching, building Geiger counters, building guitar/audio pedals); some projects are so popular that they are repeated in several iterations (e.g., pickup winding, building slot cars, building game interface devices). Participants are invited to propose topics and to facilitate workshops, although many workshops are facilitated by the author, often together with an external expert or participant. There are certain areas that prove to be popular with this particular audience and facilitators (e.g., guitar-related projects, audio hacking, game interfaces), and each of these topics has had several workshops.

Usually the workshops happen at one of the labs at the university. The university intends the workshop series, as far as can be established by the author, an open invitation for students and staff to engage with hardware in various forms, for instance, 'making' technologies such as laser cutting and 3D printing. Participation is free and usually people build and keep things; participation is also not mandatory, and neither participation nor facilitation gives formal credit.

The workshop participants are usually, by the author's estimate, more than 75% bachelor, master, and PhD students, and up to 25% technical, teaching, and research university staff; occasionally, friends, partners, and visitors from other universities attend. Students and staff of the university mostly come from IT-oriented fields such as computer science, digital media, software development, and data science. Attendance numbers vary considerably between 2 and 20 participants. A handful of enthusiasts are workshop regulars, more or less regardless of the specific project, but most participants are quite selective in the workshops they attend. The number of people who know about the workshops is without doubt much greater than the number of people who attend. Workshop invites are disseminated through a mailing list, a university-internal event calendar and weekly info e-mail, and info screens in the building.

The specific observations are made and the photos taken during six seasons of *BreakIT* from March 2014 to December 2016. The method of data collection is participatory observation by the author in the roles of workshop host, facilitator, and participant. The photos are taken regularly by the author to document the workshops.

2c. Organisation of the Practice

Several tangible effects of material construction for the learning process can be identified in the workshops.

Construction provides direction

Constructing an artefact can provide the people involved with a strong sense of direction, because, as Damşa (2014:252) posits, the object assumes *"both projective and objective value"*; that is, *"it represents both the goal to be pursued and the material outcome to be achieved"*. In a learning situation, this sense of direction can be expressed and perceived by the learners as (1) an aim to reach, (2) a reason to learn, and (3) hard success criteria.

(1) An aim to reach. Drawing on experiences and observations made during the workshop series, participants often appear to feel a strong sense of direction when engaged in the process of constructing an artefact. An artefact can act as *"an anchor for an activity"* (Damşa, 2014:252) in that it serves as a shared focal point and centre of gravity towards

which progress is measured. The artefact offers directions when it answers the questions *what to do* and *where to go*. It almost takes over from the learners and asks for the next step to be performed; the process is driven forward and deeper (see Figure 1).

Figure 1: Object orientation: The guitar in which the pickups will be mounted for testing is kept on the table (Guitar Pickups, November 2016).

Very often, the construction of an artefact is only a starting point for a journey of discovery. The artefact serves as a milestone on the way. It may answer some questions but also raises new ones. People are or become curious and want to find out more. Constructing artefacts becomes a method and mode of exploration.

(2) A reason to learn. Building something is a reason to acquire competencies. When people create something, they need to know a lot about it. The artefact defines a range of specific problems to be addressed. The construction of artefacts also often invites or necessitates collaboration. People know exactly what to look for in concepts, materials, tools, skills, and collaborations. The immediate temporal proximity between the gain

and the application of knowledge and skills motivates learners.

(3) Hard success criteria. The construction of an artefact has intrinsic and often very clear success criteria. The challenge is genuine and is posed *by the activity and the process themselves* (see Figure 2); it is not perceived, for instance, as an artificial exercise that is evaluated afterwards from the outside through an arbitrary grading scheme. An artefact confronts the learner with the necessity to evaluate when a meaningful contribution has been reached.

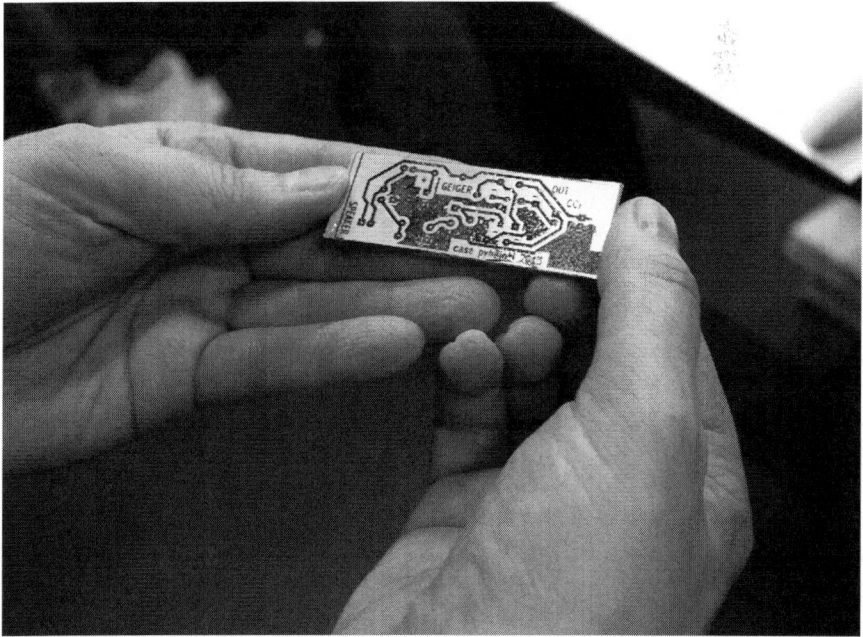

Figure 2: Hard success criteria: Is this transfer good enough? (Etching PCB Boards, March 2016).

The work structures the process

It has been observed and investigated from various angles (e.g., by Verbeek, 2005) how material and immaterial conditions shape people's behaviours. In the case of the construction of artefacts, the interaction appears to be very direct. The artefact depends on people's actions, and the actions are influenced by the artefact. What appears to be specifically relevant here is the structure that this interaction creates within the learning process. The structures created vary considerably over time and between people and artefacts, and involves many contingencies; but, by observation, it appears that certain kinds of artefacts tend to produce roughly similar kinds of structures.

Figure 3: Nobody knows if these speakers will work well enough before participants try them (Headphones, December 2015).

It has been argued that initial or basic instruction is useful and has a place in education, being then followed by, for example, more explorative forms of teaching and learning (e.g., by Bernard Robben, pers. comm., Teaching to Tinker workshop at *NordiCHI 2014*). But it appears that instruction before the learner's own activity and experience prescribes a particular experience, view, and approach, and tends to re-enact and strengthen previous, tacit and implicit positions in uncritical ways. Instruction tends to reproduce itself; by telling people what to look for, one effectively tells them what to see. Learners are then prevented from discovering learning content on their own and its structures, categories, patterns, and methods. Blikstein (2014) advises that, to learn effectively, pupils should first experiment to create a need and structure for knowledge, and only then watch a video or listen to a lecture to receive instruction. Not only should educators probably refrain from pre-shaping students' experiences on moral grounds, in explorative or research-based teaching they *do not know* what is coming and *they cannot know* (see Figure 3).

Immediate feedback

The material presence of an artefact often causes tensions between the tangible, unquestionable, and unambiguous experience and the goals, intentions, and ideas of the learners: Artefacts can appear to resist learners. The resulting questions, uncertainty, and doubts need to be competently addressed, handled, and potentially resolved. The immediate feedback that artefacts give is a way for learners to implicitly and explicitly question their understandings. An *implicit* test can happen in the form of a test, a comparison, or an experiment (see Figure 4). Depending on the outcome, their understandings needs to be extended, revised, or questioned. An *explicit* test can happen when something unexpectedly breaks, does not work, or surprises. Learners are then challenged to find an explanation for the mismatch between their expectations and the encountered results.

Without a difference such as a problem, conflict, mismatch, breakdown, error, or surprise, there would be no need to learn (Schunk, 2012:240); Overdijk *et al.* (2014:298) observe how challenge focuses and coordinates attention. Investigation to gain insight becomes a way to resolve contradictions or oppositions that learners encounter (Schunk, 2012:238). In the author's experience, ideas, theories, and investigative strategies are almost immediately formulated and proposed when a group of learners encounter unsatisfactory conditions; prior positions are made explicit and questioned.

Figure 4: Testing a handmade guitar pedal (Guitar Pedals, April 2016).

The mediating development catalyst

An artefact can act as a development catalyst for iteration and revision. Building artefacts externalises learning in that it makes positions, under-standings, and assumptions accessible within a group of people (Damşa, 2014:255). Physical activity and materials enable accidents, intuitions, and spontaneous combinations. Thus, an object can become a communi-cation device or *"mediator of group interaction"* (ibid.:274) by reformatting ongoing processes.

From the observations in the workshops, it appears that material construction can function as a mediating development catalyst in at least three ways:

(1) Negotiation. In material construction, people are pushed to find, formulate, explain, and negotiate specific, explicit, and concrete positions. An artefact thus collects and reflects people's ideas and it facilitates their negotiation (see Figure 5).

Figure 5: The construction of the first artefact serves as the focal point in the ideation process for all participants (Printing T-shirts, December 2016).

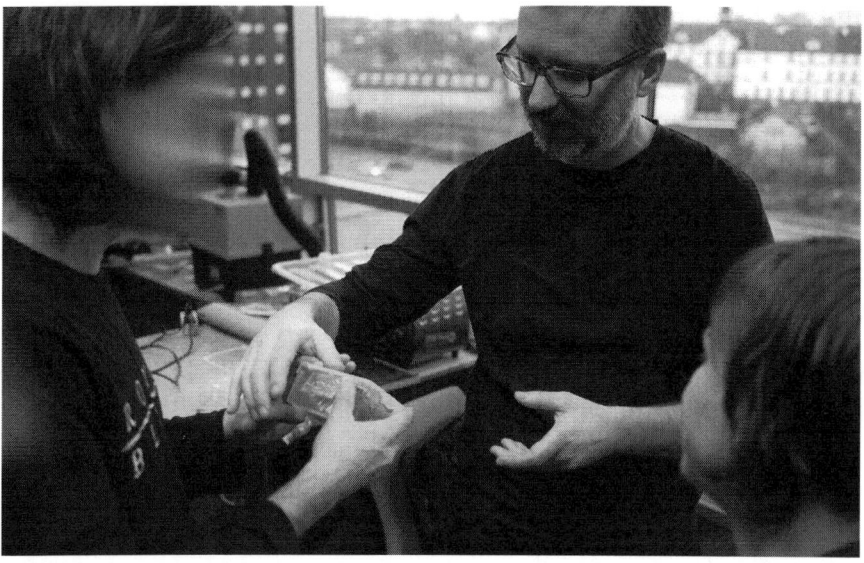

Figure 6: The artefact as an argument: Passing it from one person to another (Geiger Counters, March 2016).

(2) Association. A material artefact triggers associations by being physically present. The materiality also offers seeing it from different angles (e.g., turning it around or breaking it). An artefact can be seen in a different context (e.g., on a kitchen table) or by a person not involved in the design process.

(3) Appropriation. Many ideas for novel applications can probably be attributed to somebody misunderstanding the designers' intentions, misusing an artefact, or improvising. For this to occur, the object must be reasonably accessible (i.e., independent and free from the designers' grasp).

Attitude

Building artefacts can be fun. If it is, nothing else matters, and learning follows without effort because people want to get better at what they enjoy and apply themselves to this end. There are strong indications that emotions and attitudes such as motivation and confidence directly influence cognitive performance, for instance, attention and information processing (Schunk, 2012:23). It appears most rewarding when people learn what they are interested in, what is relevant for them, and what benefits them; and they can learn almost anything if they care (Maeda, 2006:34; Ackermann, 2001:4; People, 2016).

Material construction often involves social aspects. Building a material artefact usually involves being in the same location, working together, discussing, laughing, sweating, and eating together; helping each other, explaining, proposing, and asking things, as well as fighting with each other and with the material. Often, questions of what something is and what it means are discussed controversially.

At least three aspects of material construction can be identified that can contribute to participants' experience of fun and a positive can-do attitude: To create something that (1) participants perceive as relevant (e.g., important, in demand); (2) is difficult to create (i.e., creating it is an achievement); and (3) leaves traces.

(1) Relevance. Teaching material that is seen as relevant, necessary, and useful by the learners motivates them intrinsically – they feel the need and urge to interact with it and an internal drive to ask, discuss, make, and explore (Cermak-Sassenrath, 2015): Intrinsic motivation is

"the prototypic manifestation of the human tendency toward learning and creativity" (Ryan & Deci, 2000:69). For learners, learning something they are not interested in knowing is not a rewarding task. *"If it's not fun, if it's not creative or new, it's not worth it"* (Levy, 1994). Ryan and Deci (2000:71) note that *"people will be intrinsically motivated only for activities that hold intrinsic interest for them, activities that have the appeal of novelty, challenge, or aesthetic value"*. Obviously, many topics and subjects do not immediately appeal to students but are nonetheless relevant. An interest-driven learning approach necessitates informed learners who competently manage, direct, and evaluate their own learning.

(2) Achievement. Material construction challenges, motivates, and fuels learners' can-do attitude. Learners can perceive it as a significant achievement to have built an artefact by themselves. This (often somewhat naïve) drive can support learning when it boosts people's self-image and confidence (Schunk, 2012:22).

(3) Traces. Building something often leaves traces, and many of these are certainly unintentional side effects. But some traces appear to be purposefully constructed, and people appear to enjoy leaving traces or keeping mementos (if not the artefact itself) that witness their journey. These do not necessarily need to be graffiti on walls or tables (see Figure 7), but can be little things like changes in the environment, scratches, and by-products such as sketches, offcuts, photos, and prototypes (see Figure 8).

Artefacts, once built, can be evaluated, presented, and demoed at various opportunities – for different audiences, at different locations and points in time. Students also often assemble portfolios of their works.

Figure 7: Leftover trace: Somebody tested a star-shaped stencil on the lab's bench (Printing T-shirts, December 2016).

Figure 8: Recording the play test with a phone (Pong Games, October 2014).

2d. Preparations

Any kind of workshop works. In this chapter, the creation of all kinds of artefacts is seen as material construction, from software applications to websites, films, electronic gadgets, and wood working. The material activity itself is seen as exchangeable and arbitrary.

Section 3: Outcome

A phenomenological perspective rejects dichotic separations between body and mind, concrete and abstract thinking, practical and theoretical reasoning; rather, it sees a continuum between these positions. Here, bodily movement and interaction with material objects is not equated with cognitive processes; but it is observed how cognitive processes align with, correspond to, react to, trigger, and express bodily activity in material construction (see Enyedy et al., 2015). Mental processes are taken to be intimately intertwined with sensual perceptions and bodily actions.

When everything is learned, perceived, or observed – or rather, constructed bottom-up by individuals – there must be ways of arriving at conceptual levels of thinking from practical levels of acting. This position is shared, for instance, by Enyedy et al. (2015:8) who *"theorize that cognition is distributed and that some conceptual blends are constructed publicly in interaction and anchored by the material world"*. Lindgren and Johnson-Glenberg (2013:446) suggest that people *"draw upon [their] experience in the physical world ... when engaging in higher-order thought processes that can serve as a basis for new knowledge"*.

There is little doubt that people learn what they are doing; this is a common behavioural observation and appears to be largely undisputed. The question is, do people also learn something else? If the mental world is built purely bottom-up from sensory experiences with and reflections on the material world, transfers must happen. These transfers need to move and translate between different situations, applications, conceptual frameworks, and abstraction levels, otherwise *"all learning would be situationally specific"* (Schunk, 2012:24), and high-level mental processes and constructs would not exist. Here, three ways are observed in which conceptual reasoning and material construction are essentially connected; the occurring transfers are termed *factual*, *structural*, and *meta*. The model is not specifically focused on or limited to establishing connections between material and cognitive construction, but accommodates and integrates them naturally.

Factual Transfers

It appears undisputed that horizontal transfers (see Figure 9) happen within subject domains between similar activities, such as throwing a ball and a spear, or writing a poem and a novel.

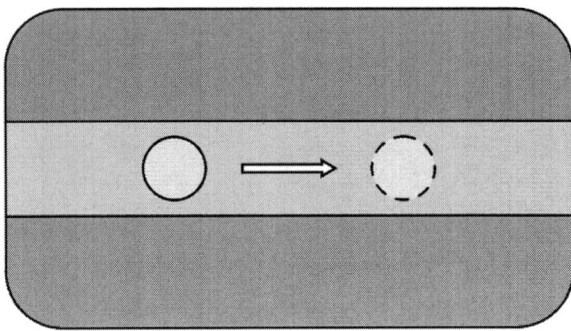

Figure 9: Horizontal transfer within a subject domain.

Factual transfers across subject domains can happen between similar or related activities (see Figure 10); the similarity and relatedness between applications, situations, and contexts can be mimetical, analogue, and associative. Examples of such factual transfers are knowledge, methods, systems, and skills, such as using scaffolding to write a text and building a model railway bridge; and students *"learn[ing] about pendulum motion"* by *"swing[ing] the forearm with the elbow fixed"* (Lindgren & Johnson-Glenberg, 2013:446).

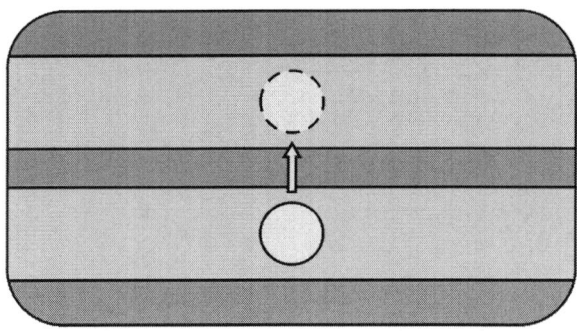

Figure 10: Factual transfer across subject domains.

Structural Transfers

Structural transfers happen vertically, between abstraction levels (see Figure 11); for instance, a pattern, semblance, or hierarchy is observed in nature and recognised or expressed in a mental construct (e.g., as a concept, cf. Dourish, 2001), or *vice versa*. Structural transfers do not rely or depend on mimetical matching or mapping; the transfer is a constructive translation and conversion from one system of reference into another. The scope, size, scale, order of source, and destination system, area, or domain differ essentially. Transfer operations include addition (concatenation, integration, combination), exclusion (subtraction), and recursion (stacking within each other).

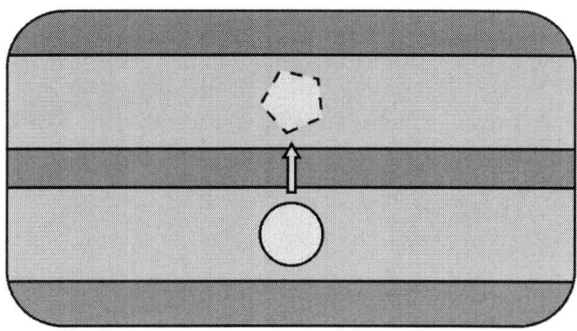

Figure 11: Structural transfer across subject domains.

Meta Transfers

Meta transfers indicate that doing something includes the reflexive experience of itself (see Figure 12): Doing and reasoning includes realisations *about* doing and reasoning (see Mercer, 2002). For instance, learning includes learning about learning: People who learn a new practical skill *experience* learning a new practical skill. It is likely that they are then more aware than before with regard to recognising and learning new skills. When people acquire knowledge and gain experience, they also learn about what knowledge and experience are; when they learn a structure, they learn that it is a structure and become aware that there might be other (e.g., valid, useful, and conflicting) structures.

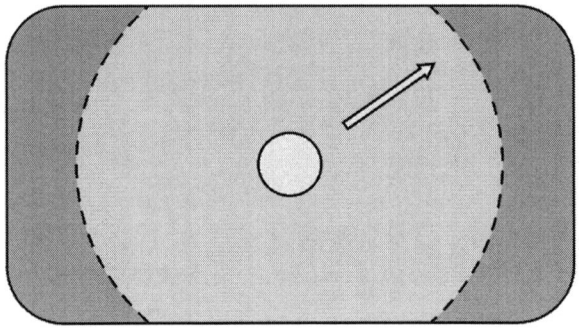

Figure 12: Meta transfer includes itself.

Conclusion

This chapter began with the hypothesis that physical making and conceptual thinking can happen together, inspire each other, and build on each other. It described hands-on experiences with material construction made over several years in a making workshop series, observed tangible effects for the learning process, and, from the basis of these experiences and observations and a dialectical constructivist position, proposed and sketched a model that identifies three kinds of learning transfers within and between subject domains and abstraction levels.

The learning process can be supported by the practical construction of artefacts through the direction it offers to learners, the structure that it implicitly introduces into the learning process when an artefact is constructed or destructed, the immediate feedback it provides, by acting as a mediating development catalyst, and by facilitating a can-do attitude in learners. Of these, the conflict that material construction introduces into the cognitive process is, seen from a dialectical constructivist perspective, essential in forming people's understanding and learning (see Glasersfeld, 1984): *"Physical making opens a distinctive, speculative pathway for reflection, communication and intuition – in Kant's or Husserl's sense as immediate, pure experience in the flesh, being confronted with rather than complemented by the material experience"* (Cermak-Sassenrath & Joseph, 2014:n.p.). Thus, the main contribution of material construction to learning is taken to be *"the tension of the challenge the existence and construction of physical artefacts poses"* (Cermak-Sassenrath & Joseph, 2014:n.p.).

The proposed model describes three specific kinds of learning transfers on a continuum between material and conceptual construction: *Factual* transfers happen across subject domains between similar or related applications, situations, and contexts, based on mimetical, analogue, and associative matching. *Structural* transfers happen vertically between abstraction levels from one system of reference into another and involve constructive translations and conversions. *Meta* transfers include the reflexive experience of themselves.

These results may motivate the inclusion of the construction of material artefacts in education at the university level to create innovative learning situations and to benefit cognitive constructions such as conceptual thinking.

About the Author

Daniel Cermak-Sassenrath is associate professor at the ITU, Copenhagen, and member of the Center for Computer Games Research (game. itu.dk). He can be contacted at this e-mail: mail@dace.de

Bibliography

Ackermann, E. (2001). *Piaget's constructivism, Papert's constructionism: What's the difference?* Online Resource: learning.media.mit.edu/content/publications/ EA.Piaget%20%20Papert. pdf [Accessed on 19 April 2011].

Baker, M. J. (1999). Argumentation and constructive interaction. In P. Coirier & J. Andriessen (Eds.), *Foundations of argumentative text processing.* Amsterdam: Univ. of Amsterdam Pr, pp. 179–202.

Blikstein, P. (2014). *Fablabs, Makerspaces in Schools: Final Revenge of Progressive Education.* Keynote speech, Key Challenges in Digital Fabrication for 21st Century Education (FabLearn Europe) conference, my notes.

Cermak-Sassenrath, D. (2015). Playful Computer Interaction. In V. Frissen; S. Lammes; M. de Lange; J. de Mul & J. Raessens (Eds.). *Playful Identities. The Ludification of Digital Media Cultures.* Amsterdam, NL, Amsterdam Univ. Pr., pp. 93–110.

Cermak-Sassenrath, D. & F. Joseph (2014). *Making as Diegesis: Material Approaches to Creativity and Learning.* Unpublished manuscript.

Damşa, C. I. (2014). The multi-layered nature of small-group learning: Productive interactions in object-oriented collaboration. *International Journal of Computer-Supported Collaborative Learning*, August 2014, Vol. 9, No. 3, pp. 247–281.

Dourish, P. (2001). *Where the Action Is: The Foundations of Embodied Interaction.* Cambridge: MIT Pr.

Ehrmann, J. (1968). Homo Ludens revisited. *Yale French Studies*, No. 41, Game, Play, Literature, pp. 31–57. English transl. Cathy Lewis, Phil Lewis. New Haven: Yale Univ. Press. Online Resource: www.jstor.org/stable/2929664 [Accessed on 6 December, 2016].

Enyedy, N.; J. A. Danish & D. DeLiema (2015). Constructing liminal blends in a collaborative augmented-reality learning environment. *International Journal of Computer-Supported Collaborative Learning*,Vol. 10, No. 1, pp. 7–34.

von Glasersfeld, E. (1984). An Introduction to Radical Constructivism. In P. Watzlawick (Ed.), *The invented reality.* New York: Norton, pp. 17–40. English translation of E. von Glasersfeld (1981), Einführung in den Radikalen Konstruktivismus. In P. Watzlawick (Ed.), *Die Erfundene Wirklichkeit*, Munich: Piper, pp. 16–38, www.vonglasersfeld.com/070.1 (25 August 2014).

Habel, C. & A. Hope (forthcoming). Little big learning: Subversive play / GBL rebooted. In D. Cermak-Sassenrath (Ed.), *The Playful Disruption of Digital Media.* Gaming Media and Social Effects series. Singapore: Springer.

Kolb, D. A. (1984). *Experiential Learning: Experience as the Source of Learning and Development*. Prentice Hall: Englewood Cliffs.

Levy, S. (1994). *Hackers – Heroes of the Computer Revolution*. 'Online' Electronic Edition, Online Resource: mitya.pp.ru/chamberlen/hackers/cover.html [Accessed on 16 August 2008].

Lindgren, R. & M. Johnson-Glenberg (2013). Emboldened by embodiment: Six precepts for research on embodied learning and mixed reality. *Educational Researcher*, Vol. 42, No. 8, pp. 445–452.

Maeda, J. (2006). *The Laws of Simplicity. Design, Technology, Business, Life*. Cambridge: MIT Pr.

Mercer, N. (2002). Developing dialogues. In G. Wells & G. Claxton (Eds.), *Learning for life in the 21st century: Sociocultural perspectives on the future of education*. Oxford: Blackwell, pp. 141–53.

Milne, A. J. (2007). Entering the interaction age: Implementing a future vision for campus learning spaces... today. *Educause Review*, Vol. 42, No 1, Jan/Feb 2007, pp. 12–31.

Overdijk, M.; W. van Diggelen; J. Andriessen & P. A. Kirschner (2014). How to bring a technical artifact into use: A micro-developmental perspective. *International Journal of Computer-Supported Collaborative Learning*, Vol. 9, No. 3, pp. 283–303.

People are Awesome (2016). *PEOPLE ARE AWESOME 2016 | BEST VIDEOS OF THE YEAR!* Video. Online Resource: https://www.youtube.com/watch?v=x3eIKSXXncc [Accessed on 20 June 2017].

Ryan, R. M. & E. L. Deci. (2000). Self-determination theory and the facilitation of intrinsic motivation, social development, and well-being. *American Psychologist*, Vol. 55, No. 1, pp. 68–78.

Schunk, D. H. (2012). *Learning Theories: An Educational Perspective* (6th ed.). Boston: Pearson Education.

Verbeek, P.-P. (2005). *What Things Do. Philosophical Reflections on Technology, Agency, and Design*. Pennsylvania: Pennsylvania Univ. Pr.

Verbeek, P.-P. (n.d.). What Things Do. Philosophical Reflections on Technology, Agency, and Design – Summary. Online resource: https://www.utwente.nl/bms/wijsb/organization/ verbeek/whatthingsdo.pdf [Accessed on 12 December 2016].

Vos, N.; H. van der Meijden & E. Denessen (2011). Effects of constructing versus playing an educational game on student motivation and deep learning strategy use. *Computers & Education*, Vol. 56, pp. 127–137.

Section 6: Curriculum Innovations

Chapter 24

Collaboration as a Vehicle to Curriculum Innovation

Rachid Bendriss, Reya Saliba, Malinda Hoskins Lloyd, Neil Ladwa
and Jo-Anne Kelder

Introduction

> *"To go fast, go alone. To go farther, go together."* (African proverb)

Curriculum alignment has become a necessary approach in higher education (HE) in order to ensure continuity in learning. Uchiyama and Radin (2009) recognise that by accepting curriculum mapping as a dynamic process, a collaborative community emerges that fosters collegiality among faculty and supports student learning. In an article on high-impact educational practices, Kuh (2008:9) describes practices that promote student learning and academic development in key skills such as critical thinking, writing, information literacy, collaborative learning, and other competencies. Therefore, curriculum alignment would not be possible without a culture of collaboration, teamwork, and collegiality.

In this introduction, we provide a brief discussion of curriculum alignment between secondary education and university study. We also describe the results of a collaborative partnership between faculty and librarians in integrating information literacy into a writing course. Furthermore, the concept of creating an active learning community through a "horizontal communication approach" is presented and, finally, the authors introduce a framework that enables collaborative and collegial evaluation of curricula for quality as well as research into its impact and effectiveness for student learning.

Curriculum Alignment

Engrained within the idea of curriculum alignment is a mission, culture, and commitment to widening participation and a high-quality experience for the diverse entrants to university undergraduate and postgraduate programmes. The goal of curriculum alignment is to enhance student access, achievement, and successful progression. Though student diversity is a strength, it can also present particular challenges when seeking to improve retention and success (Thomas & May, 2010). With increased faculty awareness of students' competencies, faculty can play a vital role in reducing student attrition and can facilitate collaborative approaches to retention and progression. One challenge that remains is evaluating the effectiveness of either creating centralised and standardised approaches to curriculum alignment or devolving decisions to schools and departments to create localised solutions. Collaborative approaches are amongst the high-impact practices related to student attrition rates identified by Kuh (2008) and are applicable to students as they transition into the university setting, as well as in improving student persistence and success (Parkes *et al.*, 2014).

At its core, curriculum alignment seeks to develop an early sense of belonging in transitioning students (Thomas, 2012; Allen & Bowles, 2012). This can be accomplished through supporting students in their transitional steps to HE by improving academic support through faculty's greater awareness and understanding of students' needs prior to their undergraduate study. Cross-sector partnerships that are student-focused can help in the exploration of barriers to learning by promoting a wider understanding of the students' learning journey in its entirety. Furthermore, promoting a wider understanding of curricula and expectations can empower and further encourage academics to actively support their students. These cross-sector partnerships provide routes for embedding the retention agenda through the establishment of dynamic and passionate communities of practice (Wenger, 1998). Thus, student retention successes utilising this approach can be attributed to:

+ strategic partnerships, as they contribute to holistic learning gains;

+ a fundamental, university-wide ethos of widening participation (diversity, inclusion, and success);

+ an integrated curriculum with teaching that capitalises on experiences across sectors, incorporating teamwork and peer support.

This approach towards inclusive practice recognises that student experiences and engagement are a collective responsibility. This nurtures both personal accountability and a culture of innovation around retention. New evidence-based approaches are encouraged and the impact of these is evaluated. Curriculum alignment can be important to facilitate innovative approaches to student success and achievement through the following:

+ developing a sense of community;

+ transition;

+ staff engagement.

In summary, student retention, progression, and achievement are continually evolving and used as benchmarks to measure student success within HE.

Information Fluency

For generation Z, which was born and raised in the midst of technological developments, finding information looks like an easy task. However, the rapidly changing technological environment to which this generation is accustomed *"does not carry over into situations requiring serious inquiry and deep investigation"* (Wiebe, 2016), specifically in the educational realm. When students are asked to do a research task, they are often content with selecting the first few references they find with no regard to the quality of the resources or their relevance (Calkins & Kelly, 2007).

Faculty members realised that college students lacked the necessary skills to successfully complete research assignments. This issue was the impetus for establishing a partnership between faculty members and librarians to enhance students' research and information literacy skills. According to Dhawan and Chen (2014:417), creating a collaboration between faculty and librarians generates a learning community that allows students to "form bonds". This also leads to a collegial atmosphere not only among the students but also faculty members and librarians, hence creating an open learning community that engages different stakeholders.

Until recent times, library instruction was still offered as a one-shot session where librarians delivered bibliographic instruction such as the use of library resources. These sessions often focused on passive learning, had no defined goals and objectives, were not linked to any classroom assignments, and thus could not measure students' learning nor assess the value of information fluency (IF) outcomes. In order to embrace affordances of new information technologies and prepare students to manage information overflow, librarians realised that library sessions should shift from bibliographic instruction to a new global IF level. The emerging need to integrate IF strategies into the curriculum and focus on information retrieval, evaluation, and creation defined a new dimension of academic libraries' involvement in HE (Bendriss *et al.*, 2015).

According to the new information literacy framework by the Association of College and Research Libraries (ACRL), the main focus is on building students' metacognitive skills, which include "reflective discovery of information", creation of new knowledge, and ethical participation in "communities of learning" (ACRL, 2016). To adopt the new ACRL framework, librarians start building effective partnerships with faculty members to become more visible on campus and play a vital role in curriculum design (McCue, 2014), thus initiating these changes and making valuable contributions to educational practice.

Active Learning through a Horizontal Approach

In many educational settings, the teacher dominates classroom discussion by determining a topic, leading the conversation, initiating questions, and providing evaluative feedback to student responses. Further, as described by Moss and Brookhart (2009), some classrooms exhibit an imbalance of power, as students are accustomed to speaking only when invited to do so. In a traditional classroom structure, teachers routinely implement a rapid firing of questions one after another without providing adequate time for responses or conversation (Gonzalez, 2008; Moss & Brookhart, 2009). In contrast, in a learning community that creates a culture of collaboration, partnerships are established to enhance student achievement. For example, as represented by Lloyd *et al.* (2016), the facilitate-listen-engage (FLE) model uses an analogy of horizontal communication in which teachers and students become equal contributors in the learning community. Framed by this horizontal approach, a traditional classroom, situated as the teacher at the front of the room with the students as a passive audience, can potentially evolve into an active learning community. In this active environment, the teacher and students engage in a reciprocal exchange of rich dialogue where learners are active participants.

Because this shift in learning and teaching is cyclical and recursive in nature, the teacher acts to facilitate student autonomy and self-regulated learning. Researchers (McElhone, 2013) describe the patterns of talk that occur in classrooms that lack the focus on engaging students in rich discussions due to the teacher's dominant role. Rather, a facilitative perspective calls for a spirit of collaboration in which the teacher and students serve as equal contributors to the educational space (Lloyd et al., 2016). Consequently, student engagement with the curriculum is increased when framed by a horizontal communication approach as opposed to a vertical communication approach, which, in opposition, is more teacher-directed.

By design, interactive learning aligns with the definition of classroom discourse as *"the interactions between all the participants that occur throughout a lesson"* (Van de Walle et al., 2014:20). Discourse involves both teacher-to-student interactions and student-to-student interactions, as well as both written and oral forms of communication. Through the completion of interactive learning log activities, for example, students engage with the curriculum, with their peers, and with the teacher as they develop self-regulated learning and metacognitive processes.

A Framework for Collaboration Focused on Quality

A pressing problem for teachers in Higher Education is how to manage the different orientations to quality attached to the task of designing, delivering, and evaluating curriculum. Academic freedom in teaching is constrained by institutional controls on curriculum design, which, in turn, are responding to external standards intended to assure graduating students have the skills and knowledge promised. The emphasis on the learning outcomes achieved on graduation implies academics need to shift from a silo approach to teaching a subject within a degree.

However, what is lacking for many teaching teams is the knowledge of how to develop a plan for evaluation of curriculum and then implement it. Additionally, academics are expected to make scholarly contributions to the body of knowledge in relation to teaching their discipline, another expectation for which they are not necessarily prepared by their academic training. In this context, a framework to guide a teaching team how to establish a scholarly evaluation-research program that meets requirements for theoretical underpinning (Laurillard, 2012), methodological rigor and that complies with ethical requirements is valuable (Kelder, Carr & Walls, 2017). A structured approach that is predicated on collegiality, and not dependent on individual motivation or capability, enables a teaching team to be systematic and align evaluation activities with research-focused activities over the life cycle of a curriculum (Phillips *et al.*, 2012).

Introduction to the Chapters Using Practice

In Chapter 25, Neil Ladwa and Chinny Nzekwe-Excel discuss an approach to improving student outcomes that uses cross-sectoral curriculum alignment to address issues related to the diversity of student populations. This approach can lead to successful student achievement and progression, capturing how institutional partnerships and collaboration can enhance the experiences and success of students.

In Chapter 26, Rachid Bendriss and Reya Saliba describe how faculty members and librarians embedded IF strategies into the ESL curriculum. They provide a ready-to-use matrix of IF objectives that can be integrated in any course that requires research and writing.

In Chapter 27, Malinda Hoskins Lloyd introduces the innovative practice of interactive learning logs, in which students interact in a discourse-intensive community as they complete in-class activities. With active learning as the goal, students complete course-related, ad-hoc activities housed in a notebook throughout the semester. In this practice, Lloyd views HE teacher candidates as valued participants in the educational setting.

In Chapter 28, Jo-Anne Kelder and Andrea Carr present their curriculum evaluation research (CER) framework as a way of thinking and method for enabling teaching team collaboration. Its focus is on the quality of a curriculum as delivered by a teaching team. Its purpose is to help a teaching team construct a plan for evaluating the content and delivery of their curriculum and align that plan with a research plan that focuses on the impact and effectiveness of curriculum innovations from a theoretical perspective.

Putting it all together, curriculum alignment and evaluation, information fluency as a 21st-century skill, and interactive learning promote collaboration and foster student engagement.

About the Authors

Rachid Bendriss is an associate professor of English as a second language and assistant dean for student recruitment, outreach, and foundation programmes at Weill Cornell Medicine-Qatar. He can be contacted at this e-mail: rab2029@qatar-med.cornell.edu

Reya Saliba is the learning and student outreach librarian at Weill Cornell Medicine-Qatar. She can be contacted at this e-mail: res2024@qatar-med.cornell.edu

Malinda Hoskins Lloyd is assistant professor at Tennessee Technological University in the Department of Curriculum & Instruction in Cookeville, Tennessee, USA. She may be contacted at the following e-mail: MLloyd@tntech.edu

Neil Ladwa is an achievement enhancement adviser at Aston University in the Centre for Learning Innovation and Professional Practice in Birmingham, UK. He may be contacted at this e-mail: n.ladwa1@aston.ac.uk

Jo-Anne Kelder is senior lecturer in the Quality Evaluation Learning and Teaching unit, in the Faculty of Health, University of Tasmania. She can be contacted at this e-mail: jo.kelder@utas.edu.au

Bibliography

Bendriss, R.; R. Saliba & S. Birch (2015). Faculty and librarians' partnership: Designing a new framework to develop information fluent future doctors. *The Journal of Academic Librarianship*, Vol. 41, No. 6, pp. 821–838.

Calkins, S. & M. R. Kelley (2007). Evaluating internet and scholarly sources across the disciplines. *College Teaching*, Vol. 55, No. 4, pp. 151–156.

Dhawan, A. & C. J. Chen (2014). Library instruction for first-year students. *Reference Services Review*, Vol. 42, No. 3, pp. 414–432.

Gonzalez, J. M. (2008). *Encyclopedia of Bilingual Education*. Los Angeles: SAGE Publications, Inc.

Kelder, J.; A. R. Carr & J. Walls (in press). *Evidence-based Transformation of Curriculum: a Research and Evaluation Framework*. Research Development in Higher Education: Curriculum Transformation. 27-30 June, 2017. Sydney, Australia.

Kuh, G. D. (2008). *High-impact educational practices: What they are, who has access to them, and why they matter*. Washington, DC: Association of American Colleges and Universities.

Laurillard, D. (2012). *Teaching as a Design Science: Building Pedagogical Patterns for Learning and Technology*. New York: Routledge.

Lloyd, M.; N. Kolodziej & K. Brashears (2016). Classroom discourse: An essential component in building a classroom community. *School Community Journal*, Vol. 26, No. 2, pp. 291–304.

McCue, R. (2014). Does a blended learning, flipped classroom pedagogy help information literacy students in the long term adoption of research skills? Online Resource: http://www.llrx.com/features/blendedlearning.htm [Accessed on 10 May 2017].

McElhone, D. (2013). Pressing for elaboration in student talk about texts. *Journal of Classroom Interaction*, Vol. 48, No. 1, pp. 4–14.

Moss, C. M. & S. M. Brookhart (2009). *Advancing formative assessment in every classroom: A guide for instructional leaders*. Alexandria, VA: ASCD.

Phillips, R.; C. McNaught & G. Kennedy (2012). *Evaluating e-Learning: Guiding Research and Practice*. New York: Routledge.

Uchiyama, K. P. & J. L. Radin (2009). Curriculum mapping in higher education: A vehicle for collaboration. *Innovative Higher Education*, Vol. 33, No. 4, pp. 271–280.

Van de Walle, J. A.; K. S. Karp; L. H. Lovin & J. M. Bay-Williams (2014). *Teaching student-centered mathematics: Developmentally appropriate instruction for grades 3-5* (2nd ed.). Boston, MA: Pearson Education, Inc.

Wiebe, T. J. (2016). The Information Literacy imperative in higher education. *Liberal Education*, Vol. 101–102, No. 1–4.

Chapter 25

Curriculum Alignment: Opportunities for Cross-Sector Collaborations

Chinny Nzekwe-Excel and Neil Ladwa

Introduction

This chapter contributes to the book *New Innovations in Teaching and Learning in Higher Education* as it presents outcomes of a project that is focused on student transition and success. The project explores how vocational and advanced level students can be supported through their higher education (HE) study, drawing insights from staff/tutor and student voices. The project, which is taking the concept of curriculum alignment even further in order to align curricula across sectors, was conducted in Birmingham, United Kingdom (UK), and involved gathering data from a variety of academic audiences (staff who teach and support vocational and advanced-level students, academics who have a keen interest on student success and the students themselves).

Curriculum alignment is a popular and possibly widely embraced educational concept that is aimed at mapping and integrating "relevant" components in the design and delivery of programmes or curriculum in an academic context. It is an academic process of reviewing a programme or course in consideration of the learning needs of students by adopting and integrating relevant strategies with the intention of progressing student success. Curriculum alignment, in this chapter, is discussed in the context of promoting collaboration across sectors (further education (FE) and HE institutions) for the purpose of adequately equipping students academically and enabling them to transit seamlessly into their HE studies. When reading this chapter, you will gain the following three insights based on project outcomes and the recommendations we discuss:

1. perceived and tangible barriers to academic achievement that students face in their HE studies from staff and students' perspectives;

2. how academic institutions and their staff can help minimise "academic remedial stigmas" and enable an academic support environment for students;

3. initiatives that HE institutions can implement so as to help students to confidently adapt to the academic demands and challenges faced in their HE studies.

Primarily, this chapter will discuss the perceptions of tutors and students on problems/barriers to academic achievements that students face in HE studies., and subsequently the proposed strategies to addressing the identified problems/barriers. The next section of this chapter will provide an overview of student learning perceptions and Biggs' 3P model in the context of curriculum alignment. This serves as the rationale for the project discussed in this chapter. This will be followed by a discussion on the research approach employed and the associated preparations made for undertaking the project. Subsequently, this chapter presents outcomes of the project and accompanying reflections. Finally, the chapter will conclude with a discussion on practical recommendations that HE institutions can embrace and implement to help minimise the key barriers to academic achievements that students face in their HE studies.

Section 1: Background

Biggs' (1996) 3P model encapsulates the concept of curriculum alignment such that it argues that there is a significant connection between a learner's prior learning perceptions/experiences, teaching methods and assessment processes, approaches to learning, and outcomes of their learning. Building upon Biggs' model, Meyer and Nulty (2009), in their discussion of curriculum design principles, highlight the importance of aligning courses with each other and the desired learning outcomes. This suggests that creating a satisfying learning experience or outcome for students during their HE studies can be facilitated by developing the appropriate learning perceptions/experiences, implementing robust teaching strategies, and enabling the students to devise applicable learning approaches before they commence their HE studies.

This chapter takes the idea of alignment across modules, programmes, and courses and extends it to include cross-sector alignment. In this way, a final-year secondary/FE-level programme would align or feed more naturally into a first-year tertiary level undergraduate programme through curriculum alignment.

The arguments and recommendations discussed in this chapter stem from the fact that we have taught in FE and HE institutions and, therefore, see the gaps in the academic preparations and support of students in both institutions of learning. Anecdotal evidence (as shown and discussed later in this chapter) suggests that there is a lack of awareness of what academic preparation pupils from schools and colleges have before commencing their HE studies. Students with vocational qualifications struggle in particular with transition into HE studies. Thus, the main argument presented in this chapter is about investigating opportunities for collaboration across sectors based on evidence generated from a series of interactive workshop and focus group sessions from January to October 2016. The workshops and focus groups were designed to capture the perceptions of all relevant stakeholders into cross-sector transitions for students. These stakeholders include students from both secondary/FE and tertiary/HE sectors, and academics from both sectors, as well as personal tutors and support staff from both sectors.

The project presented in this chapter is innovative in that it is bespoke and uses an outward market-orientated approach as opposed to an internal-facing product-driven approach. This is more meaningful than simply liaising with schools as a marketing strategy. Essentially, the project is about engaging efficiently with prospective pupils directly onto their academic studies.

Section 2: The Practice

2a. Overview

During the recent *21st Annual Admissions & HE Guidance Conference for Teachers and Careers Advisers*, held at Aston University, UK, on 7 January 2016, we delivered a session called "Supporting vocational and BTEC students through their studies". Our conference session attracted 40 delegates, comprising FE management; central and support staff, such as head of year groups; Universities and Colleges Admissions Service (UCAS) advisers; career advisors; directors of sixth forms; achievement coordinators; and head academics/principals. Through an interactive workshop session, we generated data on how well vocational students are supported through their HE studies in terms of barriers to their academic achievements and institutional strategies to enabling the students' success. Following requests from some of the delegates who attended our conference session, we organised five tailored training sessions for staff/tutors and students (BTEC (Business and Technology Education Council) and A level (advanced level)) at four specific academic institutions of learning (secondary/FE institutions).

2b. Approach

In view of the aforementioned training sessions delivered at the four institutions, we endeavoured to identify the students' problems to learning in their HE studies and possible strategies to addressing the identified problems. Precisely, data was generated through tailored interactive workshop sessions. This provided a platform to gather rich and personal information on the subject under study. Subsequently, through a voluntary focus group session, insights were drawn from the academic experiences of different levels of students who gained admission to a UK university based on their BTEC qualifications.

Tailored interactive workshop sessions

The tailored interactive workshop sessions involved exploring staff/tutors' and students' perceptions of the challenges or concerns (called problems/barriers to academic achievements for the purpose of the project) that students may have progressing into HE studies. Subsequently, the participants' views on strategies or solutions for enabling the success of students (in view of their identified problems/barriers to academic achievements) were collated during the workshop sessions. There were five different workshop sessions in total, designed and delivered between February and March 2016. The first workshop session generated data from 12 teaching staff from a sixth form college. The second workshop session generated data from 16 teaching staff from a sixth form school. The staff (participants) from the sixth form college comprised a combination of academic tutors and personal tutors; the personal tutors usually provide pastoral care to the students. However, the staff from the sixth form school comprised only academic tutors. The third workshop session generated data from 16 BTEC students from a sixth form academy. The fourth workshop session generated data from 7 A-level students from the same sixth form academy. The fifth workshop session generated data from 12 BTEC students from an FE college.

In the UK, post-compulsory education from the age of 16–19 is provided by a number of different types of institutions. These include:

+ sixth form colleges, for 16–19 year olds, offer A-level and vocational/BTEC qualifications;

+ sixth form schools, typically for 16–18 year olds, are controlled by the local council and are not influenced by business or religious groups;

+ sixth form academies, also for 16–19 year olds, are run by a governing body and are independent from the local council. They can follow a different curriculum;

+ FE colleges generally offer vocational (work-related) and specialist qualifications. They tend to provide courses for 16–18 year olds as well as adult learners, and they often have close links with the community.

Voluntary focus group

Following the identified perceived problems that students face in their HE studies and the proposed strategies for addressing the problems, in terms of the data generated from the interactive workshop sessions, it became necessary to explore the perceptions of students who have actual experience in HE studies. Thus, data for this exploration was gathered through a voluntary focus group session where the participants were required to discuss tangible problems they face as BTEC students in their HE studies and their proposed strategies (solutions) to address the problems. The focus group session, conducted in May 2016, involved a total of six male participants (students from the Business Faculty of a UK university). This comprised two second-year students, two final-year students, and two BSc (bachelor of science) graduates.

2c. Aligning Curriculum across Sectors — The Preparation

To facilitate the engagement of prospective students with their academic studies, raise awareness of secondary/FE curriculum, and to further promote opportunities for cross-sector academic alignment, a continuous professional development training day was organised at a UK university/tertiary institution. The training day, organised in October 2016, attracted 50 academic teaching and support staff who have a particular interest in student transition, progress, and retention. The training day generated further insights from HE staffs' perspective on academic preparations and support of students in HE studies.

Section 3: The Outcome

3a. Preliminary Analysis

In exploring the nature of the students' concerns to facing HE studies and proposed solutions (Tables 5-8), the tutor and student perceptions were grouped into five main categories including guidance-related, academic-related, personal and social-related, professional development-related, and finance-related factors:

- the guidance-related factors centre upon provision of advice or direction in making an informed decision regarding HE studies;

- the academic-related focus around the development or enhancement of academic skills that are required for HE studies. These factors (in view of the proposed solutions from tutor and student perspectives) indicate where the academic institutions (secondary/FE and tertiary/HE) have a responsibility to get the right academic structure in place for the purpose of preparing the students for HE studies;

- the personal and social-related focus around peculiar, individualised requirements for HE studies;

- the professional development-related are similar to the academic-related, but are more focused on practicality;

+ the financial-related focus around financial and money matters within the context of HE studies.

Tutor Perspective Voice – Secondary institutions
Conference Delegates (in view of only BTEC students)
+ Low entry levels
+ High expectation rates from HE
+ The role of the accepting university
+ Type of institution FE/sixth form
+ Balance between aspirations and educational background
+ Level of independence (independent learning)
+ Lack of basic course requirements
+ Lack of subject background knowledge
+ Single, double, triple awards… different skills/knowledge/experience
+ Insufficient career advisors/academic guidance
+ Lack of academic, research, and study skills (for example, referencing, note-making skills)
+ Poor maths/numerical skills
+ Lack of family role models
+ Poor (and difficult) links with industry
+ Unfamiliar with HE teaching delivery methods
+ Lack of awareness of HE deadline procedures
+ Transparency of HE units that have exam components – revision and exam techniques
+ Confidence – they feel like second-class students
+ BTEC access to other (wider) courses

Table 1: Problems/Barriers to academic achievement that BTEC students face in HE studies – tutor perspective (conference delegates).

Tutor Perspectives – Secondary institutions
Sixth Form College (in view of both A-level and BTEC students)

- Poor self-esteem
- Lack of self-motivation – no reassurance or not being spoon-fed at university
  - Different student/teacher relationship; not being chased up
- Writing/communication skills: lack of experience to develop such skills
  - Essay writing: the difference between writing an essay at college and in university (e.g., 3,000-word essay)
  - Lack of verbal communication/presentations in front of peers
- Literacy and numeracy standards
- Independent note-taking skills
- Unawareness of more resources for research such as databases, journals; using the web for majority of research
- Lack of confidence in mixing different walks of life
- Dealing with long days
  - New environment – greater concentration levels (3-hour lectures)
- Fear of the unknown/anxiety
- Lack of commitment to university environment
- Unfamiliar with different types of exams and coursework assessments
- Home joggling responsibilities/pressures from family
- BTEC submissions
- Lack of or no preparation for university entry requirements/interviews
- Meeting targets/time management and organisation
- Sense of independence: moving away, accommodation, travelling to university, social pressures/moving away from friends
- Financial barriers (grants/loans): money management, budgeting

Table 2: Problems/Barriers to academic achievement that BTEC students face in HE studies – tutor perspective (staff from a Sixth Form College).

Tutor Perspectives – Secondary institutions
Sixth Form School (in view of both A-level and BTEC students)

- At school, we spoon-feed students (too much help with assessments) so students are not independent learners and are not used to independent study (e.g., using the library)
- Lack of research skills: lack of skills in literature review
- Lack of social study skills
- Do not do enough wider reading
- Not used to note-taking and what to do with the notes
- Not used to travelling independently
- Change in structure of exams
- Lack of self-motivation
- Time management
- Taking responsibility
- No socialising outside peer groups; some are only good at socialising with same sex; not used to different backgrounds
- No real understanding of pressures in university environment, university expectations, course requirements and deadlines
- Cultural reasons: tend to stay at home so limited course options
- Finding quiet place to study, mixing with other people, joining clubs and societies
- Cost/financial issues: for example, pupil premium, money management
- Issue of extended writing and referencing
- Making the right choice: do they know all the options?
- Failure: and can be asked to leave
- No persistence to keep going when challenged
- Fending for themselves outside the family
- Not broadminded to accept new ideas/people, though some are prepared chronologically + emotionally

Table 3: Problems/Barriers to academic achievement that BTEC students face in HE studies – tutor perspective (staff from a Sixth Form School).

Tutor Perspectives – Tertiary institutions
Sixth Form School (in view of both A-level and BTEC students)
• Assessment alignment – weaker on exams, stronger on essays
• Assumptions of prior knowledge
• Numeracy skills – across the board problem?
• Lack of preparation
• Independent learning
• Content of BTEC – breadth and depth, style, coursework
• Level of motivation
• Proportion of BTEC population in HE
• Module design
• Late sign-up
• Unfamiliarity with large class size
• Level of English language/grammar ability
• Issue of self-study
• Differing ability within groups
• Lack of understanding of content on virtual learning environments (VLE) – Blackboard
• Issue of non-attendance

Table 4: Problems/Barriers to academic achievement that BTEC students face in HE studies – tutor perspective (staff from a UK-Based University).

Student Perspective/Voice (BTEC Students in Secondary Education: College, School, Academy)
Sixth Form Academy

- Laid back attitude – deadlines and time management
- No experience of the university environment
  - I wouldn't know specifically how to prepare
  - What exactly would happen?
  - What textbooks do I need?
  - How do I organise myself?
  - How do I access the support I need?
- Adapting to the different lifestyle
- Not all disciplines have industrial placements
- Workload
- Joggling work and fun
- Money
  - It's costly
  - What would I do with my student loan?
- Travelling
- Scared to be independent
  - What would I do with my independent time?
- Living alone/responsibility
- Not enough time with lecturers
- How can I socialise with people?
  - Different personalities
  - Fitting in
- BTEC is not the same as A level
- More knowledge in A level than BTEC
- Nervous about the support in university (I'm a very shy person)

Table 5: Problems/Barriers to academic achievement that BTEC students face in HE studies – student perspective (students from Sixth Form Academy).

Student Perspective/Voice (BTEC Students in Secondary Education: College, School, Academy)
FE College
• Dealing with Exams
• Not all universities accept BTEC students
• Foreign students don't have the required qualifications to go to university
• BTEC students feel that others think they need more student support than other students, since A-level students do more independent study than BTEC students
• Having bigger groups in universities
• Family pressures
• Academic achievements in view of grades for BTEC course
• Ability to cope with workload (support if mental health is affecting deadlines or attendance)
• Living cost
• Support with personal issues (losing someone, mental health issues)
• Choosing the right course
• Fear of getting a job at the end
• Note-taking: struggling to understand and hear lecturers
• Support with learning difficulties

Table 6: Problems/Barriers to academic achievement that BTEC students face in HE studies – student perspective (students from FE College).

Student Perspective/Voice (A-Level Students)
Sixth Form Academy
• Access to tutors
• Being independent
• Having fail/pass on own accord
• Managing money
• Living alone

Table 7: Problems/Barriers to academic achievement that A-level students face in HE studies – student perspective (students from Sixth Form Academy).

Student Perspective/Voice (BTEC Students in HE Studies)
Students/ Graduates from a UK-Based University
✦ Dealing with revision and exam techniques
✦ I wasn't as independent
✦ BTEC qualification isn't practical enough
✦ Managing the different *f* ways, we were assessed
✦ BTEC qualification didn't help with focusing ourselves to what careers we wanted to go into
✦ Interacting with college and HE lecturers is different
✦ Financial matters - Delays in processing finance resulting in "no access" to modules and VLE
✦ Losing focus
✦ Certain modules (e.g., finance modules) were challenging
✦ Dealing with essay-based questions in exams (and time constraint)
✦ Amount of reading was a lot
✦ Not taught how to analyse data/information in college
✦ Skills at BTEC don't prepare you for the in-depth level that you have to use at university

Table 8: Problems/Barriers to academic achievement that BTEC students face in HE studies – student perspective (students from UK-Based University).

3b. Reflections on Barriers to Student Academic Achievement in HE Studies

Outcomes from the interactive workshop sessions show an overlap on the barriers to academic achievement that students face in their HE studies from the staff/tutor perspective of the four different groups (conference delegates, sixth form college, sixth form school, and university). Though the data gathered (as shown in Tables 1-8) indicates that the tutors from the two sixth form institutions and conference delegates highlight a reasonable number of personal and social-related factors (e.g., *"poor self-esteem"*, *"taking responsibility"*, *"fear of unknown"*), guidance-related factors (e.g., *"insufficient career/academic advisors"* and *"unfamiliar with HE teaching delivery methods"*) and academic-related factors (e.g., *"lack of research and study skills"*) were the most highlighted as barriers to academic achievement that BTEC students face in their HE studies. A review of the comments from the university staff clearly identifies issues around academic-related factors. There is rarely any record of personal and social-related matters.

The slightly varying views between the staff/tutors from the secondary institutions and staff from the tertiary institution, in terms of tertiary institution staff rarely recording any personal and social-related factor, may be associated with the make-up of the groups; the conference delegates and secondary institution tutors comprised teaching staff, management staff, and career advisers, while the tertiary tutors mainly comprised academic/teaching staff.

From the student perspective on perceived problems that vocational students face in HE studies, the BTEC students from the two institutions (sixth form academy and FE college) recorded guidance-related (e.g., "No experience of the university environment", "choosing the right course", "Nervous about the support in university") and personal and social-related factors (e.g., "adapting to the different lifestyle", "juggling work and fun", "how to socialise with people") as the predominant barriers they will face in HE studies.

Unlike the BTEC students, the A-level students (from the sixth form academy) did not express any particular barriers to their transitioning to HE studies. Their comments suggest that this group of students feels more academically equipped and confident to face HE studies:

+ *I'm excited for the change;*

+ *I've seen all my friends going to university and I feel like it's taken me ages;*

+ *already made the jump from GCSE (General Certificate of Secondary Education) to A-level;*

+ *I know what to expect;*

+ *I'm good at managing workload;*

+ *I'm organised;*

+ *I have received advice from teachers, friends and family;*

+ *the universities provide all the information.*

A few concerns expressed by the A-level students, as shown in Table 7, were mainly guidance-related and personal and social-related factors.

An exploration of the experiences of the students (with BTEC qualification) from a UK university show that the students recorded more academic-related issues as problems that they face/faced in their HE studies (Tables 5-8), some of which are *"dealing with revision and exam techniques"*, *"managing the different ways we were assessed"* and *"not taught how to analyse data…in college"*. Interestingly, nearly all the problems faced by these students were highlighted by the staff/tutors from the secondary and tertiary institutions as the barriers to academic achievement that BTEC and A-level students face in HE studies. It is important to note that these students' comments demonstrate the lack of unpreparedness received prior their HE studies, for example: *"BTEC qualification didn't help with focusing ourselves"*, *"interacting with college and HE lecturers is different"*, *"BTEC qualification isn't practical enough"*.

On a general note, the evidence (in Tables 1-8) shows a split in perceptions of staff and students such that the staff/tutors from both sectors cite academic skills as the main issue to successful transition or barriers to student achievement in HE studies, whereas the students' comments generally identify "belonging" as the main issue.

With respect to strategies for enabling student success, there is a similarity from staff and student perspectives such that both groups propose strategies that are predominantly guidance-related and academic-related, as shown in Tables 9-16.

Tutor Perspective/Voice, Secondary Institutions
Conference Delegates (in view of only BTEC students)
<ul><li>Informed practice for the FE colleges of requirements of HE courses<ul><li>Collaborative practice between HE and FE/colleges to pass on adequate/streamlined information to the students</li><li>Keeping FE up-to-date/visits of HE to FE</li></ul></li><li>Early tailored talk sessions on HE requirements on the BTEC pathways (e.g., in Year 9)</li><li>Testimonials from past BTEC students: going back to the colleges to discuss their challenges and how they overcame</li><li>Building some level of independence in BTEC courses</li><li>External assessment</li><li>BTEC access to other (wider) courses</li><li>Tailor-made/built-in study skills strategies/schemes</li><li>Creating revision, study skills schedule</li><li>Universities delivering more BTEC-specific support for schools,<ul><li>For example, summer school</li><li>Having standard study skills/research skills units for BTEC qualifications</li></ul></li><li>Do we go for standalone or embedded units?</li></ul>

Table 9: Strategies for enabling student success: Solutions to problems/barriers to academic achievement that BTEC students face in HE studies – Tutor perspective (conference delegates).

Tutor Perspective/Voice, Secondary Institutions
Sixth Form College (in view of both A-level and BTEC students)

- Knowing who to go to for help: "buddy"/tutor system
- Fresher's fairs/taster days
- Tailored workshops on academic skills
- Getting students from local universities to speak to current college students regarding the transition from college to university
- More citizenship to improve skills
- Mandatory presentation sessions to improve confidence, presentation skills, and communication skills
- Money management workshops
- Researching workshops (workshops of searching and using resources)
- Referencing workshops
- Integrate study skills into courses (pick the right units)
- Provide academic mentors
- Keeping students informed (e.g., if UCAS were asking for attendance, we could tell the students that)
- Find out about which universities the students are going to and do some research about them
- Vocational courses should reflect assessments at university (stating the individual subject responsibility)
- Have a tutorial system/programme that enables universities to come into the colleges
- Create lecture environments/university taster days
- Prep for university focus groups
- Organise mock lecturers
- Have a learning development centre

Table 10: Strategies for enabling student success: Solutions to problems/ barriers to academic achievement that BTEC and A-level students face in HE studies – Tutor perspective (staff members from Sixth Form College).

Tutor Perspective/Voice, Secondary Institutions
Sixth Form School (in view of both A-level and BTEC students)

- Bring in students from courses/universities or ex-students of colleges to talk to the pupils about HE life/their experiences
- Take the pupils from college for university visits
- University prep activities
- Attend induction days at HE institutes
- Career advisor to prepare pupils for university choices
- Become harsher with deadlines/resits and introduce double marking
  - Stricter coursework sanctions
  - Have a submissions office
  - Have official extensions
  - Have interviews, talk to parents or examination officer, head of year
- Become more like universities in our approach through having lean deadlines
- Swap: university lecturers come into schools to teach units and school teachers go to university to teach students
  - Aston experience sleepover
- Activity-based problems based on subjects studied at university
- Reference and research workshops for subjects
- Having more university lecturers come into the schools to show off subjects
- Ditch the strict advanced subsidiary (AS) and advanced supplementary (A2) levels curriculum timetable imposed by exam boards, government, school
- Issue of time – where do you part on how to be a student
- Induction/tutorial comprehensive sessions on study skills/use of library, referencing, literature review
- Develop shorthand/note-taking skills
- Adopting mix-up groups: students are more used to being within their comfort zones
- More student shadowing
- Identify help available at university:
  - Staff
  - Tutors
  - Subject groups
  - Staff, etc.

Table 11: Strategies for enabling student success: Solutions to problems/ barriers to academic achievement that BTEC and A-level students face in HE studies – Tutor perspective (staff members from Sixth Form School).

Tutor Perspective/Voice, Tertiary Institutions
Staff from a UK-Based University (in view of both A-level and BTEC students)

- Summer schools
- University bridging exercise programmes
- Communication between HE institutions and FE providers
- Extra time in exams

Table 12: Strategies for enabling student success: Solutions to problems/ barriers to academic achievement that BTEC and A-level students face in HE studies – Tutor perspective (staff from a UK-Based University).

Student Perspective/Voice (BTEC Students in Secondary Education: College, School, Academy)
Sixth Form Academy

- Open up and get out there in dealing with the different lifestyles
- Concentrate and ask questions
  - Ask and associate with students/people who have been in the university environment before you
- Keep on top of your work (timetable, etc.)
  - Manage time better
  - Prioritise work
- Enquire about bursaries
  - Budgeting
- Get into a college that is near
  - Try university accommodation and see how it goes
- Try and be more sociable
- Have fun when you can
- Have a personal revision timetable, study method(s)
- Consult different educational resources
- Guidance on essay structure
- Self-motivation to build confidence
- *"when someone gives advice about uni, they just bombard you with info about uni as an overall thing but perhaps it is more useful to focus on uplifting someone rather than informing (specifically the advice based on the person receiving it)"*

Table 13: Strategies for enabling student success: Solutions to problems/ barriers to academic achievement that BTEC students face in HE studies – student perspective. (students from Sixth Form Academy).

Student Perspective/Voice (BTEC Students in Secondary Education: College, School, Academy)
FE College
◆ Accept BTEC students/other qualifications
◆ Support for personal issues – counselling, extra time for assignment, sensitivity to mental health
◆ Support with workload, family issues, being homesick, getting jobs, learning difficulties
◆ Help with changing course if in the wrong course
◆ Having notes/information available online to read
◆ Adopting Smaller groups
◆ Support to cope with part-time jobs + studying at the same time
◆ Provision of resource help (books, borrow laptops to take home)
◆ Sessions for students to communicate with each other
◆ More communication from the tutors to see if the student is doing well on the course
◆ Sessions to teach how to cook healthy meals
◆ University to help students to sort part-time jobs
◆ Reassurance that after university that students can get the jobs that they want

Table 14: Strategies for enabling student success: Solutions to problems/ barriers to academic achievement that BTEC students face in HE studies – student perspective (students from FE College).

Student Perspective/Voice (A-Level Students)
Sixth Form Academy
◆ Fresher's week or inductions without alcohol
◆ Information on joining societies
◆ Induction days for the students after we get our results without our parents
◆ Extra support from older students to help share their experience
◆ Form study groups – look for ways to seek help
◆ Go to advisors

Table 15: Strategies for enabling student success: Solutions to problems/ barriers to academic achievement that A-Level students face in HE studies – student perspective (students from Sixth Form Academy).

Student Perspective/Voice (BTEC Students in HE Studies)
Students/ Graduates from a UK-Based University

- Get more trained academic tutors
- Target struggling students and contact them, following them up to ensure their struggling is not long-term
- Use a more generic marking scheme for all lectures
- Stress importance/management sessions from Year 1 to build strong work ethics
  - "I have no sense of belonging to the actual university due to all the procedures"
- Build better relationship with students: offer more meetings between staff and students – personal tutoring
  - "I still feel like a stranger even in final year"
- More help on numeracy modules because BTEC does not teach many
- More implementation of group-work-related assessments (to integrate more team building assessments as opposed to getting rid of)

Table 16: Strategies for enabling student success: Solutions to problems/ barriers to academic achievement that BTEC students face in HE studies – student perspective (students from UK-Based University).

3c. Reflections on Strategies for Enabling Student Success in HE Studies

As expected, the strategies to addressing the identified barriers to academic achievement that students face in HE studies (Tables 9-16) show that the proposed solutions from the staff/tutors, irrespective of group (conference delegates, secondary and tertiary/HE staff) focused around guidance-related and academic-related factors. The only financial-related strategy (*"Money management workshops"*) can still be classed as a guidance-related strategy. The comments from the university staff reflect the need to bridge the gap between "not really understanding the university environment" and "what academic preparations students have before coming to university". Thus, the proposed solutions from the university staff focused on reaching out to or collaborating with FE colleges and sixth form schools more robustly.

There were variations from the student perspective: Nearly all the proposed solutions from the sixth form academy's BTEC students were personal and social-related solutions, as shown in Tables 9-16. However, it is important to note that the proposed personal and social-related solutions are proactive in nature, which suggest some level of taking focused/directed steps through informed practice (guidance-related). The BTEC students from the FE college proposed more of guidance-related solutions.

As shown in the confident remarks (section 3b) from the sixth form academy's A-level students, it is not unusual that these students proposed only guidance-related solutions as strategies to dealing with problems that students may face in HE studies.

With respect to the university students with BTEC qualification who have HE experience, the information in Tables 5-8 shows that the students propose more academic-related initiatives for the purpose of dealing with the problems they face/faced in their HE studies.

Section 4: Moving Forward

The next stage of this project following the outcomes of the project (barriers to student academic achievement in HE studies and institutional strategies to addressing the barriers) discussed in the preceding section will be the setting up of a professional network between the secondary and tertiary institutions used in this project and perhaps including additional FE colleges and sixth form academies within the region.

Another idea is to encourage university outreach teams (in liaison with academic staff) to collaborate more closely with the secondary or FE/sixth form sector in order to achieve a curriculum that is aligned across sectors in much the same way that modules and programmes are within universities. This idea could be a good response to opportunities identified by the university staff (Tables 9-12) in reaching out to students before they start their university study. Examples include:

- supporting and inputting directly onto the Extended Project Qualification (EPQ) scheme, with the aim of developing essential skills such as research and writing skills;

- targeted and focused/direct input onto English language and literature advanced-level courses. HE institutions have undergraduate programmes in these subjects, and the advanced levels in English language and literature have coursework and essay components that universities could help support. This support could be offered to widening participation initiatives in schools and colleges that are feeder institutions for specific universities.

What would be most important is to reach out to an increasingly diverse student population, in terms of different educational backgrounds, by engaging through curriculum alignment with BTEC students who have had a vocational education. BTEC qualifications are modular and can therefore be quite flexible in terms of content. In this way, if BTEC lecturers and academic staff in secondary/FE and HE institutions were to collaborate, this could allow institutional practices to address issues of transitions, particularly around academic skills, assessment methods, and even programme content. This flexibility in both sides of the sector could be exploited to allow greater understanding for academics and students. However, the idea can be evolved so that any collaboration is not only organised from a marketing perspective but actually has a meaningful academic engagement as the central focus.

Conclusion

Curriculum alignment in this chapter focused on the learner's prior learning perceptions before they arrive at university. The interactive workshops and focus group created a greater understanding of students' prior learning perceptions (in terms of identifying factors that impede student academic achievement in HE studies) through engaging with a very wide range of crucial stakeholders across sectors. A common theme (outcome) from the workshops and focus group was the idea of developing a better understanding of what happens across sectors concerning the transitioning student population from secondary to tertiary-level education. In this way, developing an awareness through curriculum alignment of what students will expect to study at university and also an awareness for university academics to know what skills and prior knowledge students arrive with, can make a student's learning journey smoother and more aligned.

This chapter has taken the idea of curriculum alignment and expanded it to encompass not only modules and programmes but also to ensure alignment across sectors, from FE institutions and schools to HE institutions. At its core, it is about raising awareness and promoting a better understanding of educational standards and provision across sectors. Within FE institutions and schools, the provision of education is represented by a standardised national curriculum with little room for flexibility. In contrast, HE institutions can be more flexible in moulding their provision to accommodate the skills and capabilities that first-year undergraduate students arrive with.

List of Acronyms

+ A level – Advanced level (academic qualification studied from 16–18 years of age, pre-university);

+ BTEC – Business and Technology Education Council (range of vocational, professional, career-based qualifications);

+ EPQ – Extended Project Qualification (a project-based qualification which can be taken in conjunction with A levels);

+ FE – further education (the UK education sector that is traditionally for students aged 16–18 years);

+ UCAS – The Universities and Colleges Admission Service (the UK administrative organisation which operates the university application process).

About the Authors

Chinny Nzekwe-Excel (PhD), a senior fellow of the Higher Education Academy, devotes her intellectual competence to continuous development of innovative structures/models in collaboration with recognised bodies/institutions aimed at focusing on the requirements of users, students, and concerned workers. Chinny can be contacted at this e-mail: nyerenoels@mail.com

Neil Ladwa is an achievement enhancement adviser at Aston University in the Centre for Learning Innovation and Professional Practice in Birmingham, UK. He may be contacted at this e-mail: n.ladwa1@aston.ac.uk

Bibliography

Bailey, J. & D. du Plessis (1997). Understanding principals' attitudes towards inclusive schooling. *Journal of Educational Administration*, Vol. 35, No. 5, pp. 428–438.

Beard, R. & J. Hartley (1984). *Teaching and learning in HE* (4th ed.). London: Harper and Raw Publishers.

Biggs, J. (1996). Enhancing teaching through constructive alignment. *Higher education*, Vol. 32, No. 3, pp. 347–364.

HE Academy (2012). *Employability*, Online Resource: http://www.heacademy. ac.uk/employability [Accessed on 13 June 2014].

Kuh, G. D. (2008). *High-impact educational practices: What they are, who has access to them, and why they matter*. Washington, DC: Association of American Colleges and Universities.

Meyers, N. M. & D. D. Nulty (2009). How to use (five) curriculum design principles to align authentic learning environments, assessment, students' approaches to thinking and learning outcomes. *Assessment & Evaluation in Higher Education*, Vol. 34, No. 5, pp. 565–577.

Nzekwe-Excel, C. (2012). An Exploratory Study on the Learning Needs of Foundation Degree Students. *International Journal of Learning*, Vol. 18, No. 6, pp. 199–214.

Nzekwe-Excel, C. (2014). Enhancing Students Learning Experience: Study-Techniques and Learning Development. *International Journal of Learning in Higher Education*, Vol. 20, No. 1, pp. 45–53.

Race, P. & R. Pickford (2007). *Making teaching work: 'teaching smarter' in post-compulsory education*. London: Sage Publications.

Shields, R. & A. Masardo (2015). Changing patterns in vocational entry qualifications, student support and outcomes in undergraduate degree programmes. Online Resource: https://www.heacademy.ac.uk/sites/ default/files/resources/ Changing%20Patterns%20in%20Vocational%20 Entry%20Qualifications.pdf [Accessed on 15 July 2017].

Stefani, L. (2009). Planning teaching and learning: curriculum design and development. In H. Fry; S. Ketteridge and S. Marshall (Eds.), *A handbook for teaching and learning in HE: enhancing academic practice* (3rd ed.). London: Routledge, Taylor & Francis Group.

Thomas, L. (2012). *Building student engagement and belonging in HE at a time of change: final report from the What Works? Student retention & success programme*. London: Paul Hamlyn Foundation/HEFCE.

Thomas, L. (2013). What works? Facilitating an effective transition into HE. *Widening Participation and Lifelong Learning*, Vol. 14, No. 1, pp. 4–24.

Chapter 26

The Flipped Classroom: Strategies for Building Students' Information Fluency in the ESL Curriculum

Rachid Bendriss and Reya Saliba

Introduction

This chapter contributes to the book *New Innovations in Teaching and Learning in Higher Education* as it provides second language teachers with a practical, step-by-step model on how to embed essential information literacy strategies in their academic writing curriculum. In this chapter, we define innovations in teaching and learning in higher education as critical pedagogical approaches to the teaching of key skills necessary for academic and career readiness. In a contemporary educational setting, students need to possess critical thinking skills that facilitate this desired readiness, and a vital 21st century competence is information fluency (IF). According to the Association of College and Research Libraries (ACRL, 2016), information literacy, also referred to in this chapter as IF, is defined as *"the set of integrated abilities encompassing the reflective discovery of information, the understanding of how information is produced and valued, and the use of information in creating new knowledge and participating ethically in communities of learning"*. The following chapter describes the design and implementation of an innovative curriculum that arose from interdisciplinary collaboration between librarians and the English as a second language (ESL) faculty. We integrated IF skills in the ESL curriculum in the foundation programme of the Premedical Education at Weill Cornell Medicine-Qatar (WCM-Q). The goal of this collaboration is to support faculty and students in their pursuit of excellence by building critical thinking competencies, developing metacognitive abilities and making IF skills an integral component of the overall curriculum. Reading this chapter, you will gain the following major insights:

1. establish a productive collaboration between ESL faculty and librarians to co-design an outcome-based curriculum integrating IF;

2. implement a ready-to-use IF objectives matrix that outlines outcomes, activities, and assessments;

3. create online modules and learning materials that embed IF strategies in a writing curriculum;

4. use the flipped classroom modality to deliver IF strategies and engage students in self-directed learning.

This chapter is divided into four major sections. Section 1 introduces the institutional background and cultural context of the implementation of the ESL/IF curricular collaboration. It also provides the reader with a succinct literature review that defines "information literacy" and gives examples of successful collaborations. Next, section 2 introduces an IF matrix that covers student learning outcomes, activities, supporting materials, and assessment tools. Then, in section 3, we reflect on the outcome of using the flipped classroom modality as a pedagogical approach from the perspectives of students and teachers. Finally, we conclude by identifying three long-term goals to explore future innovations.

Section I: The Background

To contextualise our study, we aim to describe the institution and curriculum where the collaboration took place as well as provide a succinct literature review that operationally defines and frames the concept of information literacy. First, WCM-Q is the first American college to offer a medical degree overseas. Established in 2002 through a partnership with Qatar Foundation, WCM-Q offers a six-year integrated medical programme that leads to Cornell University's M.D. degree. Through its mission to *"provide the finest education"* and *"improve health care"* (Weill Cornell Medicine-Qatar, 2016), WCM-Q is committed to educating and training physicians to become healthcare leaders in Qatar and the surrounding region.

Prior to joining the medical programme, some students are required to enrol in a foundation year designed to develop their basic English language and science skills and prepare them to join the medical programme. The

ESL course of the Foundation programme aims at developing students' reading and writing skills and fostering their critical thinking abilities by using learning materials that require research.

In order to develop the IF learning outcomes, we reviewed a number of resources that describe models of information literacy. After careful review, we decided on adopting the new framework by the Association of College and Research Libraries (ACRL, 2016) that defines information literacy as *"the set of integrated abilities encompassing the reflective discovery of information, the understanding of how information is produced and valued, and the use of information in creating new knowledge and participating ethically in communities of learning"*.

This definition matches Mackey and Jacobson's definition of metaliteracy as *"an overarching and self-referential framework that integrates emerging technologies and unifies multiple literacy types"* (Mackey & Jacobson, 2011:62). This suggests that the new information-literate individuals not only recognise their need for information but are also able to locate and access resources. Additionally, they can critically evaluate the information found and use it to achieve a certain task, as well as collaborate in learning environments by producing and communicating information through emerging technologies.

More importantly, as information has a dynamic content that changes constantly, information literacy teaching must also undergo a continuous evaluation to include new concepts while adopting a fresh approach to develop students' cognitive, behavioural, and affective attitudes. These attitudes, in addition to the metacognitive attitude, are used by Mackey and Jacobson (2017) to describe the four learning domains a "metaliterate" person would exhibit.

Some authors consider integrating information literacy skills into a specific discipline the most successful way to develop students' research skills (Bowles-Terry *et al.*, 2010; LaGuardia, 2011). In fact, Conteh-Morgan (2001:31) explains the importance of collaboration between faculty and librarians and the opportunity to align information literacy learning outcomes with the ESL course because theories, objectives, and practices in both disciplines overlap.

In two recently published articles outlining the partnership between ESL faculty and librarians, Herring (2014) and Bendriss *et al.* (2015) describe the successful collaboration between librarians and ESL faculty in designing and implementing library materials to strengthen *"an established ESL composition course"* (Herring, 2014:128) and integrate information literacy *"skills in a defined context to achieve specific learning outcomes"* (Bendriss et al., 2015:822).

In Qatar, the public high school system does not emphasise research skills; therefore, students enrol in the college lacking prior exposure to information retrieval and research strategies. This created an urgent need for remedial action to identify and address this issue, thereby calling for a more active role from academic librarians.

Usually, individual faculty members take the initiative of inviting librarians for a one-shot presentation during the academic year. In other cases, if librarians are lucky negotiating time constraints with the faculty, they are able to secure two sessions per semester. Librarians use these sessions to cover as many topics as possible, but they do not have the opportunity to teach more advanced skills and assess the impact of their teaching on students' information and research skills.

As a result, this model did not benefit students' learning because it did not address advanced research skills and the students' critical thinking deficiencies (Wilson, 2010). For instance, when ESL faculty assigned research papers, students were unable to identify their information need or locate reliable sources. Moreover, students were unable to evaluate information when they found it and lacked academic integrity skills such as citing sources properly and avoiding plagiarism.

Hence, to overcome this challenge and support the mission of the college, which entails students' academic integrity, metaliteracy, and life-long learning ability, an interdisciplinary collaboration between faculty and librarians resulted in a curricular innovation that allowed the integration of IF skills into the ESL curriculum. IF is a course offered every year to Foundation students at WCM-Q as an integrated component of the ESL curriculum to build their research skills in tandem with their academic reading and writing skills.

Section 2: The Practice

2a. General Introduction

To facilitate the integration of the IF strategies into the ESL curriculum, a blended-learning approach that uses the flipped classroom modality is adopted as a method to encourage self-regulated learning and use class time for hands-on activities. The flipped classroom is a pedagogical approach through which students discover and learn about a topic on their own. Reading materials and video tutorials for every module are uploaded into Canvas, the college's learning management system (LMS), and made available to students prior to the class session. Students are also encouraged to conduct a search to gather information about a specific topic, while class time is used for dynamic discussions and interactive problem-solving activities that allow in-depth exploration of the topic and immediate feedback from the faculty and librarians (Educause, 2012).

2b. The Curriculum

The following "IF learning objectives matrix" (Table 1) provides a detailed structure of the redesigned curriculum. It outlines the learning outcomes, examples of tasks and activities, and assessment tools designed to integrate IF into the ESL curriculum.

Learning Objectives	Detailed Description of Outcomes and Examples of Activities	Assessment
Understanding academic integrity and code of conduct	Explore the concept of academic integrity and WCM-Q code of ethics and recognise the consequences of academic misconduct.	Class discussion Class activity
Locating and accessing physical resources in the library	Search the library online catalogue, read a call number, and find physical resources on shelves.	Class activity
Recognising and differentiating between different types of information sources	Decide which type of information is likely the best resource to answer a specific information need.	Graded quiz Class activity

Learning Objectives	Detailed Description of Outcomes and Examples of Activities	Assessment
Locating and accessing the library's online resources	Find, access, and use a multidisciplinary database (e.g., ProQuest).	Graded quiz Class activity
Filling an information gap by searching for background information	Understand your topic by searching for background information.	Graded quiz Class activity Assignment
Planning and developing a search strategy	Decide on which relevant keywords and search terms to use and draw a mind map to generate ideas. Use a search log to document your search techniques and keep track of relevant results.	Graded quiz Class activity Assignment
Recognising popular, scholarly, and peer-reviewed publications	Understand the difference between popular, scholarly, and peer-reviewed publications and decide which ones to use for a specific task.	Class discussion Graded quiz Class activity
Evaluating resources	Assess the purpose of information resources, be able to check the credibility of the information creator, and apply sound judgment as to whether the information provided is accurate and reliable.	Class discussion Graded quiz Class activity
Understanding plagiarism and its consequences	Recognise what is considered to be plagiarism and how to avoid it by understanding that information has a value and its creation is a long process that takes time and effort. Explore some current examples of plagiarism cases to discuss and reflect upon.	Class discussion Graded quiz Class activity

Learning Objectives	Detailed Description of Outcomes and Examples of Activities	Assessment
Citing resources and acknowledging sources of information	Recognise when to give credit to information creators; how to summarise, paraphrase, and quote information from other authors into one's work using different citation styles (e.g., MLA, APA); document sources of information; and use bibliographic management tools (e.g., RefWorks) to save citations and generate bibliographies.	Graded quiz Class activity Assignment
Summarising and reflecting upon new information	Create annotated bibliographies to summarise and appraise information sources.	Class activity Assignment
Using advanced techniques to search scientific databases	Build advanced search strings using keywords, synonyms, Boolean operators, truncation, phrasing, and filters to search scientific databases (e.g., Web of Science, Scopus).	Graded quiz Class activity
Understanding the difference between Google Scholar and the library databases	Recognise the difference in using Google, specifically Google Scholar and the library databases. Set up WCM-Q library in Google Scholar to get the full-text link resolver.	Class discussion Graded quiz Class activity
Using the Interlibrary Loan service (ILLiad)	Recognise their privilege in accessing information and create an account in ILLiad to request materials not owned by the library.	Class activity Assignment

Final assessment:

Administer a survey and establish focus groups with students by the end of the academic year to collect their feedback.

Include graded activities in mid-term and final exams.

Conduct faculty and librarians' reflection and self-evaluation to identify areas of improvement.

Table 1: IF learning objectives matrix.

2c. Organisation of the Practice

To adopt the flipped classroom modality, librarians use the LMS Canvas as a platform to create and upload modules' content. Each module includes a set of resources such as reading materials, video tutorials, links to useful online resources, and practice quizzes that are made available to students for self-assessment. Students learn new skills that help them understand how to approach and perform research. They build their research competencies by applying IF skills to their essay writing assignments for the ESL course. They can access the content at their own pace; however, they are reminded of deadlines to complete a module or submit a quiz before the class session.

While in class, a graded, five-minute quiz at the beginning of each session addresses the learning outcomes of each module. Librarians use the rest of the session for hands-on activities and interactive discussions that support the outcomes of the ESL and IF components. For instance, students work in groups of three to focus their topic, create a mind map, fill in the search log, evaluate sources, and give five-minute presentations of their findings to the other groups in class (see section *2d. Preparation*). They then discuss the results and give each other feedback. While students are engaged in this class activity, librarians guide the search process and provide feedback. To conclude the class, they facilitate the discussion and summarise the outcomes of the module covered in that session.

This teaching method encourages interdisciplinary collaboration between different constituents for student success. Librarians and ESL faculty spend around two weeks prior to the start of the academic year to set up the IF learning objectives matrix that lists and matches the activities with expected outcomes of each IF component. The IF outcomes also complement the research competencies and critical thinking skills required by the ESL curriculum. Regular monthly meetings take place to follow up and realign the outcomes and activities. Moderate technical skills for faculty and librarians as well as students are essential to use the LMS and create or access the online modules and teaching materials, such as video tutorials and online quizzes. Therefore, instructional designers are provided with the content to build video tutorials covering specific topics to create and upload to the online modules.

Since this is a student-centred learning approach, students are expected to take responsibility for their own learning and access learning materials and online resources. By doing so, students also learn time management skills and develop an advanced research behaviour that becomes an integral part of their current academic life and future career.

2d. Preparation

The following supporting materials were used to prepare for the course and support the outcomes of the IF curriculum.

First, a "needs analysis" pre-test is designed for students to take prior to the start of the ESL course to help identify their basic IF skills. It is also used to revise and customise the outcomes and objectives of every module. Next, online modules are uploaded, which include reading materials, video tutorials, links to useful websites and online resources, as well as online practice quizzes. Following the completion of the modules, students participate in customised in-class activities designed to reinforce the outcomes of every module, generate group discussions, and assess the learning outcomes. To help students meet the faculty and librarians' expectations, rubrics are developed and shared with students for every essay not only to assess their writing skills but also their mastery of IF skills.

In addition to rubrics, a "search log" is developed for students to help them document their search strategy and keep track of their topic, keywords, databases used, and relevant citations. The search log helps students rethink their search by narrowing, broadening, or refocusing their topic; consider other keywords and search terms; use advanced search techniques such as Boolean operators, truncation, phrasing, and filters; and find the most relevant results through databases and search engines. Students also receive an "information evaluation form" designed to guide students through evaluating the resources found and judging the relevancy of the resource, the author's credibility, and the accuracy and purpose of the information found.

A series of "video tutorials" is created to help students understand IF concepts, introduce a specific skill (e.g., how to brainstorm and create a mind map), use a database (e.g., use the advanced search options in ProQuest) or a bibliographic management tool (e.g., create an account in

RefWorks, import citations, and generate a bibliography), and use some of the library services (e.g., request an interlibrary loan).

Finally, a "research guide" is developed for students to use for their final research paper. It covers all the skills developed throughout the academic year. It is used as a final assessment tool to evaluate the students' ability to focus their research topic (e.g., identifying the intended audience, defining the background information they need, developing two to three research questions, and creating a hypothesis), find and evaluate resources (e.g., searching for reliable scholarly resources, evaluating the credibility of resources and creating an annotated bibliography of the most relevant ones), extract the needed information (e.g., paraphrasing, quoting, and citing resources), and reuse that information to produce new meaning (e.g., producing an outline of their essay, communicating and presenting their findings, publishing the new information via multiple media).

Section 3: The Outcome

3a. Student Perspective

At the end of the academic year, students are expected to work on their final ESL essay using the "research guide" to document their progress in terms of IF skills. In order to gather their feedback and perceptions of the IF and ESL integration, students take a survey and participate in a focus group.

After completion of their Foundation programme, students are tracked throughout their first year of the medical programme. They have reported their increased confidence in their ability to find, evaluate, and use information effectively. Medical faculty members have also expressed their satisfaction with students who used these skills successfully. For example, post-Foundation students demonstrated their ability in using IF skills in their biology laboratory course research project, during which they presented a poster on their research focusing on the anti-microbial effect of phytochemicals in various herbs and spices. Not only were students able to demonstrate their competencies in experimental design and statistical testing, they were also able to show their skills in litera-ture search, citation, and scientific writing. Another example of students' success in using IF skills was their participation in the "Global Public

Health Seminar" offered by the medical programme. In this course, students were required to submit their chosen topic, an annotated bibliography, and a term paper. Based on survey results, students reported confidence in the search process, citing sources, and bibliography writing.

Overall, students developed metaliteracy skills through the use of different technological tools to search for and learn about topics, access online teaching materials, synthesise different sources of information, and collaborate with peers in a class setting through discussion and interactive activities.

3b. Teacher Perspective

The use of the flipped classroom modality helps overcome time constraints as students access the teaching materials outside class, which ensures more time for face-to-face, hands-on activities, and discussions during class time. It also helps students manage their time effectively and take ownership of their own learning.

This ESL/IF integration has proven to be an effective practice through the use of a pre-test prior to IF integration and the collection of students' feedback and comments through the use of a survey and focus groups at the end of the academic year. During focus groups, students reported the positive impact that this method had on their research skills, problem-solving skills, communication, language development, and teamwork skills. Students were also able to apply these skills by transferring what they learned in ESL/IF to other courses across the curriculum, such as writing lab reports and biology papers and producing op-eds, formal letters, or memos using relevant authoritative sources for their Global Public Health Seminar. Students also expressed an increased feeling of self-confidence in planning and doing research for their ESL essays.

Section 4: Moving Forward

This course aims at promoting metacognitive skills and preparing future students to become lifelong learners and active participants in the knowledge economy. The successful integration of IF skills into the ESL course has inspired a new phase of collaboration between faculty and librarians. To this end, we aim to achieve the following long-term goals:

1. the ESL/IF course will be offered as a credit-bearing course: Since the medical curriculum reform occurred two years ago, it made sense for the Premedical and Foundation curricula to undergo a systematic review and renewal to meet the evolving needs of students and prepare them for the rigours of the medical curriculum. For this purpose, an initial review has begun, and the ESL course will include the IF strategies as an integral component of its curriculum. This integration has already been tested, and students have expressed their satisfaction with acquiring information literacy skills, not only for future academic success but also for lifelong learning;

2. librarians and faculty members will form a taskforce: In order to identify the different levels of expertise in information literacy and research skills that medical students need, a committee of librarians and faculty will develop advanced learning outcomes. They will also map the entire IF curriculum throughout the six-year medical programme to ensure that future medical doctors are able to access, evaluate, produce information ethically and effectively, collaborate, and participate in communities of learning;

3. design a longitudinal IF evaluation: A study will be implemented to measure the impact of the IF learning outcomes on students' performance throughout the six-year medical programme. This will further enhance and strengthen the faculty-librarians' collaborations in planning and integrating future curricula and delivering instruction as a team.

Conclusion

In this chapter, we described the design and integration of information fluency (IF) skills in the ESL course for the Foundation programme of the Premedical Education at Weill Cornell Medicine-Qatar (WCM-Q). The main purpose of this collaboration was to build students' critical thinking abilities and develop their metacognitive skills towards becoming lifelong learners. By making the IF skills an integral component of the overall curriculum, we were able to:

1. set a model for a productive collaboration between other faculty members and librarians at our institution;

2. provide a sample of IF learning objectives, outcomes, activities, and assessment methods to be used by other faculty members;

3. develop online learning materials that facilitate the integration of IF outcomes in a writing curriculum;

4. apply the flipped classroom modality to engage students in self-directed learning and use class time for hands-on group activities, providing students with an opportunity for interactive participation and teamwork-building skills.

The planning, design, and implementation of this project would not have been possible without the ESL faculty member's progressive approach to education. His recognition of the importance of information literacy skills and eagerness to invite librarians to collaborate on such an initiative provided the ultimate opportunity for librarians to go above and beyond their traditional supporting role and become more invested in teaching and learning (Herring, 2014; Bendriss *et al.*, 2015).

Through this chapter, we shared practical strategies of how teachers can embed information literacy competencies in an ESL course. We demonstrated how to optimise e-learning pedagogy by flipping the classroom using LMS. Teachers seeking an innovation in teaching and learning can easily apply the learning objectives, outcomes, activities, and assessment methods described under section 2b, *The Curriculum*. In addition, faculty members are advised to set up regular meetings with librarians to communicate and ensure the smooth delivery of the curriculum and the attainment of the learning outcomes. This regular communication is fundamental to the success of this collaboration.

Teachers should also consider collecting feedback from their students through surveys and focus groups in order to improve the learning outcomes and delivery methods. For this teaching innovation to be effective, teachers should also conduct regular self-evaluation and reflect upon their teaching experience and student needs. Finally, the implementation of this innovation teaching method will better prepare students not only for their academic goals but also their career aspirations.

About the Authors

Rachid Bendriss is an associate professor of English as a second language and assistant dean for student recruitment, outreach, and foundation programmes at Weill Cornell Medicine-Qatar. He can be contacted at this e-mail: rab2029@qatar-med.cornell.edu

Reya Saliba is the learning and student outreach librarian at Weill Cornell Medicine-Qatar. She can be contacted at this e-mail: res2024@qatar-med.cornell.edu

Bibliography

Association of College & Research Libraries (ACRL) (2016). Framework for information literacy for higher education. Online Resource: http://www.ala.org/acrl/standards/ilframework [Accessed on 25 March 2017].

Bendriss, R.; R. Saliba & S. Birch (2015). Faculty and librarians' partnership: Designing a new framework to develop information fluent future doctors. *The Journal of Academic Librarianship*, Vol. 41, No. 6, pp. 821–838.

Bowles-Terry, M.; M. K. Hensley & L. J. Hinchliffe (2010). Best practices for online video tutorials: A study of student preferences and understanding. *Communications in Information Literacy*, Vol. 4, No. 1, pp. 17–28.

Conteh-Morgan, M. E. (2001). Empowering ESL students: A new model for information literacy instruction. *Research Strategies*, Vol. 18, No. 1, pp. 29–38.

Educause (2012). 7 things you should know about... Flipped classroom. Online Resource: https://net.educause.edu/ir/library/pdf/eli7081.pdf [Accessed on 12 March 2017].

Herring, D. N. (2014). A purposeful collaboration: Using a library course enhancement grant program to enrich ESL instruction. *The Reference Librarian*, Vol. 55, No. 2, pp. 128–143. Online Resource: doi:10.1080/0276 3877.2014.880317 [Accessed on 25 February 2017].

LaGuardia, C. (2011). Library instruction in the digital age. *Journal of Library Administration*, Vol. 51, No. 3, pp. 301–308.

Mackey, T. P. & T. E. Jacobson (2011). Reframing information literacy as a metaliteracy. *College and Research Libraries*, Vol. 72, No. 1, pp. 62–78.

Mackey, T. P. & T. E. Jacobson (2017). Goals and learning objectives. Online Resource: https://metaliteracy.org/learning-objectives/ [Accessed on 15 March 2017].

Weill Cornell Medicine-Qatar (2016). About us: Purpose and mission. Online Resource: https://qatar-weill.cornell.edu/aboutUs/purposeMission.html [Accessed on 20 December 2016].

Wilson, J. (2010). Information smoothies: Embedding information skills in assessed learning. *Assessment, Teaching & Learning Journal* (Leeds Met), No. 9, pp. 30–33.

Chapter 27

Student Engagement, Metacognition, and Self-Regulated Learning in Higher Education: Implementing Interactive Learning Logs as a Formative Assessment Technique

Malinda Hoskins Lloyd

Introduction

This chapter contributes to the book *New Innovations in Teaching and Learning in Higher Education* as it highlights a novel practice, interactive learning logs, which can be implemented in a college classroom setting as a formative assessment technique. I define interactive learning logs (used interchangeably with "learning logs") as a pedagogical tool used to formatively assess students. Constructed out of a simple notebook, interactive learning logs are a collection of in-class activities (housed in a course notebook) that establish an environment conducive to teaching and learning. The activities provide an opportunity for the professor to evaluate students' personal and professional reflections, professional competencies, content knowledge, as well as deficient areas that call for remediation. The professor designs these in-class activities as assessment measures throughout a course and to increase student engagement and participation. The activities may be pre-planned or may occur as the result of student deficiencies or misconceptions related to the concepts being taught that day; in which case, the professor may choose to pose an impromptu question to the students and have them respond in writing in their learning logs. Students engage in discussions in conjunction with their written responses. As a result, interactive learning logs become the formative assessment vessel through which writing, rich discussions, student-student interactions, and teacher-student interactions occur.

Interactive learning logs, albeit simple in design, serve a multifaceted purpose of transforming a potentially passive, inactive, lecture-based course into an active learning environment with the intent of increasing students' critical thinking and engagement in class. As such, interactive learning logs also function as a means of increasing students' metacognitive skills as well as self-regulation. The goal of learning log activities is to engage students in active learning techniques during class, while allowing professors the opportunity to formatively assess students via in-class activities. As will be evidenced throughout the chapter, research supports the significance of formative assessment as a way to foster advanced cognitive functioning, and interactive learning logs serve as a vehicle for this goal.

Ultimately, interactive learning logs serve as a formative assessment tool to gauge students' metacognition, self-regulating learning, and reflective practices. Additionally, the activities are designed and serve the following purposes: to engage students in personal and professional reflections (Stephens & Winterbottom, 2010), to develop professional competencies, to increase content knowledge, and for remediation of deficient background and/or course knowledge.

While reading this chapter, you will gain the following insights regarding the use of interactive learning logs in a higher education setting:

1) how they establish an active learning environment;

2) how they serve as a formative assessment instrument in the higher education setting;

3) how they increase students' metacognitive skills, reflective practices, and self-regulated learning.

This chapter includes the following sections: Introduction, The Background, The Practice, The Outcome, Moving Forward, and Conclusion. The introductory section explains the premise of interactive learning logs and includes a definition of the practice. Section 1 provides background information and research behind the practice and explains what prompted my design and implementation of interactive learning logs.

Section 2 describes the alignment with the university curriculum and the preparation and organisation required for implementing interactive learning logs. Section 3 describes the outcome of my experience with interactive learning logs and highlights student and teacher perspectives. Section 4, Moving Forward, provides reflections on advancing the practice in order to optimise the effectiveness of interactive learning logs.

Section 1: The Background

Transitioning from a teacher of elementary students to a university professor taught me numerous lessons. Over the years, I learned that when students attend their first day of a college course, they are primarily interested in two things: what are my assignments, and when are they due? One of the struggles I faced as a new professor, however, was having an entire 15-week course designed and "set in stone" before the semester began. The constraints of the required formal course outline (referred to as a syllabus at many universities) prevented me from inserting creative, flexible, and adaptable activities that were tailored to the cohort of students with their particular skill sets. Consequently, I evolved into an extremely detailed syllabus designer for each of my courses, but my syllabi often lacked some of the ad hoc activities I decided to use in class based on my students' needs. My syllabi became extremely lengthy and possibly intimidating to students, but adding each and every in-class activity to this already lengthy document would only increase the complexities of the syllabus and, therefore, the stress level of the students.

What if I needed to add activities for my students based on their misunderstandings during class? What if my students were not understanding concepts during class? As I formatively assessed my students during the semester, I noticed numerous competencies that lacked development or called for reinforcement. I also noticed numerous opportunities for my students to reflect and engage in discourse. Through the use of formative assessment, I recognised the need for altering my instruction to better meet the diverse needs of my students; however, I still felt confined by the syllabus, which caused me to question the implementation of new ideas and making adaptations to my instruction as the semester progressed. Nonetheless, I continued to add in-class activities along the way based on students' progress. Although the activities were completed in class,

I noticed students became frustrated when the assignment or activity was not specifically included on the syllabus. I needed a document that was framed in a way to enhance motivation and connect to my students' learning.

How could I alleviate feeling bound by this constitution-like document – a syllabus? Why should a syllabus stifle students' learning? How would I include new resources and related activities that I discovered my students needed after the semester had begun and do this in a way that the students perceive as beneficial? How would I react when I noticed students struggling with particular assignments? How could I scaffold my students' learning as they prepared to complete key assignments and projects? How could I justify holding students accountable for in-class activities if they were not officially stated on the syllabus? All of these concerns implored a resolution – a resolution that would encompass all of these peripheral in-class activities. An epiphany occurred to me – as long as information was stated on the course syllabus, students would be less likely to contend. However, as I reflected on my instructional practices, the goals of my courses, and the varying needs of my students, I came to the realisation that not all assignments can, nor should, be included on a syllabus in an explicitly detailed format. It was imperative, though, that I have the autonomy and inventiveness to embed formative activities in my courses to help my students achieve at a higher level. Thus evolved the implementation of, and addition to each course syllabus, interactive learning logs.

In essence, interactive learning logs, from my personal experience, were prompted by my use of formative assessment and my desire to create an active learning community based on my students' particular needs. From this perspective, interactive learning logs help to establish an educational space that increases student engagement and serve as a tool for creating an active learning environment. As students complete the in-class activities, they engage in written and oral discourse with their peers, strategies that elevate their learning.

The literature regarding the use of learning logs represents numerous benefits of their implementation. In their study, Stephens and Winterbottom (2010) explored how learning logs could increase students' cognitive control of their learning experiences while escalating cognitive functions. Along these lines and from my perspective, one of the goals of interactive learning logs is to engage students in activities within the academic environment, which removes them from their comfort zones, while feedback, scaffolding, and coaching are readily available. The activities designed for completion in students' learning logs often require extensive thought processes and "struggle time." Based on the definition of metacognition as "thinking about one's thinking," interactive learning logs allow students to develop their metacognitive skills, which requires an awareness of their cognitive functions and takes learning to a higher level.

Prior research (Park & Choi, 2014; Patrick *et al.*, 2016; Choi & Anderson, 2016; Hudesman *et al.*, 2013; Kim *et al.*, 2013) reveals that active learning is paramount in higher education and has a positive effect on student achievement. Park and Choi (2014) explored the effects of an active learning classroom (ALC) and found that such an environment was inspirational to students and that all students, regardless of their grade point average (GPA), participated more actively in this setting. Additionally, students in the ALC showed more interest in the content, increased their interactions with peers and faculty, and asked questions more frequently and willingly. Perhaps the most notable findings were that students' viewpoints changed as they began to accept and convey new ideas, knowledge, creativity, and information via peer-peer interactions.

Others, such as Patrick *et al.* (2016:62), explored faculty and student perceptions of active learning techniques and found that some faculty may need a change in mindset to overcome the barriers of implementation of active learning strategies. In doing so, reticent faculty will optimistically begin to perceive active learning as a means of developing students who are *"active architects of their own learning."* Choi and Anderson (2016) claim that active learning, as opposed to the more traditional passive and lecture-based models of learning, is more student-focused, develops students' critical thinking, and leads to cognitive autonomy. Subsequently, a social learning theory approach is achieved through the use of interactive learning logs in that students engage in interactive discourse as they complete activities. Kim *et al.* (2013) view students' dialogue and social interactions as a type of scaffolded instruction, leading students to a new and elevated level of cognitive processing.

Historically, some educational spaces in higher education have consisted of immobile chairs and desks with a teacher positioned at the front of the classroom and students situated in a position from which the teacher delivers content to the students. Educational spaces have evolved, however, particularly for college teachers whose instructional approaches advocate for a more engaged group of students who are viewed as active members of a learning community. In their conception of the facilitate-listen-engage (FLE) model, Lloyd *et al.* (2016) argue for a bidirectional instructional approach to increase student-student and student-faculty interactions and dialogue rather than viewing students as impassive participants in a learning community. In this approach, the teacher serves as the facilitator who builds on the importance of metacognitive competencies, listens to the students' conversations, and provides feedback as an engagement technique during in-class activities. Subsequently, professors who approach instruction through a more active and engaging philosophy strive to create an environment that reflects this methodology, particularly in comparison to a more traditional college classroom in which students are subjected to lectures by the professors. Again, interactive learning logs align with this model of instruction.

Self-regulated learning (SRL) is also an important part of an active learning environment. Hudesman *et al.* (2013) conclude that self-regulated learning is more highly correlated with students' college grade point average than their scores on standardised exams. Additionally, due to its recurring nature, the SRL model increases learning as students complete various assignments in phases. One example of this is found from my implementation of interactive learning logs in which students are required to complete various segments of assignments in stages, based on their developmental readiness for each phase. For example, students perform a demonstration in class, reflect on their progress in their learning logs, complete an extension activity based on their demonstrations, provide feedback to each other in their learning logs, and then complete their capstone assignment. Completing smaller segments of assignments with feedback along the way helps students to reflect on their learning – a fundamental element of self-regulated learning.

Perhaps the most notable benefit of using interactive learning logs in a higher education setting is the powerful formative assessment support. Formative assessment, a process that occurs during instruction, is heavily dependent on effective and timely feedback. In the context of higher education, professors and their students benefit from immediate feedback during active learning. As claimed by Hudesman *et al.* (2013), both faculty and students are recipients and providers of feedback during a learning segment. For example, the professor receives feedback based on students' responses to activities and then uses this feedback to alter his/her instruction. As a result, the professor can then provide feedback to students, which creates a cyclical process within the educational setting. Further, formative assessment is markedly a vital contributor to achievement gains; therefore, interactive learning logs, used primarily as a formative assessment instrument, provide a rich platform from which effective feedback is received, provided, and applied by all stakeholders. Thus, students' learning experiences related to course content are optimised, as students are also *"learning how to learn"* (2013:3). Kim *et al.* (2013) argue that even well-designed courses that encourage critical thinking are not exhaustive but must also include an assessment component to monitor students' levels of thinking and development. Interactive learning logs are a good fit for this type of assessment.

This practice was designed at Tennessee Tech University (TTU), a state-funded institution in the south-eastern region of the United States. With the aim of enhancing professors' instructional practices and increasing student engagement, TTU's Center for Teaching and Learning Excellence (CTLE) began in 2016. The mission of the CTLE is *to create an environment which encourages student engagement through innovative, transformative, and purposeful teaching and learning* (CTLE, 2017). I have attended and conducted workshops supported by our CTLE, all of which have emphasised the use of formative assessment and innovative practices to increase student engagement. Additionally, I serve on a faculty panel working with faculty from the College of Engineering. Through collaborative efforts, our main focus is on increasing student engagement and critical thinking through the implementation of formative assessment techniques. Based on recent research by our team, we discovered the need for increased student engagement in some areas, as well as the call for formative assessment techniques. As an associate professor in the College of Education at TTU, these topics are the main focus of my courses and are what I strive to model for my students who are teacher education candidates with the expectations of their applying the strategies. Both of these university-led initiatives align with the implementation of interactive learning logs, all supporting a theory-to-practice application.

Section 2: The Practice

2a. A General Introduction to the Innovative Practice

Interactive learning logs are a set of in-class activities implemented as a means of formatively assessing students and increasing student engagement in university-level courses. Some activities are planned in advance, while some ideas are prompted by an in-class discussion or by a concept on which students need additional reinforcement. The activities completed in learning logs provide a context for students to engage in both written and oral discourse. Students are typically given the opportunity to write about a concept and are then expected to engage in some type of dialogue – with a partner, in a small group, or as a whole-class discussion (or all three, sometimes in this order). These activities substantially increase student engagement and participation, while holding students accountable for their thinking and reasoning skills. Inaccuracies and misconceptions related to course concepts may occur; however, this is to be expected and is part of the goal of using the learning logs as a formative assessment tool. Some course assignments are more formal, with specific requirements and explicit directions stated on the syllabus; however, other activities are more appropriately embedded into the structure of a course based on students' developmental levels and conceptual understandings related to course content. Activities such as these are the premise of the interactive learning logs.

The following are examples of learning log activities: writing activities; activities based on deficits of students; parallel and open tasks in math; inquiry-based activities in science; student-led activities on demonstration days such as responding to a discrepant event or an inquiry-based science lesson; in-class responses to the viewing of a video or the reading of an article; journal entries based on students' personal experiences; responding to an open-ended question, etc.

Most interactive learning log activities require approximately five to thirty minutes to complete; however, the activities can be easily modified to accommodate students and course variations. Although I teach elementary methods courses in the College of Education that prepare candidates to become future teachers, the use of learning logs could be implemented in various university courses and across multiple disciplines.

As represented in Table 1, the activities that students complete in their learning logs vary in their outcomes and types of interactions. For example, some activities require that students reflect on personal experiences, while others require that students reflect on course demonstrations or phases of an assignment. Depending on the learner outcomes of the activity, interactions may be student-self, student-student, student-teacher, or student-group-teacher. For example, when students are asked to reflect on personal experiences, this originates as a student-self interaction; however, when asked to share experiences with a partner or small group, the interactions then become student-student. Completion of some activities also requires that students broaden their interactions to include the entire class and the teacher. These interactions help the students to demonstrate to the teacher their understandings of the topic at hand.

Activity with Directives	Type of Interaction	Outcome
Written response to a personal experience (students respond to a prompt presented by the teacher).	• Student-self (if only completing a written reflection) • Student-student (if students share their responses with a partner or small group) • Student-group-teacher (if students share their responses with the entire class and teacher)	Students reflect on a personal experience related to the course. For example, students provide a written account of their experience in learning how to read.
Students bring to class a rough draft of an upcoming assignment and provide peer-to-peer feedback in a step-by-step progression. During the process, the teacher is modelling for the students and providing additional guidance to extend students' learning.	• Student-student as peer feedback is provided • Student-teacher as the teacher circulates and discusses with individuals	Students will use peer feedback as a scaffold to their learning before submitting their final assignment. This is an opportunity for the teacher to circulate and provide feedback to the students and formatively assess the students during the process.

Students are presented with a topic to debate (as prompted by the teacher). Using various course-related sources (such as the textbook, journal articles, or online sources), students provide a written account of pros and cons prior to class discussion.	• Student-self • Student-student as they discuss their findings and perspectives in small groups • Student-group-teacher as they support their findings through an interactive debate	Students engage with the content and, by reflecting on the pros and cons of the topic, express their perspectives in written and verbal form.
Summary of a scholarly article (students read a scholarly article and complete an "article summary template").	• Student-self as they provide their personal reflections to the article • Student-student as they discuss their readings with a partner • Student-group-teacher as they discuss their readings with the entire class and the teacher	Students are exposed to scholarly literature related to the course content. Students reflect on the contents of the article and provide a written account of their reflections.

Table 1: Dimensions of engagement through interactive learning logs.

2b. The Curriculum

The curriculum for Tennessee Tech University's Teacher Education Program is guided by the Interstate New Teacher Assessment and Support Consortium (InTASC) standards (2016), which are designed by the Council of Chief State School Officers. InTASC standards, found on all course syllabi, state the competencies required of teacher candidates such as the knowledge, dispositions, and essential performances they must demonstrate as a requirement for licensure as a teacher. Interactive learning logs are an effective pedagogical tool to assist in the delivery of these standards and principles. In particular, interactive learning logs help to develop the following InTASC principles:

1) *The teacher understands the central concepts, tools of inquiry, and structures of the discipline(s) he or she teaches and creates learning experiences that make these aspects of subject matter meaningful for students;*

2) *The teacher understands how children learn and develop, and can provide learning opportunities that support their intellectual, social, and personal development;*

3) *The teacher understands and uses a variety of instructional strategies to encourage students' development of critical thinking, problem solving, and performance skills;*

4) *The teacher uses an understanding of individual and group motivation and behaviour to create a learning environment that encourages positive social interaction, active engagement in learning, and self-motivation;*

5) *The teacher understands and uses formal and informal assessment strategies to evaluate and ensure the continuous intellectual, social, and physical development of the learner;*

6) *The teacher is a reflective practitioner who continually evaluates the effects of his/her choices and actions on others and who actively seeks out opportunities to grow professionally.* (InTASC, 2016:1–4)

Additionally, the conceptual framework of Tennessee Tech University's teacher education programme states that the graduates of our programme must *demonstrate skills of reflection that promote self-evaluation and growth; understand and establish an effective learning environment and possess the skills, techniques, and strategies to do so, including those that provide opportunities for student intellectual, social, and personal development; and, use reflection continually and improve outcomes assessment, resulting in improved learning experiences.* Interactive learning logs contribute to the achievement of these goals. The objectives of my courses focus on teacher candidates building these essential competencies needed as future educators; thus, the interactive learning logs have somewhat of a multi-generational effect for my teacher candidates as I "teach them how to teach." For example, my goal is to model interactive and engaging activities for my teacher candidates with hopes of creating transferrable skills that they will later need as they enter the field of education as teachers themselves.

Interactive learning logs can be executed with the goal of building on or extending course-related content knowledge. These types of activities require students to summarise content, discuss various approaches and theories, and formulate personal reflections based on the new information. Additionally, some college students enter courses with deficiencies or content-related misconceptions. Through mindful assessment of students and careful design of interactive learning log activities, many of these misunderstandings can be alleviated before moving forward with instruction.

Interactive learning log activities enable students to engage in personal and professional reflective practices. Students are given prompts to which they reflect and respond in writing. Some prompts may be related to their personal lives and experiences, while others may be related to professional topics as future educators. For example, in their reading methods course during which they will learn instructional strategies for teaching children how to read, students are asked to reflect on their childhood memories of learning how to read. Many of their reflections contradict the contemporary pedagogical models they are learning or will learn in their courses. As the professor, this inspires my instructional approach for my students as I set in place the desire for my students to apply research and theoretical perspectives to their future instruction.

2c. Organisation of the Practice

The information that follows describes my personal preferences for organising interactive learning logs; however, their construction is quite simple and could easily be modified to accommodate diversity among professors, students, and subject matter. I routinely include a 3-ring notebook as part of my course requirements. Within this notebook is housed each student's interactive learning log activities. These are in addition to other out-of-class reading response activities completed throughout the course. Students are required to bring these notebooks to class each day, and I collect these notebooks as a midterm check and a final check, which are part of the students' overall grade. The interactive learning log section is evaluated based on the effort that the students put into their responses and on the completion of each activity. Students are expected to complete interactive learning log activities in class. Some of these activities include on-the-spot reactions to discussions, or they may be pre-planned activities related to the course content. These activities encourage student-to-professor and student-to-student engagement in discourse and interactions. If I notice students are having difficulty with concepts, I pose a question or activity to which they respond in their learning logs. I compile a running list of the activities written on the board or on chart paper for the students to refer to throughout the semester. I also provide a digital copy of this list to the students as a checklist when submitting their learning logs.

If a student is absent and misses a learning log activity, he or she is required to complete the activity outside of class by consulting either the professor or a peer for directions. This ensures student accountability and participation. I also provide the students with a rubric and a checklist for organising their notebook and ensuring that they have all the required components. As students work on the activities in their learning logs, I move around the room and read and respond to their responses, which allows me to intercept any concept-related misconceptions that may occur. Students often discuss their responses with partners or in small groups prior to whole-group discussions. I have noticed this substantially increases the engagement of students in whole-class discussions compared to solely posing a question to the whole class and asking for volunteers. For instance, when I pose a question to the group and have them write a response in their learning logs, discuss with a partner, discuss in small groups, and then share with the whole class, individual contributions are much stronger and occur more frequently. This increases critical thinking by *all* students rather than only by the one student who volunteers to respond.

2d. Preparations

Students are required to have a 3-ring notebook with blank paper in class each day which houses their interactive learning log activities (and are completed in class). The professor designs activities before class to which the students will respond and/or complete during class. The professor, however, may also decide to engage his/her students in an impromptu activity during class based on students' responses (and/or lack of responses) to course concepts. Occasionally, depending on the objective of the activity, handouts and other materials may be provided for the students to utilise during the completion of a learning log activity. In addition, I embed learning log activities within my PowerPoint presentations. This, along with their simplicity and on-the-spot implementation, is the beauty of the interactive learning logs.

Section 3: The Outcome

3a. Student Perspective

As evidenced in students' comments regarding interactive learning logs, students view the learning log activities as a positive component of their courses. Students learn to focus less on a grade and more on their thought processes, which alleviates many of the stress factors associated with the more formal assignments explicitly listed on the syllabus. Students also appreciate feedback during class rather than receiving feedback after a concept has been taught. I observe students during the completion of learning log activities and notice lively conversations and interactions, often prompting further questions, laughter, and the development of relationships during our classes. Students' voices are valued as they express their opinions and personal experiences in their learning logs and then share them with their classmates. Leadership skills are developed as students engage their peers in learning log activities during their class presentations. For example, in our science methods course, students are required to plan and lead an inquiry-based science lesson as if teaching it to a group of elementary students. During this demonstration, they are also required to have their peers complete a learning log activity related to the demonstration. Overall, students become more fluent in their reasoning skills and learn to approach concepts through a teamwork perspective.

I routinely do a mid-semester check-up by asking my students to provide some qualitative feedback to me. I ask questions such as: What is going well this semester? What is helping you to progress in your learning? How could I make this course better for you? When I have asked students their thoughts on learning log activities, I have steadily received positive feedback. I have not received any negative comments, which provides evidence to me, based on student feedback, that the interactive learning logs will remain an essential component of my courses. The following are students' comments regarding interactive learning logs:

+ *learning log activities engage you to participate in the activity and provide your own thoughts and reasoning;*

+ *they are quick and to the point. I like that I have them to look back at to help me understand or refresh my memory about an activity or topic;*

+ *it allows me to put my thoughts on paper before learning more about that subject or idea;*

+ *the learning log activities engage me, and I am not stressing out about a grade as long as I complete the activity;*

+ *they serve as a guide for the learning. They allow me to apply what I know and practice these concepts;*

+ *I have enjoyed the Learning Log activities for every class. They break up the lessons and let students have a few minutes to focus on something besides the lecture;*

+ *I really like the learning log activities. They help me visualize, and I can go back and look at the to help jog my memory of what our class was about for the day. Sometimes, there is so much information in a day, it all gets a little jumbled. The second reason I like them is they are FUN;*

+ *learning logs help me to be able to refresh myself about the topics and discussion we have had in class when preparing for a quiz or when completing homework;*

+ *I like how learning logs keep us up-to-date on our abilities and what we're learning.*

Overall, students describe the interactive learning log activities as engaging and fun, stating that they help them to revise for upcoming quizzes or homework. They also claim that the activities help to "break up" the class time, stimulate the visualisation of concepts, and provide a time to put their thoughts into writing. Students speak positively about the learning log activities not counting as a formal grade, which removes some of the stress from the course. Most importantly, students affirm that the in-class activities help to guide their learning.

This innovative practice is different from most traditional college classrooms in that students remain engaged and are held accountable for much of their learning as it is presented to them in class. Traditionally, many of us, as college students, may have experienced the professor lecturing as we took notes, rarely initiating dialogue related to course content, yet we were expected to know the material for an upcoming test. Discussions, if any, were typically done outside of class on assignments on which we were expected to collaborate with peers. There was very little collaboration or discussion among small groups during class time. Also, in my college experience, most written responses were expected to be completed out of class, and professors seldom allowed time for students to engage in writing in class. On the contrary, interactive learning logs serve as a thermostat to gauge how students are progressing. The professor is able to formatively assess learning patterns of the class and individuals in an ongoing manner rather than waiting until a mid-term or final exam to assess students.

3b. Teacher Perspective

In the spirit of transparency, I must admit that my first intention for implementing interactive learning logs was to please the masses! "I want my college students to be upset with me," said no professor ever! After all, these are the students who would be completing my evaluations at the end of the semester – evaluations that would be considered in the decision for my tenure and promotion! My second goal for the use of interactive learning logs was to formatively assess my students throughout the semester. Since implementing this innovative practice, I have yet to have a student exhibit any type of pushback toward the in-class activities. From the first day of class, the students are informed that interactive learning logs are an essential component of my courses and, therefore, as evidenced by students' affirmative comments, they embrace the in-class activities.

As the professor, learning log activities allow me to extend assignments. For example, students often need additional time throughout the semester to extend their learning. They are sometimes not ready for a task that can be too cognitively demanding at the beginning of the semester. For this reason, I sometimes add a reflective piece based on an assignment to be completed in their learning logs at a later time in the semester. Some formal assignments specifically listed on the syllabus have a high difficulty level and push the students to their highest potential; however, to avoid pushing students to a level of frustration, interactive learning logs enable me to embed extension activities to deepen students' learning. Because the activity does not count as a distinct grade, the stress factor immediately decreases, and students tend to reflect more transparently as a result. For example, in my readings methods course, students are required to do a read-aloud demonstration (as a formal grade) at the beginning of the semester during which they demonstrate for their classmates specific instructional techniques related to the teaching of reading in an elementary classroom. I provide qualitative and quantitative feedback to the students based on their demonstration. I video the demonstration and then have the students reflect on it later in the semester (in their learning logs) after they have been exposed to additional strategies and concepts. Additionally, after receiving my feedback, they take the demonstration a step further and transform it into a formal lesson plan (which is another formal grade). The completion of the formal lesson plan is quite challenging to a first-semester junior in our programme. Because of this, the completion of some parts of the lesson plan are delayed until later in the semester and completed as a learning log activity after students have mastered the foundational components of the lesson plan.

Adding subsequent components to an assignment as a learning log activity allows me to scaffold students' learning and to adjust the timing of the activity based on students' readiness. This also allows me to assess their growth on certain concepts at various points throughout the semester. Students' developmental progressions evolve throughout the semester as they gain new knowledge and are exposed to new concepts and strategies; therefore, learning log activities work well as scaffolded activities to formal assignments, allowing students the opportunity to apply their new understandings before submitting final assignments.

My syllabi are extremely detailed and include explicit guidelines for the major assignments of the course. Some students are encouraged by and prefer these lengthy descriptions, while others become intimidated. Rather than including additional items that will be completed during class to the syllabus, I include a requirement of the interactive learning log. This is a way to eliminate the need to explain each pre-planned activity for the course (which can be overwhelming to students) but maintains student accountability for completing the in-class activity. In addition, this increases student attendance, since students are required to have completed each learning log activity even if they are absent, in which case, it is their responsibility to contact the professor or classmate for directions and materials to complete the activity.

In addition, I have witnessed other professors' complaints concerning reticent students and a lack of participation by their students. I have also heard of students sleeping, texting, or exhibiting numerous inattentive behaviours during class; however, the use of interactive learning logs lessens some of these distracting behaviours and emphasises the most optimal use of class time, while allowing me to formatively assess each student each day in class.

As previously mentioned, I initially included interactive learning logs as a means of appeasing students, particularly from the viewpoint of a novice professor who was not quite equipped to "commit" to a 15-week course. However, after implementing interactive learning logs in my courses as a trial run and tracking their effectiveness for over a decade, I have been pleasantly surprised by their beneficial unintended consequences and how they serve much more of a purpose than appeasing students!

Section 4: Moving Forward

As I move forward, my next steps will be to continuously add to my repertoire of learning log activities for each of my courses. I keep a running list of all activities from semester to semester and tweak them based on my students' varying needs and the varying course content. I also remove activities as I find more beneficial ones to add. As I model the implementation of interactive learning logs for my pre-service teacher candidates, I have also begun expecting them to use them during their in-class demonstrations and presentations. To do this, the candidates design their own learning log activities to engage their audience (their peers). This increases student accountability and validates them as members of the learning community.

Another consideration for future use of interactive learning logs is to have students complete them in a digital format. This would enable students to interact online when face-to-face interactions are not possible or to interact with multiple classmates through discussion boards, blogs, or other digital avenues. Interactive learning logs are flexible in their design and may be modified based on course content, which indicates that they are a sustainable formative assessment technique.

As a professor of elementary education methods courses, engaging students in learning is the key focus of my instruction; however, professors in other disciplines are often more content-focused, which may present challenges in implementing active learning techniques. At the university level, my goal is to impart this innovative practice with other discipline areas by providing professional development workshops for faculty members. This goal aligns with the Center for Teaching and Learning's agenda for increasing student engagement across campus.

Conclusion

Interactive learning logs, unassuming from a surface-level view, are a worthwhile tool for the higher education learning environment. They serve as an uncomplicated method for engaging students and provide numerous opportunities for professors to formatively assess students. The activities consume a minimal amount of instructional time, yet they reap great rewards in terms of enhancing students' cognitive processing. As students complete in-class activities for the purposes of reflection, for extending course-related knowledge, or for alleviating misconceptions, they also use metacognitive skills to evolve into self-regulated learners.

Interactive learning logs require minimal preparations by professors, which increases their benefits and ease of implementation. Over the past decade, interactive learning logs have served as a key component of my courses and have been viewed positively by the students. Students deem the learning log activities as advantageous, as they use them to study for upcoming exams and to help scaffold their learning throughout the semester. The activities also encourage reticent students to interact more frequently with their peers and, as a result, gain new perspectives on course-related topics. Students also appreciate the stress-free factor of learning log activities, since the individual activities are not graded.

The most beneficial aspect of interactive learning logs is their ability to engage students in activities during class. Informing students at the beginning of the semester that they will be completing entries in their interactive learning logs removes the limitations of a syllabus and allows a professor to embed additional course-related activities into the daily learning environment. By utilising interactive learning logs as a formative assessment tool and to increase students' metacognitive skills, professors cultivate learners who are reflective practitioners and self-regulated learners. Using one phrase to describe interactive learning logs, I would say they are "simple yet superior" and are a quintessential feature of an active learning environment.

About the Author

Malinda Hoskins Lloyd is associate professor at Tennessee Technological University in the Department of Curriculum and Instruction in Cookeville, Tennessee, USA. She may be contacted at the following e-mail address: MLloyd@tntech.edu

Bibliography

Choi, Y. & W. Anderson (2016). Self-directed learning with feedback. *Journal of College Science Teaching*, Vol. 46, No. 1, pp. 32–38.

Center for Teaching and Learning Excellence (CTLE), Tennessee Tech University, Online Resource: https://www.tntech.edu/ctle/ [Accessed on 17 April 2017].

Hudesman, J.; S. Crosby & D. Clay (2013). Using formative assessment and metacognition to improve student achievement. *Journal of Developmental Education*, Vol. 37, No. 1, pp. 2–13.

Interstate New Teacher Assessment and Support Consortium (2016). Online Resource: http://documents.routledge-interactive.s3.amazonaws.com/9781138888296/other/INTASC_Standards_Information.pdf [Accessed on 17 April 2017].

Kim, K.; P. Sharma & K. Furlong (2013). Effects of active learning on enhancing student critical thinking in an undergraduate general science course. *Innovative Higher Education*, Vol. 38, pp. 223–235.

Lloyd, M.; N. Kolodziej & K. Brashears (2016). Classroom discourse: An essential component in building a classroom community. *School Community Journal*, Vol. 26, No. 2, 291–304.

Park, E. & B. Choi (2014). Transformation of classroom spaces: Traditional versus active learning classroom in colleges. *Higher Education*, Vol. 68, pp. 749–771.

Patrick, L.; L. Howell & W. Wischusen (2016). Perceptions of active learning between faculty and undergraduates: Differing views among departments. *Journal of STEM Education*, Vol. 17, No. 3, pp. 55–63.

Stephens, K. & M. Winterbottom (2010). Using a learning log to support students' learning in biology lessons. *Journal of Biological Education*, Vol. 44, No. 2, pp. 72–80.

Embedding Evaluation and Scholarship into Curriculum and Teaching: The Curriculum Evaluation Research Framework

Jo-Anne Kelder and Andrea Carr

Introduction

This chapter contributes to the book *New Innovations in Teaching and Learning in Higher Education* as we present a conceptual framework and practical approach for embedding evaluation and research into curriculum and teaching. Our curriculum evaluation and research (CER) framework facilitates academics to collaboratively engage in activities that are focused on the quality of the curriculum they design and teach. It applies to any substantive body of curriculum, typically a course of study leading to the award of a qualification, and any group of academics (the teaching team), who are collectively responsible for administering and teaching it.

We expand the definition of innovation to encompass a new way of thinking about how to organise the work of teachers to assure quality teaching and learning in higher education. When referring to "teaching", we include three fundamental activities that occur over the life cycle of a curriculum: design, delivery, and evaluation (Phillips, McNaught & Kennedy, 2012). We understand "design" to be an ongoing activity comprising teachers' decisions about content, learning environment, learning processes, intended learning outcomes, and methods of assessing learning (Phillips *et al.*, 2012; Laurillard, 2012). "Delivery" is how those decisions are enacted so that students are taught, whether by a traditional face-to-face mode or some level of technology enhanced learning and teaching (TELT): blended or fully online mode of delivery. The focus of our innovation is to foreground the "evaluation" activity; thus, we provide a framework to embed evaluation into routine teaching practice in a way that also builds teachers' capacity to practice scholarship of teaching and learning (SoTL).

Our innovation, the CER framework, is designed to harness teachers' intrinsic and extrinsic motivations so that they can work collectively to achieve and demonstrate excellence in scholarly teaching practice. It is also intended to enable teachers to effectively respond to external drivers, for example, an institutional quality management framework. The CER framework helps teachers engage efficiently with quality management practices expected as part of their role, including monitoring curriculum performance and teaching against external metrics.

This chapter presents the process for developing, implementing, and disseminating the CER framework over three phases. The range of natural data produced during the process of curriculum delivery is described. "Natural data" are the data generated by students in the course of undertaking their studies and generated by staff in the process of developing and delivering curricula and assessing student learning (e.g., assessment tasks, feedback, peer-review activities). The chapter also outlines the practical resources that the authors have developed for use by teaching teams. These resources are a set of documents that codify the knowledge developed by the authors through designing and implementing evaluation and research plans, with ethics applications, for three curricula innovations. They are written generically and are easily adaptable by a teaching team for their own curriculum. The outcome of adopting the CER framework is the ability to ethically gain consent of staff members and students to use their natural data for research purposes. This is in addition to having in place a system for routine data collection and analysis that can be used collaboratively to address sector, institutional, and personal expectations of evidence-based teaching practice and quality improvement.

A process account is important for understanding how the framework is grounded in the practice of the first author in developing evaluation and research plans for new curriculum initiatives in her institution and, of both authors, in developing the CER framework. A challenge within the higher education sector is how to facilitate disciplinary-trained academics, normally not trained in the education discipline, to be effective in curriculum design and delivery and also able to provide evidence of its impact. This challenge is linked to the broader higher education sectoral challenge where institutions are required to demonstrate that their courses meet national standards, for example, Australian standards such as the Higher Education Standards Framework and Australian Qualifications Framework (Australian Qualifications Framework Council, 2013) and international standards such as Tuning (Wagenaar, 2008).

A process account is also important for understanding the conceptual nature of the CER framework, the rationale for each stage of its development and dissemination, and how each element is related and interacts to develop a collaborative culture of teachers working on improving the curriculum in response to the evidence of their students learning (via analysing assessment and participation) and experiences (via informal and formal feedback).

The overall aim of this chapter is to present the CER framework as an innovative approach that assists academics to develop skills and knowledge in curriculum design and teaching. It can be used to build a collaborative culture within and across the teaching team and support members to engage in purposeful activities that achieve short- and long-term goals to improve their curriculum.

When reading this chapter, you will gain an understanding of:

1. the CER framework as a way of thinking about the teaching (curriculum design, delivery, and evaluation) components of academic work;

2. how to use the CER framework as an approach for embedding evaluation and research into a substantive body of curriculum taught by a teaching team;

3. the key cultural and political elements that are important for successfully implementing and benefitting from applying the CER framework (distributed leadership, teaching-team collaboration, students' participation and institutional support).

This chapter has four main sections. In section 1, we describe the changing academic workplace as the context for developing the CER framework. In particular, growing expectations of academics to provide robust evidence of the quality of curriculum and demonstrate scholarship in their teaching practice was a driver for the development of the features of the framework. Section 2 provides a process account of the CER framework during the development of three innovative curricula for the Faculty of Health, University of Tasmania. The CER framework was forged from an action research project in which three tailored evaluation and research plans were developed on behalf of teaching teams. These plans were designed to ensure the collection of relevant data that each team could use to improve their curricula; evaluate outcomes against standards; and, longer term, achieve scholarly outputs (e.g., publications). This section concludes with a reflection on the value of the plans from the perspectives of a range of stakeholders and the process of codifying plans into the formal conceptualisation of the CER framework. It also outlines our approach for engaging teaching teams in evidence-based practice. Section 3 details the outcomes for each of the three phases of the CER framework's development and dissemination. Taking a future focus, section 4 sets out the hopes and expectations of the authors for the CER framework and our approach of freely sharing what we have developed and our ongoing practice of inviting collaboration. We encourage others to apply the framework in their different teaching and learning contexts and to further develop our resources in innovative ways that support teaching teams to embed evaluation and research.

Section 1: The Background

In the academic workplace, academics are increasingly expected to provide robust evidence of the quality, effectiveness, and impact of their work. Academic work typically flows in four broad streams of activity: disciplinary research, teaching, institutional service, and community service (University of Tasmania Staff Agreement 2013–2016, 2013). Increasingly, each of these areas involves a commitment of time and effort that is devoted to documenting the evidence in terms of impact, effectiveness, and relevance to national and institutional priorities.

Similar to higher education authorities in the UK, Europe, Canada, and the USA, the Australian Tertiary Education Quality and Standards Authority (TEQSA) places strict obligations on Australian higher education providers. Thus, academics are expected to have, or acquire, appropriate qualifications and develop expertise in the design and delivery of curriculum. Additionally, higher education providers are expected to have evidence of the quality of curriculum and teaching.

This focus on standards and compliance means planned evidence collection and analysis of a range of educational data are critical for demonstrating the impact and effectiveness, relevance, and value of education. Brookfield (1995) advises a multi-dimensional approach to understanding impact and effectiveness using four lenses (self, peer, student, and literature) to ensure a scholarly approach to curriculum design and delivery. These lenses are also applicable as evidence for quality assurance and quality improvement purposes.

The CER framework is a response to multiple, often competing, expectations of academics regarding the teaching component of academic work. This framework is presented as a conceptual guide for teaching teams to help them link the evidence-base that underpins their quality improvement and quality assurance activities, and leverage that evidence as data for scholarship of teaching and learning. It provides a compelling value-proposition to academics: that a collaborative, teaching-team approach to planned evaluation of curricula is an efficient and effective approach to organising and using data as evidence that feeds institutional monitoring and reporting functions as well as underpinning scholarship. This is critical in the context of students' expectations of high quality and relevant learning experiences and the standards specified by external higher education authorities. Our approach is a response to national standards that are inherently focused on curriculum at the level of whole-of-course (programme of study leading to a qualification).

Section 2: The Practice

This section provides a process account of the development and implementation of the CER framework. The initial conceptualisation was forged from an action research project that provided support to the teaching teams developing three innovative curricula for the University of Tasmania's Faculty of Health. The first author's brief was to develop tailored evaluation and research plans for each curriculum. Each plan included research aims and rationale, research questions, data sources, data collection, and data analysis method. The plans were translated into an ethics application for each curriculum. This provided the teaching team with a framework for routine, ongoing data collection that they could collaboratively analyse to improve their curricula, evaluate outcomes against standards, and, longer term, achieve scholarly outputs (e.g., publications). The section concludes with a reflection on the value of planning for evaluation that is aligned to planning for scholarly research. It also sets out how translating the research plan into an ethics application was the impetus for formally conceptualising the CER framework as an approach for engaging teaching teams in evidence-based practice and developing a generic ethics application template as a resource.

2a. The CER Framework: An Overview

The CER framework provides a context in which teachers' horizons are expanded. It shifts the focus from individual academics and single units of curriculum (subjects and units) to whole-of-programme curriculum (course) delivered by a teaching team. The outcome is to reduce the reporting overhead for individuals, to create a whole-of-course (programme/degree) data set that all academics can use to scaffold a scholarly approach to teaching, and to support broader scholarship of teaching and learning (SoTL).

The CER framework (Figure 1) guides a systematic approach, usable by a teaching team, to address a range of quality agendas in curriculum and teaching. A key aspect of the framework is that national higher education standards and institutional quality management systems primarily refer to a course (programme of study leading to a qualification). The course and its teaching team are thus the relevant scope for the CER framework because its goal is to guide academics to organise their teaching and learning practice so they can evaluate their work in a way that is useful for making improvements and is also aligned to external reporting requirements. A second consideration was to think of quality improvement (QI), quality assurance (QA), and SoTL as three orientations to evidence-based decision-making for curriculum design and delivery. In this framing, QI and QA are guided by an evaluation plan; SoTL activities are governed by a course-level research plan with institutional ethics approval. Members of a teaching team have differentiated responsibilities to either participate in, or lead, quality activities depending on the scope of their role and personal motivation.

Ensuring that a curriculum meets minimum requirements typically involves collecting evidence and reporting actions, outcomes, and impact. Institutional information systems provide a quantitative snapshot and trend data, but contextual information and evidence of pedagogical effectiveness and impact are also important to understand the landscape of learning and teaching for each course of study – information that is held by teachers. The CER framework enables teachers to demonstrate that a curriculum meets expected standards using a multi-lens, scholarly approach (Brookfield, 1995). The CER framework (Figure 1 adapted from Kelder, Carr and Walls (2017)) has three core components that need to be present in some measure: essential activities, relationship elements, and enabling resources, including the institution's learning management system (LMS).

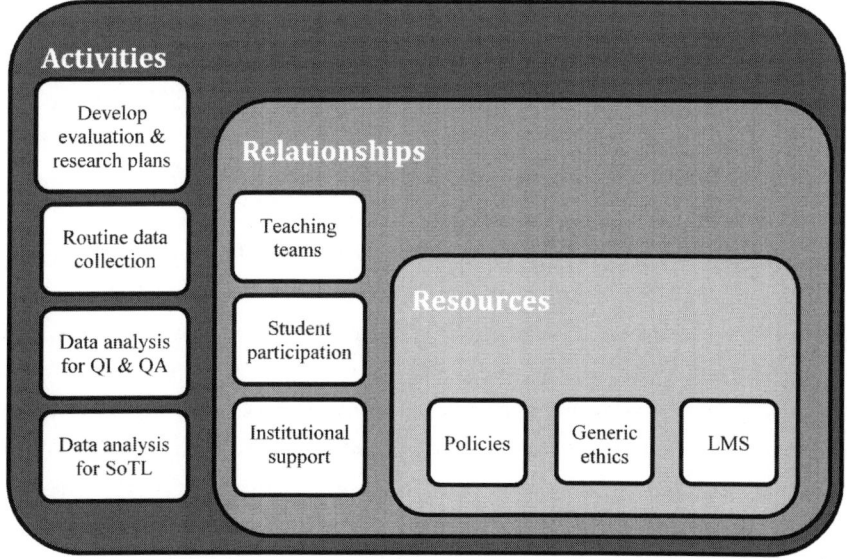

Figure 1: CER framework. (Adapted from Kelder, Carr & Wall (2017)).

The essential activities are all related to planned, purposeful, and collectively organised evidence-gathering and analysis. The relationship elements are essential if a teaching team is to collectively apply their knowledge to inform their understanding and decision-making in relation to the quality of their curricula. The CER framework is thus deliberately designed to provide a social structure and context in which a culture of evidence-based teaching practice can be built. It extends to scholarly outputs, building a collective commitment to good practice in designing and delivering curricula, as well as developing personal and collective staff capability. It functions as a guide for academics in *how* to engage with the body of knowledge in higher education literature. In summary, the CER framework brings evaluation for quality improvement and quality assurance as well as the scholarship of learning and teaching to the forefront of academic thinking when designing curriculum.

The key stakeholders relevant to the CER framework include institutions, academics, and students. The CER framework is a conceptual tool for academics that supports planning and executing collaborative activities that are directed towards the quality of curriculum. In particular, the framework guides the development of an evaluation plan that ensures data are collected for QI and QA purposes. It also prompts a research plan that leverages this routine data collection into scholarly practice and outputs (SoTL).

Academic practice is at the heart of the CER framework; it is essentially a guide to transform teaching practices from individual responsibility for the quality of units of a curriculum (detached from course learning outcomes) to a teaching-team approach that values collaboration and develops a culture of distributed leadership (Pearce, 2004) in which both individual and collective efforts are rewarded. The evaluation plan focuses attention on student learning outcomes and learning experiences and ensures that feedback in many forms is collected, analysed, and acted on to renew and refresh a curriculum. It also embeds awareness of external standards and the benefit of regular and targeted internal and external peer review. The culture-building elements are enabled by a value proposition that SoTL, via a research plan, is facilitated by longitudinal and comprehensive data sets that include student assessments available for research purposes. Students are invited to participate in the curriculum as research participants, and teachers provide feedback to students regarding the outcomes of their scholarship following each round of data analysis.

2b. The Curriculum: Developing the CER Framework – A Process Account

The process account of the CER framework can be divided into three broad phases. In Phase 1, the CER framework was developed as a conceptual framework (a way of thinking to guide action) for a teaching team. It incorporates a practical and efficient method to collaboratively plan, organise, and integrate the outputs of individual activities to facilitate QI of units of curricula and QA of the course curriculum, with the opportunity for SoTL. The goal was to develop a holistic, systematic, and organised approach to ensuring quality curriculum with QI, QA, and SoTL, conceptualised as three orientations to evidence-based decision-making for curriculum design and delivery. Phase 2 was characterised by the authors making a conscious shift from tailored solutions for individual curricula to articulating a general version of the approach and codifying our knowledge into various resources that enable teaching teams to have an ethical underpinning for routine collection and analysis of natural data. Phase 3 was indicated by a further shift in focus, developing a dissemination model for the CER framework that included ongoing development via interactive workshops and inviting teaching teams to adopt the CER framework for their curriculum and, ongoing, to collaborate in further developing resources, shared under a Creative Commons Attribute Share-Alike licence.

Phase 1. The conceptual framework

Curriculum development and delivery in Phase 1 of this design-based approach (Anderson & Shattuck, 2001; Phillips, McNaught & Kennedy, 2012) included three case studies that each had an evaluation-research plan, with an accompanying ethics application as a foundation. We decided that a design-based research approach was appropriate for the iterative development of the CER framework, as well as for curriculum development (Anderson & Shattuck, 2011). This is because it is grounded in real-world settings and allows systematic, iterative development with flexibility to respond to emergent problems and opportunities. Phase 1 involved identifying and applying key elements of the CER framework and articulating their relationships. The CER framework was iteratively developed through its application in three curriculum case studies (a learning module, bachelor degree, and a MOOC).

The figures below outline the conceptualisation of the CER framework and its meaning.

Figure 2: Representations of the relationship between QI, QA, and SoTL. (Adapted from Kelder, Carr and Walls, (2017)).

Figure 2 (left above):

> *"highlights the concept of nesting for leveraging the outcomes of routine QI activities into QA and SoTL activities and outcomes. A design-based approach to curriculum evaluation and research can simplify data collection and analysis by ensuring alignment of educational research questions. Figure 2 (right above) highlights the cyclic aspect of QI, QA and SoTL activities and the possibility of coordinating these differently oriented quality activities to link and leverage outputs. It also highlights their inter-connectedness in the context of a teaching team focused on quality enhancement of a course. Teaching team members can have different orientations for their teaching and curriculum design, but overall the team effort can be coordinated to ensure all quality activities are supported."* (Kelder, Carr & Walls, 2017)

Figure 3 (below) highlights how, within a teaching team, different staff roles can be oriented to different aspects of assuring the quality of curricula, each member having differing levels of interest, and opportunities to engage, in scholarship. All members of the team are required to engage in QI activities as they teach their students, and also to participate in QA activities (e.g., peer review and external benchmarking). The collective activity builds toward overall outputs that include evidence-based changes to the design, reports against standards, and publications related to the impact and effectiveness of various aspects of the curriculum.

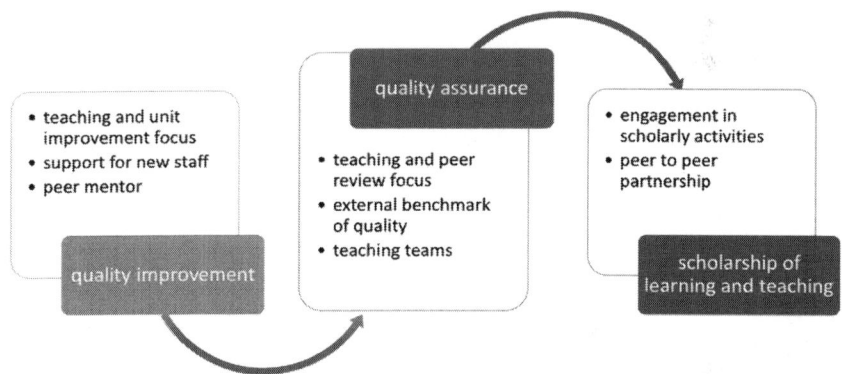

Figure 3: Relationship between QI, QA, and SoTL activities.

Phase 1 concluded with a critical review of the three original ethics applications in consultation with the chair of our institution's Social Sciences Human Research Ethics Committee. We analysed the content of each ethics application from the following perspectives: research questions, data types, data management, recruitment of participants, and the establishment of consent. We evaluated the content by dimensions of relevance, sustainability, and scalability. The aim was to codify the learnings from the process of submitting an initial ethics application, followed by multiple amendments as we learned in-practice what was actually needed for a whole-of-curriculum approach.

This method allowed the generic ethics application to be developed as a transferable resource, compliant with all ethical requirements (Australian National Statement for Ethical Conduct of Research 2007, Updated May 2015). The rationalised ethics application is now a customisable template that can be applied to any substantial body of curriculum delivered by a teaching team. Importantly, this work also encompassed the development of an online mechanism for ethical management of consent and data.

Phase 2. Local dissemination and ongoing refinement

Building on Phase 1, Phase 2 began the process of formally articulating the CER framework as a method to coordinate evidence-gathering and analysis for QA with the opportunity for SoTL. The emerging framework for evaluation and research also provided explicit opportunities to build a teaching-team culture in which collegial and collaborative academic work occurs and is focused on a shared goal of evidence-based curriculum design and delivery. Phase 2 was primarily "within-institution" dissemination via workshops and iterative refinement of the CER framework in response to feedback. Feedback was sought from participants at each workshop's conclusion on the relevance and effectiveness of the workshop and suggestions for improvement.

Attention transitioned from the impact and effectiveness of each case's curricula on student learning and experience to the impact and effectiveness of the CER framework in driving scholarly approaches and outputs in a body of curricula. This change in focus necessitated additional research objectives to document the uptake, investigate the process and outcomes of implementing the framework and evaluating its impact and effectiveness, as well as develop dissemination methods and resources. Feedback on the CER framework design, the associated resources, and the process of adapting and implementing it was collected during follow-up meetings and provided by self-nominated participants. These meetings were designed to support them to implement the CER framework in their context. We documented CER framework design refinements arising from these collaborations.

Achieving these objectives was facilitated by an *Embedding Evaluation and Research into Curriculum Design and Delivery* workshop that was designed to:

- value academic professionalization as an important element of curriculum quality;

- offer the CER framework as a valuable and collegial solution to a range of issues that academics face in their day-to-day workplace (e.g., casualisation of the workforce and management of workload);

+ facilitate the application of the CER framework in different contexts

+ share resources;

+ invite further development and dissemination of the CER framework through collaboration.

We delivered four workshops to graduate and postgraduate teaching teams within our university and facilitated the implementation of the CER framework in two whole-of-course programmes and one unit of study. We also began to investigate the benefits associated with open educational resources and sought advice on the most appropriate approach that would enable our resources to be made available more widely and without restrictions. The conclusion of Phase 2 was marked by a mature workshop design that was the result of several presentations within our university and invitations to provide feedback and share innovations.

Phase 3. A national focus

Phase 3 (national dissemination) was indicated by the authors expanding their focus to a national context and seeking to build a national conversation with interested institutions. This activity began with the delivery of a workshop at an international learning and teaching conference (HERDSA, 2016). We encouraged participants to consider how the CER framework could be adopted, adapted, and applied in their context, resulting in invitations to present tailored workshops at five higher education providers across Australia.

Collegial activity and distributed, or shared, leadership (Pearce, 2004) provide the underpinning philosophy of the CER framework design with ethical guidelines for its application. Our approach to disseminating the CER framework is also underpinned by this philosophy. As a result, we adopted a model for sharing based on an open educational resource approach guided by a Creative Commons Share-Alike licence. This approach encompasses invitations to colleagues to collaborate and build on the CER framework, adapt it to their context, provide feedback, and feed forward to an expanding community of practice. While the CER framework facilitates routine data collection, efficient management of the substantial data sets it generates is yet to be resolved. The current approach is manual management by an independent third party.

2c. Organisation – Using the CER Framework

Often, the horizon of an academic as teacher is limited to the unit of study (subject) for which they are responsible, with little opportunity or formal requirement to operate as part of a teaching team working towards course (programme, degree) learning outcomes (Brown, Kelder, Freeman & Carr, 2013). The CER framework facilitates a *teaching-team* approach that focuses on whole-of-course outcomes.

A philosophy of shared leadership (Pearce, 2004) underpins this explicitly collegial and collaborative approach. It is applied to curriculum delivery and quality improvement, which provides professional development and career opportunities for all staff. This approach allows innovations in learning and teaching explicitly aligned to a programme of evaluation and research that draws upon routinely collected natural data.

2d. Preparation – Essential Requirements for a CER Framework

Alongside the development of the CER framework, a range of supporting resources have been developed to facilitate its uptake. In particular, two practical resources were developed by the authors to remove a significant barrier to uptake of the CER framework: the time required to plan an effective whole-of-course evaluation and research programme and the time and expertise needed to translate an evaluation and research plan into an ethics application.

These resources have been refined through several iterations within the curriculum cases, continue to be refined with each implementation, and are available via a Creative Commons Share-Alike licence. They are designed to be sufficiently generic in order to provide a useful starting point, and they provide guidance in how to customise for specific teaching and learning contexts (e.g., scale of curriculum, composition of teaching team, and characteristics of student cohorts). The resources include:

Generic ethics research application template

The generic ethics application template resource is based on our institution's minimal risk application form for social sciences research (http://www.utas.edu.au/research-admin/divisional-resources/forms (Accessed on 18 March 2017)). This form complies with the Australian National Statement for Ethical Conduct of Research 2007 (Updated May 2015).

The generic ethics application template was developed as a starting point for teaching teams to develop an application for their own course. It is written to comply with the Australian National Statement for Ethical Conduct of Research 2007 (Updated May 2015) and provides a structured set of answers that, in effect, set out the research plan for a course from an ethics perspective. This includes research aims and objectives, rationale for the research, research questions, selection and recruitment of participants (students and staff members), participant information sheets and consent management, and ethical management of the data and reporting compliance. The generic ethics application template embeds two other elements – the institutional policies on research and curriculum management and the use of the institutional learning management system (LMS) as a mechanism for recruiting participants and establishing their consent status via an *opt-in* online process.

The generic ethics application template provides content for each section and can be easily tailored for a specific curriculum. The teaching team is required to name the curriculum they are researching and add any additional research questions (and therefore additional data sets they wish to collect). The wording has been vetted by this institution's chair of the Social Sciences Human Research Committee. The content is usable for translation to other Australian institutions or international context in which course-wide research takes place.

Evaluation research committee (ERC) structure and terms of reference

Embedded in the generic ethics is an explanation and justification of the governance for the curriculum evaluation research project: an evaluation research committee (ERC). The ERC is a mechanism to ensure the research plan is followed and all activities fall within agreed ethical practice (e.g., decisions related to authorship of publications arising from research, additional research questions and data analysis).

"Research room" concept

The research room concept is an innovative solution to the problem of ethical recruitment of students and staff, engaging staff in educational research, dissemination of research outputs, and providing staff with resources to develop capacity for scholarship. It uses an institution's learning management system to provide accessible and anonymous provision of consent for participants and allows data matching of a range of student and staff-related data over the life of the curriculum.

Evaluation research planning tool

The evaluation research planning tool is a document for teaching teams to support them in planning ethical management of their CER project. The tool provides a set of diagrams that establish the relationship between the key components of the CER framework (QI, QA, and SoTL); the underlying principles (strategic priorities, distributed leadership, and collaboration) and the intended goals (quality programmes and services for students, meeting higher education standards and frameworks, and development and innovation).

Interactive workshop

The authors developed an interactive workshop for teaching teams that can be adapted to a one-hour didactic presentation. The *Embedding Evaluation and Research into Curriculum Design and Delivery* workshop provides a comprehensive overview of the CER framework and resources, demonstrates its practical application and outcomes for exemplar courses, provides participants with electronic copies of the workshop PowerPoint and resources, and concludes with an invitation to collaborate, under a Creative Commons Share-Alike licence, to adapt and further develop the framework resources.

Section 3: The Outcome

The factors indicating the success of the CER framework are recognition and broadening uptake beyond the originating faculty/institution. The CER framework has allowed for the collection of evidence to support multiple teaching and learning awards for the three original curriculum cases in their institution and nationally. As the CER framework has been disseminated nationally through workshops, momentum has grown and a network of interested adopters is developing (five national institutions at the time of writing). Direct evidence of substantive outcomes of the CER framework is associated with teaching staff.

Aligned with the iterative development of the CER framework, benefits to teachers and teaching teams also developed and emerged. Different kinds of outcomes can be discerned from each phase of the development.

The key outcome of Phase 1 was a well-developed conceptualisation of the relationship between QI, QA, and SoTL in the context of a teaching team responsible for a coherent body of curricula (e.g., course, major, programme, or unit). The three curriculum cases underpinning and informing this conceptualisation (see Figure 2 and 3) formed the impetus for synthesising and codifying the learnings from each case. The case studies represented different curricula types (learning module, degree course, and MOOC). Each increase in scale of *curriculum* design prompted consideration of the impact on *evaluation research* design related to: increasing scale of data collection, data management and consent management, and managing ethical dilemmas associated with routine collection of sizable data sets that allow data matching (re-identifiability).

Specific and direct benefits for teaching staff are evident in the outcomes of the CER framework for the degree course case study implementing the framework. The course has received institutional, community, and national awards for the quality of its curriculum. Each application has been solidly supported by the breadth and depth of data available to demonstrate quality processes and outcomes. The CER framework enabled a culture of scholarship with increasing capability demonstrated in the increasing number of publications, including peer-reviewed. Aligned, the authors collected a growing body of evidence of the value and impact of the CER framework when applied by teaching teams to curricula. Between 2012–2016, the three curriculum cases produced more than 25 scholarly outputs (publications, conference presentations across the curriculum cases), successfully applied for over $100,000 grant funding, and collectively received five awards, including one national award for programmes that enhance learning.

Phase 2 was indicated by the authors stepping aside from hands-on involvement in the curriculum cases and changing focus to disseminating the formalised CER framework and generalising and refining the supporting resources. The benefit to teachers of this phase was synthesising the specific elements in the case-relevant ethics applications to create a generic ethics that was applicable across a broad range of curricula types and could be easily tailored to other contexts.

The expansion of the CER framework to a national context signalled Phase 3, with the authors engaging in a conversation with interested higher education institutions. Developing and delivering a workshop at an international learning and teaching conference, Higher Education and Research Development Society of Australasia (HERDSA), was a key activity. Workshop attendees considered how the CER framework could be applied in their context and, as a result, targeted follow-up presentations were given at five higher education institutions. A collaborating colleague indicated the value of sharing the CER framework within her institution:

> "[It is] a model of building scholarship on a foundation of compliance and quality improvement … the resources and processes that you have developed over time, has meant that we are able to get a framework in place here very quickly … [your] open[ess] in sharing the developmental journey, meant that you were able to answer our questions authoritatively, with a high degree of contextual understanding, and your responses offered much more than our sometimes naïve questions asked … your willingness to collaborate with us as a non-university Higher Education provider was refreshing … It is a significant efficiency for the sector." (Personal Communication, 31 January 2017)

Section 4: Moving Forward

The future focus for the CER framework is national and international dissemination underpinned by a programme of evaluation and scholarly research. Our aim is to document both the uptake of the CER framework and how it is adapted within different contexts and for different purposes. Each teaching team that has collectively decided to adopt the CER framework into their practice has developed resources and made suggestions that improve different aspects, removing barriers to implementation. We aim to investigate the CER framework in order to evaluate its impact and effectiveness for teachers in the hopes of addressing the following question: to what extent does it support building a collaborative culture of evidence-based and scholarly practice in relation to curriculum and teaching? The evidence of the impact of the CER framework will include a number of teaching teams adopting and adapting the framework. Qualitatively, the judgement of the relevance, value, and ease of use of the CER framework will be the feedback from teaching teams and their contributions to the refinement and development of the CER framework.

As for the first three cases of adopting the CER framework, we expect that each course underpinned by the CER framework will provide evidence of enhanced learning of students and of scholarship by teachers. Long term, we expect to have evidence of the impact on students of agreeing to be participants in the research into the curriculum they study and its delivery. Curriculum with an embedded CER framework have evidence of a range of positive impacts on teaching staff with flow-on effects for students. Data collected and analysed under the auspices of the CER framework were used to understand students' experiences of learning and to ensure the curriculum was relevant and effective for learning. For example, design changes to improve and ensure students' level of achievement and ability to meet the learning outcomes through improved scaffolding of curriculum content and assessment.

Enabling evidence collection for recognition by peers of the high standard of curriculum and delivery is an aim of the CER framework. The range of data available through the CER framework has already been used as evidence to justify successful applications for institutional and national awards for excellence in curriculum design and teaching, leading to enhanced student experience and learning. The three curricula, from which the CER framework was developed, demonstrate that a mature teaching-team culture with a strong commitment to evidence-based quality improvement can ensure that students experience well-designed curricula that are continually adapted. A course-level focus by a teaching team results in alignment of core elements and consistency of the learning environment.

Routine data collection aligned to reporting requirements for national standards (evaluation planning) enables staff to articulate and justify their curriculum, which includes, for example, student surveys, peer-review reports, and benchmarking activities.

Conclusion

In this chapter, we described the development of the CER framework as it occurred over three broad phases. The process account was provided to reflect that the framework is grounded in the teaching practice of the authors and that it is an attempt to codify and share our own learnings of the benefits of collegial work focused on curriculum quality. From our experience, we argue that it is critical to leverage the intrinsic and extrinsic motivations of teachers to design a curriculum that meets external standards, delivery that satisfies students and enhances learning, and overall job satisfaction.

Through this chapter, we have presented the CER framework as an effective solution to the problem of competing priorities (in particular, research vs teaching) that many academics find challenging to resolve satisfactorily. Our aspiration, driving the development and sharing the CER framework, is that it will provide a context in which academics can purposefully collaborate to design and deliver a curriculum that is transformative for students. We argue the CER framework facilitates collecting a wide range of data for broad and deep analysis of curriculum and learning. It guides academics to work collaboratively within a culture of continuous review and quality improvement, making evidence-based design decisions. Data used for QI and QA purposes can be leveraged by applying a scholarly lens, resulting in publications. The ability to coordinate evidence-based activities, intended to provide quality learning and teaching for students, has direct impacts on student learning outcomes and experiences.

About the Authors

Dr Jo-Anne Kelder is senior lecturer in the Quality Evaluation Learning and Teaching unit in the Faculty of Health, University of Tasmania. She can be contacted at this e-mail: jo.kelder@utas.edu.au

Associate Professor Andrea Carr is the deputy principal of the University College at the University of Tasmania. She can be contacted at this e-mail: A.R.Carr@utas.edu.au

Bibliography

Anderson, T. & J. Shattuck (2011). Design-Based Research: A Decade of Progress in Education Research? *Educational Researcher*, Vol. 41, No. 1, pp. 16–25.

Australian National Statement for Ethical Conduct of Research 2007 (Updated May 2015). Online Resource: https://www.nhmrc.gov.au/book/national-statement-ethical-conduct-human-research [Accessed on 18 March 2017].

Australian Qualifications Framework Council (2013). Australian Qualifications Framework Second Edition January 2013.

Brookfield, S. (1995). *Becoming a Critically Reflective Teacher*. San Francisco: Jossey-Bass.

Brown, N.; J. Kelder; B. Freeman & A. R. Carr (2013). A Message from the Chalk Face – What Casual Teaching Staff Tell Us They Want to Know, Access and Experience. *Journal of University Teaching & Learning Practice*, Vol 10, No. 3.

Kelder, J.; A. R. Carr & J. Walls (2017). Curriculum Evaluation and Research Framework: facilitating a teaching team approach to curriculum quality. *Higher Education Research Development Society of Australasia*. Sydney: HERDSA. Conference proceedings, 27–30 June 2017.

Laurillard, D. (2012). *Teaching as a Design Science: Building Pedagogical Patterns for Learning and Technology*. New York: Routledge.

Phillips, R.; C. McNaught & G. Kennedy (2012). *Evaluating e-Learning: Guiding Research and Practice*. New York: Routledge.

University of Tasmania Staff Agreement 2013– 2016 (2013).

Wagenaar, R. (2008). Learning Outcomes a Fair Way to Measure Performance in Higher Education: The Tuning Approach. *Outcomes of Higher Education: Quality relevance and Impact (IMHE 2008 General Conference)*.